# IT POLICIES & PROCEDURES

## Tools & Techniques That Work

2003 EDITION

George Jenkins ◆ Michael Wallace ◆
Larry Webber

ΛSPEN

PUBLISHERS

1185 Avenue of the Americas, New York, NY 10036
www.aspenpublishers.com

This publication is designed to provide accurate and authoritative information in regard to the subject matter covered. It is sold with the understanding that the publisher is not engaged in rendering legal, accounting, or other professional services. If legal advice or other professional assistance is required, the services of a competent professional person should be sought.

—From a *Declaration of Principles* jointly adopted by
a Committee of the American Bar Association and
a Committee of Publishers and Associations

1 2 3 4 5 6 7 8 9 0

# HIGHLIGHTS

The role of IT management is changing even more quickly than information technology itself. The 2003 edition of *IT Policies and Procedures: Tools & Techniques That Work* is an updated guide and decision-making reference that can help you to devise an information systems policy and procedure program uniquely tailored to the needs of your organization. Not only does it provide sample policies, this valuable resource gives you the information you need to develop useful and effective policies for your unique environment. For fingertip access to the information you need on Policy and Planning, Documentation, Systems Analysis and Design, and much more, this ready-reference desk manual comes with a policy manual CD-ROM to help you find what you need quickly and easily. You or your staff can use the CD-ROM or the book itself as a model or a template to create similar documents for your own organization.

The 2003 edition brings you up to date on the latest developments including:

- The latest best practices tips updated for every chapter
- Exploration of Business Continuity Planning (BCP), the outer shell of Disaster Recovery Planning, as a way of planning business processes to drive out problems and to keep running
- New chapter walking you through how to plan a technology relocation project and successfully move your IT operations
- Explanation of the most current issues and strategies for handling the Internet, project management, and mobile devices
- Sample policies, proposal templates, checklists, tally sheets, worksheets, tables, logs, questionnaires, and agreements are included for quick reference and adaptation to your particular needs

---

**For questions concerning this shipment, billing, or other customer service matters, call our customer service department at 1-800-234-1660. For toll-free ordering, please call 1-800-638-8437.**

3/03

# About Aspen Publishers

Aspen Publishers, headquartered in New York City, is a leading information provider for attorneys, business professionals, and law students. Written by preeminent authorities, our products consist of analytical and practical information covering both U.S. and international topics. We publish in the full range of formats, including updated manuals, books, periodicals, CDs, and online products.

Our proprietary content is complemented by 2,500 legal databases, containing over 11 million documents, available through our Loislaw division. Aspen Publishers also offers a wide range of topical legal and business databases linked to Loislaw's primary material. Our mission is to provide accurate, timely, and authoritative content in easily accessible formats, supported by unmatched customer care.

To order any Aspen Publishers title, go to *www.aspenpublishers.com* or call 1-800-638-8437.

To reinstate your manual update service, call 1-800-638-8437.

For more information on Loislaw products, go to *www.loislaw.com* or call 1-800-364-2512.

For Customer Care issues, e-mail *CustomerCare@aspenpublishers.com*; call 1-800-234-1660; or fax 1-800-901-9075.

**Aspen Publishers**
**A Wolters Kluwer Company**

# ABOUT THE AUTHORS

**George H. Jenkins**, a professional IS practitioner for over 20 years, began his career as an engineering programmer with General Electric, where he wrote an engineering end-user's policy and procedure manual. As a systems analyst with Xerox, he wrote an internal manual, *The Principles of Stock Keeping*, and worked as a DP operations manager with Columbia Record Club of CBS.

As the administrative coordinator for Capital Record Club and Capital Record Club of Canada, he wrote a manual on writing policies and procedures. He was also director for systems and DP operations for Nicolson File Company and an administrator for Wayne County General Hospital (University of Michigan teaching hospital).

Other accomplishments include: writing one of the first artificial intelligence programs (which designed electric motors for General Electric); designing, programming, and successfully installing the first exponential smoothing inventory control system; installing the second online real-time data collection system for production control; and converting the second-largest business unit record operation to computers.

Dr. Jenkins has been published in the *Journal of Systems Management* and *Data Management* magazine, and is the author of *Data Processing Policies and Procedures Manual*. He has also earned his CDP, CDE, and CSP.

He is currently a Professor Emeritus of Systems Analysis with the University of Findlay (Ohio) where he developed a four-year degree program for systems analysis. Hundreds of his systems graduates have achieved the highest job-placement record of any other discipline at the university.

**Michael Wallace** has over 20 years of experience in the information systems field. He began his career after graduation from James A. Rhodes State College as a mainframe operator for Super Food Services and then moved to a programming position at Reynolds & Reynolds.

He became a consultant after graduating magna cum laude from Wright State University (Dayton, Ohio) with a Bachelor of Science degree in Management Science. For eight years he was president of Q Consulting, a custom application development firm. Mr. Wallace has been an application developer, systems analyst, and technical and business consultant, and recently assisted the state of Ohio in developing statewide IT policies.

Mr. Wallace is a Microsoft Certified Professional and a past vice president of the Columbus Computer Society, and has served on the board of directors of various information technology user organizations. He is presently a member of the Association of Internet Professionals and the Project Management Institute, and recently graduated from the Executive MBA program at the Fisher College of Business at The Ohio State University.

After working as a practice manager and director for the last few years, Mr. Wallace is now the managing partner once again at Q Consulting, which now provides clients with guidance on IS strategy, disaster recovery planning, and policies and procedures. He has published several articles on business and technology topics.

Mr. Wallace can be reached by e-mail at: michaelw@qconsulting.biz.

**Larry Webber** has been working in the data processing field since 1974 beginning with digital communications system repair and then moving on to mainframe programming. During these years he has worked as manager of information centers at the corporate headquarters of a major telecommunications company, applications manager at a major law firm, and computer operations manager at a major automotive manufacturing facility. Currently Mr. Webber is employed as a project manager at a custom electronics assembly factory. Mr. Webber is also retired from the Army Reserve as an infantry First Sergeant. Mr. Webber has an MBA and BSBA from Rockhurst College and will complete a master's degree in project management from West Carolina University in the summer of 2003.

# SUMMARY OF CONTENTS

# CONTENTS

*A complete table of contents for each chapter is included at the beginning of the chapter.*

# PREFACE

*IT Policies and Procedures: Tools & Techniques That Work, 2003 Edition* is a comprehensive update to *IT Policies & Procedures Manual, Third Edition.* While many of the basic principles of superior IS operations have not changed over the years—we still have to do backups, service business users, and so on—the Internet and an explosion of connectivity options have added new challenges to running an effective IS organization.

## WHAT THIS MANUAL WILL DO FOR YOU

No two information systems operations are alike, but many do share some basic elements, such as hardware, software, and personnel. This manual defines the common threads that link all information systems operations, providing for a variety of situations—not as a one-size-fits-all model, but instead, as an updated guide and decision-making reference that can help you to devise an information systems policy and procedure program uniquely tailored to the needs of your organization. Rather than simply providing sample policies that will not encompass what is unique to your organization, this manual gives you the information you need to develop useful and effective policies for your unique environment.

## ORGANIZED FOR QUICK ACCESS

For fingertip access to the information you need on policy and planning, documentation, systems analysis and design, and much more, this ready-reference deskside manual comes with a policy manual CD-ROM to help you find what you need quickly and easily. You or your staff can use the CD-ROM or the book itself as a model or a template to create similar documents for your own organization.

"Simplicity is the ultimate design." Often, a multitude of forms is included in policies and procedures handbooks. This manual, however, provides a minimum of forms with the understanding that a well-written memo or e-mail message can take the place of a form and reduce the complexity of an IT operation. As an operation grows in complexity, the challenge to keep it running smoothly grows, and thus the need for a formal system of operations becomes a necessity. IS operations that have a formal systems and procedures manual in place are noticeably more efficient.

## ADDED STRATEGIC VALUE

The role of IT management is changing even more quickly than information technology itself. Today the IS operation is no longer found in some obscure corner of the corporate organization. Instead, it plays an interactive role in global systems. This manual will help you to formalize policies and procedures that are needed to formally document the IS operation. Doing so will save both time and effort. This manual will help you identify standard operations and procedures, documenting as needed, but still allowing for special needs.

Reality check: End-user computer systems will grow with or without the guidance of corporate IS, but the two working together will provide synergistic dividends. This manual updates the policies and procedures that can expedite your objective.

Our research discovered many well-run information systems operations and some real disasters. The better ones had noticeably good management and practical documentation. Expensive consultants, fad innovations, and cutting-edge technology did not always produce the desired IT results.

*IT Policies & Procedures: Tools & Techniques That Work* is a compilation of systems policies and procedures—the best practices within the industry—in current use. This manual is a process development tool that any seasoned information systems manager, working in a large or small IS operation, will find useful.

## SAVING YOU TIME

To make the manual even more valuable, a CD-ROM is included, containing the manual's forms and text. Because the format of the manual itself follows the structure of a typical looseleaf procedure manual, you can use it as a starting point for developing your own, by importing it into a word processor on a PC. Of course, you can also make needed changes and post the manual on a local area network or even a company Intranet site.

Writing this book has been a challenge because of the explosion of IT technology. By the time you finish this book, technology changes are already being developed for the next edition.

## WHAT'S NEW IN THIS EDITION

In addition to updating the material in the previous edition, this book contains new information on developing an effective disaster recovery plan, and provides useful tools and techniques for planning and executing a technology relocation project. Sample policies are also now included on the CD-ROM to further assist you in the development of policies appropriate for your organization.

# ACKNOWLEDGMENTS

Dr. Jenkins would like to make his dedication to Edith Ann Paetow, whose memory has provided a catalyst for his success for the past 40 years.

Michael would like to dedicate this book to his mother, Ruth Ann Wallace, whose encouragement and support has been invaluable over the years, and to his wife and best friend, Tami, for all her support during his many projects.

Our extended thanks to John Hiatt, who helped us start this project, and to Gina Spiezia, who helped bring it to completion. Special thanks also to Chuck Carlos, Brenda Luper, and Greg Pinchbeck for providing insight into IT policies and procedures from their unique points of view.

**1**

# POLICIES AND PLANS: SETTING THE FRAMEWORK

# § 1.01   PURPOSE AND SCOPE

*IT Policies & Procedures: Tools & Techniques That Work* offers you examples and templates to follow when setting up comprehensive and vital processes for developing, adopting, and distributing uniform IT policies and procedures to aid in information technology resource management and deployment. Comprehensive policies and procedures are critical for ensuring that your investment in IT is best used to support the overall strategy of the enterprise. They help ensure that all area of IT are working toward the shared goal of supporting and enabling the mission of the organization.

Policies discussed here are general statements of direction and purpose that provide guidance so users may exercise good judgment in the daily operation of the business. Well-written policies provide boundaries for independent action and facilitate the delegation of authority throughout an organization. They also promote the efficient use of resources in the organization. Policies explain *what* and *why* things are done. They are not, however, a substitute for sound judgment and common sense.

*Setting policy objectives*
- Differentiates between the corporate, local area network, and workstation or PC operations.
- Provides structure to the interface of various workgroup information systems, and to the relationship of workgroups and stand-alone PC systems with the company's corporate system.
- Assigns the responsibility and defines the authority for controlling all computer and network standards, operational standards, and training.

Procedures, on the other hand, are specific statements designed to provide direction in actions necessary to support the policies of the organization. Procedures explain *how* things are done.

This manual provides guidelines for policies and procedures related to information systems functions at the corporate, local area network, and PC workstation levels. It is not intended to replace instructions by various vendors in the operation of their software or hardware. Although the examples used here could be adapted to fit your unique circumstances, there is no "one size fits all" solution.

A policy manual must be kept current, ideally reviewing every section at least once per year. An out-of-date manual or one with too many gaps in it will not hold employee interest. After its review, the company executives should approve it and ensure it is properly presented to the relevant employees through presentations explaining its changes and by providing printed copies.

# § 1.02   ORGANIZING A MANUAL

## [A]   Manual Organization: A Living Example

A fundamental step to assigning structure is to develop a policies and procedures manual for quick reference and easy updating. This is true whether you create a paper version or post an electronic version to your corporate intranet. Building such a volume can be very time-consuming. The extent to which your company will benefit will be determined by how it is used. If the managers refer to it, so will the employees. If the managers ignore it, so will the employees (see a pattern here?).

This book is divided into chapters as a "living example" of manual organization and style. Remember that unlike a novel, a manual is not intended to be read from front to back. A manual must be organized for the quick location of pertinent information. Fortunately, this is made much simpler with modern word processing software, which can automatically build tables of contents and indices for you.

The chapters are subdivided into sections. The sections are subdivided into subsections. The manual opens with a table of contents displaying the chapters, sections, and subsections. Contact information for the person responsible for the policies should be included in the front of the manual so users may request updates or get clarification, if needed.

---

### A TYPICAL STRUCTURE FOR FAST RETRIEVAL

*"Nested" Style*

The reference index is in the form of:

N. CHAPTER NUMBER

   § N.N SECTION NUMBER

      [A] Subsection number

         A. First-level subdivision

            1. Second-level subdivision

               a. Third-level subdivision

                  (1) Fourth-level subdivision

                     (a) Fifth-level subdivision

---

## [B]   Type Styles and Page Numbering

Most manuals use type styles to aid in fast information retrieval. For example:

[**CHAPTER** titles will be uppercase and bold.]
[**Section** titles will be bold.]

[The subsequent text's first character will be uppercase.]

Pages are numbered within each section as page x-x. For example, if the last page of section six is four, it would be numbered 6-4. The placement of page numbers, headers, and footers needs to be consistent from section to section.

### [C]   Printing Policies and Procedures

If the policies and procedures manual is printed, use 20-lb white paper. Temporary policies or procedures should be printed on colored paper—light blue is a good choice—and should show the duration time in the "effective date" box at the top of each page (MM/DD/YY–MM/DD/YY).

### [D]   Page Layout

A clean, uncluttered layout encourages one to read the material. Experiment with different formats to find the one that works best for you. Exhibit 1-1 shows some possible header and footer formats to use.

## § 1.03   SETTING THE STANDARDS FOR RESPONSIBILITIES

### [A]   Who Has Management Authority?

Information systems policies typically flow top-down from the highest level of authority in the organization affected by the computer procedures. This person should designate a policy manager or team to develop and oversee the implementation of the policies. Note that imposing policies "from on high" without involving those affected can inhibit acceptance and compliance.

For consistency, it is important to designate a single corporate computer systems manager with the authority to implement all company computer systems policies. This person will receive policy mandates from the firm's delegated operations policymakers. These policies will be defined in writing and dated, signed, and forwarded to the corporate computer systems manager who will incorporate these policies, along with his/her own, into the company computer policies.

> ## COMMENT
>
> The first policy developed for the organization should be to designate the authority for the establishment of IT policies and procedures. This policy should outline who has the authority, from what that authority is derived, explain the importance of compliance with the policies that are issued, and describe how policies are created and revised.

Financial aspects of the firm's computer systems will require the co-approval of the firm's auditors, both in-house and outside, if applicable. The

**EXHIBIT 1-1.**   Headers and Footers

*Headers*

| Policy and Procedure Manual | | Page: | 2 of 3 |
|---|---|---|---|
| Chapter: | 1. Organizational Responsibility | Issued by: | |
| Section: | 2. Manual Organization | Approved: | |
| Effective Date: | 03/01/2003 | Supersedes: | |

| Subject: | Organizational Responsibility | Policy #: | 1–2 |
|---|---|---|---|
| | | Page #: | 2 of 3 |
| Covers: | Manual Organization | Effective: | 03/01/2003 |

*Footers*

| Revision #: | Issued by: |
|---|---|
| Revision Date: | |

| Revision #: | Supersedes: | Date: |
|---|---|---|
| | | |

responsibilities of the corporate computer systems manager are defined in the corporate policies and procedures manual.

*Local network manager within corporate IT.* The manager of a workgroup using a local area network or individual PCs within a corporate information system operation is typically the authority for such systems. If the company has a corporate system with a network or PC policies and procedures manual in place, its maintenance will be the responsibility of the corporate information systems management. Policy enforcement will come under the authority of the manager of the workgroup whose responsibilities are defined in the corporate information systems policies.

Where the manager of a local area network or individual PCs receives only policy guidance from the head of corporate information systems, he/she needs the flexibility to adapt these policies, as needed, into the PC policies and procedures manual.

*Local network manager outside corporate IT.* Managers of local area networks or individual PCs that are not part of the corporate system are the authority for the systems in their area. The company must create a combined policies and procedures manual formulated to carry out the firm's policies for the company network, local area networks, and stand-alone PCs. The manager of local area networks or individual PCs will be responsible for the procedure development, maintenance, and enforcement within his/her area of authority. The respective responsibilities for the PC policy and procedure manuals will be documented in the Corporate Policy and Procedures Manual. Any financial transactions or data access of the company's computer database systems by local area networks or individual PCs will require the co-approval of the firm's auditors, both in-house and outside, if applicable.

*Local network manager with no corporate IT.* Managers of local area networks or individual PCs in a firm that has no corporate information system will be the sole authority of the systems in their area. They are responsible for policy and procedure development, maintenance, and enforcement. The person approving will be so noted at the top right-hand side of each section's first page in the manual. This will be the same person who provides the policies, or their designated representative.

## [B]   Policies and Procedures Responsibility

All computer operations, software, supplies, and supporting hardware for the firm will be the responsibility of the head of the firm's corporate computer and/or PC operations. In most organizations, this will be the CIO or the IT enterprise architect. The authority to enforce policies and procedures is defined in the manual. This person has the responsibility to approve and sign all issued and all temporary policies and procedures and his/her name will be noted at the top right-hand side of each section's first page in the manual. The person writing the policies and procedures will be designated by the head of the company's information system, or they may elect to write it themselves. The writer is identified at the top right-hand side of each section's first page after the word "By:" and under the name of the person noted as approving.

Firms without a corporate computer and/or PC operations head will require a designated person for the PC policies and procedures responsibility. This person's authority may be defined from information provided herein.

## COMMENT

The higher up the approval authority, the more likely the policies will be followed. In addition, "buy-in" from users will help policies take root quickly. Also, if you do not assign responsibility for enforcing a policy to someone, then it will not be enforced, as being the naysayer to someone is never a popular or rewarding task.

### [C]  Implementation

All corporate and workgroup managers using the information systems department's management personnel are responsible for ensuring that the provisions set forth in the Information Systems Policies & Procedures Manual are complied with. These management persons:

1. Ensure that all application standards are followed in their respective areas.
2. Inform the person in charge of approving the procedures if there are any problems with a procedure or if inputs from other sources do not comply with the defined procedures. This should be done in the form of a memo.
3. Provide new employees with instruction and/or documented procedures that relate to their job descriptions.
4. Provide an annual "refresher" for current employees highlighting the changes made or problem areas during the previous year.

All stand-alone PC operations will be covered by a user's procedure manual provided by the supervisor. This manual will contain all procedure information needed for the authorized PC user to be in compliance. Also, the help-desk contact will be identified for any needed assistance.

## § 1.04  IT POLICY APPROVAL PROCESS

### [A]  Overview

An official policy creation, review, acceptance, and update process should be created so that everyone in the organization understands and participates in the policy process. The life cycle of a policy is:

**EXHIBIT 1-2.** Sample Policy

| Subject: | Software Copyright Compliance | Policy #: | 1–2 |
|---|---|---|---|
| | | Page #: | 1 of 3 |
| Covers: | All departments | Effective: | 03/01/2003 |

**PURPOSE:**
This is where you document the purpose of this policy.

**REFERENCE:**
If this policy references any other existing policies, document it here.

**BACKGROUND:**
This section is for background information on what brought about the creation of this policy.

**POLICY:**
The actual policy is documented in this section.

**PROCEDURES:**
Any procedures that were specifically created in support of this policy are documented here.

**INQUIRIES:**
This section tells the reader where to go for additional information on this policy.

**APPENDICES:**
Any material necessary to support the policy can be placed here.

| Revision #: | Supersedes: | Date: |
|---|---|---|
| | | |

**EXHIBIT 1-3.**   Policy Approval Process

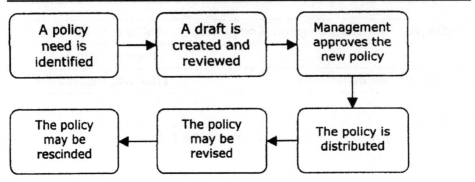

1.  A policy need is identified.
2.  A draft is created and reviewed.
3.  The appropriate level of management approves the new policy.
4.  The policy is distributed.
5.  The policy may be revised.
6.  The policy may be rescinded.

Policy additions or revisions are communicated using the form shown in Exhibit 1-4, either as a hardcopy form or as a Web page on the corporate intranet. If a Web page is used, a link to a Web page showing the acceptance criteria should be included.

## [B]  Policy Creation Process

The policy manager identified above is responsible for developing and following a standard process for creating new policies. This process should be similar to the following:

1.  A policy suggestion is made. Policy suggestions may originate from the policy manager, users, or management mandates.
2.  Is there a need for a new policy? The policy manager works with management to determine whether there is a need for a new policy (see § 1.04[C], "Policy Acceptance Criteria"). If the suggestion is rejected, the requestor is notified of the reasons for rejection. Alternatives to a new policy should be suggested to the person making the request.
3.  The policy manager assigns a priority to the policy. The policy manager works with management's input to assign a priority to the development of the new policy.
4.  The policy manager or an assigned policy analyst performs required policy research. The policy manager or an assigned policy analyst researches the requirements for the new policy. This research includes reviewing existing policies, obtaining examples from outside the company, and conducting interviews with stakeholders affected by the new policy.
5.  A draft policy is created. The draft policy is reviewed by others in the policy department, if applicable. Some firms have a formal policy review committee for review and change control; for others, this is ad hoc.
6.  The draft policy is reviewed by management. The draft policy is sent to upper management and important stakeholders for review.
7.  Revisions are made to the draft, if necessary. Revisions may be made after input is received from upper management and important stakeholders.
8.  Is this a mandated policy? If management mandated the new policy, then go to Step 14. Mandated policies are typically those required by law or requested by upper management.
9.  The draft policy is sent to all affected stakeholders for review and comment. This can be done by hardcopy, e-mail, or placement on

the corporate intranet. The quality of the final policy can depend on the number of people who review the proposed policy.

10. Stakeholder comments are incorporated into the draft, if appropriate. Incorporating as many suggestions as possible from users will help in gaining acceptance of the new policy.

11. Determine if additional research is required. A large percentage of negative comments may suggest additional research is required.

12. Revised policy draft is sent to management for review.

13. Make any revisions suggested by management.

14. Send the new policy to the appropriate person for signature.

15. The new approved policy is sent to stakeholders. This should include anyone affected by the existence of the policy.

16. Update the master policy manual.

## [C]   Policy Acceptance Criteria

Policy suggestions are made either by filling out the Policy Suggestion Form and delivering it to the policy manager or by filling out a form on the corporate intranet. The form must be filled out completely in order for the policy to be considered. The policy manager will use the following criteria to determine if a suggestion is accepted and a new policy is written or changes made to an existing one. Few suggestions will meet all criteria; the policy manager must balance strengths against shortcomings in evaluating each suggestion. Any of the following criteria may provide an overwhelming reason to either accept or reject a specific suggestion. Policy suggestions made by upper management will be automatically accepted.

1. **Purpose.** The purpose of the policy suggestion must be stated clearly and be relevant to the mission, goals, and operations of the organization.

2. **Audience.** The suggestion must address and identify the intended users of the policy, and satisfy some real or perceived need of this audience.

3. **Authority.** The policy manager must have the authority to issue policy for the area in question.

4. **Currency.** The suggested policy must apply to current and/or future activities.

5. **Scope.** The scope of the suggestion must match the expectations of the intended audience.

6. **Uniqueness.** To avoid needless duplication of effort, the information contained in a new policy should not already be covered in any existing policy.

7. **Organizational impact.** A new policy suggestion should have a positive impact on the operations of the organization. Suggestions with a greater impact will have a higher priority than those with a lower impact. Impact assessments must address cost-benefit and forecast return on investment.

8. **Urgency.** Suggestions with a higher degree of urgency will have a higher priority than those with a lower one. Policy requests mandated by law or upper management will have a higher priority.

### [D]   Manual Maintenance

Permanent manual revisions will be sequentially identified, after the word "Rev.," at the top right-hand side of each section's first page. Temporary policies or procedures supersede permanent policies and procedures, which will remain in the (three-ring) manual binder; they can only be replaced by the issuance of replacement policies and/or procedures. In the event a policy and/or procedure is to be discontinued, an order will be issued by the person who originally approved the policy and/or procedure or by a successor or agent in memo form. Requests for temporary or permanent policy and/or procedures will be handled as follows:

1.   Any user, management person, information systems person, work-group head, or manual holder may submit a request for a temporary policy and/or procedure or for a permanent revision to the Information Systems Policies & Procedures Manual.
2.   Revision requests will be handled in the following manner:
     a.   Request a revision using the Policy Suggestion Form in Exhibit 1-4.
     b.   Submit one copy to the approving authority (or successor) for the policy and/or procedure.
     c.   The final authority will review the request and approve or deny it, providing a reason for any action taken. The person assigned to investigate the request will be identified. The person assigned to determine the course of action necessary might also be the approval authority. The recommended course of action can result in a feasibility study if the required undertaking is large or expensive enough.
     d.   If the initial request is denied, the person requesting the change may move up the chain of command to the appropriate level needed for resolution.
3.   Revised documentation will be issued simultaneously to all affected manual holders using print or electronic means. The person responsible for maintaining the manual and any local area network or stand-alone PC policies will keep a current list of all manual holders with a partial or complete manual. Partial manual holders, who will have identified which sections they receive, will be cross-indexed by those sections. When a particular section is replaced, a list of appropriate manual holders may be provided for distribution. Note: The lists may be maintained in a computer database and distribution lists printed as needed.

When permanent revisions are issued, all pages for the given section will be reissued. If corrections to current procedures are required and numbering is not affected, only the affected pages need be distributed. This applies to both temporary and permanent policies and/or procedures. All releases will have a cover memo noting:

1.   The person issuing the release
2.   The effective date(s) of the release
3.   The reason for the release

**EXHIBIT 1-4.** Policy Suggestion Form

## POLICY SUGGESTION FORM

NAME/TITLE: _____

DEPARTMENT: _____     DATE: _____

**MANUAL AREA:**

CHAPTER: _____     ❏ New Policy

SECTION: _____     ❏ Change Existing Policy

PAGES: _____

**SUGGESTED POLICY/CHANGES:**

Write the proposed needed revision. Attach any necessary details, along with supporting documentation.

**RATIONALE:**

Describe the problem and how it is affecting the current operation or will affect future operations. How will the proposed revision resolve the problem?

Signed: _____     DATE: _____

Approved By: _____     DATE: _____

Approved/Disapproved: _____     DATE: _____

Date Revision Completed: _____     By Whom: _____

**COMMENTS:**

# § 1.05 IT STRATEGIC PLANNING PROCESS

## [A] Overview

The IT strategic plan is the major vehicle for articulating the information systems needs of the division and the associated resource requirements. The entire division must be involved in the creation of the IT plan, as it will shape the IT resources available for delivering the business objectives of the division. If left solely to the IT organization without business unit input, it will not provide maximum value to either part of the organization. The plan must reflect the business drivers for the organization, the relationship of those drivers to the intended IT activities, and the resources required to support those activities.

The head of the firm's corporate computer and/or PC operations takes responsibility for developing an effective IT plan for the organization. The corporate IT plan must integrate with the overall business strategies, goals, and objectives. Division-level plans also must be created, showing how the corporate objectives will be carried out. The head of the firm's corporate computer and/or PC operations reviews the division plans, ensuring these objectives are met, and provides support. Plans also will be reviewed to evaluate their technical feasibility and assess achievability of the planned benefits.

## [B] Policy and Procedures to Submit a Strategic Plan

Each division prepares an annual information technology strategic plan including strategies, goals, objectives, and performance measures. The division's plan must integrate with the overall business strategies, goals, and objectives. The plan also must consider the overall IT plan, developed at the corporate level.

*Submittal schedule.* Department/division-level IT plans must be submitted at the beginning of each fiscal year to the head of the firm's corporate computer and/or PC operations. Each division should review its plan status quarterly and update corporate every 6 months.

*Submittal procedure.* The plan must be submitted to the head of the firm's corporate computer and/or PC operations in electronic format, PDF version, with one unbound paper copy.

The sections described below are required, with subsections or appendixes added, if necessary.

1. **Executive summary.** This is a 1- or 2-page summary that provides a general understanding of the division's IT plan, and a frame of reference for understanding the overall objectives of the plan. It also may include information on who developed the plan and how the plan was created.
2. **Division mission.** This section discusses the mission of the division and how it fits into the organization. Each major functional area of the division and its role in fulfilling the division's mission should be discussed.
3. **Goals and objectives.** This section describes the major goals and objectives of the division and how they will be achieved. *Goals* are the long-term results that the organization will achieve as it fulfills its mission. *Objectives* are the near-term results that are attained as the organization

meets its goals. Measurements used for determining whether or not the goals and objectives are met should be included in this section.

4. **External factors.** This section discusses the division's business drivers. The division's business drivers are derived from the mission, goals, and objectives, and define how the division operates. Identify the external forces such as the economy, technology changes, political environment, and so on, which drive the business.

5. **Internal factors.** This section identifies the factors internal to the division that affect the division's IT activities. This may include organizational structure, personnel capabilities, management strength, facilities, training needs, and financial resources. Describe the organization's strengths and weaknesses and how they affect IT programs and management. Include an IT organizational chart and discuss personnel factors such as recruitment, retention, and training.

6. **IT architecture.** This section discusses how the division's IT planning supports its business drivers. A diagram showing the division's current architecture, including internal and external linkages, should be included. If there are plans to significantly change the architecture during the current year, a diagram of the proposed changes should be included. This section also should describe how the division's architecture fits in with the overall corporate architecture.

7. **Technology initiatives.** The major technology initiatives of the division are described in this section. Examples might include e-commerce programs, ERP implementations, wireless initiatives, etc. Business resumption plans and the division's project management methodology also should be included in this section.

8. **Project plans.** A project plan for each major new or maintenance project should be presented in this section. Minor projects may be grouped together into one or more general support projects. Each project plan should include the following information:
   a. A brief statement of the project purpose.
   b. A reference to the goal or objective from the section above that the project supports. This section should describe the scope of the project, the expected benefits, the implementation timeframe, the resource requirements for the project, and the expected impact the project will have on the organizational goals. Also describe the impact on the organization if the project is not undertaken.
   c. Describe the success criteria for the project. What metrics (return on investment, service level, system performance, and so on) will be used to measure the success of the project?
   d. Describe the technical approach employed on this project. Include hardware needs, software to be used (including operating system and development tools), and any telecommunications requirements.
   e. List any additional concerns about the project, such as staffing and training needs, schedule, integration with other divisions, etc.
   f. Document the estimated costs by fiscal year for staffing, hardware, telecommunications, etc., needed to complete the project.
   g. Estimate any future maintenance costs for the life of the system once the project is completed.

9. **Project summary.** Document a summary of each project planned
by the division in this section. This should list the project name, estimated costs, projected start and completion dates, and the estimated
benefit in dollars.

## COMMENT

### How Policies Begin

Start with a cage containing five monkeys. Inside the cage,
hang a banana on a string and place a set of stairs under it.
Before long, a monkey will go to the stairs and start to climb
toward the banana. As soon as he touches the stairs, spray
all the other monkeys with cold water. After a while, another
monkey makes an attempt with the same result—all the
other monkeys are sprayed with cold water. Pretty soon,
when another monkey tries to climb the stairs, the others
try to prevent it.

Now, put away the cold water. Remove one monkey from
the cage and replace him with a new one. The new monkey
sees the banana and wants to climb the stairs. To his surprise and horror, all the other monkeys attack him. After
another attempt and attack, he knows that if he tries to
climb the stairs, he will be assaulted.

Next, remove another of the original five monkeys and replace him with a new one. The newcomer goes to the stairs
and is attacked. The previous newcomer takes part in the
punishment with enthusiasm! Likewise, replace a third
original monkey with a new one, then a fourth and then the
fifth. Every time the newest monkey takes to the stairs, he
is attacked. Most of the monkeys beating him have no idea
why they are not permitted to climb the stairs or why they
are participating in the beating of the newest monkey.

After replacing all the original monkeys, none of the remaining monkeys have ever been sprayed with cold water.
Nevertheless, no monkey ever again approaches the stairs
to try for the banana. Why not? Because as far as they
know, that's the way it's always been done around here.

And that, my friends, is how company policy begins.

# 2

# DOCUMENTATION: GETTING EVERYONE ON THE SAME PAGE

# § 2.01  PURPOSE AND SCOPE

Well-written systems documentation presents a clear, accurate picture of the process or system documented. The documentation detail must be tuned to the technical skill level of the reader, who should be able to understand a system or operation through this method. This is especially true when users are non-data-processing people. Yet, user documentation is often left until the last minute, written hastily by nonprofessional writers, and most often is considered an after-the-project nicety rather than a requirement of the project itself. For these reasons, company information systems policy requires that documentation explaining a computer system's use and internal workings be an integral part of any undertaking. This effort will be budgeted and the assigned funds are to be used for documentation only. Users of computer systems will approve all documentation developed for their use.

Documentation of policy often gets short shrift, tacked on as an afterthought, but it is critical as a permanent record of operation methods, development techniques, and organizational policies. Documentation is institutional knowledge, a record of procedure development, design, implementation, operation, and revision data that successors can follow. It incorporates policies, rules, and information that must be distributed properly to all users associated with information systems operations so that energies are directed and coordinated correctly.

Technical documentation of a system's internal workings is the starting point for programmers to investigate problems or make changes to the system. This is best written during system roll-out so as to capture a fresh understanding of how the system works. Without technical documentation, every debugging effort must start with a time-consuming analysis of how the system works, where each data element originates from, how data is manipulated, etc.

Every company keeps some sort of documentation library today. In some cases, it is in a dusty bookcase. More often manuals and system documentation are scattered around the various work areas and programmer cubicles. All of these documents vary in how current they are. In many cases, no one knows what another person may have on their shelves and must search around even to borrow an old book. Most hardware and software vendors would be very happy to provide their documentation electronically (on an optical disk or via an Internet link) since printing mounds of manuals only distracts them from what they do best.

A well-maintained documentation library will provide an IT manager with ready access to the latest information, saving on storage space since so many copies of so many things are not floating around, and greater agility for responding to user problem reports.

## COMMENT

Well-written software documentation is the bread and butter of a help desk. When users call, help-desk analysts can answer most questions if they have access to current user documentation and can look up more detailed questions in the system documentation. The more information the help desk has, the fewer distractions will be passed on to your technical staff. Oh yes, and the callers appreciate the quick answers to their questions!

## § 2.02   POLICY ORGANIZATION

### [A]   Overview

IT documentation policy adds formal structure to the documentation of various IT processes within the organization. Among the benefits:

- Added flexibility to allow for changes
- The ability to adapt temporary procedures
- Greater benefits of minimizing cost and confusion, while maximizing the return on investment in software, hardware, and related items
- Standardized formats to make cross-training easier and to allow a wider range of people better access to technical details
- Standardized handling to keep documentation up to date

### [B]   Scope

All processes touching on IT functions within the organization should be documented. Areas requiring policies and procedures documentation include, but are not limited to:

- Procedure development
- Computer management operations
- Computer users
- Computer user support
- System analysis
- Special areas (redefining vendor software, hardware documentation, etc.)
- Internet and e-mail usage
- Security procedures

## [C]    Policy Objectives

User documentation should be written following specific standards defining the content, approach, and objectives. The standards provide a uniform plan for handling every aspect of documentation. Standard formats allow all readers to focus on the content of the document and not waste time trying to decipher different document layouts.

However, information systems policies and procedures are only as good as the effort to correctly maintain and enforce them. User documentation must be kept current or it is useless. Out-of-date documentation can be worse than no documentation at all, as it may cause users to make errors or to make decisions based on incorrect data.

## [D]    Some Basic Groundwork

Documentation is intended to tell the story about how something works or how to use it. It is a shame to spend days writing a document that is useless to your audience. So begin your writing with some document standards. Most word processors will easily accommodate these format steps:

1.   Every page will have the date they were approved in the lower-left corner. As pages are updated, this date will change so there may be more than one date in the same document.
2.   Every page will have a page number in the bottom center of the page.
3.   Every page will have its system name in the lower right corner of the page.
4.   Every document will have a table of contents.

## [E]    Document Management Actions

Someone in your organization must be tasked as the official keeper of all documentation. This person will hold the password to the Network Directory where all documentation is stored. Anything to be added to the library will pass through this person who will ensure:

1.   The documents conform to your documentation standards.
2.   The documents have been properly approved.
3.   The documents have been stored in the proper location.
4.   The proper security is applied for reading by authorized personnel.

In addition to the document library, this person should also establish a Web page with links to the documents of all key vendors of hardware and software. This will assist in reducing the number of hardware and software manuals floating around the company.

## [F]    Know Your Audience

Before writing the first word, begin with a review of who will be reading this document. Rarely are these booklets read from cover to cover. Instead, someone will be looking in here to find something. Make it easy for them by including a table of contents. For just a few additional steps, most word processing programs will build these for you.

*User instructions*. People will read the documentation to gain some overall understanding on how the system works or to look up solutions to problems. They also will depend on the documentation to help train new employees. The better the user instructions are, the fewer the calls for help! User instructions should include illustrations of screens, reports, and lists of valid edit codes. Also include what could cause any error message that a user might see so they know what they need to do differently.

*Technical explanations*. These will be used for debugging programs—often under great pressure. At a minimum, they should include an overall diagram of the system modules and data flows; a list of all file layouts; a list of where major outputs come from, such as reports; and a narrative of how it all fits together.

## [G]  Procedures

Documentation has a problem. How do you know that you are reading the latest information on the topic? The document may be 4 years old but the latest word—or 1 week old and completely revised since then. Maintaining multiple copies of system and user documentation can be a major undertaking with issuing page changes to all copies, hoping they are updated, etc. Multiply this by the number of systems in a large company and you can easily see why some companies do not even bother to try.

Documentation will reside in two places. The master copy is kept in the documentation library previously mentioned. This should always be the most current copy. To save on the effort to update multiple copies around the company, documentation users are asked to view what they need to see online rather than printing it.

## COMMENT

Several software vendors provide tools that make it easier to collect policy and procedure information and make it available over the corporate intranet. Some packages to check out include Zavanta from Comprose, Inc. (*www.comprose. com*) and onGO DMS from Uniplex Software (*www.uniplex. com*).

However, the documentation custodian also should maintain a printed copy in a standard three-ring binder (or on a CD) for times when the online system is not available. Workgroup managers will be responsible for ensuring the accuracy and currency for all policies and procedures that affect their area. The person responsible for PC administration and control, or an authorized agent, should maintain a complete information systems policies and procedures manual. If the firm uses an off-site records backup resource, it too should have a current copy of all the information systems policies and procedures. If a separate systems and procedures unit exists, it should keep an appropriate number of printed manuals.

## § 2.03 FEASIBILITY STUDY DOCUMENTATION PROCEDURE

### [A] Overview

A feasibility study is conducted to determine the practicality of changing, developing, or acquiring a system or computer program. Such studies can be omitted when a project is mandated by top management and/or outside regulatory agencies. Each feasibility study, which consists of a small-scale systems analysis and a feasibility report, will require a binder to contain such documentation as memos, correspondence, vendor literature, and detailed information about the system.

The analysis section is a scaled-down study of a current system and a determination of the practicality of the request. The feasibility report contains documented findings as to the request's feasibility. The final feasibility study report is prepared based on these two sections and any other pertinent information.

## COMMENT

Always keep a copy of every feasibility study in your documentation library whether it was implemented or not. It can provide valuable technical and business process information for future projects.

### [B] Feasibility Study Request Memo

Each feasibility study request will be initiated by an authorized person using a printed or e-mail memo form. The firm will identify the individuals authorized to initiate such requests. The memo will state:

- The nature of the requested system or software
- The expected tangible and intangible benefits from the new or revised system or software
- The date by which a reply to the report is needed

- The contact person for further information about the request
- The approval of the IT manager

## [C]  Feasibility Study Binder Contents

If the approving authority denies the feasibility study request, a notification is sent to the person requesting the study, explaining the reason(s) why the request was not approved. Both the requesting and reply memos will be filed in a "feasibility reject file" in the area of the systems and procedures unit. An approved request for a feasibility study will trigger developing a feasibility binder labeled with the title of the study. It will include the following:

- An accumulated table of contents or index, as needed
- All memos and correspondence related to the study
- Vendor correspondence and literature
- Accumulated cost data
- A log listing the calendar days and hours worked on the study
- Documentation of all meetings
- A telephone log regarding all phone calls made and attempted
- A copy of the final report

## [D]  The Final Feasibility Study Report

The final feasibility study report will be formatted in the following manner:

- Cover page, containing project title, author, and date
- Overview of the request
- Rationale for initiating the information systems project or for changing an existing system
- The body of the final report providing the details of the project/program
- Exhibits
- Summary, including recommendations, estimated costs, estimated calendar time needed, and estimated work-hours of all persons involved in the project

## COMMENT

Remember, calendar time and labor time are not interchangeable. If it takes one person 100 hours (12.5 days) to paint a barn, 100 people cannot paint the barn in one hour.

# § 2.04   PROJECT DOCUMENTATION

## [A]   Overview

Project documentation includes instructions, charts, a copy of the feasibility study, correspondence, and other material dealing with a specific project. It provides a permanent description of the undertaking along with the solutions to problems and the methods used to resolve them.

A project binder is created at the start of a project to provide an ongoing record of pertinent information. It should include all related material and vendor information and correspondence throughout the life of the project. It is important to know which document supersedes another. Therefore, each document must be dated before placing it in the binder.

At no time are the contents to be removed from a project documentation binder. If necessary, a copy may be made of any needed part(s) of the binder contents and both the date and the word "copied" posted on each reproduced page.

## [B]   Identification and Responsibility

In order to stay organized, project number and title are used to identify each project binder. Responsibility for initiating and maintaining the binder rests with the project leader/manager or other responsible person as designated by the information systems head or systems manager.

## [C]   Project Binder Contents

The binder for a proposed project contains:

1. **Table of contents or index.**
2. **Project proposal.** The project report may be in the form of a feasibility study or a systems design, or may specify software requirements. The project proposal should contain:
   a. **Description of the project.** A brief statement describing the scope of the project, its key objectives, and a copy of the feasibility study. The project manager drafts the project description, which may be more detailed than a feasibility study.
   b. **Major project tasks.** An outline of the steps necessary to complete the project.
   c. **Estimated costs and benefits.** Computed estimated costs for each major task and/or items to be purchased. Costs should be identified as "estimates" obtained at the time the proposal was written and subject to revision. Any assumptions made in determining these costs must be stated. See Exhibit 2-1 for one format for reporting proposed project costs. Consistency of format, once established, is more essential than individual style and saves time when reviewing the contents.

**EXHIBIT 2-1.**   Format for Project Proposal Costs

Description of Project
(Brief description. Use a separate sheet if needed.)

(Major Project Tasks (Use only those applicable to this project.)

|  | START DATE | FINISH DATE | ESTIMATED COST |
|---|---|---|---|
| Preliminary Analysis | xx/xx/xx | xx/xx/xx | $xxx,xxx |
| Systems Analysis/Design | xx/xx/xx | xx/xx/xx | $xxx,xxx |
| Programming | xx/xx/xx | xx/xx/xx | $xxx,xxx |
| Data and File Conversion Costs | xx/xx/xx | xx/xx/xx | $xxx,xxx |
| System and Program Testing |  |  | $xxx,xxx |
| Training Costs |  |  | $xxx,xxx |
| Hardware Purchase |  |  | $xxx,xxx |
| Software Purchase |  |  | $xxx,xxx |
| Administrative Costs |  |  | $xxx,xxx |
| Miscellaneous |  |  | $xxx,xxx |
| TOTAL COST |  |  | $xxx,xxx |

Estimated Annual Operation Cost

|  |  |
|---|---|
| Data Entry | $xxx,xxx |
| Processing | $xxx,xxx |
| System/Program Maintenance | $xxx,xxx |
| Administrative | $xxx,xxx |
| Other (specify) | $xxx,xxx |
| TOTAL ESTIMATED ANNUAL OPERATIONS COST | $xxx,xxx |

Project Staffing

(Name the project leader and state the estimated number and competence level of personnel assigned to work on the project.)

Personnel to Contact

(List names of people best able to answer pertinent questions about the various tasks within the project.)

d. **Time estimate for each task.** Estimated dates for inception and completion of each task, based on the needed resources being available as scheduled.

e. **Project staffing.** The full-time equivalent (FTE) personnel assigned to the project by job title and name. Dates of commitment for anyone assigned only for a portion of the project are also listed.

   Competence levels of personnel assigned are identified. This is essential when personnel, such as vendors or consultants, are on loan from user areas and outside sources. The caliber of personnel can determine the success of the project.

f. **Project contact personnel.** A list of persons (names and titles) best able to answer pertinent questions about the project. This is most important when dealing with vendors who may be inclined to contact persons in the organization who will benefit them most instead of the project leader or designated person.

3. **Systems concept.** A paragraph or more, written for nontechnical, management-level personnel, that provides a detailed overview of the project objectives. For larger projects, the systems concept paragraph(s) specifies the objectives, scope, and methods to be employed. A short descriptive paragraph suffices for smaller projects.

4. **Project resource schedule.** After the project proposal worksheet is prepared, a Project Resource Schedule (see Exhibit 2-2) is developed to show the estimated hours per week each task will require. Once the work is completed, actual hours spent on each task are recorded.

## [D]   Project Progress Folders

Project progress documentation folders, maintained during the life of the project, contain the history of the project and copies of all relevant correspondence filed by date. They also provide a complete historical record, which becomes a source of information when writing a project completion report, and should reflect any agreements between the project group and users or vendors. The folders should include:

1. **Correspondence**
   - Memos and letters
   - Project status reports
   - Minutes of status and problem-solving meetings
2. **Workerpower utilization record.** The estimated hours per task versus the actual hours per task are posted to the Project Resource Schedule (see Exhibit 2-2). Any line-item variations that reflect a cost of over $2,000 are explained in memo form at the time of the actual expense posting.
3. **Project documentation checklist.** To ensure that documentation is being completed, a Project Documentation Checklist is used (see Exhibit 2-3). This will be a source for what documentation is to be done.

**EXHIBIT 2-2.**    Project Resource Schedule

Project Name _____    Project Number _____

| Direct Expense | Period 1 | | Period 2 | | Period 3 | |
|---|---|---|---|---|---|---|
| | Estimated | Actual | Estimated | Actual | Estimated | Actual |
| Project Manager | | | | | | |
| Systems Analyst | | | | | | |
| Developer | | | | | | |
| Administrative | | | | | | |
| Other | | | | | | |
| Training | | | | | | |
| Total Hours | | | | | | |
| Total Dollars | | | | | | |
| Cumulative Hours | | | | | | |
| Cumulative Dollars | | | | | | |

Project Leader _____    Date _____

# § 2.05  SYSTEMS DOCUMENTATION

## [A]  Overview

Systems documentation records activities associated with systems analysis and design efforts. It provides proposed system design specifications in a format that management can easily evaluate for approval. It also provides required specifications for software and vendor bidding. Systems documentation and its maintenance are vital to the success of a project and future systems maintenance.

## [B]  Systems Documentation Binder

A systems documentation binder is maintained for each project, but is distinct from overall project documentation. Forms in this section (Exhibit 2-4 and Exhibit 2-5) are examples of standard formats to be used as needed. This binder is maintained by the lead systems analyst for the project and contains:

1. **Title page.** The first or title page contains the project name and identification number, effective dates, and the lead analyst's name and title. Names and responsibilities of all other persons assigned to the project are listed on the second page.
2. **Table of contents.** This reflects the specific contents in the systems binder and requires updating as changes and/or additions are made.
3. **Revision sheet.** Included in every systems binder (see Exhibit 2-4), it contains columns for:
   a. **Number of revisions.** Revisions are numbered sequentially starting with 1.
   b. **Revision date.** Effective date of the revision.
   c. **Portion revised.** The specific part of the system under revision, including all areas of documentation such as procedures, flowcharts, reports, etc.
   d. **Name.** The name of the systems analyst making the revision.
   e. **Authorization.** The name of the person authorizing the revision.

## [C]  Systems Concept

The systems concept is prepared by the lead systems analyst, from specifications provided by the requesting authority. This section will include copies of correspondence or written requests, which outline the requirements of the system. Once approved, it serves as a guide for analysts to design the technical specifications of the system and includes:

1. **Approval.** The first page lists the project name, the requesting authority's name, and the title of the person approving the project.
2. **Project history.** This section states the background that justifies the project.

**EXHIBIT 2-3.** Project Documentation Checklist

Project Name _____ Project Number _____

| Date Required | Actual Date | Item | Responsibility |
|---|---|---|---|
| | | Request Evaluation | |
| | | Design Specifications | |
| | | System Definition | |
| | | System Flowcharts | |
| | | System Inputs | |
| | | System Protocols | |
| | | System Processing | |
| | | System Outputs | |
| | | File/Database | |
| | | System Controls | |
| | | System Test Plans | |
| | | System Audit | |
| | | System Recovery | |
| | | Nomenclature Glossary | |
| | | Software Description | |
| | | Software Controls | |
| | | Software Tests | |
| | | Help-Desk Assignments | |
| | | Operations Instructions | |
| | | System Acceptance | |

Project Leader _____ Date _____

**EXHIBIT 2-4.**   Revision Sheet

Project Name _____   Project Number _____

| Revision Number | Date | Item Revised | Revised By | Approved By |
|---|---|---|---|---|
|  |  |  |  |  |
|  |  |  |  |  |
|  |  |  |  |  |
|  |  |  |  |  |
|  |  |  |  |  |
|  |  |  |  |  |
|  |  |  |  |  |
|  |  |  |  |  |
|  |  |  |  |  |
|  |  |  |  |  |
|  |  |  |  |  |
|  |  |  |  |  |
|  |  |  |  |  |
|  |  |  |  |  |
|  |  |  |  |  |
|  |  |  |  |  |
|  |  |  |  |  |
|  |  |  |  |  |

Project Leader _____   Date _____

3. **Project objectives.** The details of project objectives are presented. All functional areas affected by this project are listed, and any problems with overlapping lines of authority are noted so the required coordination can be established. In addition, anticipated results from the successful completion of the project are detailed. To ensure complete understanding of the system by management and users, what the system will not accomplish is also noted.

4. **Requirements.** The documentation requirements necessary for proper completion of the project are:

   a. A brief explanation of the work to be done during each phase.

   b. A schedule for inception and completion dates of each phase and the key tasks within each phase. To help picture the overall schedule, project management software is recommended for reporting the schedule and actual completion times of project steps.

   c. Special requirements for project software from vendors and/or for in-house programmed software.

   d. Special requirements for outside acquisitions such as equipment, consultants, contract personnel, and/or vendor services.

   e. Current in-house equipment resources that will be committed to the systems project.

   f. Worker-hour resources, by names and titles, to be committed to the project.

   g. Resources expected from the requesting authority, including hardware and personnel assistance, such as training of extra personnel during conversion of the system.

## [D]   Systems Specifications

Systems specifications provide a means of communication between the designer and the software providers, who may be in-house programming staff or outside contract workers. The systems specifications provide a record of the structure, functions, flow, documentation, and control of the system and include:

1. **System narrative**
   - Current date
   - Descriptive title of system
   - General requirements with description of each and sources cited
   - Source, expected schedule, and volume of input data
   - Size and characteristics of the data
   - Sample exhibits of input documents
   - Outputs indicating volume and due dates (This may be a monitor display and/or hard copy.)
   - Sample exhibits of outputs
   - References to material or organizations that may furnish additional information (This may include vendor-supplied information.)

2. **System flowcharts.** Graphics or flowcharts can identify the processes performed and the steps involved. Each symbol within a flowchart identifies a process as manual or computer. Each system flow-

chart is contained on one page. If greater detail is required of any given area of the system, a subsystem flowchart is drawn in a way that both nontechnical management and computer programmers can understand.

3. **Program specification requirements.** These define the environment within a system in which a subsystem or a single program operates. They describe:
   - Inputs and outputs, including source, format, disposition, retention method, and time period.
   - Processes controls, functions, and limitations. These specifications, prepared by the systems analyst for the programming staff, need to be confirmed by the person responsible for programming so that they may be accomplished by this staff.

4. **File/database specifications.** Complete and detailed specifications of the files and/or databases used in the system are identified. If a database is employed for storing data elements, the database administrator maintains a data dictionary, and the systems project should comply with appropriate procedures. This applies to file specifications if they also fall under the jurisdiction of the database administrator. A reference sheet describes the file layout, field definitions, and source references. A sample file layout is shown in Exhibit 2-5. The file layout contains:
   - File name
   - File number or label
   - Current date
   - File label
   - Record size
   - Storage medium
   - Record length required
   - Blocking factor (tape only)
   - Retention requirements (daily, monthly, etc., and expected currency in number of days between cutoff date and completion of update). "Monthly 5 days" means file is updated monthly with 5 days required to complete update.
   - Security level
   - File sequence

## COMMENT

The ERwin Modeling Suite from Computer Associates is a great tool for designing databases and business processes. It can be used for creating much of the documentation discussed in this section. Computer Associates can be reached at their Web site, *www.ca.com*.

**EXHIBIT 2-5.**   File Documentation

| | |
|---|---|
| File Name: | |
| File Number: | Date: |
| File Label: | |
| Record Size: | File Size: |
| Disk:          CD:          Tape:          Blocking: | |
| Retention Requirements: | |
| Remarks: | |

5. **Input description.** This is the format for all the data going into the system, both as a data file and as entered from a screen. It provides the following information for each input record:
   - Name
   - Date
   - Status (raw data or in computer media form)
   - Each field, identified within a record, its type, and length
   - Number of records per cycle (day, week, etc.)
   - Disposition after it is received by system
6. **Output description.** The layout of each output should be displayed in monitor or hardcopy format and is part of the systems documentation. Forms designed for this purpose include:
   - Name of report
   - Number of report
   - Location and length of each item within report layout
   - Number of copies
   - Relationship of items in report to source of item information in input description

# § 2.06   SOFTWARE DOCUMENTATION

## [A]   Purpose

Software documentation serves various functions. First, program maintenance has become a major expense. The investment and effort required to document software is rewarded by reduced maintenance costs, faster response to user requests, and possibly management job security. Second, it communicates to the systems analyst or project leader that the programming has been properly done. Program documentation also provides systems operators and users with the information needed to operate the software. It furnishes the auditors with information about the controls that have been established. Finally, it shows management what exactly has been accomplished with the money spent.

## COMMENT

A key aspect of object-oriented programming is the reuse of code. If the purpose, inputs, and outputs of a software object are not clearly documented, then how can you reuse it? Establish a standard format for all reusable objects as soon as possible and ensure all future documentation conforms to it.

### [B]    Software Binders

Information about developed programs and purchased software is maintained in "software binders," one for each written program or purchased software package. They contain:

1. **General information.** This section identifies the software and its objectives. Each program should have a unique identification number. The programs may be grouped together using any of the following categories:
   - Low-level written programs
   - High-level written programs
   - Reusable code
   - Object modules
   - CASE tools
   - Operating software
   - Database software
   - Network software
   - Purchased mainframe programs
   - Purchased LAN software
   - Purchased PC/workstation software
2. **General objectives.** The general objectives include a brief narrative statement of each program's purpose or use. It also addresses what passes data to it, how the data is transformed, and what passes out of it.
3. **Purchased software.** Any license agreements connected with the programs, including the number of copies purchased and the last date of purchase. Any "beta" operating software will be so identified, and its agreement information placed in this section. The license for all purchased software should be maintained in a "licenses" folder in the IT department's vital records storage area.
4. **Program's systems specifications.** Vendor-supplied information also will be included.
5. **Program flowcharts.** Flowcharts will be drawn by hand or flowcharted using available software that employs the American National Standards Institute (ANSI) symbols (refer to § 2.08, "Flowcharting Standards"). There are several commercially available software programs that can generate the ANSI symbols and facilitate the drawing of these charts.

## COMMENT

Visio from Microsoft is probably the most popular program for technical drawings. The latest version contains different editions for technical and business drawings. Microsoft can be reached at *www.microsoft.com.*

6. **Written program documentation**
   - Overall flow of program showing data going in, how it is transformed, and to where it is passed
   - Source code listings
   - Source of input and format, to include all combinations of data strings into and out of modules
   - System naming conventions—needed for database, inputs, outputs, and controls
   - Hardcopy layouts
   - Screen display layouts
   - Screen layouts displaying control buttons, text boxes, and screen labels
   - Database layouts, definitions of field items, and naming references
   - Data element cross references
   - List of all validation codes used by the program
   - List of all error messages that can be generated by this code and what causes them (do not include ones generated by operating environment, just the ones you can send to the screen)
   - Formulas used in any critical calculations
   - Subroutines, sources, and listings
   - Index of table field names—names used in databases, programs, and input/output locations (useful when programming and doing maintenance later)

## [C]  Operations Specifications

The programmer or analyst is responsible for preparing operating instructions that can be used by the help desk, central computer operations staff, client/server users, LAN systems, end-user systems, or stand-alone PC users. This documentation should contain detailed instructions on how to operate the program and handle any exceptions that may occur. It will require the signed and dated approval of the highest authority in the unit for which it is intended. Local area network (LAN), wide area network (WAN), or client/server user instructions will require the approval of the head of information systems or his/her designated representative. The types of information to be included are:

1. **Cover page information**
   - Program number
   - Program description or name
   - Name of programmer or help desk contact
   - Type of program
   - Priority requirements
   - Estimated processing time
   - Date prepared and revision dates
2. **Input/output requirements**
   - Keyboard instructions
   - Scanning instrument instructions
   - Removable disk and/or CD instruction
   - Form number
   - Number of copies required
   - Portrait or landscape printing

- External label
- Internal label
- Other input/output devices not listed

- Report disposition
- Printer(s) required

3. **Magnetic tape instructions**
   - External label
   - Internal label
   - Input or output usage

   - File protection requirements
   - Tape disposition

4. **General operating instructions**
5. **Restart procedures**

## [D]   Program Test Data

Listings of input used for testing and the resulting outputs are kept in the program test file. Screen displays are screen-printed or drawn for documentation.

## [E]   Backup and Recovery

Procedures are written for corporate and other operations for each running system. All changes are noted with the date and the name of the person responsible. Each program must have a recovery procedure in the event of a computer failure. Each backup procedure will be tested after it is placed into operation and every time maintenance is performed. Backup procedures require the following:

- When and how backup was done
- Location where backup programs and data are stored
- Number of backup generations required. If more than one, they should not all be stored in same location.
- If outside backup facility is available, a complete written procedure is required for its operation
- Any special recovery instructions to ensure data consistency
- How to quickly verify that recovered data is properly in place and program is using it

# § 2.07   COMPUTER OPERATIONS DOCUMENTATION

## [A]   Purpose

The operating procedures necessary to initiate, schedule, process, control, and restart all phases of the system(s) while it is in operation are maintained in a binder for the operations personnel. All the documentation must be kept current. The project leader is responsible for compiling and validating new systems. Maintenance information systems personnel typically update existing manuals.

The computer operations documentation procedures can vary depending on the configuration of the system's hardware. The corporate computer center operation, with hardware in the form of a mainframe, minicomputer, or PC, is under a corporate computer operations head, who is also in charge of client/server operations. This person is part of the corporate information systems and officially accepts the operations documentation. The acceptance of documentation is noted on the upper right-hand corner of each procedure section's first page.

The head of corporate computer operations can have responsibility for workgroup systems manual maintenance or this can be the responsibility of the workgroup management, whichever better serves the users. The authorized person notes the acceptance of documentation in the upper right-hand corner of the first page of each procedure section.

If PC operations, stand-alone or LAN, has a PC manager, this person may approve operator manuals for his/her area of jurisdiction. In the absence of a PC manager, a user area manager will be assigned the task of approving the operation manuals. This task may be delegated by the manager and, if need be, the help-desk person(s) may be consulted or so delegated. The acceptance of documentation is noted by the authorized person in the upper right-hand corner of the first page of each procedure section.

## [B]   Corporate Computer Center Operation Procedures

This section details the information systems operations procedures for the corporate system, which cover general information pertaining to the overall corporate system(s), backup and recovery, and job procedures.

1.  **General information.** This includes a narrative description of the overall operation, system hardware, operating system, the purpose of the system, and the methods used to accomplish the tasks. The users of this documentation are information systems operations personnel. Gathering and maintaining the following general information, which could apply to all runs, is the responsibility of the head of corporate information systems:
    * Overview and purpose of operation procedures
    * Names, titles, and home telephone numbers of all operations personnel
    * Published shift schedule
    * Contact person for operating system problems
    * Contact person for hardware problems
    * Gantt chart illustrating all scheduled runs and their start times
2.  **Backup and recovery procedures.** Documented by the systems unit in close collaboration with the firm's auditors and corporate computer center operations management, the ongoing maintenance of these procedures by the systems maintenance people is essential to the organization. Off-site backup and recovery emergency procedures also are maintained. The firm's auditors and corporate computer center management must approve all changes. Included in these procedures are:

- List of authority hierarchy
- Backup and recovery on-site procedures
- Backup and recovery off-site procedures
- Steps to safeguard backup media to and from off-site storage facility
- Disaster plan and procedures

3. **Computer operation procedures.** Job instructions should include the following:
   - Job setup instructions
   - Sources of originating data
   - Media used for inputting data
   - Output media
   - Output forms and their disposition
   - Sample of output forms
   - Sample of monitor displays
   - Corrective action to take for error messages
   - Expected job run time
   - External file label instructions
   - Input and output retention procedures
   - Computer log procedures
   - Contact person's telephone number for run problems

4. **Terminal user procedures** for users who operate terminals and/ or client/server PC systems. These users are not always familiar with information systems terms, therefore, operations documentation must be absolutely clear. Possible educational and/or physical limitations of users should be taken into account. User procedures should be simple to read and follow (eighth-grade level for nonprofessional personnel). The monitor screen also can be a source of helpful instructions. Terminal users' instructions should include:
   - Startup steps, password, etc.
   - Corrective action for error messages
   - Proper method for signing off system
   - Method(s) to obtain hardcopy output
   - Help-desk contact

## [C]  Workgroup Computer Systems

A workgroup (client/server) computer system can be under the information systems or corporate computer center operations head. It also can be a self-contained unit that may or may not rely on the information systems organization for its policies and procedures documentation. This is a management decision.

The design of workgroup systems will be under the control of the corporate information head to ensure that corporate policies are followed. The design and documentation process can be performed by the information systems unit, contracted out, or undertaken by the workgroup itself. The corporate information unit will continuously monitor the operational documentation procedures to ensure that maintenance procedures comply with the corporate standards. The workgroup computer system's communication network will follow policies and procedures instituted by the corporate head of computer networking.

1. **Workgroup general information.** Includes a narrative description of the overall workgroup operation, the system hardware, the operating system, the purpose of the system, and the methods used to accomplish the tasks. The users of this documentation are, most often, more familiar with the efforts of the group than they are with computer technology. The following general information items apply to the workgroup computer operation and the tasks of the file server computer:
   - Overview and purpose of operation procedures
   - Contact person for software problems
   - Contact person for hardware problems
   - Startup procedures for system
   - Shutdown procedures for system

2. **Backup and recovery procedures.** When the workgroup (client/server) system uses and produces financial and/or proprietary information, a close collaboration with the firm's auditors and corporate information systems management is required. Both groups must give their approval to all backup and recovery procedures. The ongoing maintenance of these procedures also will require approval of both groups. If an off-site backup and recovery operation is in place, procedures for this operation also are maintained. Changes to these procedures require the approval of the auditors and/or corporate computer center operations management. Included in these procedures are:
   - A list of who has what authority
   - Backup and recovery on-site procedures
   - Backup and recovery off-site procedures
   - Disaster plan and procedures
   - Off-site network access for on-site operations

3. **Workgroup computer operation procedures** for users of PCs who are networked into a workgroup system. These users are not always familiar with information systems terms, therefore, operations documentation must be absolutely clear. Possible educational and/or physical limitations of users must be taken into account. User operations should be simple to read and follow (eighth- to tenth-grade level for nonprofessional personnel). The monitor screen also can be a source of helpful instructions. Operators' instruction procedures should contain the following:
   - Procedure for turning on PC (password, etc.)
   - Accessing program or data from file server
   - Sample of monitor displays
   - Corrective action for error messages
   - Expected job run times
   - Input and output retention procedures
   - Telephone number for help desk
   - Shutdown procedure
   - How to access tutorial information

## [D]   Stand-alone PC Systems

Stand-alone or networked PCs that are not part of a workgroup or a corporate information system fall into this category. These are PCs throughout a firm that may not have any relationship to other PCs. But, to maintain order, consistency, and a higher level of overall efficiency, their documentation process requires a central source. The corporate information systems unit has the responsibility for companywide "independent" PC documentation, maintenance, policing, and training, as well as help-desk operations for the procedures issued.

1.  **PC general information.** Includes a narrative description of the overall corporate policies and procedures pertaining to the operation of PCs. Users of this documentation are, most often, more familiar with the duties of their own jobs than with computer technology. Their educational levels will vary widely, from the factory floor to the CEO's office. Therefore, it would be prudent for the writer of this documentation to address more than one reading level. The general information part of this documentation should apply to all users of independent PCs throughout the firm, and should include the following information items:
    - Corporate policies governing PCs
    - Procedure for turning on PC (password, etc.)
    - Daily PC housekeeping procedures
    - Overview of operating system
    - Accessing needed programs or data
    - Getting on network: LAN, WAN, or Internet
    - Shutdown procedure
    - How to access online tutorial information
    - Resources for additional specialized training
    - Frequently Asked Questions (FAQs)
    - Contact person for problems

2.  **PC operation procedures.** For given kinds of software or special hardware for a particular PC user, this documentation is in module form, one module for each given piece of software or hardware. The PC documentation manual contains the PC general information portion and as many operation procedures modules as required. Copies of vendor information are included whenever it is considered helpful to the user. The following items should be considered for each documentation module:
    - Program or hardware operating instructions
    - Corrective action for error messages
    - Backup and retention procedures
    - Telephone number for help desk
    - Shutdown procedure
    - How to access tutorial information

## § 2.08   FLOWCHARTING STANDARDS

### [A]   Purpose

Flowcharts perform several functions in the systems investigation, analysis, design, development, and installation phases. They provide a quick visual overview of a process so that you can quickly locate the part of the process of greatest interest to you. There are several good software flowcharting programs available for PCs. These can be used for drawing organization charts as well. Using a software package to draw flowcharts allows them to be easily and neatly changed.

## COMMENT

Most word processing programs can be used to draw simple diagrams.

Flowchart diagrams range in complexity from global system flowcharts to procedure step detail flowcharts. The levels of flowcharting are:

1. **Global systems.** These interrelate with other computer systems outside the organization.
2. **Total systems.** These have an interrelationship with more than one system within the internal organization.
3. **System.** This is confined to one area of operation (as in a billing system).
4. **Subsystems.** Subsystems may appear at more than one level, with the first subsystem being part of a system flowchart. (See § 2.08[D], "System Flowchart.")
5. **Program or procedure flowcharts.** Both flowcharts depict detail logic or operation steps at their lowest level. Most often, program flowcharts (see § 2.08[H], "Program Flowcharts") are used for programming instructions, while procedure flowcharts (see § 2.08[E], "Procedure Flowchart") are used for manual procedure steps.

### [B]   Global System Flowchart

A "global system" is identified here as an interaction of systems, with one or more systems outside the organization. One example would be a travel agent's system, interacting with both an airline ticket reservation system and the various credit card systems. The reservation and cost information must be approved before the travel agent can issue a ticket and charge the customer's credit card account. This is a global interactive system in operation.

The flowchart exhibit(s) will be on one page. Since there are no recognized standard symbols for global system flowcharts, the manner in which the flowchart is illustrated will depend on the IT technical skills of the viewers. Such charts are most valuable when they are rendered in the simplest terms for the whole group.

### [C]  Total System Flowchart

A "total system" is identified here as an interaction of two or more systems within the organization, which requires the interaction of all participating systems to function. One example occurs when the production control system interacts with the incentive payroll system of manufacturing, which then interacts with the inventory system for inventory control. The payroll is affected by the worker's scrap rates, which affects inventory and scrap rate report counts. The production unit count credits the worker's pay, but also affects the PM (preventive maintenance) schedule, etc.

The flowchart exhibit(s) will be on one page. Since there are no recognized standard symbols for total system flowcharts, the flowchart should be illustrated in the simplest form.

### [D]  System Flowchart

The system flowchart shows how the information flows through the system. It is all on one page, allowing the system to be viewed in its entirety. If greater detail is required of any given area of the system, a subsystem or lower-level flowchart which illustrates only the desired detail is drawn for that purpose.

System flowcharts are not governed by any national standard. Since they are intended for a diverse audience, from top management to programmers, flexibility is needed to be able to target a presentation appropriately. While programmers can follow a system flowchart drawn for top management, top management may have a problem with one drawn for a project team of systems analysts and programmers because it will often utilize standard programming flowchart symbols.

Systems flowcharts are often viewed by a whole group of people at one time. There is almost no limit to the size of a flowchart and the viewing distance of the audience governs the symbol size. With large groups, it is better to use overhead projection since anything larger than a flip chart becomes a problem to transport and store. Symbols may be used to depict such items as machines and buildings to help top management understand the system, and may, in turn, help sell it. Color also is a good tool to make the system flowchart easier to understand and more interesting to read.

### [E]  Procedure Flowchart

Procedure flowcharting is useful for illustrating manual office procedures and is easy to follow, even by people outside the data-processing area. It confirms to the operations personnel that the systems analyst has recorded the procedure correctly. It also gives the systems analyst an easy-to-follow source of information when writing or dictating documentation procedures.

Six symbols are used to draw the procedure flowchart. They represent:

1.  Original information placed on document
2.  Addition of information to document
3.  Physical handling of document
4.  Document inspection to render a decision
5.  Document holding or storage
6.  Document leaving procedure area

These are illustrated in Exhibit 2-6. A sample procedure flowchart is shown in Exhibit 2-7.

If a new, changed procedure contains manual operations, it too can be drawn as a procedure flowchart. In this case, both the old process flowchart and the proposed process flowchart are drawn on the same page for comparison. When preparing a procedure flowchart, the following must be taken into account:

1.  The direction of flow is left to right.
2.  Charts are drawn with a number 2 pencil, if done by hand.
3.  The procedure flowchart is identified in the lower left-hand corner with the following:
    *   Project name       *   Project number
    *   Date               *   Name of person who produced flowchart
4.  All input documents have a receiving point, a starting point, and a disposition. Documents may be sent to a file, disposed of (disposal), or sent to someone else.
5.  Each line represents a document flow. If a line represents one or more documents, it should be kept at the same level as long as practical.
6.  Process steps are described briefly by printing the information to the right of the symbol.
7.  When a multicopy form is originated, the parts are illustrated by the inspection symbol and the form title or number is printed inside the square.
8.  When the same activity affects two or more documents simultaneously, it is shown by drawing a vertical rectangle around a symbol indicating the activity. The flow lines are drawn to meet the rectangle.
9.  The charting of one document affecting or creating other documents is shown on the line of the affected action. A "V" line coming from the original document is dropped or inverted to meet the affected document line. After the action shown by a symbol is completed, the last leg of the "V" returns the document to its original level.

## [F] Dataflow Diagrams

Dataflow diagrams are replacing the more traditional systems flowchart. Like the system flowchart, they have not been guided by any one national standard. There is more than one proposed set of symbols, but all share the same concept and objective. The four diagramming symbols used in this text are based on work by C. Gane and T. Sarson. Their book, *Structured Systems Analysis and Design Tools and Techniques,* is the source of the concept and symbols represented here.

Dataflow diagrams, which have been around for some time, are familiar in the academic environment. They have many advantages over traditional systems flowcharts when presenting graduated levels of overviews for both current and proposed systems. Because the documentation system is so simple and employs so few rules and symbols, there is little variation between textbooks illustrating its use. Its simplicity provides for a more uniform pictorial presentation of systems that can be followed by systems analysts, programmers, operations personnel, and most users. There are commercially available dataflow diagram templates and PC drawing software. See Exhibit 2-8 for the dataflow symbols. The standard programming flowcharting template may be used with some minor substitutions. The auxiliary operation symbol can replace the dataflow environmental element symbol. The process symbol can replace the dataflow process or procedure symbol. The programming or procedure flowcharting templates can be employed to draw the data storage symbol.

The dataflow diagram illustrates the system's flow and transformation process all on one page, allowing it to be viewed in its entirety. Subsystems requiring greater detail are drawn at the next level, also in their entirety, one per page, with an identification number linking them to their source. This is illustrated in Exhibits 2-9, 2-10, and 2-11. This procedure can be repeated until the final, lowest subsystem level. The complexity and number of subsystems within the undertaking determine the number of levels that may be "exploded." The dataflow diagram levels may be defined as follows:

1. **Context diagram.** The total system concept is drawn as the "large picture," illustrating all dataflows into and out of the system. The processes themselves remain unnumbered and are not described in this general overview. The context dataflow diagram would be the one most likely considered for use in a management presentation (see Exhibit 2-9).
2. **Level 0 (zero) dataflow diagram.** This level represents the total system, numbering and describing each process. Data storage symbols are used to depict the movement of data to or from storage (see Exhibit 2-10).
3. **Level 1 dataflow diagram.** This level represents one of the processes or procedures found at the zero dataflow level that has been exploded into its own subsystem detail (see Exhibit 2-11).
4. **Level 2 dataflow diagram.** This level represents the further exploding of a given process found at level 1 into its own subsystem detail.

## COMMENT

The ease of freehand drawing of this kind of flowchart lends itself well to prototyping. The user working with a systems analyst can easily follow the procedure and the concept of what the four dataflow diagram symbols represent.

## [G]   Supplemental Dataflow Conventions

The dataflow diagramming procedure can get complex with successive levels of explosions. To help clarify the diagram, each of the four symbols employed can use supplemental conventions. Their use is illustrated in Exhibit 2-12. Following are additional conventions that may be of help:

- Entity symbols that are duplicated contain a diagonal slash in the bottom right corner. This can reduce the complexity of dataflow lines.
- Process symbols contain the process number in the top part of the symbol. When a diagram is exploded, a decimal representing the current level is added to the process number to provide for an audit trail of the related detailed processes (see Exhibit 2-12).
- Data storage symbols have a boxed area on the left side of the symbol in which to write the data storage ID. A vertical line drawn to the left of the ID indicates a duplicate data storage location.
- When dataflow lines cross each other, one of the lines may use a small crossover bridge to illustrate that the lines do not intersect.

Dataflow diagrams may be drawn by a single person or a group. If prepared by a group, a chalkboard or whiteboard can be used. Or, use a flip chart to keep a record of what was drawn. A board that can reproduce hard copies would be the most ideal instrument.

Using dataflow diagrams is good for both documenting a current system and developing a proposed system.

1. Implement dataflow diagram development procedure. Develop a free-hand context diagram. This can start with on-hand user input.
   - List external entities, dataflows, and processes.
   - Determine scope of system being charted.
   - Draw context diagram.
2. Develop a level 0 dataflow diagram.
   - Apply detail to each process or procedure.
   - Identify and post data storage. Note data storage types such as hard drive, floppy disks, file drawer, etc.
   - Identify process exceptions and post to diagram.
3. Draw the diagrams with the aid of a template. Relabel any symbols requiring more meaningful text and clean up the arrangement of the symbols.
4. Explode to the next level and repeat 1, 2, and 3 above.

## [H]   Program Flowcharts

A program flowchart shows operation steps and logic decisions to be followed by the computer for a given program in the processing sequence. All the symbols employed should conform to the ANSI standards. These symbols are shown in Exhibit 2-13.

Follow these rules in preparing the flowcharts:

1.  Draw charts on white, 8½- by 11-inch or 11- by 17-inch, 20-lb paper.
2.  Draw charts with a number 2 pencil, if done by hand.
3.  The general direction of flow is top to bottom, and left to right.
4.  When the flow is not specified or whenever increased clarity is desired, use arrows to indicate the direction of flow.
5.  Identify each page with:
    *   Project name
    *   Project number
    *   Name of person who produced flowchart
    *   Date
    *   Page X of X
6.  The terminal connector showing that a line is carried to a following page is identified with an uppercase alphabetic character in the center of the connector symbol. The line being continued on the following page starts with a connector symbol and the same character in its center as the departing connector. If that line does not continue on the following page, post the page number to the right of the connector symbol and post the departing page number to the right of the receiving connector.
7.  Describe process steps briefly by printing the description within the symbol. If necessary, print additional information next to the symbol to clarify a step.
8.  When changes are made to the flowchart at a later date, the change should be noted, dated, and signed by the person making the change.

## [I]   Unified Modeling Language™

The latest method being developed for documenting object-oriented systems is the Unified Modeling Language™ (UML). Rational Software Corporation developed UML, with contributions from other leading methodologists, software vendors, and many users. UML is based on extensive use of the Booch, OMT, and Jacobson methods to document business processes and objects, and for component modeling. The UML provides the application modeling language for:

*   Business process modeling with use cases
*   Class and object modeling
*   Component modeling
*   Distribution and deployment modeling

The Object Management Group (OMG) is developing UML into an industry standard. OMG is an open membership, not-for-profit consortium that produces and maintains computer industry specifications for interoperable enterprise applications. This standard is still in the process of being developed; for the latest information on UML, go to the OMG Web site at *www.omg.org*, or the Rational Software Corporation Web site at *www.rational.com*.

**EXHIBIT 2-6.**  Procedure Flowchart Symbols

| Process or Element | Symbol |
|---|---|
| Original operation, the first time information is placed on a document. | ◎ |
| Adding information to a document in a later procedure step. | ◍ |
| Handling the document, such as sorting, matching, separating or stapling. | ◯ |
| Inspection of a document for a decision to be made. Two or more courses of action will follow. | □ |
| Storage of document(s) as inactive, delayed, filed, or held. Also used as a destroy symbol. | ▽ |
| Sending or moving the document from one area to another. Also used to show document being sent outside. | ◯ |

**EXHIBIT 2-7.**    Sample Procedure Flowchart

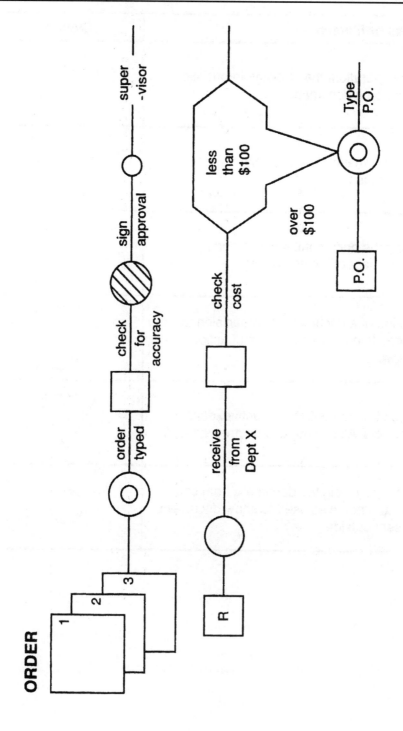

**EXHIBIT 2-8.**    Dataflow Flowchart Diagram Symbols

| Process or Element | Symbol |
|---|---|
| Entity, an environmental element, can be the source or destination of data to or from the system or subsystems. | |
| Process system or procedures that act on data being received from an external source or an internal file (hard copy or computer database or file). | |
| Data storage. This can be a computer file or database, hard copy, microfilm or COM, reference lists or tables, even the back of a tablet. | |
| Data flow. This can be in many forms, such as LAN or WAN systems, direct computer communications, the US mail, UPS, courier or what have you, between the process system (symbols) and data storage or external source. An arrow will be drawn at the contact point of the receiving symbol to denote the recipient of the data. | |

The diagramming symbols used for data flow diagrams are based on work by C. Gane and T. Sarson, *Structured Systems Analysis and Design Tools and Techniques,* Prentice Hall, Englewood Cliffs, NJ, 1979.

**EXHIBIT 2-9.**   Context Dataflow Diagram

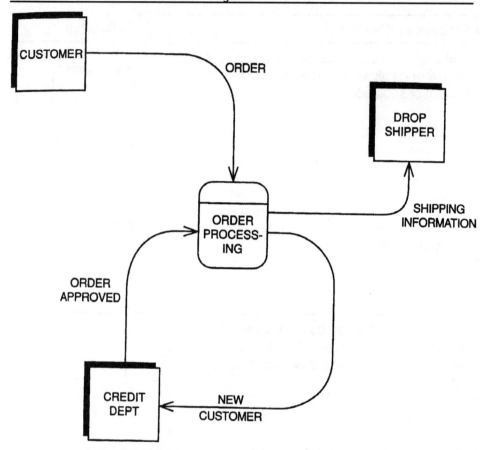

**EXHIBIT 2-10.**   Level Zero Dataflow Diagram

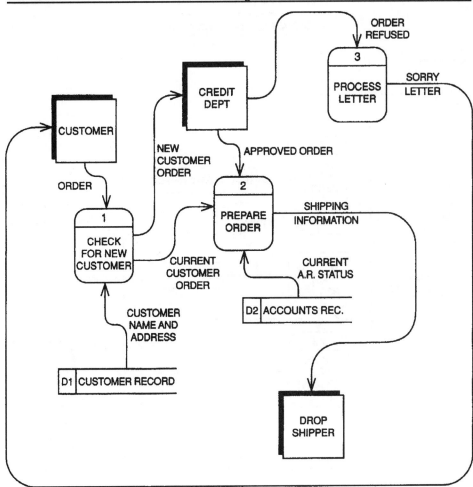

**EXHIBIT 2-11.**    Level 1 Dataflow Diagram

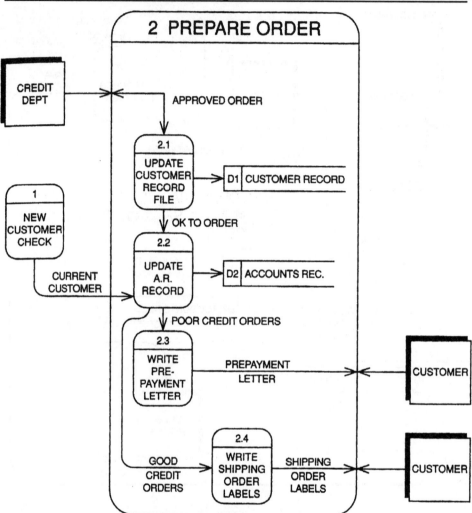

**EXHIBIT 2-12.**    Supplemental Dataflow Conventions

SLASH IN THE LOWER RIGHT HAND CORNER TO INDICATE A DUPLICATE ENTITY.

2.1

EXPLODED DIAGRAMS USE DECIMALS TO INDICATE RELATED DETAILED PROCESS.

D1

DATA STORAGE NUMBER.

D1

USE A LINE TO INDICATE DUPLICATE DATA STORAGE.

USE A CROSS ◯ OVER BRIDGE FOR LINES THAT DO NOT INTERSECT.

**EXHIBIT 2-13.**    ANSI Flowchart Symbols

| | |
|---|---|
| **Diskette Input/Output**<br>This symbol is used for floppy diskettes of all sizes. (Not ANSI standard.) | |
| **Hard Disk**<br>This symbol is for hard disk input or output. | |
| **Magnetic Tape**<br>This symbol is for magnetic tape cartridge or reels as input or output. | |
| **Auxiliary Operation**<br>This symbol is for an off-line operation such as downloading a magnetic tape to microfiche. | |
| **Preparation**<br>This symbol represents the modification of an instruction or group of instructions which change the program itself. | |
| **Manual Operation**<br>This symbol is used to show a manual operation which is limited to the speed of a human being. | |

**EXHIBIT 2-13.** *(Continued)*

| | |
|---|---|
| **Process**<br>This symbol represents a processing function. It can also represent a system symbol for a central processing unit. | |
| **Decision**<br>This symbol represents a decision step, with one or more alternative paths to be followed. | |
| **Input/Output**<br>This symbol represents the input or output of data. | |
| **Flow Lines**<br>Flow lines are used to connect the symbols and show the process flow. | |
| **Annotation**<br>This symbol is used for adding comments to an operation step. | |
| **Connector**<br>This symbol is used to exit to or enter from another part of a flowchart, especially when using another page. | |
| **Terminal Point**<br>This symbol is used to start or stop a flowchart. | |
| **Communication Link**<br>This is used to show data being transmitted over communication channels. | |

**EXHIBIT 2-13.** *(Continued)*

| | |
|---|---|
| **Sort Symbol**<br>This is used to represent the arranging of a set of items into a particular sequence. | |
| **Predefined Process**<br>This symbol is used to illustrate a sub-routine that is specified elsewhere. | |
| **Document**<br>This symbol represents a printed document output. | |
| **Display**<br>This is to show output displayed on a CRT. | |
| **Off-line Storage**<br>Any storage that is not directly accessible by a computer. | |
| **On-line Storage**<br>This symbol is for input or output which uses direct access storage such as hard disk, diskettes and so forth. | |
| **Scanning document**<br>This symbol is used for source documents which are to be scanned as input. (Not ANSI standard) | |
| **Manual Input**<br>This symbol is used for manual input entered from on-line keyboards. | |

# 3

# SYSTEMS ANALYSIS
# AND DESIGN:
# STAYING ORGANIZED

§ 3.07    SYSTEMS MAINTENANCE
          [A]    Modify or Redesign?
          [B]    Types of Maintenance Projects
          [C]    Requirements and Responsibility
          [D]    Control
          [E]    Revision Conventions

# § 3.01  PURPOSE AND SCOPE

## [A]  Planning Ahead

Most projects begin at the beginning, with an initial project planning stage, and then progress logically through each succeeding phase. However, some projects are not that neat and tidy, and begin later in the process. Either way, it is the responsibility of the project leader or systems analyst to make certain that the project has had the required planning.

A plan is required to manage any project in the most efficient manner. It provides a "roadmap" to the journey toward project completion. Without a good map, you will not know where you are or where to turn next. Establishing a policy to guide the format and development of project plans will allow others to pick up a project if you must move on, since everyone uses the same basic approach.

A properly written project plan keeps management informed on the status of each project with periodic progress reports, starting with the first phase, and following through to the end. The plan should aim for those results that are achievable with the resources management allots.

Remember that a project plan is a written document—not something simmering in the back of your mind. A project plan also is a communications tool between the project manager and the team members, the project's sponsor, and any other interested stakeholder.

## [B]  Policy Objectives

The policy governing project development requires the following:

1. Organize systems projects into manageable major phases.
2. Establish a timetable that specifies both chargeable and calendar time.
3. Stipulate the format for progress reporting, which can be arranged by task phases to be completed or by target completion date.
4. An overall plan contains the principal ingredients required for an acceptable undertaking. These are:
   a. **Economic feasibility.** Will the new system pay for itself in its expected lifetime?
   b. **Organizational feasibility.** Will the system operate within the current organizational structure?
   c. **Technical feasibility.** Will the proposed system actually work?
   d. **Operational feasibility.** Can the system work within the environment for which it is designed? If applicable, will it successfully operate outside the firm?

## [C]  Avoiding "Scope Creep"

The scope of a systems project is typically identified by its constrained elements (its boundaries). First, the relevant activities of the project establish limits confined by time, dollar resources, required changes, and/or systems or organizational boundaries. Second, the subject itself can identify and restrict the project scope. If expanded beyond its subject area, the project loses its frame of reference, unallocated resources are likely to be expended, and the objective of the project becomes less clear. Therefore, a policy that contains the scope of a project is essential to its success.

Begin every project with a written scope statement. This is a summary of what this project is supposed to achieve. A well-written scope statement is used to develop a list of "success criteria" (or features) that the project is intended to achieve. Together, the scope statement and success criteria provide an anchor for your project. Anything beyond what is in these statements is to be considered an expansion of the project and requires additional resources. The project plan is your roadmap for how these features will be created. These statements must be approved by the project's sponsor before you begin writing the plan.

## COMMENT

Many IT or systems managers attribute late, over-budget, or uncompleted projects to wandering into unrelated areas of user needs. Objectives and careers are jeopardized if control of a project and resources is not retained. This lack of control may help explain some of the management turnover in the information technology profession.

## § 3.02   SYSTEMS DEVELOPMENT AND PLANNING

### [A]   Project Planning

The system project's organization requires a standard procedure to ensure proper planning, control, and status reporting. These defined procedures provide standards to: (1) assess a project in progress, (2) assess the merits of one project over another, and (3) provide a tool when reviewing employees for merit rewards.

The following tasks are included in project planning:

1. **Definition of project goals**
   - Systems output
   - Data manipulation processes
   - Systems throughput process
   - Systems control mechanism
   - Systems requirements
   - Implied major tasks
   - Calendar time needed to complete project
   If any of these areas can be subdivided into measurable milestones for reporting, it should be done. (For example, throughput processing may entail more than one manual procedure or computer program.)

2.   **Project plan preparation.** A brief plan and schedule are developed outlining the requisite tasks and timetable to accomplish the project goals. These include:
     • Identify the work necessary to accomplish each of the project's goals. This includes tasks applicable to projects not initially identified as work to be covered in planned goals. These should be divided into measurable units or milestones. Break down tasks into functional requirements small enough that you can identify the resources required and the length of time necessary to complete them. Beware of the overlooked or hidden technical requirement!
     • Develop detailed database, file, report, and program specifications.
     • Establish a budget to implement your plan. State every cost assumption you use.
     • Assign responsibilities. To a great extent, time estimates are based on the expertise of the person working on the task. Most projects involve people "loaned" from other departments and who bring with them their usual workload. The sharpest people will be the hardest to get.
     • Prepare workload schedules.
     • Prepare appropriate project documentation. This can be time-consuming but essential when looking back to see the basis used to make a decision. It will also provide some actual performance history useful in planning your next project.
     • Develop Gantt charts from project schedules for planning and reporting the status of project tasks. If possible, use a project management software package to build these charts, identify resource conflicts, and help to track the project's progress.
     • Prepare a format and schedule for project status reports.

## [B]   Analysis of Requirements

The project leader or lead systems analyst works closely with the project sponsor to ensure that the systems requirements are defined and understood, and that the user does not expect system revision in the near future. It is a rare business manager who knows exactly what he or she wants. Business managers need software developed to meet specific business goals. Take time to understand what they want to achieve and what they visualize it will look like. During these meetings, you also will educate them on technical capabilities and cost. They may feel that specific features are "nice to have" but have no idea of the cost to develop them. Separate the essential project elements from the "nice to have" features. The smaller your project is, the more likely it is to succeed. Add nonessential features to later releases of the product.

A number of techniques exists to ensure that all systems requirements are precisely defined. These are:

• Determine capabilities of project team to achieve given system objectives
• Establish operating parameters

- Organize all pertinent data elements
- Define processing requirements
- Determine output requirements
- Determine required database or file needs
- Determine required data input requirements and method of input

To ensure all requirements are defined prior to the systems design phase, use a checklist similar to the one shown in Exhibit 3-1.

## COMMENT

You can't get there from here! Always beware of the implied tasks to accomplish a goal. The more detailed your analysis is, the more of the "implied tasks" you will uncover. For example, if the request was to develop software for use in a warehouse, there may be an implied task to run electricity and network connections to distant places. Another example might involve an implied requirement to maintain a database in sync with another database on a different hardware platform and software engine.

### [C]   Estimating Resource Requirements

A resource estimate, prepared for each project, is used to allocate resources and provide a basis for project financial control. Estimates may also provide a basis for preparing user service charges. The person in charge of planning should:

1.  Estimate the worker-hours required for analysis and programming. This estimate may be revised as programming proceeds. If you did a thorough job extracting system characteristics from the project's sponsor, you will know what is needed in terms of people, expertise, equipment, and time. It is not unusual to miss an item or two but always hope they were small ones.

    Establishing good worker-hour estimates is an art since different people have different productivity levels. Therefore, time estimates are either based on a job description (anyone with these qualifications should be able to work at an estimated rate) or based on specific people. If you are using contract workers yet to be hired, then the job description approach is used. If the team member is already on staff, ask them to estimate a time. Where possible, use the actual hours required from previous projects of similar complexity.

    After all of the time estimates are rolled up, add a percentage for contingency time to each task, depending on similar past experience

**EXHIBIT 3-1.** Systems Development Checklist

### A. Data Input Editing

1. Does editing look for missing data?
2. Does editing include verification of format?
3. Does editing include verification of codes through the use of drop-down lists?
4. Will editing be completed field by field as the data is entered?
5. Will all data rejection messages clearly state why a field was rejected?
6. Will there be a supervisor bypass procedure?

### B. Database and File Updating

1. How frequently are backups done?
2. Are partial updates done?
3. Must source data be corrected prior to update procedures?
4. Are files purged periodically?
5. Are there legal data retention requirements?
6. Are purged data files transferred to inactive files?
7. Will a transaction backup file be online?

### C. Output Preparation

1. Is the output viewable online?
2. Is the data real time or updated daily?
3. If the output is hardcopy, how many copies are needed?
4. Is the hardcopy output a regular report or only provided on demand?
5. Do the reports contain summaries and intermediate summaries?
6. Will output be made available over a network or the Internet?

### D. Error Correction

1. Will the error correction routines require rewriting the source document?
2. Is it possible for uncorrected data to enter the processing system?
3. Can an error be corrected after it has been placed in a file or database? How?

and/or the past performance of the person assigned the task. If the project covers an extended calendar time period, this becomes even more important. This can help avoid a possible late or over-budget project. If a project is late or over budget, as most projects are, this budgeted extra time will be welcome. Convert the worker-hours needed to dollars. If the project finishes ahead of schedule and/or under budget, this can reflect well on the project leader.

Use a software package to prepare Gantt charts for the worker-hours required, indicating the calendar time when personnel will be available since not all project personnel are available full time. Set milestones within each Gantt chart to identify the status of each project task. This status can be plotted against the budgeted allotted time to determine whether the task is on schedule.

2.  Most project-tracking software packages also will provide a financial report on the project's status. This report compares the amount spent to date to the budgeted amount at any given point in the project.

3.  Identify and estimate all equipment, software, and service costs required for the new system. A dollar contingency amount should be added to cover any unforeseen expenses.

## COMMENT

Contingency times should be held in reserve by the project manager and not handed out to the workers. Some people will act as if the contingency time is something to be frittered away at the beginning of the task and only begin work when time is short (similar to the student who only studies for a test the night before). Then if a problem arises, the time set aside for them to deal with the issue is gone and tasks will always run over in spite of contingency time.

### [D]   Risk Analysis

All IT projects involve some degree of risk. Risk management should be a proactive process, part of the overall project. Risk is not to be avoided, but managed. To manage risk proactively, identify and analyze risk continuously in the normal course of the project. The following steps can be used to manage the risk in a project:

1.  **Identify the risk.** Discuss risks early in the project. The sooner risks are identified, the sooner solutions can be found.

2.  **Analyze the risk.** Determine how risk can impact the project. What

effect will the risk have on cost, project duration, or the ability of the project to satisfy the user's requirements?

3. **Prioritize.** Determine which risks deserve the most attention, and which risks can be safely ignored.
4. **Follow up.** Keep track of all risks and what is being done to mitigate their impact.
5. **Control.** By making risk management part of day-to-day project management, you control the risk, rather than it controlling you.

## COMMENT

A CEO study by the Gartner Group reveals that change initiatives are most likely to fail because of such problems as resistance to change, lack of sponsorship, and unrealistic or unknown expectations.

There are several areas of risk that can influence an IT project:

1. **Economic.** Economic fluctuation can change the value of the project to the firm or affect funding available for the project.
2. **Government.** Changes in government regulations can impact the cost or utility of the project.
3. **Marketplace.** If the project is meant to support a new product, consumers' acceptance or changing needs can affect the project.
4. **Technology.** A project's technology may not work as advertised or may change during the course of a long project.
5. **Organizational.** Lukewarm management support, changes in management, unrealistic expectations, etc., can all adversely affect the project.

Exhibit 3-2 is an example of a form used to track and manage the risks identified in a project.

## § 3.03  SYSTEMS ANALYSIS

### [A]  Overview

Systems analysis is the process of analyzing a system that is operational. Of course, if a new system neither replaces nor alters one already in place, there is no need for this analysis. In that case, only the requirements for the new system are needed for the systems design.

Prototyping a new system may not require a thorough systems analysis by the IT design person, but any information he or she can obtain about the user area will be helpful. This information can reduce the time needed for the prototyping development. Also, the user will have more confidence in the systems analyst if he/she "speaks the user's language," which could enhance the final design.

Systems analysis has changed little over the years. Some new to systems analysis and others who do not want to allocate resources and/or costs to this effort, avoid it, or limit its scope. This lack of analysis leads to a process of "code and fix," whereby coding begins before user requirements are fully known, and accounts significantly for new system failures. It is common for established consulting firms to relegate this task to their lower-priced help, with predictable results. There also can be a problem of "paralysis through analysis," spending too much time on this phase. But this is seldom the case.

This section on analysis provides the traditional, proven procedures. Knowing the steps will not guarantee success, but knowing and practicing the procedures can produce the desired results.

## [B]   Preanalysis Survey

Before attempting to contact the user for an analysis of the current operating system, gather as much knowledge about the unit as possible. A feasibility study is a good place to start.

Identify the unit's head and subordinates, if possible, from an organization chart for large units. One Fortune 500 firm employs organizational charts with pictures to go along with the names and titles. Try to remember the names of personnel and their respective titles. Also, know the corporate hierarchy. Any information about personalities and the unit's organization status that can be discovered beforehand can help. Become aware of the unit's corporate politics; any hidden power structures can be a minefield, delaying the system's progress.

Examine current procedural documentation. This provides the systems analyst with the formal procedures of the current operation. Later, the analyst will have an opportunity to confirm if the procedures are still valid, and, if not, what has changed. The operating procedures should include forms used. If it does not, obtain copies. They will help you understand their role in the operation.

## [C]   Initial Unit Visit

Call the unit's head for a first meeting in his/her office. If he/she is not in, leave a voice-mail message to return the call.

## COMMENT

Prepare for the visit. Dress in a manner appropriate for management. If the area being visited is the manufacturing operation's spray-painting section, do not wear your new $500 outfit.

**EXHIBIT 3-2.** Risk Analysis Form

| ID | Description | Severity | Probability | Value | Plan |
|----|-------------|----------|-------------|-------|------|
| 1 | Database designer with required skills not available when needed. | 8 | .2 | 1.6 | Work with DBA group to make sure resource is available when needed. |
| 2 | Learning curve for new version of report writer steeper than expected. | 5 | .4 | 2.0 | Send member of team to training before start of project. |
| 3 | User resource not available when needed. | 9 | .5 | 4.5 | Work with senior management to ensure resource availability. |

ID—A unique identifier for the risk.

Description—A description of the risk.

Severity—The effect on the project on a scale of 1 (low) to 10 (severe).

Probability—The probability the risk will actually have an impact on the project; 0.0 (none) to 1.0 (certain).

Value—Severity, probability. Used to rank the risks.

Plan—How are we going to deal with this risk?

During your first contact, the art of listening becomes important. It has been said, "You cannot be a listener with your mouth open." Ask about the operation, the unit's problems, and the unit's people. If time and conditions permit, include a little social chatter, along with a cup of coffee. Later, have the person introduce you to the employees. Set up "the best time" for the return visit. If this person cannot see you within a reasonable time, ask to speak with someone lower on the organization chart, or start with the first person in the unit working with the current system.

## [D]  Information Gathering Interviews

It is wise not to spend too much time on the first visit with any one person. Speaking with a person six times for ten minutes each is better for the systems analyst than a single one-hour visit because the analyst will learn more and also develop a closer relationship with that person. Remember, when conducting an interview:

- Start at beginning of an operation flow.
- Interview person at his/her place of work or meet at neutral place.
- If person is ill or has a problem, come back later.
- Develop listening skills.
- Do not repeat rumors; sidestep any local office politics or personality clashes.
- Interview all people in unit, if possible. No one will be seen as a favorite, and more will be learned. Even if several people perform the same job, each may see it from a different perspective. One may contribute something the others overlooked. Each person will add something that leads to another question for someone else.
- Be open with your note-taking. Shorthand pads work well.
- Do not jump to conclusions.
- Listen carefully for what person really means.
- Leave your information technology jargon at the door.
- Be aware of interviewee's body language.
- Look for content, not style of delivery of information.
- Do not assume anything.
- Avoid playing favorites with workers.
- Define what tools are employed: hardware, software, files accessed, and such.
- Ask questions, but be aware of who may have a stake in or have developed the current system.
- Give people time to answer correctly.
- Collect copies of documents and ask:
  - What is daily volume of forms, reports, and so on?
  - From where do documents come?
  - Who originates first inside document?
  - Why is document used?
  - How is document completed?
  - Where are documents filed?

- Other questions:
  - Has worker come up with his/her own procedures to make things work?
  - How often and when are backups done?
  - What is security procedure?
  - What problems are there with operating instructions?
  - Whom do you contact for help?
- Conclude interview by thanking person.

## [E] Document the Interviews

After the interviews are over, analyze the information gathered. Draw (freehand) flowcharts from the data collected.

Return to the unit and authenticate the flowchart(s) by observing the actual people doing the jobs. If necessary, send a follow-up memo verifying approval of the documented information by the person or persons interviewed.

Document present procedures to be included in the final systems report. Prepare the final flowcharts and make necessary copies.

## [F] Work-sampling Studies

Work sampling is a tool used by the systems analyst to find out how people spend their time at work. Since labor costs are a significant part of operating cost, it is essential to know how that time is spent. To justify the cost of new procedures or hardware investments, work sampling is used to study a current operation. It is a simple procedure and, when properly used, can reveal the areas that require further study.

For example, take the question, "Should the company purchase a second copy machine?" The systems analyst performs random observations of the number of people waiting in line to use the copy machine, then turns that number into hours per day of wait time. These hours represent dollars: the cost of an employee waiting instead of working. This cost, plus the price of acquiring a new machine, along with the additional cost of operating a second machine (floor space, etc.), determines the write-off time cost for the acquisition. This information helps management decide whether to make the purchase.

Another focus of this work-sampling information might be the travel time of people who use the copy machine. Ask people who are waiting the location of their work units to help compute this travel time. Perhaps the second machine could be better located to reduce travel time costs.

This is a very simple example. More complex studies yield other kinds of information. One undercover study in a department of 16 people revealed that each person was spending 35 percent of the time doing no work at all. The reason was a lack of supervision.

Another study was set up in an engineering support unit of a Fortune 500 firm to find out how people spent their time, and what new equipment was needed to reduce the heavy overtime. The result of the study showed that employees were not working so hard or so efficiently because they enjoyed the overtime income too much. These findings enabled the company to eliminate Saturday overtime costs.

Other information can help address specific problems. In one instance, discovery of a new government regulation that required a ratio of hours to workers that equaled three persons made it possible to cost justify these three people quickly and cheaply.

A work-sampling study involves the following:

1. **Observation times.** Observations of the work area studied are performed at random times and dates. Random numbers can be generated by computer software, taken from a random number table in a math book, or drawn out of a hat. It is suggested that two sets of observation times be drawn: a small sample of 50 to 100, and a larger sample later. The specific sample size is dependent on the number of items and people observed. About a hundred observations per item type observed is typical. There are formulas available used by industrial engineers to compute the number needed for the required confidence level.

2. **Preliminary observations.** Compose a list of tasks for the preliminary study of the initial observations. Personal time and miscellaneous should always be included. "Out of the area and available, but no work" may in some cases be selected, too. These tasks are posted to the tally sheet for observations (see Exhibit 3-3). The observations are performed only by the systems analyst and no one else, especially not the boss. People are not usually identified by name.

   The observations are taken in a split second and tally marked (i.e., a mark is made for each observation; four in a row, with the fifth mark across the other four). The tallies are counted and posted in the total column on the right-hand side. After the tallies are posted, each total value is divided by the total number of observations. For example, with a preliminary observation of 50, divide each task total value by 50 to get the percent of time spent with that task. Added together, the percent values will total approximately 100 percent.

3. **New tally sheet.** Using the results of the preliminary observations, add or delete items from the final observation study. Those with less than a 5-percent tally are normally deleted from the final study. When the miscellaneous category is very high—over 20 percent—try to identify a category or categories to be removed and placed under their own tasks. Then construct a new tally sheet for the final study.

4. **Final observation study.** The final observation study is made at the random times and dates selected. Complete the tally sheet as explained in Step 2. Then divide each task total by the total number of observations to get the task percentage. The total number of observations for the final study, as shown in Exhibit 3-3, will be no less than 10 times the number of observations in the preliminary study.

> # COMMENT
>
> People tend to act differently if they feel they are being observed or their work output evaluated. The more often you are seen in a department, the less of a stranger you will be and the less this effect will be apparent. Most workers will view work sampling as something that will change their environment for the worse and may exhibit negative behavior toward you.

## [G]   Final Report

Place the procedure text and flowcharts in a binder with a cover sheet entitled Final Analysis Study Report, and a name to identify the study. The cover memo summarizes the study, including any recommendations and any additional comments the analyst may make. This memo is not placed in the report binder, but sent to the project leader, along with the feasibility study and the report. The dates and hours expended on the analysis should be reported in the format required by the project leader.

When the final analysis report is submitted, the project's sponsor will issue a decision to proceed with the project or to drop it. Dropping a bad project is a good thing to do. Proceeding with a bad project will generally result in failure at some point in the project so this is the best time to "keep it or kill it."

# § 3.04   SYSTEMS DESIGN

## [A]   Overview

The objective of systems design is to take the systems parameters as defined in the development and planning phase and create a system to the degree allowed, given the allocated resources and timeframe. The defined scope of the project determines the resources and time limitations. If a systems analysis final report is available, use it as an information base in designing the new system.

The systems analyst synthesizes the elements of several design alternatives and compares them with the design criteria. Compare them with each other and with the current system. The system closest to achieving the defined objectives, with the best utilization of resources, is the best choice. This decision is not the systems analyst's alone; management and/or the user will have an impact on the final selection of the "best" solution. The analyst may design the alternative systems, but management and the user have to live with the selection long after the analyst has moved on to other projects.

The procedure steps required to achieve optimal design are:

- Establish detailed system design specifications for selected design.
- Determine proper utilization of software, hardware, assigned personnel, and contract services.
- Prepare final systems report supported with documentation and system flowcharts.
- Gain acceptance of proposed system from requesting authorities and users.

## [B]   Systems Design Specifications

The development of systems design specifications includes any refinements incorporated into the design as requested by users and the requesting authority. Final design documentation will include input, output, database, and software specifications to meet the design requirements. Above all, backup and recovery procedures, along with security requirements, are a must.

1. **System specifications.** The details for this phase are determined by what is needed to communicate the system requirements to programmers or software vendors. Following are guidelines for developing these specifications:
   a. **Develop output requirements,** first based on user report or workstation display needs.
   b. **Develop file specifications.** Develop an Index of Table Field Names—the names used in databases, programs, and input/output locations. The specifications include all data elements required for present or anticipated needs, and a data dictionary to provide their specifications. Most installations already have a standard naming convention for you to follow.
   c. **Define the input layouts.** This is the format of all data to be captured for use by the system. This input can be source documents coming into the information systems data entry unit or input received as captured data from outside the computer operation. The source of captured data received by the system is input from terminals or other, nonkeyed data, and is of major concern to the systems analyst who must ensure that only the required input gains entry to the system.
   d. **Develop the processing requirements.** Describe in detail the processing operations required by the software. In addition, general guidelines may be required for some functions, such as:
      - Procedures for entry of corrections
      - Controls to monitor out-of-balance conditions (e.g., a minus payroll check or inventory balance)
      - Editing routines for missing or incorrect data entering system for first time
      - Proper restart procedures for user

**EXHIBIT 3-3.**   Completed Sampling Tally Sheet

Date(s) _1/10 – 1/20/03_   By _Mary Smith_

Unit observed _Billing Support_                    Number of people _4_

| Task | Tally | Total | % |
|------|-------|-------|---|
| Filing | ||||| ||||| ||||| ||||| ||||| ||||| | 30 | 30 |
| Telephone | ||||| /// | 8 | 8 |
| Reading | ||||| ||||| / | 11 | 11 |
| Writing | ||||| ||||| ||||| ||||| / | 21 | 21 |
| Personal | ||||| ||||| | 10 | 10 |
| Misc. | ||||| ||||| ||||| ||||| | 20 | 20 |
|  |  |  |  |
|  | TOTAL NUMBER OF OBSERVATIONS | 100 | 100 |

2. **Manual procedures.** All data processing begins and ends with a person. The computer sits in the middle digesting what the input person tossed in and spitting out the result on the other side. If you ignore the people part of your process, you are ignoring two-thirds of the process and the best-made system will fail. Clerical tasks are included to:
   - Review data to ensure it can be entered. Bad data will make a good program act in unusual ways.
   - Correct input data. At any place where someone is entering or scanning data, validate each field as it is entered. If the data is not valid, immediately send a message to the operator as to why it was rejected.
   - Change data already in system.
   - Hold or dispose of input data. Some data source documents must be retained for business or legal reasons.
   - Distribute output (printed, CDs, or LAN file).

## [C]   Utilization of Resources

Understanding the availability of hardware, software, and personnel resources is essential to preparing the system design specifications. Analyze these to determine their adequacy to fulfill the systems objectives. If any of the three is inadequate, changes are required. If the resources cannot be changed, it may be necessary to alter the system's scope or objectives.

Often, the availability of scarce resources is contingent on when the project will begin. If a project's approval is delayed for a significant amount of time, or if other critical projects have begun since the original estimate was made, you should review the assumptions used for estimated resources required.

## [D]   Final Systems Report

The proposed system design is documented in the form of a final systems report that defines objectives and states how the proposed system design meets them. The scope of the undertaking is defined, along with a proposed timetable for installing the new system. It contains proposed costs and return expected, in both tangible and intangible benefits, for the resource investment. Its purpose is to inform and gain acceptance of the proposed system, and the report is hand-carried to the proper individuals one to two weeks before the verbal presentation is to be made.

The report contains the following:

1. **A summary of full systems study**
   - Overview of events leading up to study
   - Subject of study
   - Objectives and scope of proposed system
   - Statement of recommendations and justifications for proposed system

2. **Body of report**
   a. Description of current system, including:
      - Brief description of current system and its use
      - Purpose of current system
      - Problems with current system (if any) and rationale for new system
   b. Description of proposed system, including:
      - Overview of proposed system
      - Scope of project
      - Exhibits of all reports and screen displays
      - System flowcharts
      - Systems documentation of proposed system and any vendor-supplied material that provides additional information
      - Summary of proposed recommendations
      - Summary of assumptions that recommendations are based on
      - List of personnel needs:
        i. Workerpower required to install new system
        ii. Workerpower required to maintain new system
      - Proposed timetable for installing suggested system and work-hours required to complete project
      - List of special equipment or software that must be purchased for project
   c. Financial information section, including:
      - Present system operating cost
      - Proposed system operating cost
      - Installation cost of new system and its estimated useful life
      - Tangible and intangible benefits of proposed system
   d. Proposed system summary: A positive statement of rationale for installing proposed system, summary also contains any concerns that exist about timetable, funds, software, hardware, outside contractors, or personnel available for undertaking.

3. **Appendix**
   a. Prior reports
   b. Memos and letters
   c. Other supporting documents not included in body of report:
      - Sample documents and forms
      - Charts
      - Graphs
      - Gantt charts
      - Tables of data
      - Vendor literature

## [E] The Acceptance Presentation

Gaining acceptance is the last step before systems implementation. All concerned are brought together for a verbal and visual presentation. Everyone attending should have had enough time to read the report. This presentation is used to confirm that the proposed system will meet its objective and stay within the defined scope. Although not requisite, the presentation to gain final acceptance can be just as important as the final written report that serves as a basis for the verbal presentation. However, reading the report itself is not enough.

Therefore, a different approach must be adopted to resolve any problems, whether political or technical. It is very important that the presenter know the attitudes, political positions, and status of all those attending the presentation. Not everyone present may be supportive; some may object to possible added demands on their areas, loss of present control, or loss of operations.

Here are some suggestions on how to sell your proposal:

- Be relaxed. Otherwise, people may think you are trying to hide something.
- Gain approval by seeking support from people before the meeting. If possible, contact each of the key managers before the meeting to discuss any questions they may have about the report. This will allow you time to send out any clarifications before the meeting.
- Decide whether you want credit for your innovation or acceptance. You may not get both. This is corporate politics.
- Do not expect others to think like you.
- Never have surprises at this presentation. People do not like them. Address all known problems before the meeting begins.
- Never expect that people want change or innovation simply because they may have indicated they did in the past.
- You may have a compelling story to tell but keep the entire presentation to under an hour. If someone wants to know more, they will ask you.

Well-planned audio and visual aids help to create a positive impression on the audience. Flip charts particularly add visual interest by providing step-by-step information with graphs, flowcharts, and text materials. You can write notes on the edge of each page to assist you.

In-house graphic arts departments may be of help in producing the visual aids you require. They may have a PC or notebook PC and a portable projector for running your presentation using Microsoft PowerPoint or similar software. Vendors may be a source of visuals, too.

Make sure you are comfortable with whatever materials you use. New, untried hardware or software can spell disaster. Check out the room the day before and have a dry run, if possible. To ensure everything is ready on the day of the presentation, arrive no less than an hour before the presentation. Test any equipment to make sure it works. Your high exposure may not spell a promotion, but a disaster is something you may have to live down.

The presentation should help gain as much support for and acceptance of the new system as possible. In some cases, it may even wrap up the sale. Following is a basic presentation outline:

1. **Introduction.** The introduction consists only of preliminary descriptions: Introduce yourself and the subject. Explain how the system study began and progressed, and how the presentation will be made. Include:
   - A statement defining the need for a new system. Gain their interest!
   - An explanation about how alternative systems were reviewed before selecting the one being presented
   - An explanation of the format that follows the introduction

2. **The body.** The body is the heart of the presentation. Use terminology familiar to your audience, especially management and users. Those attending will be more interested in what is done than how the technology works. Emphasize the benefits of the new system and not its hardware or software. Have a positive attitude about the benefits (such as faster processing or response time, better accuracy and control, and, maybe, reduced costs). Reliable information and honesty about any drawbacks are necessities. The body should:
   a. Briefly describe current production system.
   b. Describe proposed system and any alternate proposals.
   c. Present economic information:
      - Current system operating costs
      - Proposed system operating costs
      - Cost of installing proposed system (Be conservative with cost claims.)
      - Intangible benefits and/or requirements imposed by customers, vendors, or government
   d. Provide recommendations for proposed selection.
3. **Summary of the presentation.** All tangible and intangible benefits of proposed system should be stressed.
4. **Discussion**
   a. Open meeting for questions.
   b. Keep discussion going; call on people who support proposed system for input. You don't have to answer every question yourself if some attendees helped provide that technical aspect.
   c. Be aware of attitudes of people and have a strategy ready to handle any negative comments.
5. **Conclusion.** End your presentation on a positive note.
   a. Summarize areas of agreement brought up during open discussion.
   b. Make a positive statement as to what will happen with project and how those involved will be kept informed of its progress.

# § 3.05   SYSTEMS PROTOTYPING

## [A]   Overview

This section covers ideas and procedures for using prototyping to design a working systems model. Prototyping is an analysis and design technique involving end users in defining the requirements and developing the system according to their needs and desires. It helps define the end-user requirements more quickly than the traditional analysis and design approach. A complex system can involve a number of (modular) prototypes.

Prototypes can be hand drawn (see the dataflow diagrams, Chapter 2) or developed with computer software tools that are available for PCs. Computer-aided systems and software engineering (CASE) technologies automate the analysis and design process using modeling tools and other techniques.

Another useful technique is Joint Applications Development (JAD). If you plan to use JAD, start with a "safe" project, one that has very little chance of failure with the following characteristics:

- The user is skillful and cooperative.
- The application is a one-user and/or simple application.
- Minimum of hardware/software changes are needed.
- A top-quality team is assigned to the project.
- There is an adequate budget.

A well-selected user is essential.

The systems analyst working with the user can develop an iterative series of prototypes that can be viewed and revised interactively. This reduces both the calendar and chargeable project time.

Prototyping is best suited for developing systems that are not well defined, or for exceptional, smaller systems applications. It allows for the visualization and conversation required for quick systems development. All too often users request something they cannot define, or they cannot see how changes will satisfy their needs. This type of situation would be a candidate for a prototyping effort.

The characteristics of systems that are likely candidates for prototyping are:

- User requirements are difficult to define.
- The application has few users—often only one.
- The application may be ad hoc or even parochial in nature.
- The application has a low volume of input and/or output.
- The application requires a minimum of editing controls.
- User(s) may only require a stand-alone PC using their own files or database.

## [B]  Prototype Development

The systems analyst needs to consider what kind of system requires development since not all undertakings are suitable for prototyping. A traditional system that cuts across two or more departments would probably be a poor candidate. Another poor candidate would be an order-processing or payroll system. Rather, single-user, novel, and/or complex applications, and semi-structured or even unstructured applications are all good candidates for this kind of approach.

The systems analysis management also must evaluate the environmental conditions where the systems analyst will operate. The political climate and the user's personality play a major role in the success or failure of this kind of undertaking.

The lead systems analyst maintains a prototype project folder, containing all papers related to the project, and an activities diary for which a shorthand pad can suffice. The diary should be hand-posted while the information is still fresh and should contain such information as the day's activities, time spent on each activity, and any other information the analyst deems relevant. The diary is not for publication; it is only a reference record to be placed in the prototype project folder after the effort is completed.

The procedure for prototyping is as follows:

1. **Estimate project expense.** Both direct and indirect costs are computed. This includes the chargeable time of systems analysts and programmers, along with other development costs. Software and hardware costs are generally considered indirect costs, but a one-time-use software package required for the project is a direct cost.
   a. The information system's personnel define the calendar timeframe, as well as the estimated worker-hours. If costs and time requirements are agreeable to both the user and information systems management, the project will proceed. The costs may be charged directly to the requesting user's budget or applied to an information systems budget for such projects.
2. **Develop manageable modules.** Module size is reduced to a manageable level so that each module can be built separately from other system or subsystem modules. Each is also designed to allow other modules to interact with its features. This development is done in concert with the end user(s) and the systems analyst.
3. **Build the prototype.** As the systems analyst gathers information about the user's requirements for the application, he/she assesses user feedback about the developing prototype to better visualize the systems requirements. Successful prototyping depends on early and frequent end-user feedback to the developing process. User changes made early in the development process will reduce costs and total project development time.

   The systems analyst illustrates to the user(s) as early as possible how parts of the system actually accomplish their objectives. This early construction of an operational prototype allows early user feedback so the systems analyst can gain valuable insight into the direction of the prototype construction. To develop the prototype as quickly as possible, the analyst uses whatever special tools are available, such as personal, workgroup, or even organizational databases, computer software, and other prototype design tools. Access to databases, other than personal ones, will require the permission of the data administrator and/or the database administrator.

   Rapid prototyping development reduces the chance of changes imposed by the user. The longer it takes to develop a system, the more the system is susceptible to changes imposed by the user and/or the operational environment. Rapid prototyping development safeguards against overcommitting resources to a project that could eventually become unworkable.

## COMMENT

The saying "strike while the iron is hot" applies here. The hotter the iron is, the easier it is to work. The longer a project is stretched out, the less chance it has to succeed.

4. **Complete the prototype.** The prototyping is complete when the user has what he/she wants and the systems analyst is willing to sign off on the prototype. The sign-off can take two forms:

   a. **Scrap the prototype** when the user(s) is not satisfied with the finished product or the requirements are beyond what can be reasonably provided.

   The systems analyst is the representative of the systems department, the database administrator, and the data administrator. These areas require limited access by the end users. The systems analyst is required to police the needs of users so that they do not violate any policies or procedures that are in place for these areas.

   b. **Accept the prototype.** Operationally completed prototypes require sign-off by both the user(s) and the systems analyst. This might be a joint memo from both to the users' management and the head of the systems department. The user(s) by this time will have been trained in the operation of the prototype system, and an operation manual will have been completed and put in place. This training and documentation is the responsibility of the lead systems analyst assigned to the project.

   The lead systems analyst sends a final project memo to the systems manager within a week after the prototype has been signed-off. This allows for follow-up to confirm that all went as planned. The memo is a summary report on the effective utilization of information systems resources on behalf of the prototype effort. The report may end with an editorialized summary by the analyst responsible for the prototype. The prototype project folder and its diary are sources of information for this report.

## [C]   Types of Prototyping Methods

Due to different needs, a single "all in one" prototype model is not realistic. However, there are four tools available to the systems analyst. All four follow the same prototype development procedures as outlined in § 3.05[B], "Prototype Development." They are:

1. **First-of-a-series prototype.** A pilot prototype is developed as a full-scale system, can be made up of subsystems, and is a "true" prototype, i.e., one that is developed and debugged at one site. The following prototypes are modified to further improve the system. The first-of-a-series is volume tested after it is debugged, ensuring that the prototype can be replicated at other sites with a minimum of effort and problems.

2. **Modular prototype.** This prototype does not contain all the attributes that the final system version will have. This allows for the rapid development of less complex prototypes. After the first has been developed, another similar-featured one is developed and joined to the first to construct a finished product. There can be any number of designated prototypes connected to complete a final version.

3. **One-shot prototype.** This prototype does not have to be efficient because it will be used only once. (It could be used later, but seldom is.)

Such a prototype can afford to be inefficient, as long as the development cost is less than what would be gained from a more efficient operating model. The retrieval, storage, and computation can be primitive, if workable. If this type of prototype were popular, time and effort to develop a "user/request" form would make sense. This form would save time for both the user(s) and systems analyst or programmer analyst.

## COMMENT

Using such a form for one-shot programs is not a new idea. One of the authors developed one for a General Electric Engineering department over 30 years ago.

4. **Input-output prototype.** This is a scale model prototype, without an operating program, used to save the cost of developing an expensive process program. This prototype has well-defined input and output formats, like those used for a model car. Management may gain enough information from this scale model to determine that the cost of the process development is worth it. A software tool used for this prototype could simply be a good word-processing program. Of all the prototype methods, this is the one least used.

## COMMENT

A simple input-output prototype observed by one of the authors was one constructed by a group of students working on a systems project. The students were to write a CO-BOL program that would produce a printed report. Instead of having the program perform the calculations, they hand-calculated the results from input test data, and then used WordPerfect to print the report. There was no operating program, just an output prototype.

## § 3.06   SYSTEMS IMPLEMENTATION

### [A]   Implementation Prerequisites

This section covers the procedures governing implementation of the proposed system. This is the most challenging task of any information systems undertaking.

The following must be completed before a system is implemented and approved as operational.

1. Systems documentation conforming to the standards defined in Chapter 2
2. A system walk-through
   a. **Purpose.** The purpose of a systems walk-through is to prove the logic of the system with another systems analyst or with users. It must be proven that data records are compatible between operations and/or programs. "Index of Table Field Names" is referenced, updated, and corrected at this point. The walk-through starts with input and is followed through to the required output. This is your last chance to catch system problems before functional users begin to report bugs and lose confidence in your project.
   b. **Input requirements.** Input requirements for walk-throughs include:
      • Raw data or machine-usable input
      • Batch or online input
      • Control totals or record counts
      • Database elements chosen or generated to provide realistic test data
   c. **Anticipated processing.** This includes the process steps required to provide output of data or update of the database or files.
   d. **Anticipated outputs.** These are normally classified into categories and followed through ensuring all the data elements are available in the forms required. The following actions are taken:
      • Total record counts, units, dollars, or other data are checked against expected values.
      • Contents and format of monitor displays and reports are checked against stated requirements and precomputed results.
      • Error criteria and messages are identified for those items expected to be rejected by system.
      • Output data elements that will become input to other systems are checked for compatibility.

## [B]  Implementation Procedures

The following actions are taken as part of the implementation phase:

• Develop implementation plans, estimates, and conversion procedures.
• Review and update systems specifications to reflect requirements developed during programming.
• Develop test data for program and systems testing.
• Evaluate results from program tests, systems tests, volume tests, and any parallel testing operations. This is done with users to ensure that test specifications and system requirements have been met.
• Update schedule changes.

- Develop training procedures for systems operations and user personnel. Give everyone some systems documentation to refer to as they are learning the software.
- Confirm that all operational procedures and manuals are in place.
- Confirm that all operational personnel have been trained.
- Request systems operations and/or user sign-off.
- Perform any tests that auditors have requested.
- Follow up very quickly on end-user questions and defect reports.

# § 3.07   SYSTEMS MAINTENANCE

## [A]   Modify or Redesign?

Before a request for any maintenance is approved, the system is examined to determine if it should be modified or redesigned. The presence of three factors tends to favor redesign instead of modification:

1. The cost of maintenance of a project exceeds 30 percent of the actual development costs.
2. The existing system has been patched extensively or modified over a period of 2 to 3 years.
3. The existing system lacks proper documentation and there is sufficient factual information to justify redesign of the system.

## [B]   Types of Maintenance Projects

Maintenance efforts may originate from one or more of the following sources:

- Change in policy
- Change in procedure
- Change of system flow
- Change of program instructions
- Change of operation requirements
- Change of operating system
- Hardware changes

## [C]   Requirements and Responsibility

The systems manager defines the responsibility for coordinating requirements for system maintenance and establishes tasks to be performed.

1. **Review and estimate of work required.** The standard task list is reviewed to determine which tasks are necessary to satisfy the maintenance request.
   - Identify problem to be solved by maintenance project.
   - Define scope and limitations of maintenance effort.
   - Rewrite operational procedures as required.
   - Redesign input-output documents, files, or database requirements, and monitor displays or reports as required.
   - Correct Index of Table Field Names, as needed.

## COMMENT

The results of a programmer's decision **not** to test a "too-simple revision": It cost the programmer his job and the firm over $1 million. Always test revised programs.

- Designate programs and procedures that require modification.
- Make needed program changes.
- Test revised programs.
- Document revisions.
- Perform system tests.

2. **Management and/or user approval.** Management and users are responsible for the following tasks:
   - Approve intent and objectives of system modification.
   - Help develop test data for system modification.
   - Review and approve test results.
   - Make operational personnel available for any retraining required.

### [D]  Control

Control checkpoints are established for each maintenance project. Their purpose is twofold: to ensure the quality and completeness of the maintenance project, and to make sure the changes made to the system do not alter policy or degrade the system's present performance.

Minimally, controls should be at the following points:

- Completion of program testing
- Completion of system testing
- Completion of changed documentation
- End of maintenance (for confirmation that policies have not been changed)

### [E]  Revision Conventions

These revision practices are followed:

- All binders for revisions are updated at same time to avoid any documentation conflicts.
- A revision information cover page, with revision number and date, is completed and inserted into each binder.
- Obsolete documentation is labeled "obsolete," date posted, and documentation filed or destroyed according to records retention procedure.
- Each procedure or policy affected has revision number posted at top right-hand side of each new page of documentation.

# 4

# PROGRAMMING PROCEDURES: SOLID PRACTICES

# § 4.01   SOFTWARE POLICIES

## [A]   Overview

A company's software must reflect the business user's needs in its changing and complex operations if it is to provide useful information and functionality. Creating or buying software is more than a question of resources and cost. It is also a question of remaining competitive in order to stay in business. There is a need on the policy level to provide direction for software development, purchase, and maintenance.

Creating computer software is expensive, and a company that employs its own programming staff has invested a considerable amount of money into processes to support its business. Ideally, this provides the company with an operating efficiency or other business advantage. To protect this investment, the company must have a clearly defined policy that stipulates that all programs written using company resources (such as time, equipment, utility software, books, and so on) are the company's property. Without this protection, a company may find its internal software processes being used by a competitor or generally available in the marketplace.

Software and programmers traditionally have not been subject to organizational policies. However, organizations have recently become aware of the costs and risks associated with a lack of such programming and software policy. The move toward interactive processing, client/server development, Internet applications, and PC end-user development makes clear the necessity of policy development.

## [B]   Proprietorship of Computer Software

All software developed by employees during the hours they are being paid by the company and/or using company equipment, shall be the exclusive property of the employer. Salary-exempt personnel have no proprietary interest in programs they develop. All programming effort and documentation is the exclusive property of the employer as long as the hardware/software used belongs to the firm. Many companies cover this under their employment agreement concerning development of patentable items. Be sure software ownership rights are specifically included in company employment agreements. Additionally, programs and software policies apply to purchased and unauthorized software.

*Purchased software.* Purchased software and software documentation may only be copied as specified by the vendor. No versions of any purchased software are permitted beyond the number the firm has purchased. This applies to all organization personnel.

## COMMENT

When you purchase licensed software, you are buying permission to use a product under the conditions detailed in the license. If you violate the terms of this license by making more than the stipulated number of copies of the software, then you have violated the license agreement. This may result in a lawsuit for damages as well as the possibility that you may lose the licenses for which you have paid.

*Unauthorized software.* Personnel may not purchase or write their own software for use in the organization without authorization. They may not bring to the organization any software, in any form, that is not the property of the organization. The downloading of any unauthorized software to company-owned hardware at any company site also is not permitted. Any violation of this policy subjects the offender to immediate discharge and/or the reimbursement of all costs associated with such action.

## COMMENT

Computer technicians appreciate the difficulties of keeping all the loaded systems software in "agreement" so that one program does not "crash" another. The introduction of additional software not previously tested and approved for company use exposes stable systems to the potential of a destabilizing influence. Other issues include the ability for the unapproved software to exchange files with other systems as well as the ability of the company to provide cost-effective support to users.

### [C]   Uniform Programming Practices

The IT manager is the authority both for setting standards for computer programming throughout the IT organization, and for allocating the resources for new programming development.

Uniform programming practices are maintained throughout the organization as defined in the company policies and procedures manual; only approved documentation procedures are used. Individual coding styles are not allowed, and only one style of programming is used for any one authorized computer programming language. The procedure policies that govern program development are addressed further in § 4.02[E], "Procedural Coding."

## [D]   Program Languages

Adoption or discontinuation of any program language can have serious and long-range consequences; therefore, the head of information systems must approve these actions, as well as any upgrades of any given language.

Any purchase or upgrading of operating or network systems software will require the approval of the head of information systems. This policy applies to all corporation systems: corporate, workgroup, or PC-based.

## [E]   Beta Software

In their quest for a competitive advantage, some companies reach out to the leading edge of technology. Often, this involves assisting in the testing of products that are still in development. This is known as beta testing (alpha testing is done by the programmers). Involvement in a beta testing agreement commits the company to apply some of its hardware and personnel resources to further debug a product. The advantage to the company is to gain in-depth knowledge of a leading-edge product or technology and how to best use it before it is released to the general marketplace.

However, the cost to a company can be high. One or more technical people must be dedicated for a considerable amount of time to learn a product that is still changing. The product being tested can crash at any time, corrupt company files, and even lock up the hardware platform it is running on. There is no guarantee that the final commercial version of the product will even possess the key functions your company is looking for.

In general, IT managers should have a policy that discourages beta testing products. Technical people by nature enjoy working with the latest technologies and tend to quickly volunteer for such programs. A firm policy against this will inhibit the flow of beta requests. The policy also must strictly forbid the installation of any beta products without the IT manager's approval.

## [F]   Audit Review

Rare indeed is the company that is not heavily dependent on computer technology. As business objectives and processes evolve, so must your data systems. Data systems audits are necessary to assure that the computer systems in use continue to run properly and accurately.

Management bears the ultimate responsibility for having an IT audit policy that can assure them of the validity and integrity of financial and reporting programs. Auditors determine the actual audit procedures, and either internal or external auditors perform the actual audit.

**COMMENT**

Computer-related fraud is now an everyday possibility. Because of the disturbing rise in unauthorized access to databases, computer fraud, mismanagement, and lawsuits, IT managers and auditors have to be more security-minded than ever before.

Auditors approve and oversee financial programs. They also are very concerned with data's accuracy. A savvy IT manager requires the auditor's approval to confirm reliability of financially related systems and programs. Audit reviews seek to:

1. Review all corporate computer programs under development or have maintenance performed to assure adequate and reliable audit controls are built into the system and program software.
2. Determine that specified controls are reliable within operational system programs.
3. Confirm that access to operating programs and databases by remote access or any sort of network access is continually governed by the current state of security to prevent unauthorized access.
4. Confirm that established accounting standards have been met and employed by all information systems using them.

## § 4.02   PROGRAM DEVELOPMENT

### [A]   Why It's Important

The longer it takes to develop software, the greater the chance that problems will occur. "Creeping user requirements" are the result of building software to meet dynamic and ever changing business requirements. It is simple. A company's business environment (competitive, legal, environmental) is constantly changing. Anyone responsible for software development or who is an IT manager should read Capers Jones's book, *Assessment and Control of Software Risks* (Englewood Cliffs, NJ: Prentice Hall, 1994).

After an extensive study of IT projects, Mr. Jones has identified no fewer than 50 major problems affecting software development. He notes, "Few projects have more than 15 software risk factors at any time, but many projects have half a dozen simultaneously." He points out the "five most frequently encountered risk factors for large IT shops":

- Creeping user requirements
- Excessive schedule pressure

- Low quality
- Cost overruns
- Inadequate configuration control

Application overload and the deterioration of programming quality play havoc with programmer productivity. The prudent IT manager not only has effective programming policies and procedures in place, but makes certain they are observed.

---

## COMMENT

All developers are encouraged to read *Code Complete, A Practical Handbook of Software Construction* by Steve McConnell. The sections on commenting code and code reviews are particularly important.

---

### [B]   Review of Software Specifications

The initial step in program development is a review of the system's software specifications to ensure there is no misunderstanding of specification requirements between the systems analyst, the requesting business sponsor, and the programmer(s).

*General review.* With the purpose and scope of the programs understood, the next step is determining their relationships in the total system. When reviewing each program:

1. Review program's place in system.
2. Check functions of programs preparing input for program under review. Include sequence of input elements and contents of element sets. In addition, check purposes of program(s) that will use output of this program.
3. Resolve any questions regarding system or programming requirements.

*Detailed review.* In order to ensure a complete understanding of the requirements for the program(s), consider the following items:

- **Data element specifications.** These determine the precise record formats for files and the data dictionary specifications for database systems. For example, are the "year" data elements four-numeric character fields, or is there some other solution that was used to resolve the year 2000 problem?
- **Data element flexibility** to handle impending or likely field expansions. Examples of this are the size of currency fields, foreign currency

conversions, additional tax requirements, or even an expansion of the Social Security number field.

- **Processing specifications.** These determine calculations and comparison tests of data.
- **Systems specifications.** These are reviewed to resolve any ambiguities or problems.

## [C]  Program Organization

Before the detailed logic of a program is developed, the programmer organizes the major logic functions needed to accommodate the requirements of the programming language or software selected.

## COMMENT

> Call it a module, call it an object—in programming they are essentially the same thing.

*Program logic.* This is represented using program block diagrams as logical modules for structured programming. These reflect the relationship of the logical modules and the detailed processing that occurs within each structured module. By using structured programming, the problem's solution can be divided into logical parts or routines, so each may be programmed as soon as possible. This permits complex problems to be broken down into simpler sections. Each module routine becomes a separate entity.

A building block module is created and controlled by a single routine called the main line, which provides the master control that ties all individual processing modules together and coordinates their activity.

Modification of module routines is simplified. Changing or adding new routines is accomplished by changing the main-line routine. This transfers control to the new routine.

To design a modular program, determine the program parameters. List the requirements, elements, and functions of the program as they are developed, with no attention to logical order. Next, review and revise them to determine the logical order of the processing routines and design the main line of the program. Then an overall flowchart can be drawn. Since this flowchart can reveal errors in logic, pay careful attention to it.

In preparing and using the "modular" structured programming method, the following criteria are used:

- **Structured flowcharts.** A structured system flowchart gives an overall picture of the major component elements of the routine. Program flowcharts then progress to any desired level of detail, depending on the complexity of the routine. The program coding should be referenced throughout. In this way, the programmer can easily compare the chart to the actual coding for the purposes of debugging.

- **Comprehensive narration of each routine.** The narration of each structured routine states its purpose, describes data it processes, and generally explains the program logic as portrayed by the structured flowchart.
- **Programming conventions.** The use of standardized nomenclature conventions and standardized program documentation techniques permits someone unfamiliar with the program to readily understand its content. This is very helpful for later maintenance programming.

## COMMENT

We hate to stifle your creativity, but often we are called upon to assist with programs outside of those we normally deal with. This could be to cover for a sick employee, to be promoted to a new position, or even to work together in programming teams. For whatever reason, use field names that describe their contents. When computer RAM was small (imagine a 360K mainframe), we used field names like A1, A2, etc. We worked at saving space but who knows what they meant? Reading a program meant deciphering it word by word.

The person managing the data dictionary can enforce standardized field names. They also help reduce the number of redundant data elements to maintain.

*Program efficiency.* Efficiency results from proper use of an existing structured routine to build balanced and flexible programs. Efficient programs require the following:

1. Programming so that a minimum of effort is required later for maintenance programming.
2. Fully utilizing available software and hardware.
3. Using peripheral devices to maximize capacity of the whole system.

## [D]    Reusable Component Identification

Reusable components are those having identifiable commonalities across programs of a given project. The project must be large enough or consist of several smaller projects in the same general domain to justify a reuse strategy. For reuse to pay off, a specific plan must be developed before program coding starts. Reuse planning prior to coding a new system will help organizations avoid the error of thinking about reuse too late.

A taxonomy system is needed to identify modules for reuse. No single taxonomy system will apply to all reusable component libraries.

Program module commonalities include common data, common constants, common formula process, common tables, and/or reiteration processes. Because models are built prior to coding the actual program modules, potential reuse is greater.

**One word of caution:** Make sure the module works. There is nothing worse than having reusable code that has a bug placed into your library. A list should be maintained of each module location in case errors are detected later, as well as for future update requirements.

## [E]   Procedural Coding

Standard techniques are used to code program instructions. These are the source-code instructions whose procedural language the compiler uses to generate the executable program.

*Source coding.* All coding documentation requires the programmer's name, the program name, date, and other pertinent information as determined by the project leader or programming supervisor.

Coding requirements

- Use techniques identified with the language selected.
- Use clear, descriptive comments for explaining complicated or tricky techniques. (Remember that someone else may need to make changes in the program at a later date.)
- Follow standard coding procedures.

*Desk checking.* The next step in program coding is desk checking, which is performed after the source program is written but prior to any program compiling. Desk checking includes:

- **Verification of program logic.** The programmer traces the flow of the program through each possible path.
- **Construction of decision trees.** Decision trees are constructed for both desk checking and object program testing at a later time. These trees represent data points to test for all program exceptions, as well as normal conditions.

## [F]   Testing

The purpose of testing a coded program is to detect syntax and logic errors. Syntax errors are detected while compiling a source program into an executable program, and commonly occur when program-coding rules for the language being used are not followed. The compiler following the statement that contains the error produces syntax error messages. In some cases, an executable program is not generated because of syntax errors. After all syntax errors are corrected, the compiler for testing program logic generates an executable program.

Use the test data prepared in desk checking (reviewing your code) to generate input data to test the program's functions. Several types of errors often are made by programmers and can be detected and corrected with the proper testing procedures. These errors are classified as:

1. Clerical errors
2. Logical errors
3. Interpretation or communication errors (These occur due to misinterpretation or misunderstanding of program requirements.)
4. Data type errors

After testing is complete, the auditors may provide test data to be run to confirm that auditing standards have been met. Testing is not an afterthought, but should be considered early in the developmental stage of programming.

Maintain a copy of your test plan in your program documentation. This will be handy the next time you make a quick change and need to run a test to verify the software.

## [G]   Documentation

The purpose of program documentation is to allow other programmers to perform program maintenance at some later date. It also defines the manner in which the program is to be run, outlines the controls necessary, and provides information for operations personnel. Additionally, it provides management with a means of obtaining information about the program's operation, complexity, and costs.

Programming documentation is noted here because it is a byproduct of the preceding steps. Details are provided in § 2.06, "Software Documentation."

## [H]   Nonprocedural Coding

When using a nonprocedural 4GL, one tells the computer *what* to do, not *how* to do it. Computer-aided software engineering (CASE), one form of 4GL coding, is a very helpful tool for systems development. 4GLs employed in prototyping require a different set of procedures than procedural coding. The timespan over which 4GLs are used dictates a different approach for their utilization and documentation. Before and/or during the employment of 4GLs, pay careful attention to the naming conventions, error routines, monitor screen displays, and data dictionaries.

The use of Rapid Application Development (RAD) offers a menu of precoded samples of monitor screens or hardcopy reports from which to select. On-screen prompting takes the user and programmer through selecting a database and on to specifying output content. Since this is a shell product, the programmer may need some procedural code or 4GL to custom-code the final RAD product. This procedure also may involve pulling reusable modules of code to complete the task.

Both CASE tools and RAD are used to develop programs in a manner totally different from the procedural approach. Testing, although still performed, is less time-consuming. Documentation is a byproduct of most of this effort. The following can be done for the programmer:

- Pull-down screen menus
- Pop-up screen windows
- Scrolling "help"
- Screen list boxes
- Color screen highlighting

- Dataflow diagrams
- Data modeling
- Program specifications
- Code generation
- Documentation

## § 4.03   PROGRAMMING CONVENTIONS

### [A]   Coding Conventions

There may be a different format coding convention for each programming language used. RAD and CASE tools conventions, depending on the vendor, may not be similar to procedure language software. In any case, conventions should be used consistently.

*Program coding*

- Coding format is restricted by compiler language specifications.
- All program source code should have programmer's name, program title, page number, and date at beginning of each source module.

*Character representation*

- Special care is exercised in coding to distinguish alphabetic uppercase O and numeric zero (0). To avoid confusion, never use a zero in a field name—only as a number.

*Comments or notes*

- Comments or notes are used to explain special mathematical or programming techniques at that point in the program where these techniques appear. Use them freely—especially before each major section of code.

*Names used in programming*

- Data element names and variable names are related to the type of data being stored.

COMMENT

One popular naming convention is "Hungarian notation," invented by Microsoft's chief architect Dr. Charles Simonyi, and is widely used by Microsoft. It became known as Hungarian notation because Simonyi is originally from Hungary and the prefixes give the variable names a nonEnglish look. Documentation on the use of Hungarian notation can be found on Microsoft's Web site at *http://msdn.microsoft. com/library/techart/hunganotat.htm.* This notation ties the data element to its originating field making it easy to trace data elements back to their source.

- Size of names used is limited by naming conventions of language.
- Procedure names used for programming correspond to names of those procedures used in program flowcharts.

### [B] Controls

It is the programmer's responsibility to incorporate into a program the controls specified by the program supervisor, systems analyst, or auditor. Programmers identify any additional controls necessary for proper processing of data through the system. These controls may focus on such details as:

- Specifying use of standard labels
- Sequence checking input files
- Validating vital input elements not checked by a previous program
- Showing specific control totals to be accumulated within program

## § 4.04  PURCHASING SOFTWARE

### [A]  Overview

The decision to purchase software is made when in-house development cost is prohibitive or programming talent is unavailable in the timeframe required. In addition, it is a waste of money to write software already available as an off-the-shelf, shrinkwrapped package. One type of packaged software, known as horizontal software, is widely available for PCs, such as word processors, spreadsheets, or personal database programs. Many institutions use this software. The other type of packaged software, vertical software, has a much more limited market. It is used for specific procedures by organizations that have common needs, such as a billing system for hairdressers. This type of software is more available now for PCs, minicomputers, and mainframes.

When software cannot be programmed in-house, you will have to look elsewhere. If a shrinkwrapped program is not available, you can contact outside software contractors for bids. If possible, request three bids. Contractors can work at their facilities or yours. How much control the company wants over product development will govern where the contractors work. Different procedures for requesting a purchasing order and for payment of the invoice will be required, depending on where the work is done. (See Chapter 8, Managing IT Assets, for more software procedures.)

## [B]   IT Purchased Software

IT purchased software is requisitioned against the information systems budget for software. Someone will be delegated as the coordinator for requisitioning IT purchased software, by the head of information systems, who also furnishes the software budget information. Included are the total dollars budgeted for software, a list of authorized personnel who may request the purchase of software, and the kind of software they may requisition. A dollar limit per order also will be noted. Any request for software that exceeds this limit requires the approval signature of the head of information systems.

*IT software requisition procedure.* The coordinator of IT software purchasing is sent a memo listing the software requested, the reason for the request, and the date by which the software is needed. The coordinator checks the approved software purchasing lists by name and kind of software. The coordinator then prepares a purchase requisition. If the coordinator can approve the requisition, information will be extracted for the monthly software report before the requisition is sent to purchasing. If not, it will be forwarded to the information systems head for his/her approval.

The information systems head will approve or deny the request, note the decision on the requesting memo, sign and date it, and return it to the software coordinator.

The coordinator will take the approved requests and issue purchase requisitions. Information will be extracted for the monthly software report before the purchase requisitions are sent to purchasing. If corporate policy mandates that the information systems head sign the requisitions, that signature will be needed before they are sent on to purchasing. The IT manager, providing any information as to why the request was denied, will answer the unapproved requisitioning memos. The original requesting memos, requisition copies, and reply memos will be filed in the form of hardcopies or scanned into a computer data file.

*IT monthly software report.* The software coordinator will report the following information to the head of information systems by memo on a monthly basis:

- Cumulative expenditures to date for software
- Balance of budget to date
- Name and cost of software purchased

- Total amount spent to date by kind of software purchased
- Name of software purchased by each organizational unit and dollars spent
- Total spent to date by each unit
- Monthly license maintenance fee per product (if any)
- Expiration date for each software license (if applicable)

*Payment of invoice.* For purchase orders to be paid, the IT software coordinator has to confirm the software has been received. If there are any problems, the coordinator should notify accounts payable to hold up payment to the vendor. If the software is returned, purchasing and/or accounts payable should be notified. If the vendor will not accept the returned software, and there is a problem with it, this information should be given to the systems head. If the vendor requires a rewrapping charge, the original purchase order is cancelled and a new requisition written for the rewrapping charge, which will have to be applied to the software expense list and identified as such.

## [C]   Other Unit Software Requisition Procedures

Other units that have their own budget for software will use the same procedures as for other purchases. The information systems unit will publish and distribute a list of approved software they support. Questions will not be answered and help will not be offered by anyone in the information systems unit, including the help desk, for any software not on the list.

The small print on a software package lists restrictions in force unless the vendor guarantees something else in writing. Documentation should be reviewed before the seal is broken on the program disk container since it is usually impossible to return opened software. If the seal is broken and the software does not perform as expected, ask the purchasing department to contact the vendor. Send a memo to accounts payable instructing a hold on payment of the invoice until the problem is resolved.

## [D]   Contract Programming

Purchasing contract programs or software is governed by the organization's policy for contracting outside services. The purchase order should contain a statement describing an acceptable program as noted in § 4.04[G], "Beta Software Testing and Evaluation." In addition, if this software is being written exclusively for your company, include a clause in the purchase order specifying that your company will have complete ownership of the software copyright. (It is unsettling to see a contract programmer selling on the open market the software you paid to have them develop. When in doubt, refer to your legal counsel concerning copyright ownership.)

The vendor will provide the source code, as part of the software documentation, which will be converted to executable code and tested. These results will be compared with the vendor's test output to insure it is the same. The vendor will be provided with test data that has been approved and/or generated by the user, and a copy will be used for the final (in-house) source code test.

Once the software has been purchased, there is little leverage to get corrections made (assuming the firm is still in business when corrections are needed). Therefore, the wise IT manager sends the contract and/or purchase order specifications to the organization's legal department before signing any commitments.

## [E]   Contract Programmers

Contract (temporary) programmers may or may not work in-house, but are paid by the hour to work on assigned projects. When contract programmers start, the person they are reporting to should give them a short introduction to the staff, a tour of the facilities, and information about the company's established policies and procedures for programming and documentation. Giving them samples of previous project efforts to review would be helpful. Contract persons working at the firm's IT site should be provided with a desk and required tools. Other information about working with contract programmers is provided in Chapter 15, Vendors: Getting the Goods. The contract person should be monitored closely during the first week or two to assure proper job performance, in addition to the regular progress reports filed weekly by all programmers. Any personality problems with staff or users also should be noted and addressed promptly.

## [F]   Evaluation of Packaged Software

There are some major issues to address when purchasing packaged software, which can apply to almost any type of software supplier. They are:

- Will vendor be in business next year?
- What warranty will be provided?
- Will software integrate with other software used by company?
- Will software adapt to company's information systems standards?
- How flexible is software package?
- Is current company hardware compatible with proposed software?
- Will documentation provided be user-friendly?
- What type of training is offered?
- What other expense will be required?
- Can vendor provide modifications to software?
- Is there an upgrade planned in near future?
- Is there a vendor help desk?
- Will vendor supply a copy of purchase contract?
- What is vendor's reputation?
- How many will use software?
- Is there a users' support group?
- Will vendor supply names of current users? If answer is yes, contact them and ask for names of other users to contact!
- What is major business focus of vendor?

To discover how difficult or easy it will be to implement the proposed software, the following issues should be addressed:

- How complex is installation procedure?
- Will vendor provide installation assistance?
- How easy is software to maintain?

To evaluate vendor-supplied software, ask current or former users the following:

- Would they buy from same vendor again?
- Did software perform as promised?
- Was training of value?
- Was documentation easy to follow and complete?
- Were there any implementation problems?
- Did installation or operation have any hidden costs (to find real cost of installation and data conversion)?
- Would the referenced user allow a visit to his/her site to see how software is working and talk to operations personnel?

New packaged software must be evaluated, whether for new applications or for placement on the "approved purchase list," especially if this purchase commits the company to buy in volume. Depending on the software considered, use the following procedures.

*General use software evaluation.* A person or formal committee will be responsible for general-use packaged software evaluation. A request for such evaluation can come from a user, a systems analyst, information systems management, or the party performing the evaluation. The person or committee responsible will be a source for packaged software information consulting services. Exhibit 4-1 is a sample form used for software evaluation.

Whenever possible, more than one vendor should be evaluated for the same kind of software. Computer publications, as well as their advertisements, are good sources of evaluation information. Keep an information folder for each type of packaged software evaluated.

*Client/server and vertical software evaluation.* Client/server and vertical packaged software will require a preliminary operations hands-on test followed by controlled client/server or workgroup prototype operations testing. Users' evaluation also will be required. The time required for each controlled group prototype test will vary with the complexity of the software operation and the number of planned future users. The more users, the safer the software should be, i.e., free of bugs. The time required for testing also would be limited by the vendor, the time limit on returning the software, or when the invoice has to be paid.

## [G]  Beta Software Testing and Evaluation

Any beta commitments will require the prior approval of the head of information systems or a designated agent. Any commitments to use beta testing will

**EXHIBIT 4-1.**   Software Evaluation Worksheet

Software Title _____   Version _____

Vendor _____   Software Description_____

Vendor Address _____

Contact Person _____   Phone # _____

Purchase Order # _____   Date_____

Date(s) Software Tested_____   By _____

Software Copied to Server_____   Date_____

Rights Are Assigned/Flagged (list rights) _____

Software Copied to Other Servers (list) _____

_____

Software Evaluation (attach extra pages and documents)_____

_____

_____

_____

_____

_____

_____

Documentation Evaluation (attach extra pages and documents) _____

_____

_____

_____

_____

_____

_____

_____

_____

_____

be limited to pilot operations not part of the corporate information systems operation. No beta operations will be planned beyond the time limit specified by the vendor.

Beta testing will not have access to the corporate system or database at any time but will be limited to client/server, workgroup, or stand-alone PC systems. It will not have contact with any processing or database that is under the domain of the auditors.

All costs associated with a beta testing operation will be monitored and reported monthly to the head of information systems. In addition, a final report will be submitted after beta testing is complete. The following will be reported:

1. **Personnel time.** Personnel time will be kept for IT staff, user employees, and other workers. The total time for each group will be reported. If required by the head of IT, the dollar cost by each group, the total cost, and any overtime incurred because of beta testing will be listed and identified in the report.

2. **Other costs.** Costs, other than personnel, also will be reported. This covers such items as: supplies, postage, long-distance telephone calls, costs of outside services rendered, any charge-back services (computer, copies made, etc.), and expense account reimbursements.

3. **Beta operating problems.** Any beta testing and/or operating problems occurring during the month will be reported, with the estimated total cost of each occurrence. It should be noted if any problem has occurred before and, if so, how often.

4. **Vendors' contact documentation.** Copies of correspondence sent to vendors, telephone call notes, and e-mail sent or received will be attached to the report. The person writing the report will summarize comments addressing these issues.

5. **User reports.** Copies of beta testing memos or e-mail concerning the project will be attached to the report. The person writing the report will summarize comments addressing these issues.

6. **Report summary.** The person writing the report will summarize the status of the beta testing. Any changes the vendor plans to make that would benefit the future use of the software should be noted. Any recommendation as to continuing or discontinuing the beta testing or any other comments worth noting should be included. Also, the question of whether the beta shut-down date will create any problems should be addressed.

7. **Final report.** A final report will be submitted after beta testing has been completed. Attached to the final report will be a copy of all completed Software Evaluation Worksheets (see Exhibit 4-1). Benefits derived from the beta test project should be reported in detail. The report also will include a summarized cost-benefit analysis and what final action was taken based on the beta testing.

# § 4.05   PROGRAM TESTING

## [A]   Test Planning

Software written by IT programming staff or contract programmers, or contracted with an outside firm, will require program testing according to the procedures presented here. All new and maintenance programs require testing, the magnitude and complexity of which may be determined by the auditors. User acceptance should not be overlooked. Everyone concerned in the company may be happy with the test results, but unless the user is satisfied, operation problems may occur later. A formal test plan should be composed of the following:

- General information
- Test plan
- Approval
- Test results

*General information.* This section contains pertinent information needed to identify a program and the project with which it is associated. The following information is included:

- Project number
- Program number(s)
- Date
- Programmer(s)
- Scheduled completion date
- Language program is written in

*Test plan.* This section describes the steps required for testing individual segments of each program's logic. The information includes:

- Program number
- Test number
- Function to be tested
- Test priority

*Approval.* This section contains the signature blocks required to approve the test plan and authorize the testing. The program supervisor or project manager also will use this part of the program test to indicate the type of testing to be conducted.

- **Unlimited.** The programmer may test until completion without additional review and/or approval.
- **Limited.** A specific number of tests is permitted before approval expires and a review to approve further testing is required.

*Test results.* This section reflects the progress of the program during testing, including date of the first test, systems tests, and volume test. If tests are run for the auditors, the date the auditors' presence is required will be noted.

## [B]   Test Preparation

To ensure test data is representative, all conditions shown in the program flowcharts must be included. The flowchart can be reduced to a decision tree, showing only the decision points and the conditions for the decisions. This makes it easy for users or auditors to follow the decision conditions.

Another tool for test preparation is a decision table. (See Exhibit 4-2 for a Decision Table Structure.) The box labeled "title" contains the procedure title. The area labeled "condition stub" lists all possible conditions tested. The "action stub" area lists all actions that can take place. Under "decision rules" are listed "condition entries," the actual conditions that determine how the data will be treated, and "action entries," the actions that determine which course to follow predicated on the entry conditions. A sample procedure for credit approval is shown in Exhibit 4-3. A decision table for an "else" rule is shown in Exhibit 4-4.

For best results, someone other than coding personnel should prepare the test data. ***Never use live data for testing!*** Make a copy of it and if possible, run all tests on similar but separate platforms. The coder may conduct preliminary testing, as long as someone else does the final test development. This procedure and use of the decision table enhance the potential for detecting errors.

Test material is retained and kept current for later use in testing systems and program specifications. Following are specifications for preparing test data:

- The requirements outlined in the system specifications must be clearly understood.
- The logic and major routines requiring testing must be reviewed and the findings documented.
- The test data must be filed in the library or project folder. This material is considered part of the documentation and must be maintained during the life of the program.
- The analyst or program supervisor responsible must review all system modifications to determine if any changes are required in the test data. When a change is made, the programmer or test preparer conducts tests with the pertinent data to ensure the modifications are correct and have not affected other processing areas.

## [C]   Test Analysis

The following should be carefully checked to avoid testing errors:

*Input/output*

- Proper heading format, line spacing, spelling, and punctuation of reports
- Correct data element size and content
- Report output matches expected specifications
- Correctly keyed-in data

**EXHIBIT 4-2.**    Decision Table Structure

| TITLE | DECISION RULES | | | | | | | |
|---|---|---|---|---|---|---|---|---|
| | 1 | 2 | 3 | 4 | 5 | 6 | 7 | 8 |
| CONDITION STUB | CONDITION ENTRY | | | | | | | |
| | | | | | | | | |
| | | | | | | | | |
| ACTION STUB | ACTION ENTRY | | | | | | | |
| | | | | | | | | |
| | | | | | | | | |

**EXHIBIT 4-3.** Decision Table

| CREDIT APPROVAL | DECISION TABLE | | | | | | | |
|---|---|---|---|---|---|---|---|---|
| | 1 | 2 | 3 | 4 | 5 | 6 | 7 | 8 |
| ON APPROVED LIST | Y | N | N | N | N | | | |
| PAST EXPERIENCE OK | — | Y | N | N | N | | | |
| APPROVED CO-SIGNER | — | — | Y | N | N | | | |
| SPECIAL APPROVAL RECEIVED | — | — | — | Y | N | | | |
| APPROVE ORDER | X | X | X | X | — | | | |
| RETURN ORDER | — | — | — | — | X | | | |
| GO TO TABLE A5 | X | X | X | X | — | | | |
| END OF PROCEDURE | — | — | — | — | X | | | |

**EXHIBIT 4-4.**    Decision Table With "Else" Rule

| EMPLOYMENT | DECISION RULES | |
|---|---|---|
| | 1 | ELSE |
| COLLEGE DEGREE | YES | — |
| 3 YEARS PROGRAMMING EXPERIENCE | COBOL | — |
| | | |
| | | |
| APPLICATION FORM | GET ONE | |
| INTERVIEW | SCHEDULE | |
| DISPOSITION | — | REJECT |
| | | |

*Problem analysis*

- Original specifications are understood
- Flowcharting does not have logic errors
- Coding errors are not present
- No software revision errors exist

### [D]   Operating Program Maintenance

Only maintenance programmers will have access to the software and be allowed to copy it for maintenance. The maintenance of running programs is forbidden without the approval of the operations manager, and auditor if required. A violation of this procedure is grounds for dismissal.

After the required maintenance is completed, the program(s) should be tested. The procedures described in § 4.06[B], "Review and Acceptance of Test Results" will be repeated in order for the changes to become part of the production system.

## § 4.06   SOFTWARE INSTALLATION

### [A]   Overview

Transferring a software program from developmental to operational status follows standard review and approval procedures. These procedures apply to programs developed by IT programming staff or contract programmers, or contracted with an outside firm. Purchased or completed beta tested software will follow the same procedures whenever possible. The conversion can begin only after the software or system passes all testing procedures.

Installation or conversion is placing into operation the tested software or system, which either replaces existing programs or is completely new. When discontinued software is replaced by a new system, the options are:

1. **Phased.** The new system is installed in modular fashion or in phases. When one phase is identified as operational and accepted, the next part of the installation can begin.
2. **Direct.** Direct installation is a complete, one-time conversion or installation. The old system is replaced completely by the new. Operations has to be totally involved with the installation and operation of the new system software.
3. **Pilot installation.** The new system is installed as a prototype operation in one safe location. After this operation is running properly, it may be installed in other locations. This type of installation is ideal for workgroups or independent PC operations.
4. **Parallel conversion installation.** This type of installation is most often used with corporate IT computer operations. It is the safest and most preferred method of installing a new software system, but also the most costly as it requires the business user to enter data twice—

once into each system. If, after comparing output results and the database status of both systems, the results are compatible, the new installation is considered complete.

When no existing software is being replaced, new software installation can occur as phased, direct, or pilot installation. The other procedures for software installation are the same whether a new system is replacing an old one or not.

## [B]   Review and Acceptance of Test Results

To ensure that correct results are obtained from extended program testing, a review should be conducted with users, and auditors, if they are involved. Now is the time to bring to everyone's attention any concerns by the people who will be using this product. Acceptance will be confirmed by memo from involved users and/or auditors directed to the system project manager or the program supervisor. A vendor who is involved with the project will receive this information from the system manager and/or programming supervisor.

## [C]   Review and Acceptance of Documentation

Documentation should be prepared according to established specifications. Any changes or additions will be conveyed by e-mail or hardcopy memo to the appropriate person in charge of documentation approval. Its acceptance will be conveyed by memo to the heads of programming and systems.

## [D]   Acceptance of Contracted Software

The installation of contracted software will follow the same installation procedures as in-house developed software programs. Acceptance of purchased software as operational includes informing accounts payable via memo or e-mail that the invoice can be paid. The note should contain the vendor's name, item name and description, and purchase order number. If, on the other hand, the software does not meet the standards specified in the purchase order, a memo or e-mail is sent to the purchasing and/or accounts payable departments so informing them; the purchasing department will then inform the vendor.

## [E]   Development Programmer Sign-off

After the installation of the software is completed and accepted, the development programmers will no longer have access to the production system software. Their access codes will be removed from the controlled access subroutine in the system software.

## [F]   Selection of an Implementation Day

The first day that the revised program is to be run is very important. Some companies have a policy that all changes will go in on the same night of the week, such as Thursday. Then on Friday, they are on alert to any problem arising from the change. This also allows time to alert the help desk so they can promptly call the programmer if anything unusual or unexpected is reported for that system during the roll-out day.

A very good business policy is for the programmer to walk through the program with the business department who uses the code to obtain first-hand information of any startup problems and to explain to the business users how to benefit from system changes.

# § 4.07   PROGRAM MAINTENANCE

## [A]   Types of Program Maintenance

Program maintenance tasks, maintenance responsibility, and maintenance conventions are required for program maintenance.

1.  Program revisions are changes made that do not require a major logic change. Examples are:
    - Updates of constants and other variables
    - Increases in dimensions of tables, arrays, or work areas
    - Implementation of hardware features
    - Inclusion of new mainframe software by recompiling a program
    - Correction of minor processing deficiencies
    - Conformation to programming standards
2.  Program modifications are changes involving the redesign of program logic or the relationships of the subprograms or components. They are required to accommodate changes in input or output specifications.

## [B]   Responsibilities and Controls

1.  The head of computer programming has the authority and responsibility for new programming, while the IT computer operations head has the authority and responsibility for maintenance programming.
2.  Testing or program maintenance will not be performed on any production software under the control of IT computers or workgroup systems. This will be done off-line with no access to the production system software.
3.  Testing or program maintenance should verify that changes have been made properly and that other sections of the program were not affected by the changes.
4.  The programmer and program supervisor will review the final test output and documentation for correctness and completeness.
5.  User management or IT computer operations management will require a sign-off before the modified software is placed into production. Once this occurs, the maintenance programmer will no longer have access to it. However, in case of an emergency the programmer may regain access under supervision and with the permission of user management or IT computer operations management.

### [C]   Conventions

In addition to the conventions outlined below, those established for program development (as found in § 4.03[A], "Coding Conventions") are followed in performing program maintenance.

1.  **Changes to flowcharts.** Flowcharts are modified in the following manner:
    a.  A new chart is drawn using the software used to draw the original flowchart. The changes are noted on the new chart, dated, and initialed by the programmer. Both old and new charts are filed.
    b.  Additional pages added to flowcharts because of changes require off-page connectors to direct the flow to the inserted pages.
2.  **Changes to reports.** Always retain one copy of the original report layout in the documentation.
    a.  Include in your documentation an example report that illustrates all of the totals derived.
    b.  Include screen prints of options the business user has to select reports, such as by date range or other criteria.
3.  **Changes in program coding and testing.**
    a.  A source program is copied into a new file before extensive changes are made. After testing is complete and the updated program put into production, the old source program may be saved to an archive directory or erased after 90 days.
    b.  When testing program changes, the entire program must be checked, not just the routines that were inserted, deleted, or changed. Those segments not changed are tested to ensure the program will continue to function properly. The test data becomes part of the program documentation.

### [D]   PC Software Developed by End Users

Personal computers have evolved from glorified calculators to powerful machines. Fueling this change is a wealth of powerful software that is easily customized by the person using it. This can lead a manager down a dark and slippery path.

### [E]   Just Because the Computer Said So—It May Not Be True

IT departments spend a considerable amount of time ensuring the accuracy of the reports and data issued to the business departments. Because of this, some people may assume that any computer-generated report is accurate and not question how it calculated the data or where was the origin of the data. This can lead to faulty business decisions based on bad data.

   If someone develops a spreadsheet or small database for their own use, this is their business. They know where the data came from and how it works.

But as soon as they begin using this report away from their own desk, you begin to see problems.

When training new users in your company, include instruction on data validation, editing, and how to cross-check results against samples of the input file. Most people care about the quality of their work and will appreciate this instruction.

## [F]   IT Policies for Stealth Systems

It is a rare IT department that can address every business user request for new software or additional features in existing systems. This sometimes leads to a well-meaning but hazardous growth of stealth systems throughout the company.

Stealth systems are PC code written by someone for their own use to address a specific business problem. These will range from a department's homegrown vacation schedule to a Materials Management System. You cannot stop these systems from occurring. Instead, when it is reported that a PC system has become an integral part of a department's operations, or has jumped to another department, the IT department must evaluate it validity. The IT manager must decide if there is a compelling business case for supporting such a system. If so, then that system must be removed from end-user control and subjected to the IT validation checks and safeguards. It becomes a production system just like any other. Further user changes are not permitted.

## [G]   IT Policies on Hidden Programming Staffs

Sometimes, end users frustrated with attempts to obtain data processing support within their company will hire their own programming support staff under other titles. These might be college interns or others who are trained in the basics of PC programming. The problem is the loss of IT policy control of these people.

There are two basic approaches to this—accept it or kill it.

Accepting this "secret IT staff" normally involves establishing the following policies:

1.  Create a separate computing environment for these people to work in, typically their own LAN.
2.  They are permitted to download data from the corporate files but never to upload anything to prevent them from adding back in bad data.
3.  They are not permitted to write any software for anyone outside of their department and must adhere to IT policies concerning software piracy, antivirus protection, etc.
4.  Require all code to be fully documented to the same standard as that maintained by the IT department. A copy of this documentation must be maintained in the IT library.

Quashing a secret IT staff means that the IT department must determine what business need this staff meets and then fulfill it. These people were brought in to meet a user requirement. If you take them away, the requirement is still there so you must step up and fulfill it. The easiest way to do this is to take technical control of the people but leave their work assignments to the business department. The business department will continue to carry them under their budget. Since they are under your technical control, you can better ensure their code and data integrity meets your standards and can easily move the code around to other departments as required.

# 5

# PROJECT MANAGEMENT: GETTING IT OUT ON TIME

# § 5.01   PROJECT MANAGEMENT POLICIES

Project management is the marriage of different technologies; it requires both technical and managerial skills executed in an organized, cooperative fashion. To maximize the performance of the project activities, a project manager's primary responsibility is to allocate resources for the timely completion of the assigned project. A project manager is the driving force to maintain everyone's focus on the tasks at hand to bring them to a conclusion.

A project manager does not succeed by writing the code or turning the screwdriver himself. He succeeds by coordinating the efforts of others to accomplish these tasks. A project manager who loses himself in the minutia of details will not have the time to focus the efforts of others and preside over an unproductive team. Most technical professionals lack the administrative and interpersonal skills needed to function effectively in this position. With a bit of mentoring, most technical people can rise to the challenge. Acting as the leader on smaller projects is often their first management experience. This chapter puts some basic management procedural guidelines into perspective and establishes a uniform format for managerial procedures to be followed by all project managers.

The IT organization is a focal point for most businesses and is not limited to one project in progress at a time. Therefore, a central authority is required to act as the focal point for all IT project activities. This authority is the IT systems department manager or a delegated coordinator, who settles disputes over resource allocations, monitors the progress of each project, and attends all project presentations. For the purpose of identification, the person performing this duty shall be called the *projects coordinator*. All project reporting will be directed to the projects coordinator. If this is established as a separate department, it is usually called a *program* or *project office*.

# § 5.02   PROJECT MANAGEMENT DEFINITION

## [A]   Definition

Each project must have achievable objectives that are defined by management. The success of a project assignment must be measurable and the objectives clearly defined. Under the coordination of the project manager, the combination of personnel, administrative, technical, and financial resources are optimized to achieve a definable goal within a given calendar time period. A project has a starting point defined by time and place, and an ending point—when the project can be considered complete.

Most projects live within limited resources. The primary restriction is their budget. Assigned personnel will have their time and commitments defined, because knowing the duration of an assignment is essential for proper project management. A schedule must be prepared so that work can be performed in measurable milestone units, the progress of which can be reported. Feedback requirements must be defined to meet the needs of the firm's management and the nature of the project.

## [B] The Nature of Project Management

What differentiates project management from general management is that a project is a temporary activity with a starting point and a completion point. The calendar time period is determined before the project starts, and the project only exists between these points.

The other main difference is in the way each utilizes personnel resources. Members of a project are associated with it only for the lifetime of the project, or less. Their primary obligations are elsewhere; they may be assigned to the project for a specified number of calendar days, and even allotted specific times during those days. Although they work to speed the project toward completion, their loyalty is still to their "normal" job.

At a project's completion, any unused material resources will have a predetermined disposition. They may be purchased during the project's existence or on loan to the project.

An IT project operates within defined boundaries, and has a specific scope of operation. Resources must be utilized within this committed scope. Any expansion of the scope by the project manager will dilute the effective use of the resources provided.

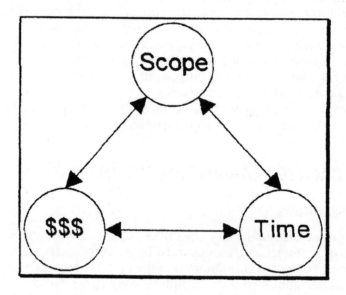

Project management requires that three important variables be in control: cost, quality (or scope), and time (or speed of completion). A project manager must have control over at least two of these variables to ensure project completion. Altering any one variable will affect the others. Generally, to improve quality (or to expand the scope), higher cost and possibly more time would be required. For example, a software project can be completed more quickly (reduce time) if I pay (increase cost) for overtime or hire more contract programmers. Or, I could cut the quality (scope) to increase the speed.

COMMENT

Lifeboats on ships have two sets of numbers painted on them. One is the identification number; the other is the lifeboat capacity. Lifeboats are resources designed for the project of saving lives, but only for a given scope, or number of people. If too many people board the lifeboat, all can be lost. That's why sidearms are issued to the ship's officers when orders are given to abandon ship.

Typical pressures are to increase the project's scope (time) or reduce its duration (increase speed to completion).

## [C]  IT Project Types

There are two kinds of projects with different purposes: a feasibility study and an implementation project. The feasibility study is a mini project, used to determine the justification of a full-blown project. Not all projects require this: some are mandated by top management or by forces external to the company.

A feasibility study informs management whether the proposed project is warranted and provides an estimate of the resources and calendar time required, information that is essential to planning and undertaking the project.

Once the decision is made to go forward, the project is assigned to a project manager to complete. The person who is responsible for the feasibility study also is a good candidate for the position of project manager. Contacts made and familiarity with the area gained through doing the feasibility study provides a solid base when the actual project is undertaken. The skills required to be a project manager evolve through hands-on experience with actual projects. More complex projects require more experienced project managers.

IT projects can run from a few days to years and involve a project team, while one person can accomplish a feasibility study in a day or a few weeks. IT projects may include:

- PC software or hardware conversions
- Mainframe software or hardware conversions
- Developing a prototype product
- Software implementation (for a wide range of systems)
- Implementation of a new operating system
- System development and implementation
- End-user system development and implementation
- IT projects involving installation of new database, e-mail, Internet, LAN, or WAN systems

- Business reengineering projects, which entail developing and implementing improved business operations with or without computers

## [D]   IT Project Components

No project (feasibility study or project) exists in a vacuum. Other components interact with it and permit its existence. One such component, representing management, is the IT *steering committee,* which is attuned to the firm's strategic goals and prioritizes projects. The committee is kept informed of the progress of each project through status reports, required at least once monthly from each project manager. Feasibility study results are delivered as only a final report. Other components in this scenario are:

1. **IT management.** The project's success will require the support of the IT management controlling the IT resources loaned to the project. IT management has a vested interest in the success of the project as well as in its assigned personnel.
2. **Project sponsor or champion.** This person or group is a party to the request. It also còuld be the one who requested the undertaking because of a government mandate. This is the business manager you go to for help in focusing support for project problems.
3. **User management.** Managers of the departments who will use the end result have a vested interest, and also can be the project champion.
4. **Other projects.** Other projects will compete for resources. Shared resources require prioritizing and queuing to gain the most overall benefit. Good people are hard to find and you will often share them with their regular jobs or other projects.
5. **Consultants and contractors.** Outside resources budgeted for a specific project also can be involved with more than one project for their firm. It is their responsibility to deliver what they promised by the time specified. The advantage of using consultants or contract people is that they can provide expertise or staffing not available in-house. Typically, there is a 10-to-1 ratio of time needed to build a software system compared to maintaining it. Contract programmers often are used to provide this short-term surge in workerpower.
6. **Corporate technical experts.** These are experts on loan from other areas of the company for a predetermined time. If these people are unavailable, outside experts may have to be employed.
7. **The project team.** The project team itself is made up of two parts: the project management and the team members. These two parts must work well together for the project to be successful.
   a. **Project manager.** The project manager must possess certain attributes required for a successful project completion. Often a project administrator will be used to handle routine paperwork such as filing reports, paying consultants, arranging meetings, etc.
   b. **Project team members.** These are people with the technical skills needed for the project to succeed. They may be available full-

time or part-time for a given time duration. They could hold any of the following titles:

- Systems analyst
- Systems and procedure analyst
- Analyst programmer
- Programmer
- User specialist
- Project librarian
- Database designer
- Network specialist
- Industrial engineer
- Project secretary

### [E]   Project Life Cycle

A project life cycle is composed of segments or phases. With the many different types of projects, one life cycle size does not fit all. There is somewhat of a consensus on the elements required, although some can be present for one kind of project but not for another.

The segments can be further defined by the internal elements. Following is a generic list of segment possibilities:

Stage I—Sharpen the idea to see if it is a good one
- Recognition of a need (we must start with an idea!)
- Conduct a feasibility study to include a return on investment analysis. (This analysis will have a great bearing on project's funding.)
- Management go or no-go decision

Stage II—Build the plan and price out the project
- Develop a detailed project plan
- Identify resources required for each step (workers, machines, and money)
- Add up costs from each step
- Prepare a make-or-buy analysis (is it worth the money and if so, do we write it or buy a package?)

Stage III—Execute the project
- Work the plan

Stage IV—Close the project
- Customer acceptance and sign-off
- Accumulate paperwork for project files
- Close budget by returning materials, paying final consultants

## § 5.03   MANAGING PROJECTS

### [A]   Overview

The management of IT projects starts with the IT steering committee of upper-level executives. The committee members align the IT projects to business priorities to ensure that IT efforts are in sync with their business strategies. They also influence which resources are allocated, and have final say regarding each project's completion date.

The steering committee follows the progress of all projects in process. Members have the authority to change priorities and completion dates of projects under consideration and in process. They also have the authority to cancel a project. The projects coordinator receives reports from each project manager, which he/she reviews and clarifies in a cover memo to each steering committee member. The projects coordinator will maintain a copy of this information. Each steering committee member receives a copy of each project status report with the cover memo from the projects coordinator. The steering committee is the court of final resort for user and project management appeals. To make these decisions, the committee has access to information restricted to the higher levels of management. It is not required to explain or justify its actions to project or user management.

## COMMENT

An interesting book on project management is Edward Yourdon's *Death March: The Complete Software Developer's Guide to Surviving 'Mission Impossible' Projects*. In it, Yourdon describes various types of project situations and advises when a project manager should bail out!

### [B] Projects Coordinator

The projects coordinator oversees all projects assigned to the IT organization, coordinating resources and the efforts of project managers and their staffs. He/she also works very closely with the steering committee. This person could be the manager of systems development or its appointed projects coordinator—the person to whom the project managers report.

When priorities change, project calendar day slippage occurs, or available personnel changes, the projects coordinator has to reconcile the resulting problems with the overall priorities defined by the steering committee. He/she has limited power to create or reallocate resources; this is mainly under the control of the steering committee.

The projects coordinator utilizes project management software to track the progress of all projects. This is critical if they are to shuffle resources among the various efforts. If someone is not needed for a project, the projects coordinator will reassign them. The assignment and reassignment is best done using project management tools.

If the projects coordinator is also the manager of systems, he/she will be responsible for acquiring new systems personnel. If not, the systems manager is responsible. If there is no systems head, the head of IT will be responsible for obtaining new systems personnel and any other IT personnel needed for projects. Whoever is in charge of obtaining new personnel will work with the human resources (HR) department. HR must have the new job requirements to set up interviews and help select new people. The projects coordinator will select the mentor for the new employees when assigning their duties.

The projects coordinator is instrumental in acquiring project consultants and contractors. He/she, not the project manager, has the authority to negotiate and sign contracts. This person will follow the procedures spelled out in Chapter 15, Vendors: Getting the Goods.

The projects coordinator writes a monthly status report. These reports are sent to the steering committee and to the head of IT. When the projects coordinator is not the systems manager, the systems manager also receives a copy of the report. Each project is reported, even if there is no activity. If there should have been activity, but there was none, the reason(s) must be reported.

An annual report is prepared at the end of each fiscal year by the projects coordinator who provides a narrative of each project, including its successes and problems, the percent of allocated budget spent versus the percent of the project completed, and a recap of the performance of each project manager. It will identify problems arising from a project manager's weakness and recommend improvements. The report also should include the next responsibility of each project manager after the project is completed. The annual report will recommend future projects for consideration, including resource acquisitions. Reports not written by the systems manager will require his/her approving signature before the annual report is sent to the head of IT. The head of IT will review and countersign it before it is distributed to the approved parties.

## [C]  Project Manager

The project's success depends on many factors, but the key element is the proper selection of a project manager. Since all participants are "on loan" to a project—they know it is temporary—they will have vested interests in other areas. Rarely does a project manager have direct authority over the team members. To overcome this, the project manager must be of dynamic personality whose force of personality can move the team forward. Project managers wear many hats:

- Leader of team (not *manager*—you must be a *leader*)
- Negotiator with team members' home department managers
- Part-time accountant to track project budget
- All around cheerleader and advocate of project's success (if you don't believe in it and work to convince others of it, then they know it is doomed)

Selecting a project manager is the job of either the systems manager alone or the systems manager with input from the projects coordinator. Choosing a candidate requires knowledge of certain attributes that have been proven to be universally successful. The only testimonial a person really needs is a successful track record with the company. However, a person being selected as project manager for the first time requires special consideration.

New candidates should have demonstrated their abilities as a project team member by contributing to a successfully completed project in which they were given increasing responsibilities. A first-time project manager's first assignment should be a project of limited scope and duration. After he/she has successfully completed a project, then longer and more complex projects may be assigned.

Keeping the position of project manager temporary is a face-saving decision made for both the project manager and the firm. If the person is unsuccessful, the problem may be more easily corrected than if he/she had been placed into a permanent position. It also provides excellent training for becoming a manager in the IT organization or elsewhere in the firm.

The selection criteria for a project manager are:

1. **Maturity.** The person must display an air of maturity. This is required when dealing with senior management and user management. It also lends credibility to the project team.

2. **Administrator.** The person must be able to routinely perform day-to-day administrative activities, such as reporting, requisitioning, memo writing, and show the ability to follow schedules, meet deadlines, and handle resources and budgets. A proactive, rather than a reactive, administrator is much more desirable.

3. **IT skills.** Because IT encompasses such vast areas today, no one person can be an expert in every area, but the project manager candidate should have a broad background and enough technical skill to gain the respect of the IT assigned staff.

4. **Company knowledge.** The person must know the company to ensure the project follows the corporate culture, and does not "rock the boat" of senior and user management. The candidate should know both the formal and informal organization to ensure the project will progress smoothly.

5. **The person who delegates the work.** The person must be able to delegate and supervise the work of others. He/she must be able to recognize when a team member is successful, and ensure that member gets all of the credit. When a team member fails, this failure is shared with the project manager. (Essentially, the phrase is, "We all succeed or the project manager fails.")

6. **Communicator.** The project manager must keep the project team, management, and others with vested interests in the project well informed. This includes informal day-to-day oral communication, written communication, formal presentations, teaching, and chairing meetings.

   As the focal point for project information, the project manager should be the most knowledgeable person about it. To gain and maintain the support for the various stakeholders (sponsors, business managers, accountants, etc.) they must regularly communicate project status (both good and bad) to all interested parties.

   When chairing meetings, an effective project manager urges all members to participate. Under the right circumstances, quieter team members will contribute valuable input. In addition, since the project manager does not want to discourage communication, he/she should never label ideas "bad."

7. **Innovator.** The project manager must not be limited to traditional solutions. He/she must be innovative and encourage others to be the same.

8. **Leader.** The project team must be led through the most trying times. The project manager must be able to work under pressure, remain calm, keep the project objective in focus, and still be sensitive to the team, users, vendors, and the corporate culture.

## COMMENT

Many new project managers mistakenly believe that merely because they are managers, they can automatically rally the support of all those assigned to them. Most seasoned managers readily subscribe to the adage that respect is earned and not bestowed by title (so hard to gain—so easy to lose). All too often, the respect of those being led is forfeited because of the lack of basic interpersonal or management skills.

Following is a list of practices through which project managers can establish and retain the respect of the team:

1. **A leader sets the example in all they do.** The question is if they are setting a good example or a bad one. The general rule is that your team will slowly rise to your high standard or quickly fall down to your low standard.

   If you demonstrate a strong work ethic by coming to work early and staying late, your team may not match your hours, but they will be less inclined to arrive late or leave early. On the other hand, if the length of your work days seem to match the weather (gone on good days, in the office on bad days), then your team will quickly match your example.

   If you focus on the work at hand, so will the people. If you stop and chat excessively or engage in idle gossip, then your team will quickly emulate you.

2. **Include others in decisionmaking.** Get the whole team involved in contributing ideas to the project. Though the final decision is not theirs, people value the opportunity to comment because it increases their feeling of worth. An environment of participation garners respect for the project manager who creates it. Due to their various backgrounds, team members will often point out pitfalls before the project encounters them.

3. **Be honest.** The project leader who is open and honest creates an example for the team members to follow and creates respect for his/her opinion.

4. **Keep promises.** An effective project manager does not make unreasonable commitments. Failure to keep promises, especially without a justified explanation, will quickly lead to a lack of confidence and respect; the project manager's word should have credibility with the project team and users.

5. **Be consistent.** Consistency in the treatment of all members of the team is a must to maintain total team harmony and loyalty. Showing preference only alienates others.

6. **Recognize contributions.** Recognition by acknowledging the ideas of all project team members promotes goodwill and loyalty. An effective project manager never takes credit for an idea that originated with someone else.

## COMMENT

Recognition of a job well done shows your appreciation. It costs nothing, but can be more valuable than money at times. A show of appreciation for the efforts of team members not only improves their output, but also increases their appreciation and respect for the project manager.

### [D]   Project Variables

Project variables include the following activities:

1. **Project inputs**
   a. Human attributes
      i. User attitude about computer systems
      ii. User attitude toward other units involved in new system
      iii. User attitudes toward firm and their willingness to participate
      iv. User educational level
      v. Value system of project team and users
      vi. Experience level of users' management
      vii. Top management's commitment
      viii. Experience users have had with current system
   b. Project team's attributes
      i. Respect for project manager
      ii. Social skills of project team
      iii. Communication skills of project group
      iv. Experience level of project group
      v. Credibility level of project group

      c.  Project variables
         i.      Size of project and project group
         ii.     Time length of project
         iii.    Value of project
         iv.    Having good measurable milestones
         v.     Budget allocation
         vi.    State of technology involved in project
         vii.   Computer program languages to be used
         viii.  Quality of acquired hardware and software
         ix.    Importance of project to company
      d.  Organization variables
         i.      Size of firm
         ii.     Type of industry of firm
         iii.    Experience with computer systems
         iv.    Span of management control
         v.     Centralization of operations
         vi.    Financial status of firm
         vii.   How progressive firm is
         viii.  Number of levels of management
         ix.    Level of management skill

2. **Throughput process of project group**
    a.  Information gathering
    b.  Information analysis
    c.  Comparisons with objectives
    d.  Economic analysis
    e.  Using systems analysis tools
    f.  Technical writing
3. **Project feedback**
    a.  Communication capabilities
    b.  Reaction to various designs
4. **Project outputs**
    a.  Goal of designed and installed running system
    b.  Timeliness of project
    c.  Maintenance of budget limits
    d.  Minimum of personnel turnover

# § 5.04  PROJECT INITIATION

## [A]  Startup

After the feasibility study has been completed, and its findings are positive, a report is written and forwarded to the steering committee for its evaluation. When the committee approves the project, the project initiation phase begins. The steering committee defines the scope and specifies the start and completion dates of the project. It will assign non-IT personnel to the project, approve the use of any outside vendor support, and provide for a project budget.

From this point IT management takes over to complete the details of the project initiation and appoints a project manager. The projects coordinator and the IT head will select the full- and part-time IT personnel for the project's duration. If any non-IT personnel, outside talent, and user people are needed, they will already have been approved by the steering committee. The assigned project manager is given the task of "confirming" the project's life cycle so that a schedule for tasks and resources can be completed.

## [B]   Project Life Cycle

Building a project plan can be very time-consuming. It requires some guess work and a lot of digging to build a good one. All journeys begin somewhere so the project manager begins by listing the major tasks necessary to complete the project. These will identify the milestones. Building a plan is easier if you have some of your project team help you. Of course until you have a plan written, it is impossible to know everyone that will be on the team.

Use your project scope statement and criteria for success as "anchors" to ensure your project plan does not drift. As your planning progresses, you will be forced to make a series of assumptions of resources that will be available. Always write down any assumptions your plan is based on, such as:

- This database will support a maximum of 25 simultaneous users.
- The new fiber network installation will be completed by January 1.
- This new payroll system will support a maximum of 10 different taxing authorities.

Next, we break down the major tasks into smaller ones so we can assemble a plan. This is easy to do with a large whiteboard and a pack of "sticky notes" since the tasks will be moved around. Under each major section begin a list of the tasks necessary to complete every milestone. Once you have a list, begin to place the tasks in a logical sequence. You will quickly see that some tasks cannot start before other tasks are finished and some can start at the same time.

Write a two- or three-line explanation of what each task is. Sometimes the short task names people use may not be clear to others.

Now under each task, list the resources needed to make this task a reality. You should list materials, special machinery, and people—anything that will be needed. The total resources from every task are what you need to complete the project and will roll-up into a budget request.

Given these tasks and these resources, make a time estimate for completing each individual task. Identify any assumptions your estimates are based on. Often this action will identify even more "hidden" work that must be completed before the project is complete.

Now that we have a task network, follow through every path in the network and determine how long each path will take to complete. The longest path is called the "critical path." The critical path is what determines how long your project will take. Any time delays along this path will delay your completion date. Sometimes during a project, work will proceed smoothly along the critical path and fall behind on one of the other network legs until it becomes the critical path.

With this network in hand, enter the task information into project tracking software. The software also will calculate your project duration and identify those tasks along your critical path. The software also will roll-up your resource requirements so you can identify the expertise needed on your team. At this point, if the key people are in-house, begin including them in the planning sessions so they can help to polish the plan.

The next step is to thoroughly scrutinize your project task network with as many IT managers and analysts that you can. Look for hidden pitfalls and any overlooked tasks and challenge every resource assumption (always document your assumptions for later review). Don't be too proud to change your plan. Project management is tough enough when you have a good plan and a disaster when you start with a bad one.

Your project tracking software will have a calendar for identifying holidays. Enter all of those along with normal working hours and any availability times for your team (they may have vacation scheduled, etc.). The software will roll-up your resource requirements and identify places where your resources conflict. These must be resolved before your plan is finished.

As any project leader will tell you, a plan is never finished. It is constantly updated as successes roll in and unknown problems arise—key people become ill, major tasks are overlooked, and sponsors demand additional features.

If major delays are expected on your project, the steering committee must resolve the problem. It can change the finish date or provide for resources to reduce the scope of the project.

## COMMENT

Don't count on overtime to meet the finish date. It only should be used for occasional catch-up of a task. Working continual overtime will only cause the people to slow down. In essence, you will be spending more time to achieve your normal 40 hours of result. If the team members become worn out on the project you will lose still further time training their replacements.

### [C]   Personnel Resource Scheduling

The context diagram further defines the tasks to be performed (see Chapter 2). The time to complete these tasks is estimated in "worker-hours" and inputted into the project management system (see § 5.07, "Project Resources"). This can be done manually for simple and small projects involving fewer than

4 people and 12 tasks. Before the project tasks can be assigned, they must be identified and detailed, and the needed skill levels for each determined so they can be matched to tasks.

Before estimating time on your project, detail the technical and business expertise level you would expect from a person holding each job title. Technical skills can be identified by job title (such as "programmer"). Level of expertise can be indicated by a title modifier, such as "Senior," "Junior," etc. (Some people prefer the suffix, I, II, III, or IV since being identified as a "Junior" might be misunderstood.) Assigning a task to an unqualified person can create delays and mistakes, while assigning the same task to an overqualified person wastes resources. When time permits, personnel development should be considered, too, by using a project task to teach team member's new skills.

When allocating task worker-hours, the project manager should note the worker's past record for finishing in the time allowed. The project manager will check with the project worker to confirm that the time allowed is reasonable. If not, a different time allowance should be negotiated. In addition, contingency time should be added, if needed, based on the worker's past performance record. If there is no previous record, time allowed should be more liberal. Ten percent above the original estimate is not unreasonable. The project manager will recompute the project time based on this new information, rearranging the schedule as needed. If a problem persists, the projects coordinator should be contacted. If necessary, he/she will assign additional workerpower to the project, possibly with personnel previously assigned to other projects. When the computer project management program has analyzed this data, the project manager will complete the final staffing plan for the project.

## [D]   Hardware and Software Delivery

Identify the required dates for the project's software and hardware delivery. Place orders in time to have the items in-house when needed. Contact the vendor a week before the due date to ensure the item will arrive on time. Take appropriate action if it will be late. Key items will have extra lead-time planned to avoid project delays. Delays may be caused by the following reasons:

- Custom fabricated hardware
- Purchased custom software
- Shipping problems because of distance (delays are more likely when items are shipped from abroad)
- Items that have to be scheduled for processing, such as custom-printed forms
- Plants closed for vacation or because of a strike

At the same time, items should not be delivered too far in advance. If bulky items come in before needed, there could be a storage problem, incurring an unnecessary expenditure. Also, items ordered too far in advance could become obsolete before being used or their costs could be lowered.

> ## COMMENT
>
> One nervous project manager was so afraid that his project budget would be cut that he purchased all the equipment his project required as soon as it was approved. Due to programming delay it was 18 months later before the time-keeping system was ready for roll-out to the customer. Meanwhile, the warranty had expired on equipment that was yet to be unpacked! Now his budget assumed the burden for repair costs for any dead-on-arrival equipment. Even worse, half of the equipment consisted of personal computers. Waiting 18 months would have almost doubled his equipment capabilities!

## § 5.05   PROJECT OBJECTIVES

### [A]   Overview

The primary project objective is to deliver a particular result or end product within the scope and timeframe originally established and budgeted by the steering committee in a form accepted by the user as operational. The final product may be in the form of a new complex system, a report, a manual operation, etc. The end result may be tangible or intangible.

A secondary objective is to utilize the resources of the project team in the most effective manner. These resources, under the control of the project manager, should be expended in an optimal manner during the project life cycle.

> ## COMMENT
>
> Information systems has earned a poor record of project cost overruns and delays over the years. The longer it takes to deliver a product, the less likely it will be acceptable to users, since business needs are constantly changing.

### [B]   Project Life Cycle Objectives

The project life cycle is comprised of tasks accomplished by the prudent use of resources available. The effort to complete these tasks requires certain managerial, technical, and/or political skills:

1. **Managerial.** The managerial skill of the project manager plays a major role in achieving the project objective. However, the IT steering committee, systems manager, projects coordinator, and sponsor can assist or undermine the project manager's effectiveness.
2. **Technical.** The number of people assigned to the project and their technical skill directly affect IT results.
3. **Political.** The project team should minimize its political "campaigning" activities, but relationships between people are not devoid of political overtones. Almost all project tasks require contact with people outside the project team. The results of these contacts may assist or hinder the project objective.

The tasks identified within the systems life cycle are divided into subtasks so that, if necessary, more than one person can work on a task. Even when one person completes the subtasks, this division provides for more convenient milestones with which to report progress.

## [C]  Project Product Objective

Standards must be set to confirm the project's product meets the product objective. Tangible objective product standards are easier to define and recognize than intangible ones.

The criteria for a project's successful completion must be defined in the scope statement and criteria for success list as approved by the steering committee. All involved management parties will have agreed to these criteria, including user management and the project manager. The project should not start the design phase until the acceptance criteria have been defined and accepted. These should include:

- List of product's key features (also known as criteria for success list)
- Validation criteria (how can we prove it provides these features?)
- Scope of product (description of product to draw boundaries around project)

The validation criteria should include the following:

- User documentation and training required are specified and in place
- Follow-up procedures are specified and in place
- Technical documentation for maintenance of software is complete
- System and volume tests meet standards set
- System downtime is not more than agreed-to limits
- Data content of the database meets agreement
- User support is in place and operational

# § 5.06  PROJECT FORMULATION

## [A]  Overview

Project formulation begins with the feasibility study. Next, the steering committee—or other decisionmaking authority—sets the project scope and finish date. Finally, project design considerations are added.

The actual finish date and final project cost are based on factors beyond the control of the project manager. The design estimate is also affected by these same essential estimating factors.

## [B]    Essential Estimating Factors

Estimating completion dates and work-hours needed becomes more accurate as the project advances. Unfortunately, this accuracy is needed much earlier in the project, when it can be the most helpful. Even the best project management software needs accurate estimates. If your organization has previously worked on a similar project, the actual times required to complete tasks will be very useful in building your estimates.

Research has shown that project members who estimate their own performance for completion times are consistently optimistic. For this reason, an independent (unbiased) group should be used on an ongoing basis to do the estimating for far more accurate results. The advantages of using an independent estimator, whether an individual or a group, are:

1. **Unbiased opinion.** An independent party will be unbiased.
2. **Estimate consistency.** Estimates will be consistent. Any discovered errors can be corrected for the person or group.
3. **Performance database provided.** The employee performance can be monitored. This also provides a source of employee information for staffing projects.

Factors affecting the estimate accuracy and ways to minimize this distortion are:

1. **Project size.** The project size can affect the time and effort needed for completion. This in turn affects the amount of calendar time needed and the final cost. Businesses exist in a very fluid environment. The longer the project takes, the more likely it is that the business sponsor will require additional changes. Changes that will be required for a usable product will also take additional time to install, which can justifiably lead to more changes. This is called the "size snowball effect."

   To reduce this possibility, the projects should be as small as possible. Changes made after project completion will then be maintenance changes to a system already in operation. This is preferable to making the same changes to a yet untested system. Large projects should be completed in phases with each phase ending in a working part of the product. They do not need to be an all-or-nothing affair.
2. **Project complexity.** The more project variables there are to manage, the more time and effort it will take to complete. The size of a forecasting project may be relatively small, but very complex.

   A complex project is more difficult to estimate. By breaking it into smaller modules it is easier and more accurate to estimate.

**COMMENT**

The validity of the user's specifications is critical. Years ago, one of the authors wrote an artificial intelligence program for a General Electric engineering department, which took 18 months to complete. It should have taken 6 to 8 months. The debugging of 45,000 machine instructions led to the discovery of a bug in the original formulas provided to the programmer.

3. **Personnel productivity.** This is a universal problem with system and programming departments. In the IT data entry unit, the output minus the errors defines the person's productivity. If the source documents are simply input, the system for judging a worker's output is simple and fairly accurate. This is not the case with the systems and programming production estimates.

   A systems analyst's past performance can be a gauge for estimating future performance for similar tasks. The difference in output of programmers has been estimated to be as high as 20 to 1 between the best and the worst.

   All too often programmers are judged by how hard they work. The lengthy hours spent and lines of code produced all too often are used to determine a programmer's contribution to the company. Yet the hardest working data entry operator, for example, may be the least productive and rewarded as such.

   When using in-house employees, take a hard look at their expertise level. Some companies are willing to pay for good contract programmers, but not willing to pay competitive wages for better in-house programmers. A poorly performing programmer can reduce the group's total output. A savvy IT manager will use the contract programmers to help raise the expertise of their employees by mixing the in-house and contract programmers in the project.

**COMMENT**

An IT manager in Ohio has two systems employees whose salaries are higher than his. When asked why, he answers, "They are worth it."

4. **Resources available.** Resources must have quality, but they must be available in quantity, too. There is no assurance that the people

promised for the project will be available when needed. The longer the duration of the project, the greater this problem can become. People leave, retire, get promoted, or get reassigned to other higher-priority projects.

If possible, make sure monies are budgeted to obtain contract help. It is better to have this money in reserve than to have to ask for it when it is needed, and be unsure of getting it.

5. **Resource technology.** The physical and technical resources available to the project team also affect the estimate. These items can include:

   a. **Work area.** The final work area can affect the productivity estimate. Is the project team housed together in a private area, or spread out into different locations without privacy?

   b. **Programming tools.** Are the programming tools familiar to the staff? If the tools are new, will training be available in time to be effective?

   c. **Computer hardware.** The workstations available will affect the project team's performance. Are notebook computers needed? What kind of networking is there? What about e-mail and voice mail?

   d. **Project management software.** Always use a project management software package. It will save time and effort needed to control the project and reduce administrative time required. (See § 5.07[C], "Project Management Tools.")

## [C] Factors Affecting Finish Date

There are factors other than incorrect time and cost estimates that affect the finish date, depending on the nature of the project, the user, corporate culture, etc. Some of these factors can be any number of the following:

1. **Adding programmer help.** If the project develops a need for one more programmer, it would be better to do without if the person being considered is not a high producer or performs poorly. In addition, the "communication factor," which will slow down the other programmers, along with the new programmer's learning curve productivity loss, would probably reduce the total programming output. Therefore, it is better to work overtime for more output than to bring in a new person late in a project. The danger is that extended overtime also will reduce programmer productivity.

2. **Project delays.** Project delays that extend the finish date can cause further delays. This is the "snowball delay effect." One delay creates other delays, which in turn create more delays, etc. Each delay will affect the time window for each succeeding task. People may be needed later than scheduled and may not be available. A new schedule must then be drawn up, based on the availability of key people. This can set a project back far enough that the user may now want to make changes, which will create more delays and increase the project's costs.

   With a delay pending, an effective project manager will look ahead to anticipate what problems might occur. For example, if you have arranged for a network team to install a new server and now you see that it will be delayed for a month, you can look ahead and reschedule that team for another time rather than let the agreed date pass.

There should be enough money budgeted for overtime. The law requires overtime pay, for hourly people, which can cover programmers. But, when an hourly person makes more money than a salaried worker does, working the same number of hours or more, there will be problems. In this case, the salaried worker should be rewarded with "comp" days off after the project is over or a monetary bonus. A better reward would include both.

3. **Staff turnover.** The loss of project members can have a significant impact on the project. The effect varies with the loss of staff. When new people come in, there is a learning curve to be expected. There will be a loss of work effort from the time a project member departs until the new person becomes fully productive. A problem can occur when a key user employee leaves, too. When anyone closely connected with the project leaves, the morale of the rest of the project members is affected. This may become a catalyst, causing others to quit, especially if problems exist with the project.

When extra effort and overtime are applied because of project slippage, there is an increase in employee turnover. There is a distinct correlation between employee turnover and overtime pressure. People have other pressures and interests outside of their employment. Overtime intrudes in this area. If it intrudes too much you may not see the danger until they have already given their notice.

## COMMENT

It is within the realm of reason that a 2-year project with 20 people could have over a 100-percent turnover before the project is completed—that is, if it is ever completed.

However, staff turnover is a normal thing and it should be anticipated. If there is a 10-percent turnover in personnel, and a 2-year project has 20 people, no fewer than 4 people will leave at one time or another. This does not count company transfers or promotions.

One solution is asking for more people to start the project. Having key players under contract is another. Paying team members a bonus and awarding paid time off at the project end will encourage salaried people to stay.

4. **New technology introduced.** When new technology is introduced to an ongoing project, it takes away available hours of time from the project, which in turn can result in calendar time lost. Training time is required and there is always a learning curve. New technology introduces a major risk of project failure that must be closely managed.

## COMMENT

If CEOs can get million-dollar bonuses with firms losing money in the United States, why can't all project members who complete a project be paid a bonus? It could be pro-rated to the finish date. This is done every day with contracts for outside construction projects. It certainly could be cost justified. Though there is a lack of research for this theory, we are willing to assist any firm willing to try it.

For these reasons, it is best not to introduce any new technology to a project past the analysis phase. If new technology must be added, it would be beneficial to have a new person join the project early who has already mastered the new technology skills.

5. **Administrative paperwork.** With the current trend to downsize secretarial staff, the project manager is now expected to perform these duties, which include word processing, filing, inputting data to spreadsheets, maintaining a project log, etc. This diverts time from the project manager's main function, which is managing the project.

A clerk typist should be assigned to the project and expected to stay until it is completed or abandoned. This person may expand his/her duties to also be of help to other members of the project. If such a person is not available in-house, contract outside part- or full-time help. This position should be listed on the staffing request for the project when the budget is planned.

Another way to address the essential paperwork load is to appoint an assistant project manager. A lot can be learned by drafting and handling a project's documents and this is a great place to start project management training.

### [D]  Project Design

The last phase in the project formulation is the design phase. At this point the feasibility study and project estimation and analysis are complete. In the design phase, details are formulated from which the program or operation will be constructed. The design can provide the criteria for writing or purchasing a computer program, or it can be a scheme for a manual procedure operation or a new report, etc.

The actual construction can begin after the design phase. It is sometimes feasible for the construction to start even before the design is complete, reducing the calendar time when there is a justifiable need.

Tools are now available that can accelerate the design function. They can be used alone or in combinations. The following is a sample of what is available:

- Prototyping
- Phased delivery
- Joint application development
- Simulation

Systems maintenance requires about two-thirds of all programming effort at most IT installations. Effort expended in design, construction, and documentation can reduce this time. This planning can help formulate a much more successful system, which will open up more time for new project development efforts.

# § 5.07  PROJECT RESOURCES

## [A]  Overview

IT project resources are comprised of people, tools, techniques, and education. These assets have a profound effect on the success of an IT project. IT organizations with continuous ongoing projects should have a source of project resource information. Depending on the size of the system, this could be the systems manager or projects coordinator with the added duties of resource person for project tools, techniques, and education.

## [B]  People Resources

People are by far the major expenditure for most IT project efforts, and a record of their activities must be maintained. A project file and a project management file must be maintained on a project management system of all current projects and their assigned personnel, as well as contract personnel and all user assigned personnel. In addition, active personnel will be entered on a personnel project display chart.

After a project is completed, data from the project file will be entered in a personnel project history file, which will contain data records of each completed project such as:

- Name
- Job title
- Project ID
- Planned start and finish dates of project
- Actual start and finish dates
- Hours committed to each project task
- Hours required to finish each project task
- Duties involved for each assigned task
- Time ratio (hours required divided by assigned hours)
- Total project time ratio

The project file of all current projects and the projects coordinator, who is responsible for allocating personnel resources for the projects, will maintain the project management file. These files are part of the project management system used for controlling people for projects.

The projects coordinator allocates human resources by job title. All consultants and contract personnel will be given the same standard internal job titles assigned to IT personnel. A descriptive narration following the job title will be used when needed. The titles are:

- Projects coordinator
- Project manager
- Assistant project manager
- Systems manager
- Project secretary
- Project librarian
- Systems analyst
- Systems and procedure analyst
- Industrial engineer
- Analyst programmer

- Senior programmer
- Programmer
- Junior programmer
- Business systems analyst
- Data manager
- Database administrator
- Database specialist
- Network specialist
- Quality assurance auditor

## [C]   Project Management Tools

There have been over 700 project management software packages produced for mainframe, minicomputers, and PCs. The prices start at shareware levels and go into the thousands of dollars. Today there are some effective packages for Windows-based PCs, Macintosh, and Unix systems.

> **COMMENT**
>
> Microsoft Project is by far the most popular PC-based project management package. There are also numerous Web-based applications available for managing enterprise-level projects.

When selecting a project management package, first look for software that will run on the hardware and operating system already installed. Second, choose the least complex package that will do the job. Other features that must be considered are:

- User support
- User friendliness
- Reliability
- Maximum number of simultaneous users
- Ability for team members to enter their time spent on a task

The package should contain:

- Work breakdown structure (WBS)
- Single-source data entry

- Calendar support
- PERT and CPM charting
- Online tutorials or help screens
- A database information repository for multiple projects

It should be able to:

- Perform "what if" scenarios
- Identify critical paths and compute slack time
- Support capture of resources for allocation to tasks
- Compare planned to actual Gantt charts
- Plot milestones

Other features worth considering:

- Can be networked
- Can handle multiple projects and roll up resource requirements
- Has resource leveling to identify people who must be in two places at once
- Training is available
- Has individual resource calendars for vacation and training times
- Can show work completed versus budgeted milestones

## [D]  Project Techniques

There is a wide range of project planning techniques. Some require a computer and supporting software, while others use manual methods. No one technique resolves all project management needs.

1.  **PERT charts.** PERT charts can display the total project with all scheduled tasks shown in sequence. These can be produced manually or by using project management software. The displayed tasks show which ones are in parallel and can be performed at the same time.

    PERT and CPM charts look alike. The only difference is how the task times are computed. The CPM method uses one value (most likely time) for determining the time each task will take. PERT requires a calculation as follows:

$$\text{TASK TIME} = \frac{\text{Optimistic Time} + (4 \times \text{Most Likely Time}) + \text{Pessimistic Time}}{6}$$

    The critical path of the PERT/CPM chart computes the project duration. This can be done manually or by using a project management program. The critical path can be worked backward from a finish date or forward from a start date.

    The PERT/CPM chart will show the slack times. Slack time occurs when a task takes less time to do than a parallel critical path task. This information can be valuable. For example, suppose the critical path needs to be reduced in total time by 2 days, and assume a critical path task of 12 days is found which has a parallel slack task of 10 or fewer days. Simply have the critical path task work overtime 2 Saturdays, and the total project time is reduced by 2 days. This is a very simple illustration; more complex solutions for reducing the total project time can be found by using a project management program.

The PERT/CPM chart can be the input for the Gantt charts. Each leg of the PERT/CPM chart can become a Gantt chart, displaying the scheduled calendar days. The chart can be available on screen from a project software package and/or placed on the office wall.

2. **Gantt charts.** Gantt charts are used to show calendar time task assignments in days, weeks, or months. Task progress and milestones can be shown on the chart. The number of days required to complete a task that reaches a milestone can be compared with the planned number. The actual worked days, from actual start to actual finish, are plotted below the scheduled days. This information can give a forewarning that the task is not on schedule, and adjustments can be made.

Gantt charts can also be used to show dollars allocated versus dollars spent. This information can be compared to the status of task work completed. Tasks also can be broken down into subtasks, and both used to identify the persons assigned. Charts can be produced showing a person's task type assignment by projects. The overall project status displayed allows the project manager to assign or reassign personnel as needed. It also shows him/her when there is a need for shifting project schedules and can warn of future problems.

Gantt charts can be produced on graph paper or magnetic boards, or by computer project management software. If the latter, the charts can be displayed on a corporate intranet for easy access by the entire team.

## [E]  Project Management Education

There is a wide range of project education resources today, from informal self-paced education to more formal presentations. Sources are available in the following forms:

1. **Reading material.** Many books and articles have been written on this subject. The local library will have a periodical index and books-in-print text. Look under "project management" for the most current source selection. Larger town libraries now have computer access to this information. If the library does not have what you need, it can copy periodical articles and obtain books through interlibrary loans.
2. **Seminars.** Professional organizations as well as others offer seminars, such as American Management Association (*www.amanet.org*); SkillPath Seminars (*www.skillpath.com*); and Project Management Institute (*www.pmi.org*). Check the library for more names and addresses.
3. **Videotapes.** There are commercially available videotapes on project management.
4. **College classes.** Colleges offer project management classes, both in engineering and business programs. These classes are often at the graduate level, most with no prerequisite.
5. **Project management professional organization.** The Project Management Institute publishes a monthly "Project Management Journal" and holds seminars.

# § 5.08  PROJECT PROGRESS

## [A]  Overview

The project progress is tracked in three ways: task completion, progress measurement, and reporting. This tracking begins when the project starts and ends after it is terminated. Not all projects are completed but all are terminated. Those that are not completed but terminated are the ones most often noted as failures.

## [B]  Task Completion

As task milestones are reached, this information will be entered into the project management program. Completed tasks are assessed for quality, completion effort required, and effect on the project schedule. The hours estimated to complete the task effort will be compared with the actual hours, and this information will be retained for correcting future estimates.

This task completion information will be used to identify the project status at different points in time, and will be discussed in status meetings. If projects start to fall behind schedule, solutions will be sought. The following are some solutions that can be used to take care of project slippage:

1. **Overtime.** Overtime should be used only for completing critical path tasks and only in the short-term. If the need for overtime becomes routine, it can affect the personnel turnover rate. The best time for paid overtime is right after Christmas, and the worst time is during the summer months.

2. **Assign more people.** Assigning people at the start of a project is less of a problem than adding more later on. The worst time is at the end. As more people are added, the communication required between project members reduces the output per worker, and the learning curve becomes a factor, too. As a result, the project effort could end up less effectively completed than if no additional people had been added.

## COMMENT

Adding more people does not automatically speed up the result. If one woman takes 9 months to make a baby, 9 women cannot do it in 1 month.

3. **Farm out a task to a vendor.** This action has merit if the vendor has reliable skills in the appropriate area. For the best results, the vendor should be given advance notice to expect the project.

4. **Reduce the project scope.** If the user management is willing to re-

duce the project scope, this may be an effective solution to project slippage, helping to keep the quality of remaining project tasks intact.

5. **Reschedule module delivery.** Delay modules which may not be required for the finish date. This could be a better solution than reducing the project scope.

6. **Request additional funds.** If you are over budget, more money will have to be requested. The sooner this is done, the better, because as the end of the fiscal year approaches, money becomes less available. If the dollars represent people cost, this is not so much of a problem. Salaried people do not require overtime pay, and both hourly and salaried people are budgeted for, whether they are working on a project or at their regular jobs.

## [C]  Progress Measurement

Items that must be controlled and managed should be monitored for both quantity and quality. It is harder to measure the quality of output than quantity at the time the work is being done, since the quality of the programming effort starts to show up only when the programs are tested and debugged. Therefore, the testing should not be delayed.

Employee time is the greatest cost of the project, and it should be closely monitored to provide information to gauge the results in terms of the effort exerted. Everyone must complete a time sheet, including the project manager and contract workers and/or consultants. Some of the project management packages collect this data online and summarize it in a weekly report, automatically applying the time and dollar values to relevant project tasks.

So as not to intimidate the employees or have them spend too much time collecting this data, do the following:

1. **Explain why the data is needed.** Demonstrate the process used to record the time and explain why it is used. Encourage the use of real numbers, not made-up ones or estimates. Stress the fact that the information is for their benefit, too.

2. **Simplify the recording.** Do not require too much detail. Let people know they may receive a telephone call from a spouse or go to the restroom. According to the time measurement people, workers are normally allowed 10 percent of their work time for personal time.

   Have the time sheets turned in or inputted to the computer daily. Efforts expended on Monday morning are difficult to remember by Friday afternoon. For forms inputted to the computer, use scannable documents. Ideally, have the worker input the data from his/her own workstation.

   Do not insist that the time used agree with the required time.

3. **Use continuous work sampling.** Note this alternative to having the employees keep track of work time would relieve them of this effort and most likely would be more accurate. (However, it would be more costly.)

4. **Confirm time estimates.** Inform employees that the time estimates on which the project is constructed need to be confirmed. Estimates

are only approximations and should be corrected, if wrong. This cannot be done without keeping track of the actual time spent.

As a byproduct, workers will be more productive if monitored.

## [D]   Project Reporting

Project members should submit weekly and monthly project reports to their respective project managers, who then forward copies to the projects coordinator. He/she will compile a monthly report of all projects for the head of information systems and the steering committee. The monthly report will also be sent to the systems manager if the systems manager is not the projects coordinator.

The project team should have a brief status meeting late Friday afternoon to summarize the week's work. Any catching up can be done on Saturday, if necessary. From this meeting and the project management program information, the Monday status report will be produced by the project manager and issued to the project team and the projects coordinator. This status report will note the progress made, what tasks are behind schedule, and what effort is being made to catch up. Tasks still to begin also will be reported.

The monthly report will recap the weekly reports and forecast the project's status for the next month. If the current month's status does not agree with last month's forecast the reasons will be given. The monthly report will provide the percent probabilities that the project will meet the finish date and the budget provided. Dollar variances of over 5 percent or more than $2,500 must be explained (your IT steering committee will set these guidelines). Any future items that may affect the project should be reported (such as people going on vacation, leaving, etc.).

A final report, written by the project manager, will be sent to the projects coordinator recapping the project's major issues. Problems encountered and how to avoid them in the future will be presented. People who did outstanding work will be noted. This report is only for the projects coordinator who will write a completed project report and submit it to the systems manager if he/she is not the project coordinator, the head of information systems, and the steering committee.

# § 5.09   PROJECT COMMUNICATIONS

Communications is a key to coordinating efforts by your team. They need to understand how the various parts of the project are progressing and problems found. If you maintain a steady flow of information to the team and the business stakeholders, you will find yourself repeating the same things over and over as managing a group of individuals instead of leading a team. The flow of information concerning a project comes in the form of written communications, e-mail, voice mail, and meetings. Each has its advantages and limitations.

1. **Written communications.** These are letters, memos, and e-mail. Letters are used for communications that go outside the firm. Memos and e-mail are preferred for written internal communications. A standard format is used for both types.

2. **Voice mail.** Voice mail is used to communicate verbal information. This can be sent to more than one receiver.

3. **Meetings.** Meetings are very important, but costly. Project managers can spend over 50 percent of their time in meetings. There are two types of meetings: the one-way communications meeting and the two-way meeting. The one-way meeting is a meeting to inform. The two-way meeting is used to resolve an issue.

   Following are procedural steps to use as a guide for conducting a meeting:
   a.  Write an agenda with time limits for each item. Ask team members for issues they want to surface.
   b.  Send out copies of the agenda to all personnel invited to attend.
   c.  Begin and end the meeting on time.
   d.  Keep minutes of the meeting and include the names of those present.
   e.  Limit the number of people for two-way communication meetings to 10 to 12. Save one-on-one issues and major discussion for after the meeting.
   f.  Arrange the seating for the best communication and control.
   g.  Place important subjects first on the agenda.
   h.  Discussion procedures:
       • Keep to the agenda.
       • Be aware of supervisor and subordinate relationships.
       • Draw out shy participants.
       • Give everyone an opportunity to be involved in the discussion.

# § 5.10   MULTIPLE-PROJECTS MANAGEMENT

## [A]   Overview

Seldom does an information systems operation have only one project in process. Therefore, multiple-project management must be considered. The systems manager is responsible for the effort, but may delegate this responsibility to a projects coordinator.

All projects must use the methodology of reporting, operation, naming conventions, and so on. This standard must be universal so that resources shared will present no problem when being exchanged. The reports received also must be consistent because of the need to combine them when reporting to the systems manager if the manager is not the projects coordinator, the IT head, and the steering committee. A database of all personnel (including their job titles) who are involved in projects will be maintained. The database will include a list of project titles, dates of assignment, and time spent on those projects. The database will identify any person(s) being assigned more than one task at a time.

## [B]   Resource Sharing

The projects coordinator is responsible for overseeing the multiple projects and assigning IT personnel to the different projects. If there is a problem with an assignment, the IT manager will resolve the problem. The projects coordinator is also responsible for overseeing contract personnel and consultants. Arrangements for others, who can be on loan, are the sole responsibility of the projects coordinator.

The weekly reports will indicate the status of each project and its tasks. The coordination of the people by the projects coordinator makes it possible for resources to be shifted from one project to another when necessary. Coordination duties also include the authorization to prioritize projects and tasks within projects.

## [C]   Backup Personnel

When a large number of people (over 30) are engaged in project activities, it would be prudent to have extra key workers reporting to the projects coordinator to provide for a needed workerpower buffer. The type of personnel that would most likely be needed in the buffer pool would be:

- Project secretaries
- Programmers
- Systems analysts
- Network personnel
- Database personnel
- IT trainers
- Documentation writers
- Systems and procedure analysts
- Project librarians

## [D]   Scope Management

With more than one project in process, there can be problems of boundary management with users. To avoid this problem, the projects coordinator must be aware of projects that have overlapping scopes. Not only can this cause wasted effort if not policed, but company political problems as well. Projects must be viewed in a proactive light to prevent this from happening.

The projects coordinator will have at his/her disposal the repository plans of all projects in process, as well as planned projects. This information should be kept on a database provided by a PC program management system.

## COMMENT

Many project management experts suggest that when a project is terminated, there should be a party to celebrate. The end of a project does not necessarily indicate that it was completed. A project's termination also may come in the form of a cancellation. Whatever the reason, it still calls for a party to celebrate the occasion.

# 6

# CORPORATE IT COMPUTER OPERATIONS: ENSURING SECURITY AND SAFETY

# § 6.01    IT COMPUTER OPERATIONS POLICIES

## [A]    Overview

This section sets down the policies governing an information systems computer center operation. The operations area is restricted to operational and identified vendor support personnel; but because of today's distributed data processing and computer networks, access is not limited to persons physically entering the area. It also can be vulnerable to unauthorized access through telecommunications, so every precaution should be taken.

Computer operations is the enabling part of data processing. Operations encompasses all of the routine efforts, such as backing up data, running a central print room, help desk, workstation and peripheral repairs, user IDs and security, etc. The primary goal of operations is stability—not optimal processes. Optimal is nice but a stable, predictable environment is more important than an optimal, but erratic service.

The computer operations manager is the "landlord" for all of the central computer and network rooms and has control over the equipment within them. This control includes physical security, logical security access, environmental controls, fire safety, operator training, and anything else required to keep them stable.

## [B]    Security and Safety in the Computer Room

To maintain proper computer room security and safety, the following policies are in place:

1.  **Restricted access.** Only authorized personnel—those persons needed to operate, supervise, or provide maintenance to the area and its equipment—are permitted entry to the IT computer operations area. Anyone entering or leaving the area must sign a sign-in/sign-out log or an alternative tracking system. Neither food nor drinks are ever allowed in these areas. No one should routinely work in these areas. The fewer people that enter these rooms, the less dirt they will track in. Given the constant movement of air in these rooms and the number of devices with cooling fans, dirt can easily build up on computer circuitry.

2.  **Restricted online access.** Online access to the system from outside the computer center is controlled with proper user and ID access codes that are changed no less than twice a year. Codes no longer authorized should be deleted as soon as possible. Telephone access will have caller ID screening.

3.  **Power supply**
    a.  The computer center area has its own power supply connected to the main power source for the building.
    b.  A backup uninterrupted power supply (UPS) or a fail-safe device is required to prevent a disk crash if the main power fails.
    c.  A self-starting generator is available to provide emergency power for work lights, room ventilation, and air conditioning.

4. **Air conditioning.** The computer center has its own backup air conditioning system.
5. **Construction hazards.** The computer room area is not adjacent to any natural gas or liquid-transporting pipes, high-voltage lines, or magnetic radiation sources.
6. **Fire precautions.** Fire extinguishers are the safest possible precaution. All materials used in constructing the computer room area are fireproof or fire retardant.
7. **Smoke detectors.** Smoke detection equipment is installed and connected to a monitoring center when no personnel are on duty.
8. **Data backup.** Database and file backups are kept as current as is reasonable. Off-site data and software backup is maintained. The off-site storage has a fireproof rating for secondary data devices. Vendor contracted backup of online real-time transaction data is recommended as demand may require.
9. **Low profile of the computer area.** The computer center area must maintain a low profile. No signs directing persons to the center should be displayed.
10. **Safe location.** The actual site of the IT computer center must not be located on a flood plain or within 50 miles of an earthquake fault.

## [C]   Housekeeping in the Computer Center

The following are policies that apply to housekeeping in the computer center:
1. No smoking, drinking, or eating is permitted.
2. Operations personnel are responsible for maintaining a clean working area.
3. Operators are not to attempt to repair any equipment without the specific authorization of the supervisor or maintenance vendor.
4. Operators are not to alter programs without specific authorization of the supervisor.
5. The computer is to be used for only assigned operations.
6. Temperature and humidity are to be monitored at all times and kept within the recommended ranges for the equipment.

## [D]   Disaster and Recovery Plans

Well-organized disaster plans help ensure the firm's continued operation in case of an emergency. Likewise, an effective recovery plan in the event of computer hardware or software failure is a necessity. The company cannot be without an IT computer operation for more than a minimal amount of time.

# § 6.02   GENERAL OPERATIONS

## [A]   Scope

This section covers general procedures to be followed by the IT computer center personnel and any visitors. Each center is an enclosed shop with operating areas restricted to only those persons required for the center's operation.

## [B]   Operating Environment

A key part of operations management is to protect the stability of your equipment. To do this the equipment must have a stable environment in which to work. This environment includes the quality and constant supply of electrical power, a stable temperature, and an acceptable humidity level. Quick reacting fire suppression (usually $CO_2$ or Halon gas) is also recommended.

1. **Power.** The power lines for your backroom equipment must pass through a line filter to protect expensive devices from power spikes. This will be done at the point where electrical power enters the computer rooms.

   Data servers maintain tables in memory to provide speedy access to files. If the server loses power before these buffers can be flushed to disk, then the server must rebuild the file indexes when it restarts. This greatly increases your server restart time. Other equipment in your computer room also performs better if shutdown is in an orderly fashion rather than "pulling the plug" on them. There are, however, some devices that a power loss is not a major problem, such as a monitor or printer (assuming it was idle).

   To ensure there is always electrical power for your equipment, you must provide an uninterruptible power supply (UPS) for all key equipment. A UPS is essentially a battery pack to supply power until either electrical service is restored or to provide time for an orderly shutdown of the servers. Most power outages are of short duration. Your UPS batteries must be able to provide power to your servers for at least 30 minutes. The time available from your UPS is based on the age of the batteries and the current draw against the batteries. For this reason, the operations manager must determine which devices will be on the UPS and make a policy that no one may attach anything to the UPS without permission. UPS batteries must be checked semi-annually and replaced every 10 years.

2. **Heating and air conditioning.** Environmental controls in a computer room are very important. Servers are designed to operate within a specific temperature range. You must ensure this is maintained or immediate steps must be taken. A policy should be established that roving security is to step inside of the computer rooms every time they make their rounds to see if the temperatures are too high. There is also remote signaling equipment available that can notify you if environmental limits have been exceeded.

## [C]   Security and Safety

Procedures that apply to the security and safety of the computer center are:

1. Lock the computer operations area at all times.
2. Restrict access to the computer center to operations personnel, approved vendor maintenance personnel, and/or operations management personnel due to report for duty at a specified time. Tours by visitors, employees, vendors, or customers must be authorized and approved by the IT computer operations manager.

3. Use a sign-in/sign-out log or a computer ID card access door-opening system to keep a record of all who enter the computer area including the time of entrance.
4. Fire extinguishers and/or their controls must be easily identifiable. Instructions should be posted next to the instruments. Ensure fire suppressing gas cautions are plainly visible.
5. Operations personnel are responsible for knowing:
   a. Location of fire alarms, extinguishers, and controls for firefighting systems
   b. Emergency power-off procedures
   c. Emergency procedures for notifying fire department, programmer on call, and appropriate management personnel

## [D]   Housekeeping Standards

Standard measures are required to maintain cleanliness and ensure safety in the computer operations area.

1. Eating, drinking, and/or smoking are never permitted in the computer center area. Post signs to this effect in the computer center and on or near the outside door of the computer center.
2. Operators under the influence of prescribed sedatives or similar medication are to be given assignments that will not endanger the operator or the operation.
3. Operations personnel are responsible for the general cleanliness in their areas. Items removed for use are returned to the area where they belong.
4. Personnel will not place their feet on top of desks or equipment. Shoes must be worn at all times.
5. Personal radios, TVs, or audio equipment are not permitted in the computer center area.
6. Personal phone calls are limited to 5 minutes.

## [E]   Downtime Procedures

When there are hardware or software failures, downtime procedures require computer operators to describe and record:

1. General conditions at time of failure
2. Unusual activity observed in any input/output device prior to computer failure
3. Information received from outside sources for correcting problem

## [F]   Disk Handling

Proper disk handling ensures data availability for jobs and reduces read-write errors.

1. Store removable disks in proper containers when not in drives.
2. File disk-storage containers in place when not in use.
3. Identify contents of disks by external labels placed on front of disk.

### [G]  Tape Handling

Following are procedures for handling tapes:

1.  General tape procedures
    - Clean hands are a must for operators handling tapes.
    - Read-write heads should be cleaned in accordance with the manu-facturer's recommendations.
    - Keep tapes in protective containers when not in use.
    - To prevent accidental recording, read-only tapes should be write-protected.
2.  Tape-handling procedures
    - Tapes must be handled gently and not slammed or dropped.
    - Tapes should be kept in environmentally friendly areas (like a computer room) or other place where they will not be exposed to extreme temperatures.
    - Tapes should be mounted squarely and evenly on the tape transport.
    - Tapes should be checked after use to discover irregular rewinding.
    - Tape drive doors are closed when tapes are not in the process of being mounted or dismounted.

## § 6.03  OPERATING PROCEDURES

### [A]  Overview

Computer room operating procedures are a combination of vendor-provided instruction manuals and programmers' instructions peculiar to each application. If any procedure appears incorrect, confusing, or contradictory, the problem should be brought to the attention of the appropriate operations supervisor.

### [B]  Process Flow

The flow of source document input and hardcopy output is funneled through a reception area or user input/output counter. This area provides a buffer to the area outside computer center operations.

Source documents are routed to the data entry unit, which enters the data and transmits it to the computer room. For purposes of control, the data entry area is separate from the computer room. As with any part of the computer center operations area, only authorized personnel may gain entry.

Data being carried into the computer room comes from the data entry area or directly from the receiving input/output counter where it is usually in the form of tapes, disks, and turnaround documents. (Turnaround documents are output documents the computer generates and sends out—for example, utility bills, installment payment documents, factory timecards, etc.) When they are returned, their computer-printed information can be read by both computer input devices and the human eye.

Computer operations keeps off-line data in a storage area called the data library, which is controlled by a librarian or computer operator who logs tapes and disks in and out. Entry to the library is through the computer room. In addition to the flow of data between operations and the library, there is a flow of backup data to and from an off-site data storage location. The library is separated from the computer room by a fireproof wall and door.

## [C]  Computer Operations Procedures

The heart of the IT operation center is the computer systems. Operation of the computer equipment is the duty and responsibility of the computer operator. His/her duties and responsibilities vary depending on the computer, and the policies and procedures of each computer center operation. In a small shop, one individual may be responsible for virtually all activities. Regardless of the size of the computer center operation or the computer system used, some duties or tasks are traditionally performed by an operator, although the computer operation may at times be run unattended.

*Daily shift duties.* The operator beginning his/her shift first checks with the one ending the prior shift to ascertain if there are any problems. Then the operator:

1. Checks for system messages on the display monitor or system message log book.
2. Checks the schedule of the previous shift. If there are any priority jobs not completed, the operator may rearrange the job schedule. If there is a major problem, he/she contacts the operations supervisor.
3. Performs housekeeping tasks such as checking the tape drives, disk drives, etc.
4. Updates the tapes' and disks' status required for the rest of the shift. Sets aside tapes and disks to be taken to the data library. Goes to the data library to exchange tapes and/or disks.
5. Checks to see if a backup is required and, if so, performs it.
6. Checks the monitor for the status of jobs being run. If the system does not generate its own processing log, the console operator maintains a written one for each shift's operation. The information logged consists of the number of the job completed, the start and finish times, and any remarks.
7. When questions arise about a job being run, the operator checks the operator's manual and related documentation for that particular job. When all else fails, contact the supervisor.
8. If an error causes a job to be terminated prematurely, the operator corrects the problem by following the restart procedure for that job.

*Other shift responsibilities.* In addition to general tasks, some other duties and responsibilities for the operator are:

1. Power up/power down the system. The operator may be required to turn the computer system on and perform an initial program load (IPL) procedure.

2.  Turn the computer off (power down) if the computer center does not operate 24 hours a day, or for other specified reasons. The operator follows standard power down procedures as listed in the operator's manual.
3.  Initiate the processing procedure required if there are any batch jobs to be run. The operator checks, before starting the job, to ensure that all the required data is available.
4.  Monitor the batch-processing job being run.
5.  Check tapes or disks into the computer center from other sources.
6.  Check in any turnaround documents using the job procedures for logging in documents.
7.  Transmit messages to online users of the system including downtime and its duration.
8.  Change the priority of jobs waiting to be printed by accessing the spooling system.

*Administrative responsibilities.* The person responsible for the computer operation performs the administrative responsibilities. In a one-person department, this can be the operator. These responsibilities include the following:

1.  Order supply items.
2.  Order and maintain technical manuals.
3.  Distribute technical briefs and standards.
4.  Schedule computer maintenance.
5.  Design and maintain special forms and logs required for computer center operations.
6.  Schedule operators by shift.
7.  Train new operators.
8.  Rotate backup media properly by storing the most recent media used and preparing the labels for the current day's backups.

## [D]   Peripheral Equipment Operation Procedures

Computer systems have a host of online and off-line peripheral devices. In a single-operator shop, the operator is responsible for the main computer and all these devices. In a one-person computer center operation, the individual responsible for the entire operation functions as the data entry person, the computer and peripheral equipment operator, the data librarian, and the center administrator. In a larger operation, these duties are assigned to different people.

Depending on the size of the operation, peripheral device operation procedures can be done by one or many operators. These procedures are defined by vendors' manuals or written by a systems analyst. They are defined as duties or tasks required by the operations personnel. Here are examples:

*Printers.* The computer spooling program controls the printing operations. The operator determines what kind of paper is required for the scheduled printouts. The center may employ more than one kind of printing device, each with its own manufacturer's operations manual. A printer operator might be responsible for any of the following kinds of printers:

- Impact printers
- Wire-matrix printers
- Ink-jet printers
- Laser printers
- Computer output microfilm

Duties required for printer operations include:

1. Change or add paper to printer following manufacturer's instructions.
2. Check print alignment before starting printer when job changes. This is very important when using preprinted forms.
3. Monitor paper supply and output stacks.
4. Remove paper jams.
5. Check output at the start of each job to determine if it is necessary to change printer ribbons, and replace toner or inkjet cartridges.
6. Perform minor preventive maintenance, as designated in the instruction manual, and clean the machine when needed. Paper dust must be vacuumed out daily, as it is a fire hazard.

*Magnetic tape drives.* Tape drives are reel or cartridge. Cartridge drives present less of a handling problem than reel drives, but with either kind, the tape should never be touched. When mounting a reel tape on a drive, care should be taken to avoid letting the tape touch the floor. The following required procedures apply to both types:

1. Tapes are never stacked on top of each other in a flat position.
2. Tapes are never left on top of tape drives.
3. Tapes are always write-protected prior to reading.
4. External labels are checked before mounting tape to ensure that the correct tape is being used.
5. Magnetic tapes are cleaned as needed.
6. A record of all tape read/write errors is maintained, i.e., the tape number, drive number, type of error, time and date of the error.
7. A record of scratch tapes is maintained. (Scratch tapes are those that have been previously used for other jobs but the data they contain are no longer needed.) All old external labels are removed.
8. Tape error messages that appear on the monitor are responded to immediately.

*Direct-access devices.* Removable direct-access storage can be in the form of disks, Zip disks, or CDs. The operator handling tape drives often handles the direct-access devices, too. Online computer systems are noted for having many direct-access storage devices. Operating procedures for the devices are defined in the manufacturer's manuals, but some duties and responsibilities are common to almost all devices. Following are duties or procedures associated with direct-access devices:

1. Floppy disks, Zip disks, and CDs are retained in their storage containers when not in use. Dust is their enemy!
2. A felt pen is used when writing on disk labels.
3. Disks and Zip disks are not placed on disk drives or close to telephones to prevent magnetic contamination.
4. Blank disks are formatted in advance and kept, ready for use, in a dust-free container.
5. The insides of disk and CD drives are kept free of foreign objects.
6. Prompt response to monitor messages is necessary. An operator takes corrective action by following the manufacturer's manual or disk operations manual. If instructions to correct the problem are not available, the operator contacts the lead operator or operations supervisor. Some of the more common problems noted by error messages are:
   - File label errors
   - Disk drive errors
   - Duplicate file names
   - Read errors
   - Write errors
   - Wrong tape loaded

*Other peripheral devices.* Computer centers today use a large variety of peripherals in addition to standard printers, direct-access storage devices, and magnetic tapes. One also may be available for a specific computer center application. Some of the more common devices are:

- Computer output microfilm (COM)
- Optical readers
- Magnetic-ink character readers
- Page scanners
- Modems
- CD or DVD writers
- CD disk arrays (a stack of CD readers)

The degree of operator involvement depends on the device. The manufacturer's manual prescribes the correct operating procedure. Any additional instructions should be available in the operations procedure manual for the job being run.

In the event of equipment failure, the operations supervisor is notified. Operator requirements of the more common devices follow:

1. **COM.** The computer output microfilm device is most often a stand-alone off-line device requiring a tape input. Tape-handling procedures have been outlined in § 6.02[G], "Tape Handling." The operator fol-

lows the manufacturer's operating instructions in running scheduled jobs. Main duties required for the device are to:

- Perform minor maintenance as required by instruction manual.
- Mount tapes for output as scheduled.
- Maintain a log of start and finish times by job.
- Clear any jams as prescribed in instruction manual.
- Check distribution counts for each job.
- Make sure supplies are available before output is started.

2. **Optical readers.** Optical reader input documents can be user-generated documents or the computer center's own turnaround documents. Operation of the device follows the manufacturer's instructions. Input is most often in batch form. The main duties required for operating the device are to:

- Perform minor maintenance as required by instruction manual.
- Maintain a log for run times of each batch of input.
- Clear any jams as prescribed in instruction manual.
- Repair or provide replacement documents for damaged documents.

3. **Magnetic-ink character readers.** This device receives input from users and may have additional information keyed in at the data entry unit. Operating duties are similar to those for the optical readers.

4. **Modems.** The modem is a peripheral device that serves as an online input/output instrument between outside users and the IT computer. For the most part, it runs unattended. If the modem goes down or is known to be out of service, the operator provides users with information about the current or pending shutdown. Pending shutdowns can be transmitted as monitor displays.

5. **CD/DVD.** CD/DVD disk burners have replaced a good deal of the microfilm output. These devices use a magazine of blank disks that are automatically loaded, the information copied, and the completed disk placed in an output hopper. Care must be taken to avoid scratching these disks.

# § 6.04   REPORT DISTRIBUTION

## [A]   Types of Reports

There are many different types of forms created for printed reports. Forms and reports are not the same. A form is a sheet of paper, containing preprinted information and providing space for additional data. Preprinted information can be logos, headings, lines, boxes, or constant narratives, such as a payroll check. A report is information printed on blank paper.

Forms can be single sheets, as used by laser printers, or continuous, as used by impact printers. Preprinted forms are usually purchased, while flat forms can either be purchased or printed in-house. COM units also can produce reports in the form of microfiche. Procedures for generating reports were covered in § 6.03[D], "Peripheral Equipment Operation Procedures."

COMMENT

Where practical, avoid using preprinted forms in your laser printer. Some large laser systems will print in several colors and sometimes the form is simply black ink. By using your laser printer to print the form while it prints the information on it, you save on the cost of preprinting and stocking a special form. This is important since if the form ever changes, the existing stock may need to be destroyed. If instead you flashed the form while printing the data, you could make changes at any time.

Preparation of reports requires knowledge of how these reports are distributed; this information provides the basis for control of both reports and forms. Therefore, preprinted forms for inventory and control are part of the preparation of reports operation. Their inventory levels are dictated by quantity discount purchases and delivery times.

"Controlled forms"—such as payroll checks, bank drafts, credit card blanks, and savings bonds—require special care to ensure their availability and security. They contain printed, usually sequential, numbers to help prevent theft. Close monitoring and storage of controlled forms is required. Discovering there aren't enough checks to meet the payroll is an unnerving experience for any IT operations manager. The report preparation area should have storage space available for both stock forms and controlled forms, with a fireproof, lockable container provided for controlled forms.

## [B]  Preparation of Reports

Computer operations personnel are responsible for loading the correct forms or microfiche into the printing device when output reports are generated. When continuous forms are used, pin-feed margins and the pages remain attached until the entire job is complete.

Laser printouts and microfiche output require different preparation procedures. COM is usually processed off-line, while impact and laser printing occur online.

*Continuous-forms procedures.* If the continuous form is a multipart form with carbon paper, the carbon paper remains between the copies. When accounts payable and payroll checks are printed, the checks are not yet signed. Continuous form documents are processed as follows:

1.  The printed reports are placed in a decollator to separate the copies of multipart forms. (See the procedure for operation in the manufacturer's instruction manual.)

2. If pin-feed margins are to be removed, the margin slitter on the decollator is turned on.
3. If multipart forms with carbon paper are used, the carbon paper is attached to carbon spindles on the decollator.
4. The forms are run through the decollator and stacked.
5. Forms that require separating into individual pages are run through the burster. Single-sheet copies are stacked after the bursting operation.
6. Checks requiring imprinted signatures are imprinted with a continuous-form imprinter or during the bursting operation. The procedure used depends on the hardware available.
   a. **Accounts payable.** The accounts payable unit provides the imprinting stamp for writing accounts payable checks. When the checks are delivered to accounts payable, the imprinting stamp also is returned. The beginning and ending check numbers are reported to accounts payable in accordance with its procedure. All damaged checks are marked VOID and returned.
   b. **Payroll.** The payroll unit provides the imprinting stamp for writing payroll checks. When checks are returned to that unit, the imprinting stamp also is returned. The beginning and ending check numbers are reported to the payroll department in accordance with its procedure. All damaged checks are marked VOID and returned.

      When running confidential payroll or expense reimbursement checks, only authorized personnel are allowed in the processing area and signs are posted to that effect.
7. When computer-printed reports have been prepared for distribution, they are moved into the distribution area. Confidential reports are placed in sealed cardboard boxes or envelopes.

*Laser output procedures.* The preparation of laser-printed reports for distribution is as follows:

1. Single-copy reports are moved to the distribution area. Reports of more than one page are stapled together in the upper left-hand corner.
2. If more than one copy of each report is required, the pages are collated and stapled in the upper left-hand corner of each report.
3. The reports are moved to the distribution area.

*Microfiche procedures.* Microfiche (COM) are processed as follows:

1. The operator checks to see if there is more than one copy of each microfiche document. If so, all copies (up to 20) are placed in one microfiche envelope.
2. When there is more than one microfiche document to each report output, or multiple copies of each, the microfiche are sorted and then placed in their respective envelopes.
3. The report name is posted on the outside of the microfiche envelopes.
4. The envelopes are taken to the distribution area.

### [C]  Report Distribution Procedure

The IT computer operations department produces a variety of reports. Some require extensive attention from the time they are printed until they are delivered.

The preparation, processing, and distribution information required for each report is posted to the Distribution Control Form (see Exhibit 6-1) which is completed by the systems analyst or programmer responsible. Procedures for processing these reports are as follows:

*Report log maintenance.* At the start of each day, a report-generation listing is provided by the console or computer operator and forwarded to the report distribution area.

1. The operator crosses off the report on the Distribution Control Form with a yellow marker.
2. The operator posts the time the report was received after the name of the report on the Distribution Control Form.
3. At the end of each shift, the operator going off duty notifies the arriving operator of reports that have not been produced, and if the business unit expecting this report has been notified.

*Distribution procedure.* The person processing the reports checks the Distribution Control Form to be aware of their disposition. If there is any variation from what is expected, that person notifies the computer operator.

Changes to the Distribution Control Form are made only when a memo is received with instructions from the responsible systems analyst or programmer. The memo is held in a file as long as the report is produced.

When the reports are complete, the operator sets them aside for proper distribution. Those requiring maximum security are kept locked until such time as the documents leave the area.

*Distribution methods.* The distribution method for reports depends on the report's security status and the distance between the user and the data processing center. The following options are available:

1. **User pickup.** Report users come to the computer center, or a satellite pickup area, to obtain their reports. Bins similar to the boxes used by post offices, but larger, are used for this purpose. Areas that require some degree of security will have locked doors on the bins.
2. **IT computer operations delivery.** Computer operations center personnel deliver reports to recipients located near the computer operations or who require special equipment for large-volume delivery.
3. **Mail delivery.** The reports are picked up or delivered to the mailroom. Mailing methods are:
   a. **Interoffice mail.** Interoffice mailing envelopes are used for interoffice delivery.
   b. **Outside delivery.** Some computer-printed reports must be mailed through the U.S. Postal Service. These are items such as purchase orders, bills, and government reports. Packing or envelope inserting is done in the mailroom. Large shipments may be sent by UPS or some other agent.

**EXHIBIT 6-1.** Distribution Control Form

---

Report Title:

Report No:                                          Security:

Effective Date:                                     Supersedes:

Description:


Form No:          Copies:          Burst:          Decollated:

Copy              Department       Title           Method

1

2

3

4

5

6

Special Instructions:

### [D]   Managing Your Output Volumes

Monitor the volume and use of paper generated by your print room. Look for opportunities to reduce it. Eliminating unwanted reports will save in the cost of paper, the cost of printing it, the cost of disposing of it, and all of the handling in between.

1.  Look in your reports distribution bins. What reports are not picked up? This could be due to someone being absent so don't jump too quickly. Often this is a sign of a report no one wants.
2.  Put a "recycling bin" next to where people pick up their reports. Look to see what reports go straight into the trash. These are likely candidates to eliminate.
3.  Reports of 30 pages or less are candidates for routing directly to a network-connected printer in the business users' department.
4.  Reports larger than 150 pages are candidates for distribution on CDs. At around this point, the blank CD is cheaper than the paper and ink.
5.  Large reports are also candidates for distribution online where they are easy to search and the business user can print just the portions they need.
6.  Institute a "sunset" check on all reports. At least once per year attach a note to every report asking the recipient if the report is still needed. You must write the report identifier on the slip and they must sign it. If they do not, then call the recipients to see if the reports can be cancelled.

# § 6.05   DATA SECURITY

### [A]   Purpose

This section covers procedures to ensure data security throughout the computer center operation. These procedures are designed to ensure that management and systems operations' audit policies will be satisfied and support their enforcement.

### [B]   Data Security Responsibility

One person is selected to be responsible for data security reports to the head of information systems and to a security committee of three to five members that authorizes the implementation of its policies. This committee will have a majority representation from the firm's audit area enabling the controller to influence policy and verify that the security responsibility is fulfilled in line with the audit and control policies of the firm. This data security responsibility may or may not be a full-time effort. The person may have a title reflecting the status of the position if it is full-time. Otherwise, the task will be undertaken in conjunction with other duties. If the latter is the case, the security position should not be subservient to the other responsibility. Suggested titles for the position are: security officer, security coordinator, supervisor or manager of security, chief of security, data security officer or coordinator, or data administrator.

## [C]  Span of Data Security

1. Data security begins at the point data is captured for the information systems operation. The actual process of receiving and capturing raw data is under the domain of data security.
2. The vehicle used to hold captured data will be returned to sender if required. The return will require a confirmation of time, date, title, and data contents. A record log will be maintained of the returns by item, date, and time, with the signature of the receiver. If the return vehicle or raw data documents are to be transported by a third party (UPS, U.S. Postal Service, or some other agent), a signed and dated receipt will be required to confirm the transaction. Receipts will be held for one year.
3. Retained hardcopy raw data will be held under the jurisdiction of the data security person or delegated authority in a secure area until there is a disposition of the material. The length of time the material is kept will be predicated on policies for the various items.

    Retained instruments used to convey data other than on hardcopy, such as tapes, disk, etc., will be kept in a secure place as other such records are kept. The length of time the material is kept will be predicated on policies for the various items.

    The internal disposition of retained data instruments depends on their source. Tapes or disks that can be erased will be erased and returned to service. A log will be maintained of the erased items by day, title, and control identification. Each batch listing of erased items will contain the signature of the operator doing the erasing. The log will be kept for no less than one year. Raw data documents will be shredded. The level of shredding will depend on the level of security required:
    a. Confidential data will be finely shredded.
    b. Classified data will be cross-shredded.
    c. Unclassified data will need only simple, one-way shredding.

    A "destroy log" will be maintained of the shredding operation. The log will contain the name and identification of each batch of raw data. Each batch destroyed will list the level of security and the name of the person performing this duty. The log will be kept for no less than one year.
4. Released data and information hardcopy will be duly recorded. ("466-1324" is data; "telephone number: 466-1324" is information.) If the report distribution procedure is not employed, a release log will be maintained for the local release of data and information hardcopy. Confidential hardcopy will be contained in a sealed envelope. The release log will record the signature of the person receiving the envelope,

date, time, and item description. The log will be kept for no less than one year. Documents or other storage devices released to outside the organization require second-party verification of the release entered into a log that will contain the item name and identification, date, time, method of shipment, the person releasing the material, and the person receiving the material. Otherwise, follow the distributions methods procedure.

5. Internal data (data on the system) and secondary storage also will be under data security care. If information systems employs a person as database administrator, that person will be responsible for the physical security of data and/or information. Required procedures for the safety of captured data and information and the policy enforcement will be the responsibility of the designated data security head.

## [D] Online Processing Data Security

Telecommunication (LAN and WAN) and online IT computer access standards and protocol are the responsibility of the person delegated to data security. This subsection defines how the online data security system operates.

Security procedures have three major elements. The first is to establish barriers so that only the people who need to do so can touch the data. The second is to establish a tracking mechanism such as journal or transaction files so you can trace who may be doing something they should not be. The third is to periodically check who has access to what and ensure this need is still valid. People move around a company and you may not always be aware of it.

1. **Access authorization for database data.** The data security person in concert with the database administrator will categorize the security access levels. The database administrator will group the records within a given database so that the record elements, as much as possible, have the same level of security. This is to prevent elements of a higher level from being accessed by a person with a lower-level access to the same record.

   The database administrator will use the data dictionary to provide the access level of each listed element. A valid security method is to group only like-level security elements into the same record. However, an element of a lesser level may be included to avoid developing other records only for the sake of common security-level confirmation.

   To enhance security, the data dictionary will list the programs authorized to access the data elements. This is to limit authorized program access to specific users, identified by the user's password. If the data dictionary does not provide for a given level of access for the user wanting the higher-level data elements, access will be denied. Assigning security access to a specific workstation (such as in the payroll department) will further enhance control by limiting which devices can access a specific program.

   Gaining access to data is one thing, but unauthorized altering of the data is something else. The data dictionary should allow access to individual data elements based on password level, as follows:

a.   Read a data element only.

# COMMENT

This system is to prevent someone from getting into highly confidential data that should only be available to the controller. There have been cases of some very interesting data turning up on workstations that should not have had access to the data.

b.   Change the data element.
c.   Remove the data element.

In cases of vulnerable data, a procedure can be instituted to off-load the old data element and to record the time, occurrence, and password performing the alteration.

2.   **Access authorization for files data.** Files must only be accessed by approved user passwords, which should be grouped by access levels. This grouping should be a joint effort of the database administrator and the data security person. If there is no database administrator, the security person alone will classify which files are to be accessed by which password level. The level of the user's password controls his/her level of access to files as:

• Read only
• Change
• Remove

A file access log should be maintained by the computer system to record the time, file identification, and user ID accessing the files. As an audit trail, if files are altered, off-load the changes. This file should be under the control of the data security person and kept for no less than one year.

3.   **Control of password file.** The vendor-supplied passwords and account numbers should be removed before a system is placed into operation. The password control file is the responsibility of the data security official with access through an encrypted authorized password program. To access a listed code, the password will first need to be decrypted. This list will be under lock and key. The encryption instrument will be in a different locked location. A log will be maintained for each access of the password file, listing the reason, code, time, and date.

4.   **Granting of data set access.** The data dictionary will list the restrictions level for each data set. Access will be granted only to those authorized for access at the given level or higher. The list of who is authorized to access what data should be reviewed quarterly to en-

sure it is accurate. If someone changes departments, they might not tell you. Business unit managers should reapprove who should have access to what information.

5. **Granting of access levels.** The security officer and database administrator authorize the granting of access levels, either for a given time period or an indefinite period. The security officer and database administrator will review the approved access levels no less than once each year. A random review will also be performed at a time known only to the security officer. The results of the review will be documented and filed.

   The access level will be commensurate with the person's need, that is, the level determined by the job description, and changeable if a job requires higher access.

6. **Termination of employees with restricted access.** An employee should not be terminated until he/she is denied all access to the system, if possible. The employee's password must be removed from that part of the system that accesses any data or program files.

7. **Restricted access after voluntary employee termination.** When an employee gives notice, a review of whether to terminate or restrict access to privileged data should take place, and a decision be made within 24 hours of receiving notice.

## COMMENT

Run a routine criminal background and credit check on anyone receiving a highly vulnerable access level before granting the access code. Research indicates that desperate people tend to be much more susceptible to taking advantage of an ill-gotten opportunity than not. Also, a person's credit rating can change for the worse at any time, and it would be wise to be aware of this before it is too late. Given access levels may require a great deal of protection because of the monetary vulnerability of the data elements. New and transferred personnel will require the appropriate screening for granting of and for determining respective levels of access.

There was a story some time ago of a U.S. government data processing clerk who spent money like a member of Congress on his yearly salary of $23,000. By the time management started wondering just how he could support his new lifestyle, he had cashed millions of dollars in checks made out to his dummy company.

8. **Data entry processing.** Data entry processing must be separate from file maintenance processing to protect the integrity of the system. File maintenance procedure is discussed in § 6.05[E], "File Maintenance Data Security."

9. **Security bypass.** Bypassing the security restrictions for online processing is not permitted, except by following the file maintenance procedure noted in § 6.05[E], "File Maintenance Data Security."

10. **Unauthorized access times.** Workstation access at other than authorized times (usually normal office hours) or on unauthorized workstations will require supervisory approval. The supervisor authorizing the access will forward a memo requesting permission to the data administrator/data security person. That person will notify computer operations when granting the request, and this unit will initiate the procedure to allow the access after the following information is provided:

    a. Person to be authorized access
    b. Information/data to be accessed
    c. Date and start/end times of access
    d. Reason for access, other than normal conditions

    Network messaging, when available, should be employed both to send the requesting memo and to notify computer operations, with the messages or memos saved for no less than 30 calendar days.

11. **Online programmer file access.** No access will be permitted whatsoever for online programming or accessing and testing of database or files. This means all live database or files access, including even live archival data. Programmers may access only files copied for their use. Using copied files will require the approval of the database administrator, with the files provided by computer operations. Any such unauthorized access of live data or files will be grounds for dismissal. Strict operations control procedures should exist to prevent such accessing.

12. **Data dictionary data protection definition.** The data dictionary will contain information about all the data elements and their respective applications. The level of protection granted or not granted will be noted in the data dictionary by element or data sets. Any corrections or changes to this information should be published and disseminated on or before the correction or procedure is performed.

13. **Maintain a log of failed data access attempts.** If possible, capture the user ID, the workstation ID (or IP address), the date, and time. Review this log at least daily. This may identify someone trying to hack into an area.

## [E]  File Maintenance Data Security

The file maintenance operation is under the jurisdiction of the database administrator. This includes the loading and maintenance of files and/or databases. The data administrator/data security person has the responsibility to establish policy for file maintenance data security, along with its privacy and integrity. File maintenance will be a separate procedure from that of data entry operations and will cover the updating of all files and databases.

- File maintenance
- Database maintenance
- File uploading
- Generating a work access file or database for a given programmer for access and the testing of programs

Confidential, classified, and unclassified file maintenance will be performed and documented under supervisory review which will ascertain:

- When the maintenance was done (date and time)
- Who performed the maintenance
- What files were processed
- What data elements were affected
- What transpired in the maintenance process
- What files were reproduced, if any, and the disposition of files
- What audit trails there are to confirm the process, such as transaction files and/or premaintenance files or databases

Very confidential file maintenance procedures require the review of the data administrator/data security person to identify what, if any, maintenance requirements were performed at the supervisory level. This file maintenance also will record the same documentation as in confidential or unclassified file maintenance.

## [F]   Password Controls

The data security person defines the password policy. The database administrator stipulates the procedure. If the data administrator challenges this, the problem is presented to the data security committee whose decision is final.

*Types of passwords.* There may be two kinds of passwords: one assigned by the database administrator or an agent, and one that is self-assigned. A person given a self-assigned password receives a temporary assigned password until it is changed after he/she first signs on. The authorization of user-assigned passwords is limited to only those persons approved by the data security person.

*Changing of passwords.* All passwords will be changed from 1 to 12 times per year by the authority of the data administrator who may call for a password change any time there is a need.

*Password display.* Computer systems will suppress passwords and IDs on the monitor screen and all printed output. Passwords are not to be displayed on or near the monitor. A second notice of a violation of this procedure requires a reprimand by the database administrator/data security person. Any serious problem will be referred to the security committee.

## COMMENT

How many times have you seen a password posted to the monitor? 3M's Post-It notes were not invented for this purpose!

*Password coding.* The systems software will validate passwords to ensure they conform to data security policies. All passwords will be limited to no less than 6 and no more than 10 alphanumeric characters. At no time will a person or department/unit name be part of the password. No whole word found in a dictionary will be used. Every password must contain at least one capital letter, one lowercase character, and one number. The remaining characters can be any combination.

*Password files.* Password files will be encrypted. The database administrator and the data security person will keep the encryption code keys. This information is placed in a fireproof and locked container. A backup copy is enclosed in a sealed envelope and placed in an off-site location. When a new encryption code key is required, the database administrator or the data security person inspects the sealed envelope ensuring the envelope has not been tampered with before the contents are destroyed.

### [G] Workstation Controls

Access to the system by workstations requires both physical and procedural operation controls for direct access to the main system or a network system. Workstations employing both WAN and LAN systems should require stricter controls than those used by workstations employed in the computer operations areas. Required controls are:

1. **Physical location.** The actual physical location of a workstation is a major consideration. Remote or secluded areas invite unauthorized access attempts and are more vulnerable to vandalism and theft. When such a location is unavoidable, the workstation should be in a room that is locked after normal business hours. If not possible, enclosing the unit or using a cable lock should be considered.

2. **Workstation locks.** Workstations that can access any databases or that are in remote or secluded areas must have locks. Personnel assigned such a workstation will be responsible for locking the unit when not in the general area for an extended period, such as more than an hour. When more than one person is assigned the use of the machine, the last to leave the area is responsible for locking the workstation and will be reprimanded by his/her supervisor of any infraction. A supervisor not enforcing this procedure will be reprimanded in writing by the data administrator, with copies of the notice sent to

the person's immediate superior and all members of the data security committee. All personnel using workstations should be made aware of this policy both in their training and in the written workstation procedures.

## COMMENT

Include in your employee orientation that a password is tied to a user ID. If someone knows your user ID and password, and uses it to a bad purpose, the company security will come looking for you! Therefore, you are responsible for safeguarding this information.

Each lock will be different from the rest. In the event a workgroup is to share a group of workstations, a common key may be used. The person responsible for issuing keys holds duplicate keys under locked conditions. The data administrator, members of the data security committee, and computer center workstation maintenance employees will each be issued a master key. The master workstation keys will never be removed from the firm's premises.

3. **Workstation operating system controls.** The computer operating system maintains a log record of each workstation sign-in, consisting of date, timeframe, and password for each access. The same software controls the access using the time-of-day frame and automatic timeouts. Any violations are logged by workstation, password, time, and date. A listing of the violation log, by date, is forwarded to the data security person and the computer operations manager daily. The database administration software ascertains which workstation, along with the allowable password, can access which file. The data dictionary identifies which users are allowed to initiate transactions. The final control will be exercised by operations program.

The database administrator confirms these controls before they are placed in service. A reconfirmation is required in the event of any program maintenance, before the program is placed back into operation, regardless of what the maintenance effort entails.

4. **User ID/password identification.** The computer operating system allows three attempts at entering a user's ID and password identification. If all three attempts are incorrect, it will allow no further access for a given time period which is determined by the data administrator/security officer.

5. **Modem access controls.** The same workstation and user ID/password controls apply to modem access. The computer dial-up telephone number(s) are changed periodically, at the discrimination of the data administrator/security officer.

The level of control for the dial-up access is determined by the data administrator, with level 1 being the lowest and level 3 the highest:

a.  Standard user ID/password and workstation control.
b.  Access confirmed by automatic callback system or caller ID hardware.
c.  Access confirmed by data center personnel by physically calling back the listed authorized number.

A computer record of all unsuccessful attempts to gain automatic access to the system is maintained. The physical callback procedure has a manually maintained log containing the same information. Computer operators assigned the task send a daily notice of the unsuccessful access attempts to the data administrator and the computer operations manager.

## [H]  Audit Trail Monitoring

A continuous audit trail monitoring program should be in place to police the access and flow of data and information to and from the central computer system. To accomplish this, the program uses the data dictionary, the database administration system, and the operating control systems. It provides for the report listings noted in § 6.05[G], "Workstation Controls" as well as other information:

1.  **A transaction detail file.** This contains the transaction detail by workstation and user (ID/password), with the date and time of each access. It can be kept on tape or disk and used to reconstruct the most recent backup file necessary to return the database/file to the point of the last transaction. A computer program is available to produce a listing of this file that can be reviewed manually by either the database administrator or the data administrator on demand.
2.  **Exception reports.** A file is maintained of daily exception reports called for by any source. A weekly report lists each exception report requested, grouped by requesting party, as well as the data accessed, the date, and time. If the computer system time is charged back to the user, the time and/or dollars also are posted.
3.  **Telecommunication report.** The computer operations manager will generate a telecommunication network report weekly. It outlines all access to the system and identifies any abnormal occurrences. If needed, an attempt will be made to explain the reported activity. The report is distributed to the data administrator, database administrator, security officer, and IT head.

    The data administrator evaluates it and compiles a monthly statistical analysis report from the weekly reports, and from any other sources deemed necessary. This Monthly Statistical Analysis Network Report is sent to the IT manager, the database administrator, the computer center operations manager, and all members of the data security committee. Each monthly report is discussed at the data security committee meeting and the discussion is recorded in the minutes.

## [I]   Data Entry Controls

User manuals that users understand will be available at each workstation. The user's name, ID, or password will not be written on the manual, which is put into a locked drawer at the end of each workday.

Training material, such as instruction manuals and tutorials, are available for any workstation operator in the language understandable to that person.

An immediate supervisor is responsible for the operator's proficiency and the data administrator/data security officer for enforcing this procedure. Any supervisor refusing to comply is reported in writing to his/her superior and the data security committee. Data entry procedures are followed to minimize the loading of incorrect data into the database/files.

---

### THE IT AUDIT MANAGER'S
### TEN REQUIREMENTS OF A SECURITY PROGRAM
### (FROM A FORTUNE 500 OIL COMPANY)

1. Establish and enforce policies on acquiring PCs. Establish network guidelines and enforce them, and enforce disciplinary actions for violators.
2. Perform preemployment checks.
3. Secure physical access to computer center.
4. Back up all data and programs, and store at an off-site storage facility.
5. Ensure adequate power, air conditioning, and fire protection.
6. Develop and enforce documentation and approval standards.
7. Establish program change controls.
8. Monitor use of computer resources.
9. Control the telecommunication network.
10. Evaluate security and control systems.

---

- Computer program instructions edit incoming data for errors before the data is uploaded to files or the database. The data may be contained in a buffer file before it is edited. The editing parameters are listed in the data description tables or the data dictionary. Also, they may be developed using data decision tables.
- Any overrides to this procedure require both the operator's supervisor and the computer operations shift supervisor's approval. The shift supervisor notes the time of the override in the shift log. Any temporary computer program patching for an override requires the normal procedure for program maintenance to be followed. In the event of an emergency, the computer manager may be contacted to expedite the maintenance programming required.

## [J]   Data Communications Backup

The person or group sending data is responsible for maintaining the data backup until notification that the original data is no longer required. This backup may be in the form of:

- Source document retention
- Captured digital data in the form of batch tape backup or secondary storage random accessed files

Data communications hardware backup provisions also should be considered, depending on the size of the operation and/or security dependency, in the form of:

- Backup modems at critical sites
- Alternate data lines available for dial-up backup
- Alternate dedicated lines available

## COMMENT

A Fortune 500 company had its alternate dedicated backup line buried in parallel when a backhoe cut them both by accident. This is some sort of message! The data administrator or his/her agent should test the backup provisions, unannounced. Perform the tests periodically no less than once per year. The test results should be documented in a memo and copies sent to the database administrator, IT manager, and all members of the data security committee.

# 7

# IT SUPPORT: HANDLING DAY-TO-DAY HASSLES

# § 7.01   IT SUPPORT POLICIES

### [A]   Overview

The IT computer center area consists of an IT computer operation and support areas. Support areas are restricted; only authorized personnel may enter. The computer room itself requires a higher level of authorization to gain entry. The main purpose in keeping the support areas apart from the computer operation room itself is to ensure security.

For better security and to prevent conflict of interest, personnel responsible for the support areas report to the IT corporate computer center manager.

### [B]   Support Area Environment

The support area must be a clean, air conditioned environment. On a daily basis, housekeeping personnel may enter all areas except the data library area and the computer room itself. A fireproof, walk-in vault should house the data library or, if the volume of data does not justify this, a fireproof safe in the data library area. An off-site fireproof vault also is required for backup programs and data.

No smoking, food, or beverages are permitted in the support areas. A separate room will be provided for the storage of personal effects, food and beverage consumption, and smoking.

## COMMENT

Fireproof safes must meet the rating requirements for IT off-line storage. Safes that normally house paper documents are rated at a higher temperature than for IT off-line storage, so they are not suitable for computer storage media. These safes tend to be larger and much heavier than standard safes. Therefore, the support flooring may be a limiting consideration, along with access needed to get the safe(s) in place, when assigning their location. This will be a determining factor for the size(s) and weight(s) of the safes that will be used.

### [C]   Systems Software Support Policies

Operations personnel, systems software support personnel, and help-desk personnel report to the technical support manager who reports to the IT corporate computer center manager. Software support responsibilities include the operating system, plus utility and compiler software, but not maintenance of any programs written by the systems or programming units. Service of both sides of a client/server system is also the IT computer center's responsibility. No one other than operations programmers or maintenance programmers may perform any maintenance on the operating software unless given special permission by the manager of the IT computer center.

## [D]   Tape Storage Policies

The limited life span of magnetic tapes mandates the close monitoring of their age and condition. It will be policy to copy all tapes to a replacement media, and have them confirmed as operational before the old tape drives are removed from service.

# § 7.02   DATA LIBRARY

## [A]   Overview

The data library is perhaps one of the most critical areas of the IT computer center. It contains magnetic tapes and/or disks and is off-line storage for both data and software. It contains data files that will be critical to a rapid disaster recovery. The data also may have legal retention, privacy, and tax data retention requirements.

Data libraries are usually enclosed within a fireproof room or large vault. In smaller operations, a properly rated fireproof safe may be all that is required. A duplicate off-site data and software library needs to be located a safe distance from the main site. The storage of the tapes, disks, and microfilm must meet the proper fire-retardant rating for such media.

A data library is responsible for several services, including:

1. **Database and file security.** All the activities associated with the protection of data from fire, nature, misuse, and unauthorized access
2. **Data control.** The activities and procedures for backing up, storing, retrieving, and retaining data
3. **Software backup.** Maintaining backup copies of all current operating software
4. **Data file maintenance.** Activities associated with keeping track of the data and software in storage (If tapes are stored, they should be monitored for condition and reproduced as needed.)
5. **Other storage media.** In some cases, the data library houses other items such as:
   - Computer-generated reports
   - Policy and procedures manuals
   - Cancelled checks or other vital documents

## [B]   Data Library Operations

The data librarian performs the data library operating procedures, but in smaller shops also may have other duties. The primary responsibility is to support the computer center operation. The storage area also may be provided for other company vital records such as deeds, titles, and other valuable documents. Following are the librarian's duties and responsibilities:

1. **Receives new storage media.** Upon receiving new off-line storage media, the data librarian:
   a. Compares quantity received with original order and billing information. If the quantity is incorrect, he/she notifies the IT computer operation's manager/supervisor.
   b. Inspects the storage media for signs of damage. If any are damaged, the IT computer operation's manager is notified.
   c. Logs in new storage media and assigns each a consecutive number. The date received and vendor are also posted to the consecutive number log.
   d. Notifies the computer operator that the storage media have been received if a storage media inventory is maintained for the computer system. If there is no such inventory, the data librarian will maintain a card or PC file for storage media issued to the IT computer center.
2. **Maintains an inventory file.** The librarian monitors the storage media inventory. Computer storage media inventory programs are available or, for smaller operations, a manual card inventory is kept.
   a. **Manual card inventory file.** A 3- by 5-inch file card is used for each storage media item, with the storage media number, file label, date, and time created, and current file name posted to it.
   b. **Computer storage media inventory program.** A computer program maintains the status of the storage media inventory. A report is available from an online file. (See Exhibit 7-1.) The data librarian:
      • Checks the status of all storage media daily.
      • Updates the storage media inventory file.
      • Maintains a sign-in/sign-out log for daily movement of storage media to and from the data library and the off-site storage area. (This log acts as an audit trail and is for updating the storage media inventory file.)
      • Updates and checks the status of the off-site data library inventory daily.
      • Randomly spot-checks off-site storage inventory status.
3. **Maintains software backup files.** The data librarian maintains backup copies of operating software at both on-site and off-site storage locations. The duties performed are:
   a. Maintains a record of all stored software. (A sample form is shown in Exhibit 7-2.)
   b. Replaces old versions of programs (both source code and an executable copy) with new versions. Authorization to replace programs comes in the form of a memo from the IT computer center operation's manager. Unless otherwise informed, the old programs will be sent to the off-site storage.

**EXHIBIT 7-1.**   Storage Media Inventory Status

**Date:**                                          **Report No:**

| Disk No. | File Label | Date | Time | File Name |
|---|---|---|---|---|
| 1 | PAYROLL | 09/01/02 | 13:40 | Payroll Master |
| 2 | ACCT PAY | 09/02/02 | 09:30 | Accounts Payable |
| 3 | INV | 10/30/02 | 10:15 | Plant Inventory |
| 4 | A/R | 10/01/02 | 12:45 | Accounts Receivable |

| Tape No. | File Label | Date | Time | File Name |
|---|---|---|---|---|
| 1 | MPT | 09/01/02 | 09:40 | Master Programs |
| 2 | XXX | 10/31/02 | 08:30 | Scratch Tape |
| 3 | XXX | 12/21/01 | 11:40 | Scratch Tape |
| 4 | PR-TRAN | 10/01/02 | 14:45 | YTD Payroll Transactions |

| CD No. | File Label | Date | Time | File Name |
|---|---|---|---|---|
| 1 | HR Files | 09/02/02 | 09:45 | Resumes |
| 2 | 2001 Payroll | 01/31/02 | 08:30 | Payroll |

**EXHIBIT 7-2.**   Program Inventory

| Program # | Name | Language | Source | Date |
|-----------|------|----------|--------|------|
| PR3 | Payroll | COBOL | Smith | 01/15/98 |
| INV-6 | Finished Goods | COBOL | Jones | 07/04/95 |
| STA | Stress Analysis | Visual Basic | Smith | 11/14/00 |

4. **Other duties**
   a. Maintains and controls the policies and procedures manual inventory
   b. Maintains and controls the "controlled forms" inventory
   c. Maintains and controls any vital records
   d. Keeps data library area clean and neat
   e. Cleans media periodically as needed

# § 7.03  DATA ENTRY PROCEDURES

## [A]  Overview

Operating procedures are a combination of vendor-provided instruction manuals and data entry instructions specific to each application. If the procedure appears to be incorrect, confusing, or contradictory, the problem is brought to the attention of the IT computer center operation's manager.

## [B]  Data Entry

Data entry procedures can cover various input methods. Processing can be done in "batches" or "online." When raw data is to be converted to "captured" data in machine-readable format, the systems analyst or programmer will provide data entry instructions. The instructions should include an example of the raw data source documents from which input information comes. Data entry procedures, with example source documents containing identified data elements for input, are placed in a folder for each job that can be performed in a centralized or decentralized data entry operation.

Both types of operation have advantages and disadvantages. The way an IT computer center handles data entry is somewhat different from a decentralized system. Decentralized data collection can then forward its information to the IT computer center. This data can be used as received or altered.

## [C]  Centralized Data Entry

A centralized data entry organization requires a unit adjacent to the computer center staffed by employees of the IT computer center processing operations. Source documents from any place in the organization (including the mailroom) are forwarded to the data entry section for processing. The advantages of centralized data entry over a decentralized system include:

1. Good use of machine resources since all data entry equipment is located in one place
2. Skilled data entry operators providing efficient use of equipment
3. Procedure for verifying input data since there should be more than one data entry operator
4. Better controls over the data entry activities (This is an important con-

sideration since data entry provides an opportunity for dishonest operators to key in unauthorized orders for goods or monies.)

The procedures for data entry processing are:

1. Each batch of source data is date- and time-stamped upon arrival in the unit. Batch numbers are sequential.
2. Each batch is logged in on the Data Entry Log (see Exhibit 7-3).
3. Each batch is identified for verification (if required) and placed with other batches of the same type for data entry by priority.
4. When a batch is entered, the operator initials and posts the time and date of completion. Source documents are forwarded to one of the following:
   - A verification holding area (if required)
   - A work-completed area
5. Documents requiring verification are assigned a priority and made available to a different operator from the one who entered the data.
6. The verification operator rekeys the data to ensure it is correct. Corrections are made, if necessary. The verification operator initials and posts the date and time on the source document with a blue marker after completing the batch. The batch of source documents is forwarded to the work-completed area.
7. The batch number, time, and date are posted to the Completed Batch Log after the documents arrive at the work-completed area (see Exhibit 7-4). The batch is then filed or returned to the originating department.
8. Filing is by source document and disposition date. When source documents are to be disposed of, the standard disposition procedure is followed.
9. By the end of each day, the numbers of all entered batches posted to the Data Entry Log will have been crossed off with a yellow marker.
10. After the Data Entry Log is posted to the Completed Batch Log, the Completed Batch Log is filed. Each sheet is held for 6 months, then discarded. The Data Entry Log is filed after all batch numbers have been crossed off. This sheet is also held for 6 months, and then discarded.

## [D]   Decentralized Data Entry

*Decentralization* means the data entry is not limited to one location. Most often, decentralized data entry activities are located where the data originates. In this situation, responsibility for them is placed on personnel other than computer operations personnel.

Those operating decentralized input devices are usually familiar with the source documents, data, or information associated with the input. There is less need to convert raw data from a familiar format to a different format for use by a centralized data entry operator because the individual entering the data is accustomed to the information.

**EXHIBIT 7-3.**    Data Entry Log

Date_____

| Source Document | Batch Number | Time Received | Initial |
|---|---|---|---|

**EXHIBIT 7-4.** Completed Batch Log

Date_____

*Batch Number*                    *Time Received*                    *Initial*

The advantages of decentralized over centralized input are:

1. Fewer content errors occur because of user familiarity with input data.
2. Data preparation is the only step in the data entry process because decentralized data entry is usually online.
3. Time is frequently saved in the preparation of data for the computer system because it is usually converted to captured data as it is originated.

Many firms employ both centralized and decentralized systems for optimal efficiency. The decentralized data entry procedures for batch processing are the same as defined under centralized data entry procedures.

The instruments providing online data to the computer system exist in many different forms; most common is the online workstation. Others are barcode readers, optical or magnetic character readers, and voice input. In addition to online procedures, keyboard input needs to have special computer operating control procedures provided for the system when in use.

The procedures for online monitor/keyboard data entry processing are as follows:

1. All personnel and terminals are identified with the proper codes ensuring that only authorized terminals and personnel enter data. This includes mobile units, too.
2. When the data is displayed on the screen correctly, the operator keys in the proper code to send the data to the computer.
3. All data is edited by the computer system to ensure that correct data is being received. If the computer discovers an error in its input editing routine, the computer will not place the information into its database but will hold the data in temporary storage and notify the workstation of the possible error. The operator can then correct or abort the input.
4. The computer system maintains a log by workstation to identify, by user ID, when each user logs on and the type of data entered.
5. At each workstation there should be a binder with general operating instructions, along with procedures for each kind of data to be entered. There will be a name and telephone number of the help desk if there is a problem.

## [E] External File Downloading

Files can be downloaded from the firm's distributed systems input, commercial databases, commercial online services, or even the Internet. Each of these downloading procedures requires a computer operations procedure, provided by the programming staff. Except for a firm's distributed system, all downloading will be under operator control.

Except for a firm's distributed system, all downloading will be to an off-loadable secondary storage device. Before this information can be placed into the main system, it must be confirmed as "clean"—it has no embedded virus or distorted data.

Computer operators will maintain a Downloading Log Book. It will record the date, time, operator name, source of input, amount of input, time required, ID of secondary storage device, and any problems encountered.

### [F]   Data Entry Administrative Duties

Data entry units with more than one person will have a supervisor or lead operator to keep track of batches and assign data entry jobs. The supervisor or lead operator will perform the administrative duties. These duties include:

1. Scheduling each batch that enters the unit. If there is a conflict of schedule and workloads, the IT computer center manager is to be contacted for permission to use overtime or to change schedules.
2. Maintaining up-to-date operator procedures and documentation for each job.
3. Checking the documentation of new jobs for possible discrepancies, unfinished work, errors, and/or ambiguity. Providing copies for each operator and a file copy of all data entry documentation procedures. Updating procedure modifications on all copies in the unit.
4. Maintaining ongoing communications with systems analysts, programmers, and users to assure a continued understanding of any new or pending changes. This includes source documents, input procedures, volume by day and hour, and schedules.
5. Maintaining data entry supplies.
6. Maintaining vacation schedules for operators.
7. Contacting the repair service in the event of equipment malfunction.
8. Ensuring source documents from batches already entered are properly stored.

## § 7.04   COMPUTER CENTER TECHNICAL SUPPORT

### [A]   Purpose

The primary purpose of the technical support unit is to provide technical services to the IT computer center area of operations. Its four sections are communications, database administration, systems software support, and the client/server help desk.

### [B]   Communications

The communications section or unit is responsible for the hardware, software, wiring, cabling, maintenance, and leasing of services for the operation of all corporate communications. Also included in this section are LAN and WAN systems. This unit will assist management with any vendor bidding for communication hardware or software. It will keep the IT computer center operations management and users informed of any planned status changes in communications. Users are responsible for informing communications in the event of transmission problems.

The communications section provides written instructions to the systems analysis and programming units regarding communications. Notice to users of operating procedures is done by e-mail or memo.

The unit is responsible for the system of wireless data transfer. This includes both the hardware and software systems. The standards developed by the Portable Computer and Communications Association (PCCA) should be followed whenever possible. With the proper standards, processing wireless data can be simplified by connecting existing applications to the wireless environment.

The communications section monitors the volume of data traffic over each "pipeline" to identify processes consuming excessive resources and to plan ahead for increased capacity. The section is always ready to rapidly respond to any network slowdowns at any time.

This unit also is responsible for the firm's telephone communications from the switchboard operator to the voice-mail system. The use of scrambled voice message coding is done as needed by this unit. The operation and maintenance of the telephone hardware and software is its responsibility as well. The following reports will be generated:

- Monthly telephone usage by phone number (see Exhibit 7-5)
- Monthly telephone usage by department (see Exhibit 7-6)
- Monthly telephone usage by company (see Exhibit 7-7)

The usage by phone number report will be sent to the person assigned to the telephone or, in the case of multiple users, to the unit's manager. The usage by department report will be sent to each department manager for his/her respective departments. The usage by company report will be sent to:

- IT computer center manager
- Corporate CIO
- Corporate controller

## [C] Database Administration

The database administrator is responsible for maintaining and controlling the data processing databases in the most efficient and secure manner. His/her duties are to:

1. Select and maintain the database software.
2. Identify personnel and control access to the database as to who can:
   - Read specific information
   - Change information
   - Add information
   - Delete information

   Not only will access to the database be controlled by a person's ID code, but also by which terminal the user is allowed access. Workstation access will be limited to given "windows of time." (This is to prevent the cleaning person from accessing data at 10:00 PM, a common problem nationwide.)

**EXHIBIT 7-5.**   Usage by Phone Number

## OCTOBER 2002 TELEPHONE USAGE REPORT

For: John Smith

Phone number: 456-3321                 Department: Accounts Payable #4311

| DATE | TIME MADE | MIN TIME | NUMBER CALLED | COST |
|------|-----------|----------|---------------|------|
| 10/23 | 9:21 | 23 | 800-431-7708 | 00.00 |
| 10/23 | 10:03 | 4 | 513-4141 | 00.10 |
| 10/23 | 14:19 | 27 | 422-313-7931 | 11.22 |
| 10/23 | 16:33 | 11 | 456-5362 | 00.10 |
| 10/26 | 8:46 | 2 | 481-6116 | 00.10 |

TOTAL TIME 1 Hour 7 Min          TOTAL COST $11.52

**EXHIBIT 7-6.**    Usage by Department

## OCTOBER 2002 DEPARTMENT USAGE REPORT

FOR: Accounts Payable #4311

| PHONE No. | USER'S NAME | TOTAL TIME USED | TOTAL COST |
|---|---|---|---|
| 456-3321 | John Smith | 14 Hours 22 Min | 47.63 |
| 456-3322 | Mary Brown | 11 Hours 14 Min | 48.21 |
| 456-3347 | Phil Montros | 22 Hours 4 Min | 67.83 |
| | DEPT. TOTALS | 47 Hours 40 Min | $163.67 |

**EXHIBIT 7-7.**   Usage by Company

## MONTHLY TELEPHONE USAGE REPORT

FOR: July 2002

| DEPARTMENT | ID NO. | HOURS | DEPT. COST | YTD COST | BUDGETED |
|---|---|---|---|---|---|
| Accounts Payable | 4311 | 48 | 164 | $ 1,741 | 2000 |
| Payroll | 4321 | 27 | 43 | $ 421 | 600 |
| Shipping | 3741 | 63 | 221 | $ 2,643 | 2500 |
| COMPANYWIDE TOTAL | | 138 | 428 | $ 4,805 | 5100 |

3. Control and maintain the database data dictionary, assisting developers in using existing data instead of creating duplicate information.
4. Maintain procedures for file and database backups.
5. Provide consulting service to data processing departments and users.
6. Provide disaster planning procedures, and test them no less than once a year unannounced.
7. Locate and set up off-site data and software backup systems.
8. Maintain directory services.
9. Promote the use of audit trails for the processed data.

Depending on the size of the database administration, this segment can be part of the database administrator's duties or delegated to a directory services manager.

A directory is a collection of information for given applications. It holds all the information relating to each application, such as user-access and user log-on IDs. Its services make it possible for all applications to share the same database of user and network information, reducing the need to replicate the same information throughout the network. Directory services can be used to find numerous objects on a given network. Developers of software systems have a need for an information tracking system for LAN-based keys.

Software to drive this system is made available by several firms, such as Novell, Microsoft, and OpenLDAP, both for network and non-network operations.

Directory services are responsible for evaluating software best suited to the firm's current needs. It will install and maintain the system, and also will provide user instruction and procedures for the software's proper usage.

## [D]  Systems Software Support

This section covers the software support of the operating system. The applications programs—in-house and purchased software—are the responsibility of the systems software support programmers. Maintenance of operating programs is the responsibility of the programming department. But the maintenance of the operating system software is the responsibility of the systems software support programmers who:

1. Make changes to operating system software when informed by memo from the manager of the systems software support section.
2. Inform by memo computer operations, programming, and affected users of any changes to the operating system software.
3. Test new operating system software before it is put into use. Also, test for changes to be made to the operating software.
4. Assist the database administrator with programming needs.
5. Write and maintain workstation procedures in the standard procedure format for operating software.
6. Review for approval the operators' instructions provided for operation programs.
7. Assist in volume program testing and auditors' studies.
8. Maintain system controls for accessing the computer system.

9.  Assist with workstation operators' training when putting new systems into operation or making changes to the current operating system.

## [E]  Client/Server Help Desk

All data systems sites have a help desk—either formal or informal. An informal help desk is where the users "know" who to call to get a problem resolved. The problem with the informal help desk is if their contact person is on vacation, or out sick, they do not know who else to call. In addition, your developers and support staff are constantly interrupted by minor problems. Since the calls go all over the department, the IT manager cannot see the sort of problems occurring with the data systems. A central help desk addresses all of these issues.

The help desk receives all incoming calls and logs them into a problem tracking database. This database allows for review by who is calling (perhaps the user needs training), the system causing the problem (the IT manager needs to speak to that programmer), and time of day the calls come in. The help desk immediately adds value by addressing the most common user questions such as resetting passwords (within the IT security policy guidelines), dispatching hardware repairpersons, and by answering data entry questions (since they have a copy of every user manual).

If the help desk cannot resolve the problem, they escalate it to the next level. The help desk maintains a list of the primary and secondary support people for each software system or hardware technology. They also are told who is absent on any given day so they can contact the next person on the support list. They also can provide early detection of a major problem as the user calls come in.

There are three basic forms of client/server help desks: a computer operator for very small operations, a full-time staffed in-house help desk, and an outsourced help desk. Which is chosen depends on the given situation. A computer operator or in-house help desk is generally for client/server systems. Other user systems tend to employ outsourced help desks. However, whatever approach is employed, one person must be responsible for a help desk's existence and maintenance. Following are basic considerations for implementing and maintaining a client/server help desk.

1.  Determine requirements for such an operation, for example:
    *   Current and future expected use of system
    *   How to evaluate user requirements
    *   How to communicate user requirements to system development or vendors
    *   Required help-desk hours of operation
2.  Seek out available vendor systems for your help-desk systems:
    *   Look at complete problem-tracking packages. Never lose track of another user's request again!
    *   Look for diagnostic and monitoring tools. Your goal is to detect major problems early and call for programmer assistance.
    *   Look at Internet services available.
    *   Look at distributive support technology available.

3.  Consider user services, such as:
    - Directory of services
    - On-site education and training programs. This will reduce your calls and increase user satisfaction.
    - Online tutorials
4.  Develop help-desk staff:
    - Develop job descriptions. This is a great entry-level job—or rotate your programmers through here so they see what their users see.
    - Determine staff requirements. Hours of operations and number of trained backup staff.
    - Prepare help-desk orientation procedure.
    - Provide a comprehensive training program.
    - Instill a proper service attitude.
    - Provide a safety net for stress and burnout. This can be a high stress job and on occasion, angry users can be rude (and swear a lot).
    - Provide for performance evaluation and feedback.
    - Monitor performance and provide feedback.
    - Introduce help-desk staff to users. Attend staff meetings in various departments to match the name to the face. The less of a stranger you are, the easier it will be to work with them when there is a problem.
5.  Management considerations for help-desk operations:
    - Develop budget requirements.
    - Use technology to enhance productivity.
    - Maintain ongoing user communication.
    - Seek out user information and training needs. These statistics can come straight out of the problem-tracking database.
    - Create and publish monthly and annual reports.
    - Create an informative monthly user newsletter. Pass along common fixes from "power users" to the less technical ones.

The day-to-day operation of a client/server help desk is routine, but unexpected events can occur. The required procedure for day-to-day operation is as follows:

1.  **Log incoming contacts on a problem-tracking database**
    a.  Ask user for user ID number and name.
    b.  Enter ID number to screen prompt.
    c.  When name of user comes up on screen, the computer begins keeping track of time user is in contact. If user's name on screen is different, ask for correct name. If this is not provided, hang up and record the event.
    d.  Provide user with help needed.
    e.  When contact with user ends, press the ENTER key on keyboard. Choose the kind of service from the appropriate menu. (Menus may vary from one company location to another.) Type short, one-sentence description, if needed, on the monitor display. Press

the designated LOG key. The help-desk operator is now ready for the next inquiry.

2. **Prevent fatigue.** Help-desk personnel should not be on the phones for more than 2 hours at a time without time off for lunch or a personal break. They should take their breaks and unwind.

3. **Compile monthly report.** The data collected for each contact will be included in a monthly report prepared by each help-desk employee. One copy will be sent to the IT computer operations manager, one copy retained by the help-desk operator, and one copy sent to user management. If there is more than one help-desk worker, a combined report will be sent to both user management and the IT computer operations manager. The report will list:

   a. The number of contacts made by each user (who needs training or is there a troublesome system that must be fixed?)
   b. Time range of all the contacts made—used to plan staffing levels
   c. The total time used by each user, sorted in descending order by amount of time spent (Big problems take a lot of time to fix. Is the help desk escalating calls properly?)
   d. Total time spent with users by each help-desk operator
   e. The count by type of service rendered

There are basic pricing options to consider. This may be reviewed when considering outsourcing the task versus keeping it in-house. When considerations are made, the following should be examined:

1. **Per-solution price.** With per-solution pricing, users pay a fixed fee for each call answered and problem solved. This fee may have to be adjusted from time to time.

2. **Per-desk price.** This is a common option that is selected. The fee is based on the number of users. The price may range from $20 to over $300 per user served.

3. **Call-block pricing.** This help-desk service comes in fixed blocks of calls (a given number) at fixed prices. This allows user management to place a usage cap on help-desk outsourced costs.

Vendor-provided help-desk service most often comes from the vendor's site. This remote service is generally less expensive than on-site service and creates fewer problems. Signing up for a vendor's price is a fixed contract cost; estimated in-house service is *just* an estimate. Like most estimates, it is likely to go up, while the service will not be as expected.

# 8

# MANAGING IT ASSETS: IDENTIFY WHAT YOU HAVE

# § 8.01  ASSET MANAGEMENT POLICIES AND OBJECTIVES

## [A]  Scope

Asset management policies address both hardware and software assets. Well-defined and maintained asset management policies and procedures will be financially rewarding, will fine-tune the companywide information systems operations, and will help avoid embarrassing litigation.

> ## COMMENT
>
> Assets are poorly managed in most IT departments. If you are looking for a way to reduce your department's cost without firing people, this is *always* the best place to start. It is the best place since most IT people take their equipment for granted and typically neglect the administrative side of their business. Often the asset manager position is assigned based on personnel availability rather than aptitude.

Top management must formally direct the asset management policies and procedures as the duty of the information systems organization. To be successful IT management should be required to:

- Inform all employees of the directives.
- Explain the need for the policies and procedures.
- Mandate that all employees should use only company-owned hardware and software. Even if their intentions are honorable, no one is to bring in their own hardware or software.
- Announce that the downloading of company-owned software is never permitted to privately owned computers or secondary storage in any form.
- Permit infractions to be noted in the employees' records.
- Emphasize that serious or repeated violations of asset management policies will be grounds for dismissal.

The policy objective of resource management, in the simplest terms, is to reduce cost while increasing overall efficiency and to avoid possible litigation. The department management cannot see the forest through the trees, and top management cannot see the trees through the forest. The asset management people should be able to see both.

A tool for controlling IT assets is the purchasing department since it controls the purchase order system. For example, use of purchase orders makes controlling the purchase of office furniture a simple process. There is seldom the problem of people making their own furniture, buying it with petty cash funds, having a "free trial," or even stealing it.

---

## COMMENT

Bygone mainframe days seldom had asset management problems. The hardware was purchased under capital expense budgets and the software was developed in-house. The hardware was unique and bulky and depreciated over time. (Today, workstations are so cheap they can be expensed.) All this activity came under the domain of the data processing department. But today, computer hardware is found throughout the company, and often there are no controls over purchase, standardization, or use. Software is even more problematic. It can originate from legitimate in-house development or purchase, or from questionable or illegal sources. This anarchy can appear insignificant because of undocumented direct expense, but the indirect repercussions can be great and the cost astronomical.

The burden of asset management for PC hardware and software assets usually falls to corporate information systems, often through default rather than proper planning. One of the authors installed an asset management program some years ago to determine what additional investment was required to "bring the resources level up to satisfy the demand." After the program was completed, it was found that there was already more invested than what was required.

---

### [B]   Policies and Objectives

Asset management is a major IT responsibility. The company depends on the IT manager to identify what is needed, to redeploy idle assets, and to save the company money. Yet when it comes to getting purchase orders signed, all the executives see is a never-ending stream of requests for expensive new equipment. If you are having problems getting your purchase requests approved, it could be because your executives do not believe you are a good steward of the company's assets. Establishing an asset management program can be a step in the right direction.

To establish an asset management program, you need to appoint someone as the asset manager for your site. As you read through this chapter you will see that this can easily be a full-time job. In some companies this function resides in the operations department since it is a part of IT's routine efforts. In smaller companies, this is an additional duty for the PC coordinator. An asset manager should be someone good at paperwork who pays attention to details. They should have a broad background so they know the difference between a terminal, a PC, and a network card.

The next step is to open a project. To begin, the asset manager should:

- Inventory assets
- Tag assets
- Establish and maintain an asset database
- Control all future purchases
- Develop a 5-year workstation planning strategy
- Reevaluate how your assets are being repaired

There are many benefits to doing this:

1. With firm numbers in hand, you can develop a long-term asset strategy to drive out variation and focus on "standard" equipment. True, you cannot standardize every item when entire technologies are replaced every 18 months, but you can drive in that direction.
2. You can evaluate your equipment repair strategy perhaps to move some categories to a "hot spare" and "service center" approach.
3. You can collect idle equipment for redeployment or disposal.

# § 8.02   STEP 1: LAY THE GROUNDWORK

## [A]   Getting Started

There are a few things to do before you stray off and start counting things. You need to figure out what to count, what data to gather on each item, how (or if) you are going to tag things, etc. Conducting an asset inventory is a very time-consuming process and you won't want to redo it anytime soon. Consider these steps before you begin. Also, run a sample inventory on several very different departments to help shake the bugs out of your process before counting equipment across your facility.

The success of your hardware inventory count will depend almost entirely on how well you are prepared before the count begins. Neglect your planning and you will find yourself making more than one inventory count per area!

## [B]   Asset Management Project Scope

The first step in asset management is to identify what you are going to manage—the scope of the project. There are many different IT assets to manage and you might want to tackle them separately. Also, be prepared for resistance, as you will be stepping into sensitive areas. The types of assets you may need to manage include:

- Workstations and peripherals
- Network devices
- Telephone instruments and add-on devices
- Servers in computer room and business departments
- Data collection devices, such as bar-code scanners
- Data output devices such as dedicated printers, CD writers, etc.
- Mainframe or server software
- PC software

This list can go on and on. The point is that there is a lot to look at. Each type of device has its own unique data elements to collect so identify these before you start. Examples of unique data elements might be the size of the monitor screen, the firmware revision level of your network devices, or the CPU speed for a workstation. For most companies, the main effort will be for workstations since there are so many of them, they cost so much, and they are very visible to executives.

Take some time to also exclude some things from your project. Keyboards and PC mice are generally disposable and not worth the expense to track. You might set a lower limit based on cost, such as nothing under $100 is worth the effort to track.

## [C]   Asset Information Database

In its simplest form, an asset inventory count could just be a count of what all you have. To move this forward into managing your assets, you need to gather descriptive information as to what you have, where it is, and how it is being used.

## COMMENT

If you have help-desk problem-tracking software, it may already have an asset management module. Help-desk software uses a key, such as the user's telephone number, to bring up a description of that person's workstation to assist in the troubleshooting process. If you have such a module already, read its manual and examine the data fields it captures to see if it is adequate. Once your asset database is populated with data, the help desk will be its biggest customer.

An asset management database can be as detailed as you want to make it. However, the more fields you have to track, the more time it will require to be kept current. Which data elements you need to track is driven by what you need to report, so the best place to start is an outline of the reports you might use. These reports might be:

- Total number of devices, subtotaled by model
- Number of workstations, subtotaled by processor speed
- Number of network devices, subtotaled by model and where they are located
- Number of devices per department
- Breakdown of processors by user type
- When each item was purchased
- Length of warranty (save in a date field of when it ends)
- Operating system
- Hardware characteristics such as CPU type, RAM, and disk space

As you can see, each of these reports brings its own data collection requirement—and each could be quite useful. The more successful your asset management efforts are, the more the accounting department will ask for data—especially data elements you did not collect during your inventory count!

Refer to Exhibit 8-1 for an example of a simple equipment-tracking spreadsheet. Below are examples of how your data tables might look for tracking assets.

**Data Table 1   User Information**

| User ID | | Dept. |
|---------|---------|---------|
| Telephone | Name | Code |
|  |  |  |
|  |  |  |
|  |  |  |
|  |  |  |
|  |  |  |

In this example, the user is identified by their telephone extension and name. The department code is used if you are looking for the amount of equipment in a given department. Other things to add might be the location by office number or column identification. You can use the telephone extension number to link to the equipment table.

**Data Table 2   Equipment Tracking**

| User Phone # | ID Tag | Device Type | Serial # | Maker | Model | Workstation Specific | | | | | | Monitor Size |
|---|---|---|---|---|---|---|---|---|---|---|---|---|
| | | | | | | CPU Speed | Hard Disk Size | RAM | CD RW | DVD | OS | |
| | | | | | | | | | | | | |
| | | | | | | | | | | | | |
| | | | | | | | | | | | | |
| | | | | | | | | | | | | |
| | | | | | | | | | | | | |
| | | | | | | | | | | | | |
| | | | | | | | | | | | | |

In this example:

| | |
|---|---|
| User phone #: | This ties to the user name table |
| ID tag: | Used if you place a company asset tag on the device |
| Device type: | PC, network hub, AS400 terminal, etc. MUST pick from a list to ensure consistency. |
| Serial #: | Essential for tracking movement and for some service contracts |
| Maker: | IBM, Compaq, Systemax, Cisco, HP |
| Model: | Gives you some idea of what is in it |
| CPU speed: | Important when estimating cost of upgrading software |
| Hard disk size: | Not so important with new 100+ GB drives |
| RAM: | Important when estimating cost of upgrading software |
| CD RW: | May or may not be important—great for making data backups |
| DVD: | May not be important |
| OS: | Type and version number are very important when planning software upgrades |
| Monitor size: | Or any other relevant fields |

To this you may add any number of other fields such as date purchased, warranty expiration date, date information was last verified, etc. Warranty is a nice way to reduce your repair costs, but you need to keep the proper records. Further complicating this—if you put a new motherboard in a PC, do you need a mechanism to track its warranty separate from the PC's?

Depending on how sophisticated you want the system to be, you also can link this record to a repair record for any updates or to a table listing every item in the machine. Although personal computers were used in the example, this is equally useful for network equipment, large printers, bar-code scanners, etc.

Consider building a table for collecting a software inventory and a table for equipment repair history at the same time.

## [D]   Asset Tagging

Many companies have a capital item asset-tagging process in place. It is supposed to deter theft, help keep track of asset location, and allocate overhead budget based on material used to support a department. Asset tagging is something that you should either do correctly or not at all. It involves a major labor investment to establish and maintain. If the resources to do this or the benefits derived are not there, then do not start it.

> ## COMMENT
>
> Asset tagging is a poor theft deterrent. One of the authors worked at a company that always stamped their name and logo on their hand tools. So many tools were stolen that it became something of a point of pride to have a complete set of tools with the company imprint on them. The removal of asset tags can mar the surface of an item that may reduce its resale value—but not by much. Stolen goods are usually sold cheaply.

Most equipment comes with a serial number from the manufacturer. However, these numbers vary widely in length, composition, and can be attached in some of the most inconvenient places. In addition, the longer the serial number, the greater the chance of incorrectly keying it into your database. Most companies attach their own asset number to expensive equipment. This makes it much easier for them to track.

The most basic asset-tracking numbering system starts at 000001 and counts up from there. Other approaches use the first two digits to identify the class of item and the remaining numbers to identify the individual item. Typical groups might be personal computers, network hubs, printers, monitors, etc. Embedding a "device group identifier" in the serial number reduces the likelihood of someone swapping asset tags on equipment. You also can get an idea of what the device is by the serial number.

The general costs for asset tagging are:

- Expense of printing or buying preprinted tags
- Expense of portable tag reader (if using RF ID or bar codes)
- Time to expand the database to accept the tag ID
- Time to gather information on each item and to attach the tag
- Time to update your asset database every time a tag moves
- Interruption of new equipment delivery to attach a tag

1.  **What to tag.** Someone must decide what you are going to track. Do not attach tags unless you are committed to tracking equipment. There is a labor cost for every device you tag and track. Base this decision on what you are going to do with the information. Are you tracking equipment to maximize your warranty coverage? Are you gathering capital item depreciation information for accounting?

    The IT department may want to manage certain classes of equipment like network cards or workstations. Anything you want to track the location of is a good candidate. Disposable items such as keyboards and computer mice are not worth the effort. Your decision of what to tag may be driven by its cost, if it leased, or under a service contract.

2.  **How to tag.** The purpose of a tag is to read it later. At the same time, the less obtrusive it is, the less likely the operator is to remove it. After determining what you want to tag, establish a procedure of where you want the tag to reside. For example, on the back of a PC makes it difficult to read since some PC system units are tucked deep under desks and held in place by too-short wires.

    A suggested place to tag PCs is near the bottom of the case on the side, such as the front lower corner of the right side of the case (as you face the unit). Network cards are usually in a rack in a locked closet and might be tagged on the front—if there is space. For items that can only be reached by technicians (usually in locked cabinets), the asset tag can be attached to a paper tag and attached to the device if there is not room for a sticker.

    However you attach the tag, take some pictures of your attachment points to standardize where to put it. Different devices may have different attachment issues but PCs should always be tagged in one space, printers in another, etc. This is a good time to write down what to put on the tag and where to stick it.

    Asset tags, by their nature, are intended to be permanent. Using an adhesive to attach them requires an idea of to what they will be stuck. The more permanent the glue, the fewer chances you have to attach the tag! All adhesives have solvents that will remove them (even if they seriously mar the surface at the same time). In some cases, you might consider physically attaching the tag with a screw, but this is a bit of overkill for electronic equipment.

3.  **What does the tag look like?** The best tags have an RF ID chip embedded in them. This way, the chip reader only needs to get close to the device and you won't need to move equipment to conduct an inventory count. A more inexpensive approach is to use bar-coded labels. Then when conducting subsequent item counts, a portable reader can quickly collect information.

    Along with the bar code, include the same number in human readable format, as you will often move equipment in a crisis without access to a bar-code reader. Also, include on the label a request to not remove it along with your company name. It may not stop everyone, but it will slow down the more honest ones.

    Bar codes and RF ID chips pay off in subsequent inventory counts. They allow you to quickly move through a department scanning bar codes instead of reexamining every device to discover who it is. You can do the same without a bar code, but you must write down every tag number and even careful people make data transcription mistakes.

4. **How to use the tag.** Before buying or attaching the tags, consider how you are going to read the bar code or RF ID chip. Since your goal is to count it without returning to your office, consider using a scanner with an RF connection to a notebook PC (this eliminates fighting a cable). When conducting a device count, the PC will be used to enter a tag's current location and then the tag number is scanned in.

## [E]   Idle Equipment Collection

1. **What is it?** During the course of your asset inventory, you will undoubtedly come across small stockpiles of equipment. Some of this equipment does not work. Some of it will be obsolete. Some is new and has never been plugged in. Now is the time to set aside an area to receive this material. Idle material is the result of a number of things. Usually, someone had a system problem and a replacement unit was brought out. No one ever came back for the old device so it was eventually shoved into a closet or under a desk in an empty office. Most companies are littered with disconnected keyboards, monitors, and computer mice. Walk around with a large cart and pick up all the obvious material. If you have a facility newsletter, encourage people to call the help desk to arrange for a pick up.

   Another type of idle equipment is the private stash of spare equipment that some people accumulate. These are computers, scanners, network cards, monitors, and a wide range of devices that are in working order but kept hidden away in case they are needed. (This is an indicator that people lack confidence in IT's ability to support them!) Expect considerable political pressure not to pick up these piles. Once they are identified, the company's accounting manager will be your biggest ally in confiscating this equipment. The problem is that all of these stashes cost money to establish. By consolidating these stashes into one place, the company saves money since fewer items are needed. These types of stashes often contain new in-the-crate equipment. The warranty clock is ticking! Over time, these new items are worth less and less as better technology becomes available.

2. **Safeguard it.** Idle equipment must be stored in a locked room. People should not be allowed to freely walk in and take whatever they want. Remember, you are now controlling the assets, not just shuffling them

around. If your asset room is viewed as a candy store, then the best equipment will quickly migrate to newly reestablished department stashes.

In this room, you'll need a large worktable, shelving for the equipment you pick up, and a cabinet for individual circuit boards. A file cabinet for keeping records will be useful as will a kit full of basic tools.

Ensure only a few people have keys to the doors. Establish a sign-out sheet for equipment taken from the room. (All equipment can enter but few can leave!) The IT manager should establish guidelines for removing equipment.

3. **Tag and test.** You will need three types of colored tags: green, red, and yellow. Stickers also can be used. You also need a stockpile of cleaning supplies. If using tags, the attachment point must be very clean. Take some rags and cleaner and begin by cleaning the dirt off the outside of each device. Attach a yellow tag. Yellow is for caution, that the device has not yet been checked. Imagine your feelings if you trucked a large monitor up 10 floors only to see that it does not work. Assume all incoming equipment is broken until proven otherwise.

Once you have collected the junk (I mean "valuable company equipment"), every item must be tested to see if it works. Sort the equipment into piles according to its value (very old workstations versus newer technology). Obviously new items can be tested quickly. It is hard to thoroughly test every item. In most cases, just turning them on and trying to use them is test enough.

## COMMENT

The best time to attach the yellow tag is when you pick it up. Write on the tag where it came from. This is most important for PCs who may have important data on the hard disks.

Every item that seems in workable order should have a green tag attached. Whoever tested the item should write their name and the date on the tag. This provides some traceability. Items that do not work go into one of two piles. One pile is the to-be-scrapped items. The other is the to-be-repaired items. Note on the red tag in which pile they belong.

Your accounting department will provide guidelines to follow for scrapping equipment. They will need to know serial numbers, make, model, etc. In most states, companies pay a "property tax" on their assets and the accounting team will want to remove these items from the books. If you have an environmental department, they can advise you on the safest way to dispose of the devices. There are other possible disposal outlets:

- Call the company you use to repair that type of device. They might buy the old equipment for use in their repair operations. This is most true with the oldest technologies where spare parts are very tough to find.

- Call a local vocational school to see if they want them for their students to repair.
- Offer them to the local computer repair shop that might be able to reuse some of the parts.

When scrapping PCs, most companies overlook recovering the software licenses. Each software company's license is different but they typically allow a company to use one copy of a program on one machine. If that PC has been scrapped, the right to use that program should be transferable within the company. You will need to show proof of your license, which is why when new software is purchased, the license notices are collected and filed.

Items to be repaired should be collected together. If the pile is high enough, the repair service may come in to work on them rather than sending them all out. Some items such as bar-code scanners are usually sent to the manufacturer and repaired for a flat rate that includes all parts and labor. The biggest problem will be the data on PC hard drives. Track down the last owner if possible or ask the manager of the department to look at the data to see what they want to keep.

When redeploying PCs, reformat the hard disk and load it with your basic software load. Most people are reluctant to delete things off their disk and this removes the accumulated program fragments and DLLs.

Try out your new inventory tag system on all the good items. This is a way to debug the tagging process without bothering anyone. This also will provide some experience in attaching the asset tags, which is never as simple as it sounds.

Working equipment should be noted on a list and provided to the IT manager. This equipment should be considered for redeployment whenever someone calls for a new purchase. Another use is to begin migrating older working equipment out of the offices by installing newer equipment from the idle equipment room. Who gets the best of the redeployable equipment is another political battle. Let the IT manager fight it!

## COMMENT

*Always* reformat a hard drive before sending a workstation out for repair or scrapping. Some companies that scrap PCs remove the hard drive and crush them since with a bit of technical know-how, the drive can still be read.

### [F]  Data Collection Forms

The last step before beginning your inventory count is to draft a data collection form to gather equipment information as you move through the facility. The form should include all of the data elements in your database table. There are also some decisions to make:

- Do you want to track PC software?
- Do you want to track circuit boards within PCs?
- What can you do with PCs that have locks or passwords that prevent you from checking them unless the normal operator is present.
- Do you want to do anything else while there, such as detect illegal copies of software?

For your machine count, you also will need a form to record idle equipment uncovered so you pick them up later. A floor plan is useful if there is a lot of area to cover. As rooms are completed, they can be colored in on the floor plan. A sheet of small colored dots can be used to mark the door of rooms that have been completed.

## § 8.03   STEP 2: CONDUCT THE INVENTORY

### [A]   Conducting the Count

***Finally!*** We are ready to begin our inventory count. Our goals here are to uncover idle assets, find hidden equipment stashes, and tag all hardware assets and to gather data on what is present in the facility.

Take some time to get (almost) everyone on your side. Meet with the facility staff and explain what you want to do and why. Issue a schedule of when you expect to visit each area. In most cases, you want to do this over a weekend so that equipment is not moving around while you are counting. Schedule times after the inventory is complete for departments to bring over their notebook PCs and PDAs for tagging.

Before the count begins, issue an announcement to the department several days in advance. The IT manager and that department's manager should sign it. It should explain what you are going to do and why. Ask people to remove any material they have placed around their equipment so you can check its serial number. Also, ask everyone to put idle assets outside their office door. Pick these up before the count to save counting them for later. The best place to test this process is in your own department.

During the count, be sure to look in every closet and large storage cabinet. If they are locked, ask security to open them. You are looking for stashes of good equipment and forgotten broken equipment. Be very thorough. Look into large boxes, drawers of empty desks, anywhere keyboards, mice, modems, scanners, etc., can be stuffed.

As the count progresses, have someone begin entering the data sheets as soon as they are turned in. A problem reading the data may require someone to revisit some areas to verify information.

Once the count and tagging is complete, run some summary reports. Provide these to the IT manager and the accounting manager. Once the data appears to be clean, provide each business manager with a recap of what you tagged in his or her department. Exhibit 8-1 is an example report that includes some accounting allocation assigned to each device. Some companies would use an asset report such as this to assign depreciation expense to their budget. The value of each unit may be a flat amount based on equipment type.

**EXHIBIT 8-1.**  Asset Report by Department

Date: 9/12/2002

Dept. Name: Tech Support

| | | | | |
|---|---|---|---|---|
| PCs | $95,950 | < 1 GHz | 1–2 GHz | 2–4 GHz |
| | | 62 | 8 | 18 |
| Notebook PCs | $6,969 | | 2 | |
| Monitors | $24,240 | 15" | 17" | 19" |
| | | 21 | 47 | 20 |
| Inkjet printers | $2,345 | HP 932c | Canon 5100 | Epson Stylus 740 |
| | | 7 | 3 | 12 |
| Laser printers | $3,214 | LJ 5000 | Lexmark 1855 | LJ 1100 |
| | | 2 | 1 | 1 |
| AS 400 printers | $2,780 | 4224 | 4230 | |
| | | 1 | 1 | |
| Telephones | $24,240 | Lucent 6224 | ATT 7406 | |
| | | 69 | 23 | |
| Fax machines | $1,295 | Intellifax 1550 | | |
| | | 1 | | |

*Total Assets*   $161,033

*Monthly Charge*   $4,473

# § 8.04   STEP 3: CRUNCH THE NUMBERS

## [A]   Set a Hardware Strategy

1.  **Identify a minimum workstation configuration.** Examine your total equipment counts by category. Clean up any data classification inconsistencies. Let's use personal computers as an example. Report them by category. What are the current operating system hardware requirements in CPU, RAM, and disk space? Does each of your workstations meet the minimum configuration? How about the recommended configuration? Some example products are:

    Windows XP Pro®, a Microsoft product, sets their hardware minimum as:
    
       CPU: minimum 233 MHz, recommended 300 MHz
       RAM: 64 MB minimum, 128 MB recommended
       Hard disk space: 1.5 GB

    Corel WordPerfect® 2002 Standard
       CPU: minimum 166 MHz
       RAM: 16 MB minimum, 32 MB recommended
       Hard disk space: 165 MB, 250 MB for a typical install

    Sun® StarOffice 6.0 Office Suite
       CPU: Pentium compatible PC
       RAM: 64 MB
       Hard disk space: 250 MB

    Using the survey together with the hardware capabilities recommended by the software that you use, a minimal standard workstation configuration can be selected. No workstations with less than this minimal configuration will be repaired. Any equipment in the idle assets room that falls below this must either be upgraded or scrapped.

    Based on your hardware survey, you can now estimate the cost to raise all of your existing workstations to the recommended hardware capability. As new software upgrades are contemplated, you now have a data-driven basis to identify workstations in the business departments that are below the minimum; these are prime candidates for replacement by any of the more capable equipment you recovered.

    Most companies have at least three desktop minimum configurations. Some workers use their equipment lightly and only need a minimal configuration. An office worker spends more time using a keyboard but their programs do not tax the equipment. The engineering team will often exercise every megahertz of their equipment with newer and more complex software. Consider establishing categories of capability for your workstations. Some examples might be:

    **Minimal User:** E-mail, Internet communications, runs basic software
       **Minimum configuration:** 1-GHz processor, 20-GB hard drive, 15″ monitor

**Office Worker:** E-mail, word processing, spreadsheet, database
  **Minimum configuration:** 1.5-GHz processor, 40-GB hard drive, 17″ monitor
**Engineer:** CAD, e-mail, word processing, spreadsheet
  **Minimum configuration:** 2.0-GHz processor, 80-GB hard drive, 21″ monitor

2. **Identify candidates to eliminate.** Are there any pockets of very old technology that should be eliminated? Electronic technologies of all types seem to reinvent themselves every 2 years. If you have clusters of very old equipment, you may not be able to get the necessary spare parts to repair them. If you wait until they break, you will be forced into making a decision in a crisis that you can make at leisure today. However, before announcing to anyone that you are scrapping his or her "old faithful" terminal, find out if there is any reason that device *must* be used. The older the technologies, the more likely it is that a specific device must be used to support a business function.

    Another type of device to eliminate is anything on a lease. Some leases allow you to return leased equipment—some are just disguised time-payment purchases. If you can return them, you will lower your monthly costs a bit (assuming you can replace them with equipment from your idle asset room). If you cannot return them early, at least now you know where they are. A procedure should be established for returned "scrap" devices that are on lease.

    Make a projection of the hardware minimums you anticipate for the next several years. Assuming your company staffing remains the same during this time, use your asset inventory count to project what you need to buy to replace equipment that will fall below the minimums for each of these years. This projection can be used in your capital budgeting process.

    The same process can be used for servers, network cards, and any other hardware device. Look at what you have, estimate what you may need next year and the year after, identify the weak, and project your capital needs.

# § 8.05   STEP 4: SET A SERVICE STRATEGY

## [A]   Developing the Strategy

Let's return for a minute to the equipment count that you made.

1. **Identify all key devices.** The first step in a service contract strategy is to identify which pieces of equipment are vital to your organization. These are machines that must be operational at all times. Where practical, you should store spare equipment for vital machines next to the machine. However, most machines can wait for an hour or so to be repaired. The operator may not think so, but it is usually true.

Ideally, critical machines have their backup device always online and in parallel with the primary unit. This allows for a quick change-over. No matter how stable the existing process is, never let the users convert the backup unit to any other purpose. If a process isn't critical enough to protect the spare machine, then it really isn't that critical at all.

2.  **Set a spare equipment stocking level**
    -   Look at your total number of machines in each class.
    -   Determine how long it would take to get one repaired. Are they sent away for repair? Does the service person come into the building to fix them? Are they common items or rare?
    -   Estimate how often this device seems to break down.

    Calculating your spares:
    a.  How many devices of this type are in service?
    b.  How many workdays between failures?
    c.  Typically, how many days does it take to get that type of device repaired?
    d.  How many workdays in a year (roughly)?
    e.  Determine your mean time between failures.
    f.  Determine the number of machines/days in week.
    g.  Divide the number from Step d by the number in Step e.

    Example:

    Say your company is using 200 PCs. You estimate one hardware problem per unit, every 2 years. You estimate it typically requires 5 working days to get a PC repaired. Given vacations and holidays, a PC is in use 48 weeks per year times 5 days per week or 240 days per year. Therefore, if you work 240 days per year, and a PC fails every 2 years, you have a mean time between failures (MTBF) of 480 days. In a given week (5 days), you have 200 machines running or 1,000 machine/days per week. Divide the MTBF by the number machine/days in a week to see you need a bit more than 2 spares on hand. Round this up to 3 as the minimal stocking level.

    If you have less than your minimal stocking level on hand, order some equipment today! If you have more than the minimal stocking level, then redeploy that equipment in place of purchasing new equipment. Another option is to scrap broken machines instead of paying to repair older equipment until your idle assets stockpile is drawn down.

    Once your emergency spares stocking level is set, lock them up! People with marginally financed projects will try to use this equipment to make their project look less expensive than what it actually costs. These machines are not to be used for anything other than spares.

3.  **Service contracts.** Here is another area where an asset management program shows its power. Compare your equipment totals with your service contracts:
    a.  Evaluate your coverage. Is everything on the contract that you think should be on it?

b. Are you paying for service support for hardware that is gone? Is everything that is listed by serial number on the contract still in-house? Before cancelling anything here, make another pass or two through the area to look for it.

c. Look at each device separately. Are you paying for the proper level of service? Do you still need that expensive "24 by 7" support?

d. Evaluate your list of critical equipment. Is it properly covered? This is not the place to cut corners!

Look for ways to lower your cost. If you have plenty of spares for a particular device type, consider establishing a quick swap/service center. In this approach, you exchange one of your spares for the broken item to restore service. The repairperson only needs to come in weekly to work on what was broken.

Are any of your older technologies covered by service contracts? How much is it costing per device? This helps to justify the expense to eliminate older technology.

### [B]   Ongoing Asset Management

Once you have everything tagged and counted, you must maintain a vigorous effort to keep your database current. This requires any equipment taken out of the idle assets room be properly entered into the asset database. Any equipment moved back to storage also is noted. Depending on their workload, the help desk can keep this up to date. The technical worker who makes the move (such as to set up a PC for a new employee) can also update the equipment inventory records.

Think a minute how far you have come. You began with running your business using "tribal knowledge" and now can proceed based on the facts! When your annual budgeting cycle comes around, you can better estimate your equipment needs for the upcoming year. When software conversions become necessary, you will know what is needed.

As you know by now, conducting a full asset count is very time-consuming. Instead of doing this every year, you can audit one department per month since you have bar codes on all the machines.

## § 8.06   SOFTWARE ASSET MANAGEMENT

### [A]   Overview

When most people think of asset management, they think in terms of physical property. For a long time, this was true of IT systems also. The software was expensive but the hardware cost much more. With improvements in manufacturing and lower prices, you can quickly have more money invested in your software than in the equipment to run it. Software asset management is quite different from hardware management yet it also can be a place to save money in your budget.

## [B]  Lay the Groundwork

Expand your asset database. The software asset database table is typically linked to the device table, since software exists to support a hardware device. In addition to the user information collected during the hardware inventory, it is useful to know the software's version number.

What information to collect?

1. **Purchased Software—PC**
   Software name
   Manufacturer's name
   Version
2. **Purchased Software—Server/mainframe**
   Software name
   Manufacturer's name
   Version
   Annual maintenance fee
   Number of simultaneous users licensed
3. **In-House Developed Software**
   Software name
   Programmer's name
   Version

Typically, the most work on collecting software information is spinning on the PC hard disks. There is software available that will check the networked PCs overnight or the next time they log onto the server. A nice feature about this type of software is that you can set it to reinventory PCs at programmed intervals. There is also software on the market that will use the network to "visit" each PC on your network. In addition, by catching PCs as they log on, you can capture data from notebook PCs when they return from the field.

## COMMENT

Examples of this class of products are iInventory at *www.lanauditor.com* and Express Metrix at *www.expressmetrix.com*.

A major benefit of this class of automatic software auditing is when you are preparing to roll out new software. You can see who has what, who might need the new version, and who might still be running an old OS version and require upgrading.

## [C]  Unauthorized Software

Dig out a copy of your company's policy concerning the use of unauthorized software. You will quite likely find unauthorized software during your inventory count and need to be ready to address it. Your searches may find anything from the company bowling team scores to pornography. Be sure you understand what the company will permit before proceeding. Based on this policy, you should copy the offending files to a secure library on the server and then delete them from the PC. Leave the offending operator with a copy of the policy.

Illegal software must be removed and reported to the IT manager. The problem with removing it is that if you have waited too long to make an inventory, this software could have become ingrained in that department's operation. Removing it is the right thing to do but will hurt your company. In that case, *immediately* purchase the necessary number of copies and assign the cost to that manager.

An exception would be computer games. Most companies have a policy of "death on sight" for computer games loaded onto their company PCs. Make sure of what you are deleting before removing it.

### [D]   Conduct the Inventory

Just as you made the rounds for the hardware inventory, so must you do the same for the software inventory. If an automated software inventory system is used, then you only need to compare it to your hardware list to determine who has been missed. The inventory must include every workstation, every server, and don't forget the all-important network software versions. Remember that notebook PCs and PDAs may not show up on your automated software count—or they may pop up over time as they reenter the facility and attach to the network. Schedule times with each department to bring in their machines for evaluation.

Although PCs have been used throughout this chapter as an example, it is important to know information about your other software. Typically, each IT section handles their own. They can continue to do so but this will allow some upper management visibility. For example, the software on network devices does not change very often but without an accurate list of what there is, there is no management oversight.

### [E]   Crunch the Numbers

Roll up the numbers after the inventory is completed. Compare this number with the number of software licenses you can prove have been purchased. Report the results to the IT manager. If more copies need to be purchased, do so immediately.

Now look for traces of "homegrown" department-written software. If someone writes a program for their own use, that is one issue. But if someone has written such as program and now it is in widespread use, then the IT department must step in and ensure it follows good data processing procedures (like all of the numbers add up), etc.

### [F]   Ongoing Software Asset Management

Cleaning illegal software one time is a good first step, but unless the people believe you are now monitoring their systems, it will all be back. Publish a clear policy explaining that installing software not purchased by the company is forbidden and that people doing so will be disciplined. In some companies, pornography on a computer is forwarded to the human resources director for disciplinary action.

# § 8.07   COMPUTER HARDWARE ACQUISITIONS

## [A]   Overview

Computer hardware acquisitions can come in more than one form. Hardware can be purchased, leased, or provided by a third-party lease. Acquisitions can come from one or more of these sources. The most practiced one is for the outright purchase of hardware. If it is more practical to lease the hardware, but the vendor will not, a third-party lease may be arranged. Vendors encounter this often enough that they may have some recommendations. Some leases cover a buyout at the end of the lease or third-party lease.

Signing a lease will require the firm's legal representative to review the documents before any commitment is made. The purchasing department also should be contacted to ensure that the company's acquisition policies are followed.

## [B]   Major Systems Acquisitions

Any project affecting more than one department and/or without budgeted funds allocated for such a system is identified as a major acquisition by the manager of information systems. User managers will send a memo to the manager of the information systems unit and a copy to the person to whom the manager of information systems reports. This memo addresses the need for a major computer system acquisition. The memo may originate from one or more user management person(s) or the systems analysis unit's manager.

The memo will cover the following issues:

- The area of the firm that will be affected by the new system
- A defined need for the acquisition
- Cost savings expected and expected life span (from the business perspective) of the proposed system
- The maximum calendar time allowed for the expected system to be operational
- A priority ranking provided for this project as compared with others under study or development (Final decision on this will be made by the IT steering committee.)

1.  **Analysis of new systems request.** The manager of information systems and his/her superior review the requesting memo. Management evaluates the merits of doing a preliminary systems needs study and the status of the total organization's budget situation. The information systems manager sends a reply memo to the requesting manager. The information systems manager sends a memo giving the rea-

son for the denial or approval for a feasibility study. If approved, a preliminary systems needs study (which is identified as a feasibility study) will be done. A memo to that effect is sent to the manager of systems analysis. The memo asks for a feasibility study and provides the following information:

- When results of study are to be expected
- The people and monetary resources provided for study
- What user personnel are to be contacted
- What level of confidentiality is expected of preliminary systems needs study

2. **Feasibility study.** An analysis of the users' areas can assist the feasibility study before it is undertaken. This information would be helpful before attempting to contact users for a formal study. Gather as much information about the units as possible before conducting a formal study.

Contact user personnel identified in the requisition memo received for the assigned project. Remembering the names of the unit's personnel and their respective titles would be helpful. Find out who controls the informal unit organization, who at times can be known as the "power behind the throne." They can influence the feasibility study, and even more so when and if a new system is in place. Any knowledge of the corporate politics involved can be helpful. The status of units in the corporate pecking order provides insight regarding the proposed computer system's chances of success.

Examine current procedural documentation. Follow up with a study of the actual procedures followed by the unit's employees. The operating procedure study should include input and output documents. All existing files will be documented—these include hardcopy and computer files.

The current systems operation studied should provide the following information needed for a final systems design to be completed later:

- System flowcharts
- Dataflow diagrams
- Document flowcharts
- Data dictionary
- Current procedure flowcharts
- Any work sampling studies done
- Current operation costs (i.e., direct costs and indirect costs)
- Generated reports and/or computer monitor displays

An evaluation of the proposed system is made for its justification. The feasibility will be determined by several factors:

a. **Operation feasibility.** Operation feasibility analysis determines if the solution will meet end-user requirements: Does the solution fit into the end-user operational environment and meet the requirements of an acceptable time schedule? It ascertains meeting the user's human factors requirements and fits into the organization's social work scene.

b.  **Technical feasibility.** Technical feasibility analysis determines if the solution is technically practical: Is the technology available or soon to be available and can the end user and the facilities accommodate the solution?

c.  **Economic feasibility.** Economic feasibility analysis determines if the solution meets measurements of cost-effectiveness. It is justified by a cost-benefit analysis. There are situations that may override economic feasibility. This can happen when government legislation, customer requirements, or union contracts mandate that it will be done.

When it is completed, the feasibility study is sent to the manager of information systems for his/her approval. When the manager of information systems approves the feasibility study, he/she writes a cover memo. The memo will be attached to the report and sent to his/her superior and all user managers involved in the original needs request.

If the feasibility study is not approved, a copy will be returned to the authors of the study with recommendations noted on the document. A cover memo will be written and attached to the returned study reviewing why the study was rejected and what is needed for approval. The required changes and/or additions to the study will be done. If needed, a revised study will be resubmitted for the final approval of the manager of information systems.

3.  **Final systems design.** The final approved system design will be one of the following:
    *   An off-the-shelf system provided and operated by a third-party vendor
    *   An off-the-shelf system provided by a vendor
    *   Company-acquired hardware with a third party providing the software
    *   In-house-produced software with company-acquired computer hardware
    *   In-house-produced software with company-acquired computer hardware with vendor assistance

    The manager of information systems will designate the system design and installation process used and financial management approval is required for the final systems design and operation.

The priority assigned by management will determine the priority of the project. The new major computer system will determine the resources and timeframe to install it. The systems designer who performed the feasibility study will (at a minimum) be available to assist the project's completion. The manager of information systems and the manager of the systems unit determine the degree the project is supported by the current resources. A project manager will be appointed to manage the project's completion. See Chapter 5 for more detailed information about project management.

## [C]   Budgeted Hardware Acquisitions

Computer budgeting can be done several ways. Hardware budgets are allocated for the entire process of designing and placing the computer system into operation. This is a budgeted item that may cover one or more budget years. Other budgeted hardware acquisitions can be found in different budgeting forms. There are several options with which to acquire computer hardware. One or more may be employed by the organization. Typically, the cost for hardware is projected over 5 years since a large part of the equipment cost is in ongoing maintenance or machine specific supplies.

## COMMENT

Don't let the total expense over 5 years frighten you. Do the same thing for your car? Yet you still drive it.

1. **Information systems hardware committee.** The manager of information systems assigns the computer hardware asset management responsibility to the information technology asset manager. An information systems hardware advisory committee is formed. The chairperson of the committee will be the information technology asset manager. The information systems manager appoints members from the programming, operations, and systems technology areas. This allows an "expert" from each department to comment on the impact of purchasing a specific device on their area and on the company's interoperability as a whole. A representative is appointed by the purchasing manager and the CFO. The committee provides information required for the maintenance of the approved computer hardware list.

No less often than quarterly, an update of any added or deleted hardware will be made to the asset management hardware database. An asset management hardware status report is issued monthly. The report is made available to committee members one week before the committee meeting. Minutes of each monthly and special meeting are kept. Approved copies of the minutes are sent to the committee members and the manager of information systems by the IT asset manager.

Any hardware that is not on the current approved computer hardware list will be flagged. The approved computer hardware list is a screening device for current computer hardware acquisitions. The information will be current and available via online access or published listings. The manager of information systems may authorize past acquisitions not on the current approved computer hardware list. Current acquisitions are required to be listed. New computer hardware acquisitions will be listed. The approved computer hardware list is updated and distributed by the chairperson of the information systems hardware committee/IT asset manager.

In cases of special one-time hardware needs not on the approved computer hardware list, an acquisition waiver may be granted. A request is sent to the chairperson of the information systems hardware committee. The chairperson brings the request before the information systems hardware committee. The committee replies to the request.

The reply memo is sent to the manager of information systems for his/her final approval.

Approved memos will be signed by the manager of information systems and sent to the person requesting the hardware. The IT hardware person is sent a copy of the memo. Disapproved requests are returned to the committee for follow-up action. These special hardware items are added to the asset management hardware database when placed into service.

2.  **Corporate lump-sum budget.** Senior management will allocate a lump-sum budget based on information provided by the information systems manager. The information systems manager may assign the task of collecting information for the hardware needs to the information technology asset manager.

3.  **IT hardware loans.** Sometimes, companies keep a small pool of equipment for occasional use such as a pool of notebook PCs to be loaned to a department so their travelers can stay in touch. The IT hardware person reviews the request in light of other approvals to the same unit. If not approved, a memo to that effect is sent to the person requesting the hardware with the reason for refusing the request. The memo may be in the form of a hardcopy memo or e-mailed to the person. A copy of the memo will be stored with the request file for that unit. The copy may be in the form of hardcopy or a file maintained in a computer database.

    If the loan of equipment is available and approved, it will be issued from the reserve equipment stock. Organizations with a computer store will provide for the loan of the hardware. Whichever unit provides the equipment will maintain a follow-up file. Further information, such as recording who signed for the equipment, the unit to which it is to be loaned, and the expected return date information, must be filed by the return date. The person making the loan will follow up on expected return dates. If the computer hardware is borrowed from another department, the information technology asset manager will be informed.

4.  **Stocked hardware.** If the information systems unit maintains a stock of computer hardware, the IT hardware person will issue the hardware from the stock supply. He/she will update the computer inventory stock file for the items taken from stock. The hardware also may be made available from the company computer store. The store's inventory record will be updated. The IT hardware person posts an approval and dates and signs the memo. He/she also records on the memo the proper item name and tag number of the hardware. The original copy of the memo is filed, a copy returned to the requesting unit manager, and a copy sent to the information technology asset manager.

## [D]   Purchasing Expendable Computer Supplies

Computer supply items cover all supplies used by computers, computer peripheral equipment, and other office support equipment. These assets must meet the required standards established by an IT supply standards committee. It is important that high quality materials be used for magnetic media, printer toner, and ink. Poorly refilled containers can severely gum up the insides of a machine and require expensive repairs. Once a standard has been set, each department can purchase their own expendable supplies. The IT operations team purchases materials for the IT department, and for emergency spares to support the facility.

The IT supply standards committee will identify the materials that are acceptable and the purchasing department will source these materials. Business departments will purchase their own supplies from the approved vendors through the company purchasing policies.

1. **IT supply standards committee.** The committee will be made up of IT operations, IT systems, and IT planning personnel. The purchasing department manager appoints a representative to this committee. The committee selects supply items and the vendors to be on the approved purchasing supply list. These items and/or vendors may change at the discretion of the IT supply standards committee. The manager of information systems will appoint the chairperson for the committee. Their respective unit managers appoint representatives of the other IT units. The committee will meet monthly and as needed.

   The committee addresses all internal correspondence and provides a reply from other correspondence. Vendors may contact the chairperson of the committee to make a presentation to the committee. Other persons within the organization may refer their received correspondence to this committee to be addressed. The committee replies to all correspondence referred to it by other departments. Minutes that will be taken at each meeting will be provided to all committee members. The minutes will be approved at the next meeting. The manager of information systems, the asset manager, and any top management person requesting it, receives a copy of the approved committee minutes.

   The committee publishes an approved purchasing supply list (expendable assets) and provides copies to the supply department, computer store manager, purchasing agents, and all unit supervisors. Any person not on the distribution list may request to receive copies of the approved purchasing supply list. Copies are for company use and no part of the list is to be made available to anyone outside the firm.

2. **Maintaining expendable supplies.** Maintaining expendable supply policies and procedures for computer and computer support devices is the responsibility of the IT supply standards committee. This covers the following areas:
   a. Maintaining quality standards for IT supply items
   b. Setting the supply product items standards and maintaining the consistency of purchases
   c. Maintaining corporate IT expendable purchasing policies
   d. Following the policies set down by the company purchasing department and/or the material control department
   e. Outlining expendable computer supply policies and procedures

Policies are recommended by the IT supply standards committee, which require the asset manager's and top management's final approval. The committee approves of the procedures required for the provision, maintenance, and control of expendable computer supplies.

For vendor contracting policies, please refer to Chapter 15. The vendors selected must meet quality standards first, and price second.

The IT supply standards committee will monitor the quality of all supplies on a continuous basis. User feedback is encouraged with all supply products. Committee members spot-check the use of the supply items within its jurisdiction. Any problem will be studied to ensure that it is not a machine, operator, or environmental problem before the problem is brought to the attention of the vendor. The vendor's reaction will determine if that item will be purchased in the future from the same vendor. It is the sole responsibility of the IT supply standards committee to decide from which vendor the supply items are purchased.

3. **Stocking expendable computer supplies.** Each department will purchase their own supplies from the vendors approved by the purchasing department. Purchasing will focus purchases onto one or two vendors to gain further volume discounts for the company. The IT department will stock material for its own use and for use in troubleshooting equipment.

   If a department has run out of an expendable supply, they can borrow a refill from IT and then return it when their shipment arrives.

## COMMENT

The downside of departments buying their own supplies is the accumulation of new toner cartridges sitting under printers awaiting use. At $100 per toner cartridge, this can quickly add up. Some companies use their office supplies supplier to stock what is needed and always deliver it the next day. That removes the need to stockpile this expensive material. Take the time to educate your users on these costs!

4. **Budgeting expendable computer supplies.** The committee uses the hardware inventory results to estimate supplies usage for input to the facility's budget. The cost of expendable materials is sometimes another nail in the coffin of a very old device.

## [E]   Procurement Process

The company's purchasing department establishes company vendor policies. The purchasing department provides a service for the entire company, just as the information systems unit provides service to the company. Information systems is the user when working with the purchasing department. Information systems should provide the same cooperation with purchasing it expects from its users. Purchasing will not necessarily be the only contact for vendors. This depends on the type of purchased item.

Purchasing requisitions used by information systems will be the same kind used throughout the organization. If there is no company purchase requisition form available, the systems unit designs a purchasing form. The managers of information systems and purchasing are required to approve the form.

1. **Purchasing expendable computer supplies.** One or more purchasing department representatives will handle computer supply items requiring custom designing. These representatives will be provided with a current copy of the approved purchasing supply list and any changes that will be forthcoming with the next issue of the list. This provides for a more efficient operation. Purchasing's contact source will be known by information systems personnel and vendors. The purchasing department will, at times, be contacting the same vendor for purchasing non-computer-related products.

   For small-item purchasing, a credit system reduces the time and cost of procurement. Charge limits and payment installments would be set covering the blanket purchases. The final procedure would be worked out with the accounts payable unit. Credit card companies provide this kind of service, i.e., American Express.

2. **Computer hardware purchase acquisition.** All purchase orders will be issued from purchase requisitions approved only by authorized information systems representatives. These purchase requisitions should be funneled to the same purchasing agents each time because of their familiarity with both the vendor and products. These purchases are for standard hardware items under the asset manager's jurisdiction. If the purchasing department can arrange for early payment to take advantage of payment discounts, it should do so. Expense records will have to be adjusted to reflect these cost savings.

   Small-item assets may be purchased with a credit card system with limits per purchase. Arrangement and procedure requires the approval of the accounts payable unit. There are credit card companies that will provide this kind of service, one being American Express (*http://www.americanexpress.com/homepage/smallbusiness.shtml*). They will provide an American Express Gold Corporate Card. A list of authorized employees should receive the cards. This is a competitive business, and it is wise to shop around for the best service.

3. **Computer hardware disposal.** The purchasing organization may be asked to assist with the disposal of unnecessary computer equipment. They may sell it or donate it to a charity. The longer one waits to get rid of used equipment, the harder it will be to dispose of. The IT asset manager and capital asset accounting unit should be contacted about the equipment disposal. They also should be contacted for any money collected or donation credit received for the hardware.

The removed hardware will be deleted from the computer hardware database. The IT hardware person removes the tags before the hardware is disposed of. The IT asset manager and accounting manager are notified by memo or e-mail that the hardware has been disposed of.

# § 8.08   COMPUTER SOFTWARE ACQUISITIONS

## [A]   Overview

The purpose of a computer software acquisition policy is to formalize a uniform standard for computer software acquisitions throughout the organization. This policy mandates the endorsement and support by the CEO/head of the organization.

The computer software acquisition policy covers all computer software used by the organization. An organization can have several kinds of computer software. The kinds of software will depend on its source. Each computer software source will require its own software acquisition policy. The sources/kinds of computer software include the following:

- Company-written software
- Contract personnel–written software
- Vendor-written off-the-shelf system software
- Purchased operating systems
- Purchased packaged software
- Leased software
- Bootlegged software
- Pirated software

The objective is to provide the guidelines for having uniform programming software, purchased operating systems, and programs. This also covers all proprietary software, including development, writing, and contracting. Sole ownership of the program's source coding ratifies the programs as proprietary. The code is loaded to a compiler. It will generate the operating program. There will be standards for proposing and recommending benchmarks, vendor selection, and contracting. Purchased software is approved for payment after passing the testing criteria. The purchasing of operating program (object-coded) software is limited to its defined purchase agreement specifications that come with packaged software.

Each type of software has its own software policy requirements. These are directives needed, in addition to the general guidelines, for all software.

1. **Company-written proprietary software.** All programming will be done in the approved programming language. All programs written using company software, hardware, and any other company-owned resources are company property. Programming documentation and operation manuals will follow established standards.

2. **Contract-written proprietary software.** All contracted programmers will employ the same programming standards and procedures as do company programmers. Documentation, test data, and drafted work information are the property of the company. The company is the sole owner of the source-coded programs.

3. **Complete system contracting.** This is a vendor-developed system, including development cost and the program's source coding, and belongs to the company. The company has the copyright and/or patent rights to the developed off-the-shelf system software. Top management can approve other contract arrangements. Any third-party add-on software used will be identified. Limitations on the use of the third-party software will be defined. Its warranties, restrictions, and operations will be fully identified.

4. **Purchased packaged operating systems software.** There will be standard uniform operating systems software. There will be no more systems in operation than licensed. The information systems committee will identify the authorized system software version.

5. **Purchased packaged application software.** Only approved application software is permitted. There will be only properly licensed programs in operation. The information systems software committee will identify the software version to be allowed. Modifications may be done at the vendor's discretion. These modifications will be provided and identified by the version number.

6. **Leased software.** Some software is only marketed by lease arrangements. There only will be properly leased programs in operation.

7. **Bootlegged software.** Bootlegged software will not be loaded onto any company computer. Repeated violations of this policy are grounds for dismissal.

8. **Pirated software.** Pirated software will not be loaded onto any company computer. Violations of this policy are grounds for dismissal.

## [B]   Proprietary-developed Software

Proprietary-developed software comes from several sources. Required software that is not listed on the asset management software database file or available for purchase or lease may need to be developed. When the developed proprietary software becomes operational, this information will be put into the asset management software database file. The information systems software committee decides if the software will be listed on the approved computer software list. The software's source will be identified on the approved computer software list. This allows potential users to contact the developers for information about the software. The company can have its proprietary software developed by more than one method.

1. **End user–developed software.** User-developed software follows the firm's policy for software development. The information systems area resources will be available, as time is available from the information technology units. Monies may be budgeted to departments for

such development. Some users can develop their own software. Depending on the area of operations, there can be different levels of skills available. Depending on the corporate culture, user activity varies. At times it would not only be faster to accomplish the task, but even possibly at a lower cost. The average IT unit is overwhelmed by backlogs. It would be helpful to have users reduce the load of the IT units. Department managers may even buy computers and vendor assistance if they are required to, hopefully not because of IT disinterest.

a.  **The inception process.** The end-user department manager is required to approve user-developed software within his/her jurisdiction. The user's department manager should receive a memo, from the requesting party, defining the need for the unavailable software. The department manager also can originate the memo. The memo will be part of the project documentation. This is required before any effort is expended developing the software.

User-developed software will be done at the user department's own expense. The information technology asset manager will be contacted before end user–developed software is produced. The user manager will be informed about available software that may assist the project. Also, user management will be informed of what is available from the asset management software database. Not all company-used software is listed on the approved computer software list. Computer programs may be available that can be used as is or with some modification. Information is available about third-party add-on module software. This module software can be part of the program being developed and save programming time. When users are writing their own software, they may find a need for third-party software. It is then that the IT asset manager should be contacted for assistance.

User-developed software is confined to accessing company files using read-only access. Under no circumstances will these programs be enabled to update corporate files. If that need arises, then IT must take over development and maintenance of that program.

b.  **End-user resources.** Consulting resources will be provided by the IT organization when time is available. User management determines what kind of assistance is required. The assistance available from the information systems organization, when needed, should be known before pursuing the project. The information systems unit may charge for this service, depending on the company policy for interdepartmental service billing. When the information systems staff has no time available, they can provide vendor sources for user assistance. Payment for this service will be from the user's budget, unless other provisions have been made. The information technology asset manager will assist end-user management with vendor negotiations.

c.  **Developing end-user software.** The user will employ an approved software compiler, for example, Visual Basic (a Microsoft product). The user should contact the help desk with any problems with the compiler software. An IT programmer/mentor will be assigned to the project. Their role is to answer questions about data files and the compiler. They are not permitted to write any of the code. Writing user computer programs should follow the procedures for programming methods provided by IT. For more information see Chapter 4, Programming Procedures.

d. **End-user software documentation.** A copy of the project, including source code, compiled software, and supporting documentation, is sent to the chairperson of the information systems software committee. The committee examines and tests the computer software under the leadership of the IT programming representative on the committee. The approved software requires a memo written by the IT programming representative describing the value of the software. The memo will be sent to the manager of information systems and the information technology asset manager. They will determine if the new software warrants being listed on the approved computer software list.

e. **End-user software completion.** After testing is completed, all software documentation is brought up to date. Test results are part of the documentation. Any operations manual needed for the operation of the software is written and tested by users who do not have any knowledge about the new software. After extensive successful testing has been completed, the user may employ the software within his/her own operation. The manager of the user department writes an authorizing memo permitting the software to be used in his/her department. The memo contains information on the software's performance. A copy of the memo is placed in the documentation folder and a copy sent to the information technology asset manager. The IT asset manager updates the asset management software database using this information.

All end user–developed software is to be maintained by the same department under the same conditions as which it was developed.

f. **User follow-up procedures.** The user developer of the software forwards a copy of the project documentation folder and the software—both the source and object-code programs—to the chairperson of the information systems software committee, who is also the IT asset manager. The copies will include both a hardcopy of the program software and the operating program on disk. A copy of the operations manual for user operation is sent with the copy of the documentation folder. The information systems software committee may elect to make the user-developed software available companywide by placing it on the approved computer software list. The software may be used by other parts of the company. The approved computer software list will identify who developed and first used the software. The IT programming unit member of the information systems software committee retains the software folder and the programs in a user-developed software file. The file contains user-developed software found on the approved computer software list and software that is not on the list, but is in the asset management software database.

g.  **Other users' involvement.** If the software will be used as part of a system employed by other users, approval is required by the IT software committee and the managers of the IT programming and computer operations units. To ensure there will not be a problem with any integrated operating software or database, a copy of the software folder is sent to the manager of the IT programming unit for his/her study. He/she reviews the information with the manager of IT computer operations. The programming unit's representative on the committee must confirm that the software meets the firm's information technology standards. Any IT unit manager may request a duplicate copy of the software folder. With the approval of the IT programming unit manager, the help desk will support the software.

2.  **IT-developed software.** The IT programming unit of the information systems department may develop software for users or its own needs. User department managers may request the software by a memo to the information systems manager. The information systems manager may have user management direct the request to the IT programming unit manager. The request will be reviewed in light of other requests and the current workload of the available programming staff. If the request is one not requiring a major new system, the information systems manager will be notified along with the requesting user department manager. A memo or e-mail message will provide what course of action the user manager may take.

a.  **New software development study.** A study to be conducted for the development of new software requires a formal request by approved user management and/or IT unit managers. The request will provide the following information:

   • When are results of the study to be expected?
   • What software may be available which can be purchased and used as is or modified for this application?
   • When will the project be completed and in operation?

   After the requested information is returned and studied, the IT programming manager summarizes the information in a memo and sends it to the information systems manager. The information systems manager decides what course of action the IT programming manager will take with the project. The reply can be a memo or e-mail. These procedures are for projects without their own budget—resources are provided from existing budgets. Major system projects, with their required software development, will be provided with their own budgets when annual budgets are granted.

b.  **Software maintenance.** Updating current software in use by information system's IT operations or user application operations will require maintenance. A software maintenance request will be sent to the IT programming manager and contain the following information:

- The completion date needed for the required program changes
- Which software programs are modified
- What the modifications will contain. Any I/O changes will have attached the current and new I/O layouts

3. **Contract programming.** Software development may be contracted for user or IT computer operations. Unless the company has already a blanket vendor contract for software development, competitive bids will be solicited from two or more software contracting vendors. The vendors will be provided with information for contract bid proposals. At a minimum, the request for bid proposals will contain the following information:

- Which contact person will be the source for more information and submitting his/her bid proposal?
- Will the contract call for maintenance of new programs?
- What type of application will be programmed? Examples would be billing, payroll, inventory control, etc.
- If maintenance programming is required, in what language is the software written?
- What language is the new software to be written in? If the vendor proposes an alternate one, what would be the benefits?
- Will the bids requested be for contract hours or a project? For project bids, interested vendors will be provided with detailed information. It is advisable that the project be well defined before requesting project bids.
- The due date for bids.
- The expected start and finish dates.
- What are the skill levels of the people who will be working for the vendor?
- What is the dollar amount of the bid?

a. **Hourly contracting.** The programming effort is paid hourly. Enough money should be available to complete the task. Have a contingency reserve set aside. For new program development, running out of money presents a far greater problem than a maintenance task. It's more difficult to finish a partly completed program that someone else has started. The purchase requisition identifies the vendor will be paid for hours worked. Purchasing requisitions identify how the vendor will bill, either lump-sum or partial payments. If something other than a monthly check is issued, accounts payable should know.

i. **Programming.** The programming can be done in-house or at the vendor's location. The programmers will submit a weekly report of hours worked by day. Each day, the work effort and persons contacted regarding that day's work effort will be recorded. If contact is not related to that day's work effort, why is it being billed? A daily log will be kept of the detail-supporting information for the weekly report. The log may be manually kept and will be the property of the company. It will be submitted weekly to the company's contact person. The vendor (for its own records) may want to make a copy of this log.

ii.   **Company contact person.** The company's software vendor contact person should examine each week's vendor billing information before approving payment. The daily detailed information will be examined weekly. As more time passes, it becomes harder to confirm detailed information. If need be, a contact may be made with the vendor for any questions that may arise. Don't delay this action too long. Vendors' memories are no better than anyone else's.

iii.   **Vendor payment.** Paying the vendor requires a purchase order. The purchase order may be in the form of a blanket purchase order, allowing the purchase order to be paid by accounts payable in installments as approved by the person signing the purchase requisition. The vendor will submit a bill to the company contact person for payment. The bill is confirmed to be correct. Approval is noted, dated, and signed, and then sent to accounts payable. A copy of the bill is made for filing. The dollar amount left that was allotted for the task is noted on the copy before it is filed. If it appears that the task will not be completed before the allotted funds run out, this is reported to the contact person's superior.

b.   **Project contracts.** Contract programming by project is for a well-defined programming project with detailed acceptance criteria. No vendor timekeeping is required. The project will have a calendar finish date.

i.   **Project tasks.** The tasks within the contracted project are plotted on a Gantt chart. The completion date of each task is reported in writing, dated, and signed by the vendor. It is sent to the information systems project contact person. If it is a user project, the information will be provided to the user vendor contact person. A copy of the Gantt chart is signed and dated for each completed week of the project. The chart represents the work plotted for the work week, Monday through Friday, and is provided to the designated company contact person who receives it by the following Wednesday.

ii.   **Project contract.** A contract is drawn for the project. It defines in detail what is to be accomplished. The authorized person signs the contract after approval by the firm's legal representative. A purchase requisition with a copy of the contract attached is sent to purchasing. Purchasing sends a purchase order to the vendor who uses the purchase order number for a billing reference. Input and output documents detail the I/O information furnished the vendor. Printed program source and object codes will be provided no later than one week after shown as completed on the Gantt chart. The user provides the test data for detail testing of all conditions that can be expected. Examples of output testing will be provided to the company contact person along with a printed copy of the actual test data used.

iii. **Penalty clause.** The contract will contain a penalty clause. The clause states the penalty for each workday the project is late. If the user would benefit from an early completion date, a bonus could be included for each workday it is finished early. The bonus clause would be after all other things are agreed upon. This avoids any padding by the vendor.

iv. **Bill payment.** An invoice/bill is sent to the company project contact person. The company has 30 days to confirm that all contract conditions have been met. Any work added by the company will be paid by issuing a separate purchase requisition and following the same procedure as the original project contract. When the project is accepted as complete, accounts payable is notified by sending them the invoice/bill with a noted approval, date, and approving authority signature. The vendor will be paid with one check for the purchase orders. If there are any unresolved disputes with the vendor, the firm's legal representative will be contacted for resolution.

## [C]   Purchased Software

This section covers the purchase and control of software. These are nonproprietary programs. The software's manufacturer is the owner of the source and object programs. When the operating (object) program and instructions are packaged for sale, it is for use by one computer. The purchaser has limited claims to the software. Most often the software, registration card, and instructions are boxed and sealed with shrinkwrap material. To accept a return without the shrinkwrap, if permitted, the vendor will require a restocking charge, including reshrinkwrapping the box. The program disks are often in a sealed envelope. The sealed envelope usually contains the printed warranties and liabilities. Included is the warning that when the seal is broken, you own the software and you agree to the terms of the license agreement. This is no longer a returnable product.

The IT asset manager chairs the information systems software committee. Its major task is keeping abreast of new acceptable vendor-provided software. The committee is comprised of the managers of IT units, with the information technology asset manager as the chairperson. The purchasing department may have a representative on the committee.

No less often than a monthly update of any added or deleted software will be made to the asset management software database. The approved computer software list is updated at the same meeting of the IT software committee meeting. An asset management software database status report is issued monthly. The report will be made available to committee members one week before a committee meeting. Minutes of each monthly and special meetings are kept. Approved copies of the minutes are sent to the committee members and the manager of information systems.

# § 8.09  SOFTWARE ASSETS

## [A]  Overview

The information systems software committee members will keep current with software developments in the IT profession and proprietary software development. If there is (IT or user) beta testing, the status and results will be reported to the members of the committee.

Selected committee members will form a subcommittee to evaluate newly marketed software. Members will read and evaluate published IT reports. Networking with other outside IT people for information can be beneficial too. This information will be reported to the whole committee. Software that sounds promising will be purchased and tested in a controlled environment. There will be an annual IT budget for this purpose. Results are reported to the whole committee. With the committee's approval, the software is listed on the IT asset management software database if it meets the testing criteria. Beta opportunities also can be considered. There will be a selection procedure, written by a committee member, for buying new software. The IT software committee approves the procedure. End users also can test sample software under consideration not currently available to them through normal IT channels. This testing is limited to sample files or databases and not online with any network operation.

1. **Approved software.** Approved software sanctioned by the information systems software committee will be found on the approved computer software list. The software has been used, tested, and approved by the IT programming unit and the information systems software committee. Being on the approved computer software list means it will be available to users or information systems staff. The only question is whether to charge the software to the information systems budget or a user budget. This question will be addressed by corporate policy.

2. **Requesting software.** The unit manager requesting the software sends a memo or e-mail to the information technology asset manager or his/her appointed representative. The memo requests the software be installed on an identified computer or computers. This is for software found on the approved computer software list. At times it may be made available from the asset management software database by the IT asset manager. The request will be for software not contained on the approved computer software list.

   a. **Other software.** If software is not on the list and is needed, look for it on the asset management software database. If the software is available and approved to be used, it will be installed on the end-user PC.

b. **Special software needs.** There can be a special need for software that is neither on the approved computer software list nor on the asset management software database. The user's manager sends a request memo to the information systems software committee asking that a waiver be granted with a request to purchase the special software. When and if the software is purchased and received, the software information is posted to the asset management software database. The end user is required to resolve any software problems with the vendor. If the software gains acceptance, it is placed on the approved computer software list and the help desk will support the software.

3. **Unauthorized software.** Unauthorized software should be of concern to the IT asset manager and the IT software committee. Employing unauthorized software can be a very expensive experience for the company. The information systems software committee is responsible for policing all company computers for any unauthorized software whether it is in use or not. Just the software's presence on the hard drive can provide a problem. If the information systems software committee has never screened all the PCs and the task seems overwhelming, contact a few vendors specializing in this. Select one who has worked with the same hardware/software environment. It will not be cheap, but it is cheaper than the alternative. If the firm is small enough, around-the-clock scrutiny over a weekend and an examination of computers may be revealing. The asset management software database should furnish a list of what is authorized on each computer, including laptops. Have all the laptop computers turned in for "upgrading" so they may also be checked.

Once the 100-percent clean-sweep is made, perform surprise checks randomly. Each PC and server should be checked no less than once a year. If the task is too large for the committee then hire contract personnel. It can be done during nonworking hours so as not to disturb the daily operation. All unauthorized software is removed, and the asset management software database list is confirmed for accuracy. Any serious violations will be reported to the information technology asset manager. If the problem is serious, the information technology asset manager reports the details to the information systems manager.

4. **Antivirus procedures.** To start an antivirus procedure, no software will be brought into the firm that does not belong to the firm. Even authorized disks will be checked for viruses before they can be brought into the firm's work area. This includes newly purchased software prior to its release to the users. The antivirus device will contain the latest version of virus protection. Downloading of any Internet information without specially granted permission is absolutely prohibited. If any virus is detected on a computer, the machine will be disconnected from the network. The computer help desk is notified as soon as possible by telephone. The e-mail service to the problem computer is taken off-line along with the LAN service. The operators will immediately write down all that led up to the problem.

The next step is the recovery process, done by a representative of information systems who works with PCs and their software. If it is a full-time job, it may be done by a PC manager, or the PC store manager may have this duty.

5. **Approved computer software list.** The approved computer software list contains software that is approved for user acquisition, including approved software operating systems and company-developed software. To discourage the use of any unapproved software, help-desk support will not be provided to any unauthorized computer/user. The list is primarily a screening device for new software acquisitions. Authorized software not on the approved computer software list, but found on the asset management software database, can still run. The asset management software database lists all software that is permitted to be in use and by whom.

Proprietary software can be on the asset management software database (i.e., software developed by members of the firm and owned by the firm). Users who may have a problem with this software will contact the person(s) who developed it. There will be a list of third-party add-on software the company has purchased and is on the asset management software database. This software has very limited use and is not supported by the help desk. If help is required, the IT programming unit should be contacted.

6. **Software purchasing.** The IT asset manager with a purchase requisition will do all purchasing of new software. The requisition will note possible vendors for the software. Software is seldom purchased directly by the user manager. If it is purchased from the manufacturer, it will most likely be an upgrade. User management may acquire this software through its own or information systems' budget.

   a. **Unproven software.** When purchasing software, avoid release of version 1.0 of the product. Any release of that kind may have undiscovered bugs. It is safer to wait until the last number replaces the zero. Unless IT programming has been a beta site for the software, try to avoid brand-new software. This software is not required to be supported by the IT help desk.

   b. **Software stock.** Some software requests can be made from proprietary stock of software. This requires contacting the IT asset manager, who arranges for the installation on the end user's computer. Purchased software also may be available from the information technology asset manager or the company computer store. The computer store will have a small inventory of purchased software. The manager of the company store sends a request to the IT asset manager for any software issuing or restocking.

   c. **IT help desk.** The help desk supports purchased software as long as it is on the asset management software database. The asset management software database lists all software permitted for use and by whom. This database is the source by which users can be identified for help-desk assistance. Also supported will be user-written software, with or without third-party purchased add-on software, if it is on the approved software list. One or more purchased add-on third-party products can be combined with an in-house written program. If the help desk has any problems with this software, the caller is referred to the IT programming unit.

The IT programming unit is the reference source for third-party-purchased add-on software. This software is not intended as a computer program unto itself. It is to be used within a main program.

## [B]   Software Copyright Compliance Planning

Software not in compliance with the authorized ownership puts the company in jeopardy of lawsuits by the manufacturer of the software and/or its distributor. It is imperative the IT organization has the full support of top management to develop and maintain a policy of software copyright compliance. The plan should be documented and publicized throughout the company. This in itself will provide credibility; the company has a policy in place and will not tolerate any infraction. Employees who knowingly violate the policy will be dealt with accordingly. Repeat offenders can be held liable for costs incurred by their actions and/or be terminated.

The IT software asset manager has full responsibility for enforcing the unwarranted use of copyrighted software used illegally within the company. There are software packages on the market that can assist this process, and vendors who will undertake a continuous or one-time contract.

The total number of software units installed should be no more than what the contract license stipulates. If the number of software units installed is greater than the license allows, consider how many have to be removed or increase the number of purchased units licensed.

## COMMENT

One easy way to control the number of copies of software is to always retain the disks after loading the programs. You can tag them with the name of the person whose machine they were installed on, along with its asset tag number.

# 9

# POLICIES COVERING PCs: MANAGING THE DESKTOP SYSTEM

# § 9.01   PERSONAL COMPUTER POLICIES

## [A]   Overview

Personal computers make up a major share of today's IT assets. In most offices, there are at least one PC per person and more if you add in the number of PDAs and notebook PCs. The cost of personal computer hardware is now over-shadowed by the cost of the software within it. The proper management of these assets is critical if companies are to gain maximum benefit. The responsi-bility for maximizing PC utilization falls squarely on the information services department.

Current technologies make PCs seem like a series of interchangeable build-ing blocks that can be mixed and matched at will. This is definitely not true. Internal software drivers, ROM-based software, design assumptions, and inter-actions with other software makes introducing new components a tedious task. The PC coordinator will carefully select hardware components that are compatible with the installed base to ensure that they will work as envisioned.

To maximize the company's benefit and minimize its cost, the PC coordi-nator will recommend to the IT manager a series of policies governing the purchase and use of personal computer assets. These policies will reduce the variation in desktop systems making their support and repair possible for lower cost and with fewer people.

## [B]   Acquisition of PCs

The information systems manager sets the standards for PC hardware acquisi-tions. The fewer the variations in personal computer hardware there are in the company, the easier it is to maintain the existing base and to test new items for future use. The PC coordinator will recommend to the IT manager a list of hardware and software that has been found to meet the company's needs in the most reliable and cost-effective manner. A policy must be written that states all PC purchases must be in conformance with the approved product list.

An approved products list allows companies to focus their buying power on a few products and drive down the price. It also simplifies support require-ments since there are fewer products for the IT support staff to master and eases the testing and roll-out of new products since the desktop units are similar.

To ensure purchases adhere to the list, the purchasing department will forward to the PC coordinator any requests for PC products they receive. Once the PC coordinator verifies that the product is on the approved list, the pur-chase request is returned to purchasing for processing.

There are many valid business reasons for deviating from the approved list. If a requested item is not on the list, the PC coordinator will call the re-questor for an explanation. Sometimes there is a valid reason to purchase cop-ies of very old hardware or software if the migration to newer technology is too expensive. Some departments such as engineering may require unique products to achieve their business goals. The approved product list is a guide-line that should restrict the majority of users with the option that the IT manager can make exceptions to meet business needs. Before approving the exception, the PC coordinator must explore standard solutions with the users to see if they fully understand the capabilities of approved products. All deviations to the list must include a plan for providing ongoing training and support for that item.

Hardware that deviates from the list must include an explanation of who will repair it and how much it will cost. If the device will support a critical function, then the user must pay for an on-site spare machine as a quick backup (a function that the PC coordinator provides for standard units). Once IT approves the purchase of nonstandard hardware, they assume responsibility for maintaining it just like any other device.

## COMMENT

Some PC coordinators take the stance that since they are unfamiliar with nonstandard hardware they should not support it. This sounds like a spoiled child. The PC coordinator exists to support the customers in satisfying whatever might be their business needs. If their needs are for an unusual item, then the local IT staff should make a "best effort" to support that item and know who to call for help if the problem is beyond their technical abilities.

### [C]    Acquisition of Software

It should be a company policy that information systems management has control over all company software. To ensure system compatibility and to avoid interoperability problems, all software must be purchased from a list of approved products. This list is drafted by the PC coordinator and approved by the IT manager. A standard software products list will enable the support staff to focus on a few vendors for better price and support.

Unlike most hardware, software typically requires training for users to become productive with it. By standardizing on a few software packages, training becomes easier to provide and employee mobility between jobs is eased since all departments use the same basic tools.

Larger companies may purchase a license for a certain number of machines or for unlimited copies at their facility called a "site license." The PC coordinator will administer any per-seat or site-licensed software according to the terms of license, to include loading software on the appropriate systems and tracking how many copies have been installed.

Departments must not bypass this process by purchasing their own software. Doing so introduces new support costs that were not apparent when the purchase was first considered.

## [D]   Personal Hardware and Software

It must be a firm company policy that no one is permitted to bring into the facility any hardware or software that was not purchased through the normal acquisition process. This is to prevent the inadvertent damage to corporate systems from well-meaning but untested equipment or software. Along this same line, no one is permitted to load personal software on company-owned hand-held or notebook PCs, or to add any hardware upgrades to them. These actions are intended to reduce the likelihood of introducing software viruses or hardware incompatibilities into the company's processes.

## [E]   PC Management and User Support

The information systems department provides strategic planning for the firm's personal computer needs. This includes responsibility for hardware, software, maintenance, user support, and training. The IT department also is responsible for maintaining backup hardware and software, which are available on a loan basis to users and for coordinating and providing PC user training. Training can consist of both formal classes and individual, self-paced instruction.

Every department's needs are unique. An advisory panel, consisting of management-level staff and line operations personnel, guides information systems management and settles disputes concerning the firm's current and strategic needs.

## COMMENT

> The firm's management is responsible for providing current policies ensuring that PCs provide the best possible service to the firm. PC anarchy has caused the demise of more than one senior executive.

# § 9.02   PC COORDINATOR

## [A]   Overview

The PC coordinator's duties and responsibilities will vary from one location to another, depending on needs. The actual title also may vary, but whatever the title, its objective is to ensure that PC policies meet existing business needs and are enforced. Many companies create this assignment to provide a single point of contact for all activities and information pertaining to PCs. This provides a "single voice" that should consistently issue the same information. The PC coordinator recommends policies relating to personal computers to the IT manager for approval.

## [B]  Responsibilities of the PC Coordinator

The PC coordinator has a responsibility to ensure that the company's investment in personal computers is maximized to its full potential. The person assigned the position of PC coordinator will have a wide range of responsibilities:

1. Recommends a list of hardware and software for the company to standardize on based on its existing base of assets, its current business needs, and the strategic business direction of the company. Each item on the list is accompanied with a discussion of why it was selected. All existing items in the same product class (such as word processors) will be grouped together with the recommended replacement. The narrative also should state which existing items in the company assets inventory it replaces.
2. Creates and maintains a 3-year workstation strategic direction list for hardware and software migration. The list is recommended to the IT manager who has final approval. The recommendation is based on the existing asset inventory, emerging technologies, and emerging business requirements. The plan is usually updated annually.
3. Processes requests for new hardware and software to ensure they adhere to the published standard, in a timely manner. (If the PC coordinator's review becomes a major delay in the process, people will find ways to avoid it.)
4. Keep abreast of the latest hardware and software technologies and problems through review of trade press and by attending PC trade shows.
5. Keep abreast of the latest user hardware and software needs by participation in the PC advisory council.
6. Provide an ongoing hardware and software troubleshooting service for users to handle day-to-day operating problems. This includes management of outside hardware repair services.
7. Provide informal and formal training assistance for PC users.
8. Enforce policies regarding PC hardware and software operations, to include actively seeking out and deleting unauthorized software.
9. Provide backup service for critical PC data.
10. Provide PC LAN service and/or supervision.
11. Work closely with the help desk to detect systemic problems with PC processes and products.
12. Publish a newsletter detailing PC user successes, known problems and their workarounds, and tips for easier computing.

## [C]  In-house Consulting Service

The PC coordinator acts as an in-house consultant for users of PC hardware and software. This service assists users in understanding the capabilities of their systems and advising them how to use them for maximum performance. In this role, the PC coordinator constantly strives to demystify the technology by using nontechnical terms to describe technical functions.

The network manager identifies the standard for PC and LAN or WAN communications to ensure continuity and compatibility of the PC systems. The PC coordinator ensures that all PCs connected to the local area network use equipment approved by the network manager.

PC access to mainframe databases requires approval by the coordinator before any contact is made with the database administrator and/or data manager. The PC coordinator tries to match requests to existing data views. End users can only access corporate databases in a read-only mode and are never allowed to update corporate databases.

The coordinator maintains a daily log, which is the data source for monthly reports of his/her activities. Depending on cost accounting practices, users may be charged for the time they use. The daily log will record, by user charge code, time spent on the following items (travel time also will be included):

- PC hardware troubleshooting
- PC software troubleshooting
- Informal and formal training assistance
- User consulting service

The coordinator's indirect (administrative cost) time is kept in the following categories:

- Reading and other education methods used to keep up with current technology
- Communication network services
- Web site use and maintenance
- Publishing newsletters and other information
- User education and training preparation when not charged to a given department
- General administration duties, etc.

## [D]   PC Training

The PC coordinator arranges for PC training on all company standard hardware and software. The goal of this training is to raise user productivity and satisfaction with the tools provided to them. It is a waste of company resources to drop off a new PC loaded with software on someone's desk and hope they can master it on their own. Training leverages the equipment investment by showing the basic as well as advanced features to all employees. Training on the standard products should be offered in three levels:

1. **Basic.** How to start and navigate through the basic features of the product.
2. **Intermediate.** How to manipulate data, import, export, and build complex reports. Most users stop at this point.
3. **Advanced.** For those users who are constantly running this software, this is a thorough explanation of all of its features.

Training is a very time-consuming process. Many people lack the patience to work through the issues with users who do not seem to understand the technology. Those people who do have the patience often find this position very rewarding. There are several methods by which training can be provided. These include:

1. **Read the manual.** Software comes with two basic types of manuals. The first type is for reference only. You use it to look up how to perform specific functions and is not very good for learning the product. The second type is a training book that walks you through the product from beginning to end. The problem with this second type of manual is that there is no one to ask questions and it may take a long time to find the answer.

2. **Self-paced.** Some companies purchase self-paced software which users use to walk through the product at their own pace. This may be available to them in a central "walk-up" facility or they might start the software from their own desk. There is the same issue of who do you ask specific questions about the product.

3. **Classroom.** This is the best way to instruct a group of people over a short period of time but there is the added expense of an equipped classroom and an instructor.

4. **One-on-one.** Personal tutoring is the typical way that executives learn how to use the features of their PCs. This is the most timeconsuming method, but the PC support staff do it all the time when providing desk-side support.

A major tool in your training program will be a dedicated training room. This room should be equipped with one PC per student, plus a PC for the instructor. The instructor will require a projector to display the PC screen on the wall where all can follow along. The classroom should be isolated on the network to prevent accidental corruption of corporate data. The training room PC hard disks should be reloaded to the basic configuration at the end of every class.

Whenever the training room is not in use, anyone would be able to walk in and access self-paced training. However, the ideal way to access self-paced training is from the individual's desktop. This way they can do small portions of the training throughout the day. However, if there are too many interruptions throughout their day, they could use the PCs in the classroom.

The PC coordinator manages the PC training room schedule. Anyone wishing to use the room for any purpose will schedule it through the PC coordinator.

PC training can be provided in a variety of ways:

1. Purchase blocks of "tickets" to a local training facility and distribute them to people who require training. This has the added benefit of getting them off-site and away from distractions.

2. Hire a full-time training company. This works if you have many people to train, you have an equipped training room, and the training com-

pany has a pool of instructors who can cover all of your primary products. When the instructors are not in class, they can be used for one-on-one instruction or to develop courses for in-house software.

3. Hire college teachers on an as-needed basis. Most college instructors are available on an hourly basis for work outside the college. For most of your PC products, these people can teach the material for what they have already developed for use at the college! They also make great people for developing training sessions for in-house-developed software or new PC software upgrades. Again, you must have an equipped training room to do this.

## COMMENT

Promote training provided in the evenings by local colleges in the standard PC tools. Make schedules available and assist employees in filing claims for tuition reimbursement.

A major issue for providing training is when people reserve seats in a class and then do not show up. This prevents others from scheduling to attend training. A training policy must be established that anyone who makes a reservation and who does not show up (and stay for the class) will still be charged for their portion of the instructor's expense.

Half-day classes seem to work best as it allows time for the students to address pressing matters in their normal job.

## COMMENT

Training is your best tool to raise user productivity and satisfactions. Good training is your No. 1 defense against a deluge of simple questions to the help desk. In addition, after the help desk solves a problem, they may recommend to the PC coordinator that specific people receive additional training.

To back up the training, the PC coordinator maintains a library of reference material for use on a walk-up basis. This allows the IT staff and end users to investigate issues and find better ways to do a task. This library also includes a complete set of manuals for every approved product (past and present).

The PC coordinator's office should be near the training center and easily accessible to all users. It is important that users feel comfortable in approaching and discussing issues at any time during business hours.

A minimum level of support equipment is needed for a PC training operation. Most of the items will be stationary, but some may be portable and loaned to users. Keep on hand more than one of each item to be loaned. The following PC training equipment is considered the minimum needed:

- Whiteboard, which doubles as a projection screen
- PC LCD projector
- Tabletop lectern
- Flip chart (floor model)
- Digital or 35mm camera
- Camera copy stand with lights [If daylight film is used, blue (daylight rendering) photoflood lights should be used to provide the correct color balance.]
- VCR and color monitor
- Supply items: nonpermanent color markers, flip chart paper, camera supplies, and erasers

## [E]   PC Newsletter

A PC newsletter is a great place to spread the good news about maximizing your desktop tools. It is also a valuable communications tool for the help desk to explain ways to address common and systemic problems. If many users are having the same problem, workarounds can be detailed here. This is a great outreach tool for proactive issues, such as pending upgrades. Let everyone know what is coming and when. Publish your training schedule so everyone knows what is available. Remember your audience and keep the style conversational; stay away from technical jargon.

The newsletter may be published monthly, but not less than quarterly. It should announce forthcoming training programs, tell who completed which particular programs, announce new hardware or software availability, and list contact telephone numbers for PC or network assistance.

An information systems newsletter may be published instead if it incorporates the information needs of the PC users.

The newsletter can be part of the company intranet or printed as hardcopy. If printed as hardcopy, the size of a newsletter should be 8½- by 11-inch: printed on 11- by 17-inch paper and folded into an 8½- by 11-inch document. If this is not possible, stapled 8½- by 11-inch paper will do. Using desktop publishing software to produce the newsletter would be ideal, but high-end word processing software also can generate a professional looking newsletter. Graphics and photos will enhance its appearance even more. The "slicker" it is, the more likely it is to be read.

## COMMENT

Remember, its readers may not call a late newsletter a "news letter."

# § 9.03   PC ACQUISITION PROCEDURES

## [A]   Scope

The PC coordinator is responsible for the inventory control of all PC hardware (desktop, transportable, notebook, and hand-held) and software acquisitions. He/she also assists users with any future hardware and software requirements, and should be attuned to PC users' expected needs.

Purchase requisitions for PC hardware, software, and service or consulting contracts are forwarded to the information systems department's PC coordinator who approves the purchase requisitions, then forwards them to the purchasing department. Purchase requisitions are used only for approved budgeted expenditures.

## [B]   Hardware Acquisition

The procedures for hardware acquisition are:

1. **Approved hardware purchases.** Departments with budget approval for hardware expenditures complete a purchase requisition and forward it to the PC coordinator, who checks the equipment against the approved hardware listing. If the equipment conforms to the current standard, the purchase may be approved.

   If not on the approved list, the PC coordinator calls the requestor for clarification as to why an exception is ended (often they do not realize what is available). If the requestor cannot provide a satisfactory explanation and is adamant about the equipment desired, then the purchase requisition is returned with a memo explaining the problem. If a satisfactory explanation is provided, the coordinator dates and signs the purchase requisition and forwards it to the purchasing department.

   However, the purchase of unsanctioned hardware requires a request either for a one-time purchase or that the item be placed on the approved list. The procedure for either action is to write an explanatory memo to the coordinator containing the following information:
   - Item name and vendor's name and address
   - Cost of the item
   - Quantity required
   - Reason special item is required
   - What happens if item is not approved
   - Personnel (or outside service) responsible for item's maintenance
   - Personnel responsible for training and operation support

   If required, the coordinator will hold a meeting with the party interested in the new hardware. If alternate approved hardware is not acceptable to the user, and the request is not resolved, the coordinator contacts the manager of information systems for disposition of the problem.

   The information systems manager informs the requesting party by memo of his/her decision. If the equipment acquisition is still not approved, the user may appeal in writing to the PC advisory panel whose decision is final.

## COMMENT

Don't be the bottleneck in the process! Promptly resolve and pass on or pass back all requests. Your users will appreciate the prompt service. Good service will raise your users' opinion of you even higher. It takes just as long to check a request promptly as it does to check it two weeks later.

2. **Hardware loans.** It is very handy to have equipment to loan as needed. It is a very unpopular job holding borrowers to their commitments to return it on time, and with all of its pieces. If you have departments who often need to borrow equipment for things such as road shows, temporary offices, etc., then consider establishing their own pool of equipment. It is usually more cost-effective to maintain your own equipment pools than it is to rent equipment.

Departments requesting a loan of hardware from the PC idle assets room send a memo or e-mail to the coordinator with the following information. (In the event of an emergency, a telephone call will do.)

- What is to be loaned? Include a checklist of accessories (consider a notebook PC and its charger cords as one kit), such as cables and power supplies that must come back with the unit; otherwise, there will be a delay before loaning it again. Be sure to include any important software beyond the standard office tools.
- Expected length of time for the loan. A firm return date is critical.
- Reason for the loan.
- The department and person requesting the loan.
- Where the equipment will be used.
- The person who will be using the equipment.

The person to whom the equipment is released completes an "out card" that shows the date, time, equipment loaned, serial number, and to whom it is loaned. This card is signed by the receiving person and is filed, by date, under the requesting department. When the item is returned, the card is signed and dated by the person returning the item. The "out card" file is reviewed once per month. Delinquent borrowers are contacted. Cards for returned items are held on file for one year.

If the item is damaged, it is noted on the card, which becomes the source for a damage memo report completed by the PC coordinator. This memo is sent to the department manager of the borrower. Arrangements are made to repair or replace the piece of equipment. The

PC coordinator decides the cost, if any, that will be charged to the borrower's account for the repair or replacement. Ensure borrowers have removed their data and reload the system's standard configuration promptly on its return before shelving it.

3. **Notebook and hand-held PCs.** Company-owned notebook and hand-held PCs are useful because they allow a user to take the computer to the problem. As prices have dropped and computing power increased, notebook PCs are now considered as alternatives to desktop units in many offices. Companies spend a considerable amount of time maintaining security on their premises. Once a notebook PC leaves this shelter, it becomes highly vulnerable to theft and damage.

Before allowing notebook PCs to leave the premises, determine whose insurance covers loss or damage. If a notebook PC is stolen from someone's car, whose insurance covers the theft? If a notebook PC is damaged (and they are quite fragile), who covers the repairs? How much responsibility does the user have for safeguarding the unit?

Besides the loss of the hardware, notebook and hand-held PCs also contain company data. This hits the company in two ways. Before a notebook or hand-held PC leaves the company premises, a safety copy of the data should be made and left inside the facility.

a. The loss of use of data will delay whatever work was being done.

b. Company-confidential data can be compromised. What seems to be a random theft may have actually been industrial espionage. Why break into a building with all of its guards and security cameras when you can read the most sensitive files by stealing the CEO's notebook PC at an airport?

There is security software available that can be purchased for the most sensitive notebook and hand-held PCs that scramble everything on the hard disk every time a file is saved. This extra layer of software may slow system performance but keep your company's secrets off the front page of the newspaper.

## [C]   Software Acquisition

Software may be developed in-house or acquired from an outside source. Only consider in-house software development if no commercially available software can be found for less than the in-house cost. Availability of in-house programming personnel is also a consideration. The coordinator, who decides whether the actual programming effort is done in-house or contracted out, makes arrangements for any in-house-developed software. The cost of this effort is charged to the requesting user's department budget.

Software can be purchased for multiple users or a single user. Most software is purchased from vendors for a one-time cost, while some is only available for an annual fee. Also, upgrades are generally available for a single user or multiusers. Purchased off-the-shelf software is available in two forms. One is for the horizontal market, for widespread use across many different kinds of firms. Examples would be word processing or spreadsheet software. The other is for the vertical market, that is, for applications pertaining to given industries. This kind of software may be more flexible, because in some cases the source code is available, making it possible to alter the program to meet the user's own needs.

It is the coordinator's duty to continually seek newer and better software. He/she maintains a published list of approved software, continually updated with equipment newly approved to respond to new needs. Only approved software may be used. In the event the coordinator does not approve the requested software, the requesting party may appeal in writing to the PC advisory panel, whose decision is final. A part of the coordinator's role as a technical advisor is to include a budget for training, especially if this software is for several people. It will reduce the number of help-desk calls, raise user satisfaction, and ensure the company's investment returns benefits as quickly as possible.

Software acquisition procedures are as follows:

1. **Specially developed software.** A user requiring software not available by purchase works with the coordinator to define the needs. The coordinator then submits a memo to the person responsible for PC programming systems and provides enough information so that a project proposal can be developed and the cost estimated. (In some cases, the PC systems programmer and the coordinator may be the same person.) Project proposal information is reviewed with the user requesting the program. If time and money are available, a formal request in writing is issued by the user management.

   Program development is handled using the standard procedures for information systems program development. As long as no security problem exists, the new software is made available to other PC users.

2. **Purchased software.** The user sends a memo requesting the approved software to the coordinator who reviews the request and, upon approval, sends the software to the requesting party. An internal charge is made to the requesting department's account. If the software license is not available for reuse in the idle assets stock, the coordinator will issue a purchase requisition on behalf of the requesting department, which is forwarded to the purchasing unit.

   When the software is ready to install, send a copy of the class schedule to the requesting department along with the software manuals. Since this is from the approved software list, a class should be available. If no local classes are available, see if local junior colleges offer continuing education classes and forward their schedule and registration forms.

   It is critical that the PC coordinator maintain software licenses in a fireproof file cabinet, preferably off-site. In case of a disaster, you may be able to use those copies as authority to reload software into your replacement PCs without repurchasing it (often the manufacturer will even send a "gold" disk if you have adequate documentation). This license file is a primary company defense in case of a software audit. From the cost side, it is evidence for buying upgrades instead of purchasing new software.

3. **Software registration.** All software registration will be handled, completed, and mailed by the coordinator in the company's name.

4. **Software library.** Copies of all in-house-developed PC programs and the original licensed software, as well as backup copies of other purchased software, are maintained in a software library. Users with one-of-a-kind software are encouraged to have backup copies here as well. All software will be the most current version in use. Disks out of the shrinkwrap may require bug fixes. The library ensures the latest stable version is provided. The same applies to manuals' errata sheets. The library is under the control of the PC coordinator.

5. **Software demo disks.** Software demo disks will be provided to users requesting them. These can be provided by vendors or developed in-house, and are not charged to the user's account. Preferably these will run on a dedicated PC, as demos may introduce subtle configuration problems and not all software uninstalls cleanly.

## COMMENT

The software library may provide an opportunity for potential users to try software before obtaining their own copies. The library also contains proper documentation and user instructions so that software may be tested. The PC coordinator may be called on to demonstrate software or demo programs to potential users.

### [D] Communications Acquisitions

The company's data network analysts will identify acceptable network cards to be used in personal computers. These cards will be selected based on industry reliability and data throughput reports. The network analysts also will document and forward to the PC coordinator the proper operating system and driver settings for these cards for each supported operating system. No one is permitted to change the operating system network settings.

PC communication systems require some planning, by both the potential user and the coordinator acting as resource person for acquisitions. The coordinator must maintain an information file of LAN (and a lesser degree of WAN) hardware and software needed when considering future acquisitions or upgrading. There are a variety of LAN systems today including wired, wireless, and even one employing power supply lines as the transmitting media. Remote network users (mobile or home offices) use modems or the Internet to link with LAN systems.

For many years, the number of modems in companies grew and grew. Eventually, modem pools were established that could be accessed over the LAN. Most of this modem traffic has been replaced by Internet communications. If your application requires modem communication, be sure you have an analog telephone at the point it will be used. Send your request to the PC coordinator along with an explanation as to for what it will be used. The user is supplied with "approved" modem hardware and software with the required (or a higher) transmission rate and installed by the coordinator.

## COMMENT

Fax-modems allow for double-duty and convenience. Also, inbound fax traffic can be routed to e-mail accounts to reduce the number of fax machines required and the amount of paper floating around the office.

PC network communications acquisitions may require approval of the person responsible for corporate communications. This is especially true with WAN system interfacing or when linking two or more LAN systems. The gateway and modem selection also will require the approval of the organizational communications person. If this is not required, the coordinator will be fully responsible for installing the micro-LAN communications hookup and for providing the users with the required instructions and operations manuals for the online communications systems.

## COMMENT

Connectivity over the Internet is replacing information systems host-based systems. The pros, so far, outweigh the cons for this trend. Remote connection to a LAN opens the door to viruses and hackers. Ensure safeguards are in place—a backdoor to loading unauthorized software, etc.

One of the remaining major areas for modem requests is for employees to remotely access their electronic mail and network files while they are away from the office. Most home PCs come with modems and these people require access through the firewall via a login process. Some companies automatically set this up in all notebook PCs assuming they often will be used away from the office. When the modem is installed in their PC be sure all the necessary software to manage it is loaded as well.

Acquisitions and ongoing support of a LAN-based e-mail system fall under the domain of the coordinator who also is responsible for its maintenance, upgrading, and support.

### [E]   Database Access Acquisition

Database access is an important part of the personal computer since most end user–written PC programs are for report writing. Database access should always be arranged through a database administrator to ensure the query is efficiently coded. All database updates must be by way of IT developed or approved programs.

PC users requiring access to a mainframe database will consult with the PC manager regarding their needs. The manager reviews the user's needs and contacts the database administrator and the data administrator, if there is one, for user access. Both the database and data administrators' approvals are required for the user to access the information system's database. If another user (in the same workgroup) owns the database, or part of a network of PCs, the coordinator contacts the data administrator for written approval. If there is none, the coordinator resolves the problem with the user and sends a requesting memo to the database administrator for access.

The coordinator also arranges for new PC users to access the database and provides them with training and an operations manual that explains the programs being used and what each of the data elements represent. Normally, database access front-ends are provided to prevent the uneducated user from "dimming the lights" with poorly designed queries. Including a data dictionary explaining the contents of a field will improve reporting. Ambiguous field names cannot be used.

## § 9.04   PC OPERATIONS

### [A]   Overview

PC (desktop, transportable, notebook, and hand-held) operations use recommended manufacturers' operations instructions as outlined in the manufacturers' manuals. These manuals are to be supplemented with those provided by the information systems PC coordinator, which are both purchased and written in-house.

### [B]   PC Security

Theft of hardware is bad, but the cost to reproduce the data lost with the unit could be more than the value of the equipment. Desktop PCs or any stationary PC should be located in a safe environment. The person assigned nonstationary equipment assumes full responsibility for safekeeping both the hardware and the software. Preventing unauthorized access of any PC system should be of utmost concern to all employees.

Due to their light weight and small size, notebook PCs are very vulnerable to theft. A special pass should be attached to notebook PCs with the owner's photograph on it so guards can easily check them out of the facility.

*Physical location.* The room where computers are kept should be locked when not in use. If not possible, seriously consider employing a cable lock to deter any removal of the desktop computer hardware. Keep portable computers in a safe place at all times, including when the hardware is in transit. All portable computers must be handled as "carry-on luggage" while on public transit. When PCs are being transported for a special event that does not permit them to be carried individually, permission must be requested in writing from the coordinator. Approval is granted in writing, along with the special one-time procedures to be followed for the event.

Today's technology encourages the use of the PC as a user information and learning instrument with the aid of self-paced tutorials or even the HELP key. The person responsible for the organization's PCs should not overlook this technology.

Various operations within the company may have differing degrees of autonomy, but the PC policies, enforced by the coordinator, apply to all PC users.

If a desktop PC is moved to a new permanent location within an area under the jurisdiction of the coordinator, the coordinator is informed in writing within 24 hours of the move. If the new area is not under the jurisdiction of the current coordinator, he/she must approve the move before it takes place and inform the asset manager and the new area's coordinator. The PC coordinator will in turn ensure there is adequate electrical and network connection available in the new location prior to moving the equipment.

*Access security.* Stationary PCs with a modem or network and/or hard drives with any restricted information will be required to have one of the following:

- A lock
- An access security board with a lock-slot, so the board can use a cable security system
- Personal access code software (in the event the PC does not have an available slot for an access security board) or use of a screen-saver password
- An access security board with a motion alarm (In the event a building alarm is available, and the situation warrants, an external connection to the building alarm system should be made. The alarm may be set to notify IT operations, and the firm's own security force, or an outside security service.)

*Software and data security.* Software disks held centrally are stored in a locked place. Data disks and backup tapes and disks are stored in a PC media safe or other such comparable device if so warranted by the data administrator or coordinator. Where practical, data backups are stored off-site for protection. Encourage users to back up their data directories to the LAN, which is in turn backed up daily and the media stored off-site. Off-site may just be a different building in the same complex.

## [C] Daily Operating Procedures

There are standard operating procedures applicable to all PC operations:

1. **Turning on the system.** To turn on the system, the operator follows the manufacturer's prescribed procedures. PCs should be rebooted at least once per week for reliable operation. Daily rebooting is recommended for critical systems.

# COMMENT

Approved power backup hardware is highly recommended in case of a power failure. If there is no backup, do not use the machines if a power failure is likely.

The operator checks to see that the monitor display and all peripheral equipment are operating properly. If not, consult the operating manual. The operator proceeds when the system is ready.

Check the batteries of portable computers having access to AC power supply. If the batteries require recharging (or to prolong battery life), use the available AC power supply. If the power supplied is outside the United States, be sure it is compatible with the hardware requirements.

2. **Turning off the system.** When turning off the system:
   - Remove any removable media.
   - Exit from operating system.
   - Turn off peripherals.
   - Turn off computer.
   - Turn off surge protect switch.
   - Check battery-powered PCs for recharging needs and, when necessary, recharge batteries as soon as possible.

3. **Daily operations.** Systems are checked daily by the administrator or user for:
   - Paper supply in printer. Add paper as needed.
   - Quality of printing. Replace ribbons or printer cartridges as needed.
   - Quality of monitor display. Adjust as needed.
   - Cleanliness of the computer equipment. Cleaning the equipment as needed may be done at the start or end of each workday, and at other times during the day when there is high-volume use.

4. **Weekly housekeeping.** The administrator/user vacuums or dusts off the keyboard and wipes clean the monitor glass once a week. If the heads are not often used, a once per month cleaning will suffice.

5. **Dust covers.** In areas with a higher than normal amount of airborne dust, dust covers should be used for PCs, keyboards, monitors, and other attached devices when not in use. For very dusty areas, use special keyboard covers that can be employed while using the keyboard. These require periodic replacement; the coordinator/administrator must maintain a supply.

## [D]   Operation Rules and Procedures

The following rules and procedures apply to the operation of all PCs:

1. No food or beverages on or near the hardware or software.
2. No smoking near the hardware or software.

3. A clean, cool, and dry air working environment is recommended for the computer.
4. The computer disks and reading heads must be at least 2 ft from telephones. Keep other magnetic devices away from the computer, disks, and tapes.

## COMMENT

One of the authors demagnetized some videotapes over some just-purchased software that was hidden under some papers. The new software disks were demagnetized, too.

5. Plug all computers and peripheral equipment into a surge protection unit. Noncomputer electric devices should not be plugged into the surge protection outlet or into the same wall plug with the surge protection device. Use only grounded electrical outlets. Plug company-critical equipment into a UPS with a signal to shut down the PC before the UPS batteries die.
6. No illegal copying of software is ever permitted.
7. No hardware or software may be removed from the firm's premises without the coordinator's written permission for each occasion. Portable computer systems used outside the workplace require a permission letter or ID card signed by the manager to be kept with the system at all times. The permission letter/ID card identifies who has permission to use and carry the authorized equipment and software. It also will contain the serial numbers of the units authorized and identifies the software contained in the system.
8. No personal hardware, software, or disks are allowed on the premises.
9. No hardware or software (including portable equipment) will be loaned to noncompany persons.
10. Removable media labels will be written with a permanent marker before they are applied to the media.
11. Removable media will be kept in their disk containers or storage unit when not in use.

## [E]   Backup Procedures

Backup procedures may vary within the same company. Not all data and software have the same value (although it is better to be safe if not sure). The following procedures are recommended:

1. **New software.** The PC coordinator who retains all the original media installs new purchased software. If subsequent upgrades require access to the media, they must be coordinated with the PC coordinator. This step is to reduce the company's liability of someone making illegal copies of the software that it owns.

2. **Hard drive backup procedures**
   a. At the end of each workday, all new data should be backed up onto LAN disks or tape. Some active transactions (such as word processing, billing, etc.) will need to be backed up more often.
   b. A backup copy of the hard drive data should be maintained on the LAN disk or tape.
3. **Removable media data.** When data is kept on removable media (floppies, Zip disks, CDs, etc.) and not on a hard drive, the disk is copied for backup. The two copies of the disks are never stored together. It is recommended that the backup copy be write-protected, if applicable.

---

## COMMENT

A small company in Florida had its PC system stolen along with the AR file, and no backup. It placed an ad in the newspaper promising it would not press charges and offering a reward if the PC was returned undamaged. The company got no response.

The U.S. Post Office in Washington backed up its PCs daily. But when the ninth floor of the building burned, so did its PCs and the backups that were stored in the desks under the PCs.

---

### [F]   PC System Crash

In case of a PC system crash, the operator writes down what occurred just prior to the crash and the time of the crash, then calls the coordinator/administrator for assistance. The machine should be left on, ideally with the error message displayed. Post a sign on the computer stating that the system has crashed and it is not to be used. Portable computers should be taken to the coordinator.

### [G]   Hardware Problems

For hardware problems, the operator refers to the operating manual. If the problem cannot be corrected, the problem and its effect on the hardware are noted, and the help desk is contacted. Post a sign on the (desktop) PC indicating it is not working and is not to be used. If a peripheral device does not work, a sign is placed on the device noting that it is out of order and indicating whether or not the computer is usable without the device.

### [H]   Software Problems

For software problems, the operator contacts the help desk. If the help desk cannot resolve the problem, the operator contacts the coordinator.

Before contacting anyone for assistance, the operator will:

1. Write down the details of what happened.
2. Make a list of what corrective measures were tried.
3. When assistance becomes available, bring the software up on the computer at the place where the problem occurred.

## [I]   Accessories and Supplies

PC accessories can improve productivity, reduce fatigue, and improve morale. These accessories and supply items are on a "recommended" or "approved list" provided by the coordinator. The approved vendors will carry listed items. This information helps when ordering through the purchasing department. The approved list will be published, updated, and distributed by the coordinator.

---

### COMMENT

PC supplies and minor accessories can, over the course of a year, amount to a large expense. Still, given the size of the items and the volumes, it is much easier to treat them as you would the pens and pencils in your office supplies. The PC coordinator should identify what items are acceptable (inkjet refills, toner cartridges, etc.) by brand and model, and purchasing will provide these items through their office supplies program.

---

The items can be purchased with the user's department petty cash fund or a budget requisition. Supply items are requisitioned from the unit responsible for office or computer supplies according to standard operating procedure.

Accessories are classified in two groups: ergonomic devices and productivity aids. (The following items are not identified by brand name.)

1. **Ergonomic devices.** PC ergonomic devices are to help the human body interact with the PC system and function with the least amount of fatigue, error, and bodily harm. The following types of ergonomic devices are available on the "recommended list" provided by the PC store:
   - Keyboard wrist rest
   - Mouse wrist rest
   - Foot rest
   - Ergonomic keyboard
   - Arm support
   - Ergonomic adjustable chair
   - Adjustable workstations for special employees
   - Radiation and/or glare monitor screen

**COMMENT**

Remember the requirements of the Americans with Disabilities Act!

2. **Productivity aids.** The following, if used properly, have been known to increase productivity:
   - Tilt 'n turn monitor stand
   - Copyholder (flex arm, attachable, or standard)
   - Copyholder light
   - Diskette storage devices
   - Cartridge storage devices
   - Desktop printer stand and/or organizer
   - PC roll-out keyboard system
   - Keyboard with mouse
   - Keyboard labels for F keys and/or other keys

## § 9.05  END-USER COMPUTER COMMITTEE

### [A]  Responsibilities

A committee provides policies and procedures to guide the selection, use, support, and training for end users of computers and peripheral devices. The end-user computer committee represents the users and their computer needs along with their needs concerning office equipment. The committee's duties include being a source of information for users, providing management with user needs, and policing operations to ensure that policies and procedures are being followed.

### [B]  Committee Organization

The committee is made up of no more than seven or fewer than three end-user unit managers. It provides the "voice of the customer" back to IT to assist them in managing a tool that they all use daily. The purchasing department furnishes a representative to the committee, as will the information systems unit. The chairperson is the information systems representative. If the company has an office manager, he/she should be a member. If the company has a graphics unit, the manager of that unit will be on the committee. Most companies have an engineering department with very unique technical needs, and it should be represented on the committee. The size of the committee will vary depending on the size and complexity of the company.

The committee provides policies and procedures to standardize training, and assistance and training for end users of computers and peripheral devices for the company. The committee will meet no more than once a month and call special meetings as needed. The committee will have notes taken of the meetings. A copy of the approved minutes will be provided to each committee member, the committee's file, the information systems manager, the information technology asset manager, the information technology end-user computer technician unit, and the administrative VP.

### [C]   Secondary Committee(s)

If the company has other sites in different cities, it will have a person, or chairperson, from each site reporting to the corporate committee. If the site is small enough, it will have only one person appointed by the local plant or operations manager. This person does the task for the corporate committee. He/she provides the committee with the location needs and the degree of compliance with the corporate policies and procedures. A copy of the information also will be provided to the local plant or operations manager. If a site is large enough, it will have a committee to resolve local problems and needs. The committee has three to nine members. The site's office manager, graphics unit, purchasing unit, and information systems units will each have a representative on the committee. The local plant or operations manager appoints the committee chairperson.

The committee provides policies and procedures to standardize and provide assistance and training for end users of computers and peripheral devices at the local level. The committee meets once a month and calls special meetings as needed. Notes will be taken of the meetings. A copy of the approved minutes will be provided to each committee member, the committee's file, the local information systems manager, the local information technology asset manager, primary company end users' computer committee, and the local plant or operations manager.

## § 9.06   END-USER TECHNICAL SUPPORT

### [A]   Overview

End-user technical support is available in several forms. The information systems organization provides some forms of support. Different vendors provide other end-user support. End-user support will be provided in one form or another for stand-alone computers and networked PC systems.

Payment for these services depends on company policies. The payment can come from one central source and/or department budgets. Whichever method is used, a record system will be maintained.

### [B]   The Resident Expert

Every business department seems to have at least one person with an aptitude for all things technical. This person is usually looking over your shoulder whenever you come to resolve a problem or to tune a system. Early on you can chose to fight this person (and lose) or enfranchise them as an extension of your staff. The resident expert concept means that you will ask them to handle all of the simple problems that arise in a department. They probably already do so. In exchange, you will give them priority service, first chance at new software classes that open, ready access to your technical library, and help with tougher problems. A thorough resident expert program will reduce the volume of simple user error calls and open a wide channel of business user feedback.

## [C]   Computer Technician

Computer technician is the title of the IT person who provides desk-side help with end-user computer and equipment problems. In either case, the person in charge of this unit reports to the manager of information systems. The end user contacts this unit when there is no help desk or the help desk cannot solve a problem. The problem may be with hardware, software, or a supply item.

The computer technician is always dispatched by the help desk (users are never given their direct telephone number). The problem-tracking database then provides utilization tracking. The computer technician should carry a cell phone or pager so they can proceed to their next call without always returning to their desk first. This communications path also allows them to "drop and run" when critical systems are having problems. If you have multiple PC technicians, consider assigning them to the primary support of specific areas to better understand the users' needs. They can still support other areas but will have deeper knowledge of specific departments. Another way is to assign them by technology but this will confuse your users. By nature, a PC technician is a generalist.

*Computer technician skill requirements.* The computer technician has general knowledge of the users' PC hardware and/or software uses, including supply items. The hardware and software are identified under their respective approved lists. For large, complex organizations, there are specialists for lesser-used equipment. The computer technician is called by the help desk if the computer operator has a problem the help desk cannot walk them through. It could be a problem where the computer technician requested a call to them the next time it happened. The computer technician will more often resolve end-user hardware problems than the help desk, while the help desk will more often solve the end-user's software operations problems. Help-desk personnel and computer technicians should get to know each other for their mutual benefit.

It is important that computer technicians have a good understanding of their users' business to recognize a priority call. This helps focus them on critical issues and less on "squeaky wheels." The technicians need patient temperaments so they can help users through basic and embarrassing mistakes without alienating them. Computer technicians are your primary trainers since they can provide a steady stream of tips to users with whom they are constantly in contact. The technicians who run calls must have a quick connection to someone they can refer to for priority resolution (who do I see next?) and for backup in a crisis. This person also is a prime source of feedback to your training and newsletter and should refer troubled users to the trainers.

*Computer technician resource requirements.* The computer technician will be provided with a tool kit to cover the kind of hardware he/she will need to resolve problems. This will be carried in an attaché case provided by the company. There will be a minimum of space for spare parts. Supply items that are often used should be stored close to the computer operation. Other items needed may be obtained by someone else, from the source, to save the technician's time. The computer technician also will be provided with a pager or mobile phone.

*Computer technician's responsibilities.* The technician will maintain a daily activity log. The computer technician should perform the following computer tasks at the user's site:

1. Replace faulty computer parts.
2. Perform hardware upgrades.
3. Check connection cords.
4. Run a virus check and remove any viruses.
5. Check operation of modem.
6. Reformat hard drive.
7. Reload operating system.
8. Load new software and confirm it is operational.
9. Install hardware accessories.
10. Perform routine diagnostics.
11. Remove any unauthorized software from computer.
12. Disconnect and/or remove unauthorized hardware. The unauthorized hardware device will be turned over to PC coordinator.

At times there may be hardware problems requiring the user's computer or attached devices to be taken back to the repair shop. If the time the equipment is away from its operating area becomes a problem, the computer technician will arrange for a loaner to be provided. The loan will be only for the time the user's equipment is not available. If the loaner is the functional equivalent to the old one, then leave it. Expect loaners that are superior to the old unit to be difficult to get back. Given the time necessary to copy files from the loaner back to the old unit, it may not be worth the fight.

*The computer technician's work log.* While working, the technician should look for any bootlegged or pirated software. Any that is found is immediately deleted. If any is found, record it in the log. If any unauthorized hardware is attached to the desktop computer, it will be confiscated and delivered to the IT manager. It also will be recorded in the daily log sheet. The superior will acknowledge acceptance of the equipment by signing the computer technician's daily log sheet.

*Weekly computer technician's report.* The charge time will be portal to portal. The charge time is summarized by user, user's unit, and other duties not charged to a user. Any administration or other nonuser charge time is prorated to service calls. If the company has an interdepartmental charge system, the end-user's department is charged for the service time for the maintenance. How these costs are handled will depend on the company's accounting practice.

The computer technician writes a short weekly report to the technical unit's manager. The report notes any special hardware or software problems occurring during the week. Any operator problems needing resolution will be recommended. Can the operator problems be remedied with operator training, new operation manuals, or equipment? If the operator problem deals with an ergonomics issue, state what the problem is in the report.

## [D]   Software Support

There will be software that is not on the current approved computer software list, but is in the asset management software database. PC end users who employ the software must have it approved for support before a computer technician can help with the problem. Some of the end users using software will be assigned to a computer technician if the help desk cannot be of assistance. The technician will pull the software file folder for the programs and review the documentation before going to the end user's workplace.

Computer technicians are not expected to solve all the end-user problems they encounter. There will be special hardware and/or software technicians who are not generalists. They will work at the company sites needing their special skills. When the help desk contacts the IT unit for computer support, they will need to provide information to have the proper technician answer the service call.

### COMMENT

Consider an outside support contract for critical software you cannot support. For example, two vocal users needed PageMaker to build company newsletters. It was not feasible to train or hire a support person for them. Instead, an open purchase order was arranged for outside support as needed.

The asset management software database has the inventory information of legally owned company software. All software on the approved computer software list is on the asset management software database. Not all asset management software database programs will be found on the approved computer software list. The technician will not resolve all software problems for these programs. The kind of software will determine its solution source.

1.  **End-user computer software.** The software for end users is found on the approved computer software list. The help desk and the IT technical support unit support this software.

2. **IT computer software.** The software for the IT units is on the approved computer software list. The IT programming unit supports this software. Obviously, games, football pools, questionable photographs, etc., are not a part of the company's business and can be removed.

3. **Company IT unit's computer software.** Other IT units using purchased packaged software may call on the IT technical support unit for assistance. If the IT programming unit developed the software, it should be contacted for support. This software is in the asset management software database, but seldom found on the approved computer software list.

4. **Special computer software.** All software is required to be in the asset management software database. This software can include several types of programs and may be supported by information systems. If the software is not found on the asset management software database, it will not be supported. The question will be asked: How did the user come into possession of the software?

   Some special computer software, not on the approved computer software list, but on the asset management software database, can be identified as follows:

   a. **End-user software still in use.** End users can use software that is no longer available but is still supported. The software may no longer be available on the market or is about to be replaced. There is no need to replace the software at present. This software will be supported. Often this software was on the hard drive of the last PC which was on the hard drive of the PC before it. . . . Users don't know why it is there but are afraid to remove it.

   b. **Mainframe computer operations software.** This software is used for mainframe operations and is not available to end users of PC systems. IT operations programmers support this software. The IT programming unit may help IT computer operations if it developed the program(s).

   c. **Software for special applications.** This software is purchased for specially approved application and/or hardware. The software will not be supported. The department that arranged to acquire the software is responsible for obtaining the needed support.

   d. **Software testing.** Purchased software for testing for possible future use will not be supported. The person who acquired the program(s) will seek his/her needed support from the vendor.

   e. **Turnkey software operations.** The vendor will support contracts drawn for vendor-developed, turnkey-operated systems.

## [E]  Network Computer Technical Support

Networked PC systems and workgroup systems are more complex. Their hardware configurations and support needs are more intricate. The network of computers depends on the system server. A network is unique; by itself it can shut down all computing in an enterprise—a single point of failure. The system server computer may have a database. All this requires more support from the information systems' IT units than what the stand-alone PCs require. There will be the need for support from the following IT units:

1. **IT technical support unit.** This unit support is available for network or workgroup operations. The IT technical support unit can store more spare parts for the system at the user site. There should be a more technically knowledgeable person, such as a lead administrator, of the system operation to resolve some day-to-day operation problems.

    The technical support unit provides communications support for a local area network system. If a gateway connection is needed, that technician will handle it.

    The technical support unit works with the workgroup's lead administrator for any training needs. If the technical support unit has an IT trainer, this person will provide assistance. If there is no IT training unit, the company training department or a training vendor can be used. The following types of assistance could help with training:
    a. Vendor tutorial software
    b. Third-party videotapes or CBTs
    c. Programmed instruction packages
    d. Audio instruction procedures
    e. Operator instructional manuals
    f. Troubleshooting program instructions
    g. Lectures and demonstrations
    h. Pretest assessments for end users
2. **IT programming support.** The network or workgroup system developed by IT programming will be supported by them.
3. **Database support.** The information systems database unit will be fully involved with any database problems. The database unit representative can restrict access to database file information to prevent files being corrupted. Database support personnel are available to help with any backup and recovery procedures.


## [F]  Computer Ergonomics Support

If the company has an environmental ergonomics unit, it should be available to provide service to the information systems units. If the service is unavailable, consulting firms are available for this kind of support. Most ergonomic problems do not require a consultant. Someone is selected in the end-user technical support unit and trained. This person will provide support to IT units and end users of computer devices. College courses and short commercial programs on ergonomics are now available. Books and periodicals also are available.

COMMENT

The Human Factors and Ergomonics Society is a national organization with local chapters. They can be reached at *www.hfes.org.*

AliMed publishes an excellent ergonomics and occupational health catalog. They can be reached at 800-225-2610 or at *www.alimed.com.*

## [G]   Help Desk

A help desk provides a central point of contact for all users who are experiencing a problem. A well-run help desk is critical to user satisfaction. In years gone by, users "just knew" who to call. If they had a computer problem, they left a message on a specific person's phone (usually a programmer) and waited for them to call back. If that person was on vacation or out sick, they had no way of knowing. If that person did not know how to solve the problem, it did not matter, as they would find someone for the user who did. This was very personal customer service. A very hit-or-miss situation.

A help desk acts as a buffer between the users and the IT department. The help desk should be informed who will be out of the office, and when. They should have a matrix of who to call for support for each system first, who to call next, etc. The help-desk technicians should resolve all of the simple calls that used to interrupt the kindly but very busy programmer. In an emergency, such as a network outage, all users call the help desk to get updates instead of each user calling their favorite programmer.

An early decision is the level of service you want the help desk to provide. Your staffing level will determine how quickly a call will be answered. Certain times of the day will be busier than others so use your call-tracking database to chart the time of day and the day of week when your call volume peaks. You will have greatest customer satisfaction if the telephone is answered within five rings and the technician answering the phone resolves the problem.

The second decision ties closely to the first in that now that the phone is answered promptly, can the technician resolve the call? How much technical depth do you want on the help desk? One strategy is to use nontechnical (low-paid) people to answer the telephone, ask a few questions to identify whom to refer the call to and then pass on the message. In this model, the customer twiddles their thumbs and awaits a call from a technician. Another approach is to use technical people to resolve the questions as they come in and refer difficult problems to the appropriate technician. Both approaches work but which one is right for your facility?

Another question is if the help desk resides in your facility or is provided by an outside company. The advantage of the inside help desk is that the people learn about your facility's operations, insider jargon, who works where, and allows the technicians an opportunity to be on a more personal basis with your users. The help desk also can take walk-up requests. Using an outside provider allows them to staff for the peaks and valleys but you lose a great deal of control over who is answering the telephone.

With this tradeoff in mind, consider that the person answering the help-desk telephone will have more one-on-one contact with your users than you will. A bad experience calling the help desk will translate into a black mark on your IT department no matter how many times you explain that these people are a contracted service.

Help-desk calls tend to come in waves. During the quiet periods, the technicians can get a bit of rest and monitor vital system activities. This monitoring of network volumes, mainframe job flows, and the pattern of incoming calls provide the IT manager with some early warning of data system problems.

Some companies rotate their programmers and PC technicians through the help desk during peak periods so they can listen to some of the user calls. This is a valuable opportunity for the help-desk staff to learn more about their systems and for the programmers to hear some of the problems their systems cause end users.

Contracted help-desk service arrangements will require an accurate assessment of the level of help needed by end users. Determine the costs involved before soliciting bids from vendors. Requests for vendor bid proposals are sent to three or more vendors. The request letter identifies the contact person for the service. Include an expected date for the bid proposal to be submitted.

A key cost driver for contracted help-desk services is the level of service provided. If all that is expected is taking a message and asking a few scripted questions, then just about anyone—anywhere—can take your call. The result is to dispatch a technician. This is synonymous with a simple answering service. Another cost driver is the required response time—how many rings before the call must be picked up?

But if help-desk staffers are expected to provide some level of problem resolution during the initial contact, they need the ability to access your data systems for troubleshooting. This may require an on-site office or a dedicated high-speed data line. They must be dedicated to your company's support so anyone answering the phone can be anywhere to take the message.

Security also is a major concern. High-volume calls for help desks are password problems. Since the desk needs access to change these, they may pose a security risk.

*Vendor contracting.* After the bid proposals are received, they are compared with each other. Lowest bidders do not always provide the best service. Beware of startup companies without verifiable experience. Calculate the costs for providing the service in-house. This provides a baseline to evaluate the bids.

Write a short-duration flexible contract when beginning a relationship with a new vendor. This provides information to both the vendor and the company about the contents of the final contract. The company's legal representatives review the contract and make recommendations before it is signed.

*Budgeting proposal.* Budget proposals for vendor service per call or in-house help-desk operations require a large contingency budget—50 percent or more of the original amount is not unreasonable. A contingency amount should be budgeted even for a flat-sum contract. An amount equal to 10 to 20 percent should be sufficient.

*In-house help desk.* An in-house help desk often starts as a pilot project. As the bugs are worked out, it can accommodate more internal customers. Start an in-house help desk with a lump-sum budget. Record the number of contacts by unit and the time spent per contact. This will be helpful for future planning.

There are several ways to operate an in-house help desk. Which one you use depends on corporate culture, union concerns, etc. The following things should be considered when operating an in-house help desk:

1.  **Operations.** Record conversations to provide an audit trail of the dialogue between the user and the help-desk technician. This reduces and simplifies note-taking by the help-desk staff. Use a voice-mail system to avoid busy signals or no answer when calling the help desk.
2.  **Facility.** The help-desk work area provides rapid access to information needs. It is ergonomically suitable for the tasks of the help-desk staff. The job is confining and any ergonomic assistance would help reduce the burnout rate for this job. Any change or rotation of duties also would prolong the life of the help-desk technician.

A help desk is a built-in feedback mechanism for finding out how your systems perform. Use the data!

The help desk's demeanor is critical. Users' opinion of your department will be greatly shaped by the help desk; they are the ones users talk to most. The help-desk staff must be able to work under pressure. Abusive callers should be forwarded to the help-desk supervisor.

## [H] Maintenance Contracting

All hardware may not be maintained in-house. In some instances, vendor equipment service contracting for some devices might be a better solution. Some peripheral devices are best maintained using vendor contracts. Some leased items include service agreements. Contracts can specify an unlimited number of service calls or charges on a by-call basis. Contracts can provide for spare parts or parts can be charged as installed. Some vendors can offer an array of equipment they can service. Service can be provided for normal working hours or around the clock.

There can be one or more service vendors. There are firms providing a full-service blanket for most all hardware. Other firms service one or more machines. Consider these options when deciding the service best for the company.

If considering vendors, solicit bids. The IT manager or his/her representative and the end-user committee review the bid proposals. The optimum vendor is selected and receives the contract. The end-user charges for this service will be determined. There is no problem if company policy dictates how costs are internally handled. If no such policy exists, the end-user committee and information systems management resolve the issue.

Before any maintenance contracts are signed, the legal representative of the company reviews them. Upon approval, the authorized management personnel sign them. Purchasing is contacted regarding such contracts. The procedure followed will be the corporate procedure for contracting services.

Sometimes you must outsource repairs for:

- Parts availability—they won't sell them to you.
- Technical expertise.
- Warranty work—usually only good if you pack it up and deliver back to the factory or a rep. This may not be worthwhile in the case of PCs unless you can afford to remove them from service and send them away.

Equipment with moving parts (like printers) has a higher ongoing maintenance cost than solid-state devices.

Using your asset database, compare the cost of a maintenance contract to the cost of buying several spare devices. Use your spares to replace broken equipment and then send the damaged material out for service on a time-and-materials basis.

A key component of maintenance contracts is the hours of coverage. Normal working hours coverage is cheapest and "24/7" is very expensive. Keep in mind that this is response time—not maximum resolution time.

# 10

# LOCAL AREA NETWORKS: KEEPING THINGS RUNNING

# § 10.01  LOCAL AREA NETWORK POLICIES

## [A]  Overview

A local area network (LAN) can be from as small as a few personal computers connected together to all of the PCs in a huge building. A wide area network (WAN) is another term for a network covering a larger area. Whichever term you use, they mean that you are providing a shared service through a central server (few companies use peer-to-peer). Some LANs are intended to serve a single department or workgroup. This arrangement may provide some performance protection from the rest of the facility. This also may be advisable for security reasons.

It is important for IT professionals to remember that this is a service business. The LAN is considered in most companies to be an essential IT service. If the LAN fails, it is a major crisis. The reason for this is the tremendous strides made over the last two decades in LAN reliability. In the past, if the LAN worked at all, workers were happy. Now if the LAN is dead, people become very angry. They expect it to be as reliable as electrical service—plug in and there it is! LAN administrators are victims of their own success.

A LAN is popular because it makes so many things accessible to desktop PCs. In a sense, it is a doorway into all of the data processing tools. Some of these capabilities include:

- Mainframe access—instead of a separate dumb terminal on your desk, now your PC runs a terminal emulation package.
- Print sharing—allows the company to buy fewer and faster printers. Also frees space on every desktop.
- Sharing files and folders—a central repository for shared information sources, similar to a department's filing cabinet and bulletin board.
- Shared modem and fax pools—this is a big improvement over every person needing their own equipment.
- Internet communications through high-speed lines—research is quicker; applications can be more easily distributed.
- Electronic mail—virtually eliminated the mail clerk and a lot of the secretarial work in many companies.
- CD farm with multiple CD drives always loaded.

This list could go on and on. The key element is the sharing of resources is enabled by the use of a LAN. If the LAN does not work, then all sharing stops.

Workstations connect to the LAN server using wire (coaxial or twisted pair), radio frequency communications, or fiber optics. The type of connection is important for planning future expansions or upgrades. It is quite likely that your LAN uses a combination of all three. Your type of connection determines your maximum data communications capacity—the bigger the "pipe" the more water that flows.

A data network is a hugely complex thing. When you consider all the different components of it each with its own potential to fail, and that all of these items are working in sync despite who the manufacturer may be, it is a truly amazing thing.

Like all good things in life, bad things can happen to LANs. Problems can include:

- PC viruses—these spread quickly through a LAN. Just as fast as someone can send a file or open a program, viruses can spread. To protect your equipment against PC viruses, ensure that all data traffic passing into your LAN pass through an antivirus firewall. Similar to a firewall in a building (which stops the spread of flames), a LAN firewall provides a barrier against incoming viruses.
- Illegal uses—the faster the communications, the faster that someone can make illegal software copies.
- Access to confidential files—an electronic filing cabinet is much less secure than the metal cabinet in your office. Ensure that user-specific and departmental file folders have security to keep out the curious.

### [B]   LAN Policies

A local area network of connected PCs used by a department or workgroup can be to some extent autonomous from the rest of the organization. However, the more the workgroup using the LAN relies on corporate information systems for assistance, the less autonomy it has. Even with "total" autonomy, a LAN needs to comply with universal standards for hardware and software use. It does not have any more autonomy than that found with any stand-alone PC operation.

A local area network system can be a client/server operation employing an information systems server, or an autonomous local area network with its own server system. It can be a closed system or provided with a gateway for external network access. There is no restriction as to the hardware configuration of the group, as long as the equipment is justifiable.

The company is responsible for complying with certain industry practices. Responsibility for assuring that these practices are followed is delegated by management of the corporation to information systems management.

Policies common to all LANs:

- A person's user ID and password must remain confidential.
- All folders will default to full security for the author and no access by anyone else, unless granted by the folder owner.
- Outsiders cannot connect into the line at any time. They may not plug their own PCs into the network and be provided with LAN security. This is very important when consultants work in your facility.

## § 10.02   LAN COMPLIANCE PROCEDURES

### [A]   Overview

LAN computer systems can vary in configuration and process within the same corporation. However, all LANs within the corporation will follow the LAN compliance procedures applicable to "common procedures." When operation needs are expanded beyond the common procedures, procedure documentation will conform to the requirements set by information systems.

## [B]  General Operations

This subsection covers general operations to be followed by the workgroup when operating its own local area network. Each has a person appointed as the workgroup's LAN computer coordinator (full- or part-time duty).

A LAN coordinator position is technical by nature and is concerned with the LAN networking components and server(s). This position typically does not deal directly with end users. In a small office, this position may be merged with the PC coordinator position and then they will both manage the LAN and users.

A LAN coordinator is often a network analyst with a detailed understanding of networking equipment capabilities and topographic design. This person would be expected to monitor and troubleshoot network traffic throughput problems. They would also monitor server usage (CPU and disk) to ensure adequate resources are always available and that anyone using an excessive amount of resources is investigated. (It could be an early indication of a serious problem.)

In most facilities, the LAN coordinator is dispatched by the help desk to address technical issues and reports the results back to them.

A LAN coordinator establishes and maintains the antivirus firewall, ensuring that all traffic is properly filtered. This tool will require regular updates. In addition, the coordinator schedules off-hours scans of the LAN server to protect against "infected" files that may have been loaded onto the LAN by authorized users.

The LAN coordinator establishes and maintains trusted connections with other LANs in the company for the easy exchange of information. These connections are still via the firewall.

They establish quotas (maximum amount of disk storage allowed per person) on the disk drives to ensure there is space for all users. They monitor file usage to identify candidates for archival from the disk onto tape or CD storage. The coordinator also schedules off-hours defragmentation of all server disks to ensure peak performance.

User security is an ongoing task. New users must be established and the files of departing employees must be reassigned to their replacement.

1.  **The LAN computer coordinator's responsibilities are to:**
    - Analyze current usage and project future growth to ensure adequate hardware, network, and software capacity.
    - Provide information and service for users.
    - Provide for informal and formal training.
    - Oversee operation policies.
    - Be a source for operation documentation.
    - Disseminate new operating information.
    - Provide for needed backup hardware and software.
    - Be the liaison between the LAN computer operation and corporate information systems.
    - Be a knowledge source for user applications.
    - Perform hardware maintenance.

- Manage server disks by archiving old files, defragmenting disks, and performing daily data backups.
- Maintain security for folders, establish new shares.
- Perform software updates.
- Ensure the physical security of the LAN server and network components.
- Establish the security profile for all new users, make changes as required, and remove security access from departing employees.
- Be the facilitator for disaster recovery.
- Be on call for after-hours problems.
- Maintain computer security procedures.
- Police system for unauthorized software.
- Maintain an operation performance problem log.
- Write a monthly exception report to the unit manager and IT computer operations manager.

2. **Workstation operations.** In most companies, the workstations require users to "log in" or identify themselves with a user ID and password. Based on this login, they are typically given access to the workstation as well as the LAN. Most of the LAN's operation (from a user's standpoint) is transparent.

3. **Operation rules and procedures.** When providing the rules and procedures to be followed by all system users, the LAN coordinator explains the rationale behind them.
   - No food or beverages close to the workstation area.
   - No smoking near software or hardware.
   - No telephones near computer media.
   - No illegal copying of software.
   - No personal software allowed.
   - No personal use of computer system.
   - No personal media allowed.
   - No hardware may be removed from department.

   Operators will inform the local area network computer coordinator of needed ergonomic devices. Those available are:
   - Keyboard wrist rest
   - Mouse wrist rest
   - Foot rest
   - Ergonomic keyboard
   - Arm support
   - Ergonomic adjustable chair
   - Adjustable workstations for employees with special needs
   - Radiation and/or glare monitor screen cover

# § 10.03  LAN SYSTEMS PROCEDURES

## [A]  Overview

In a local area network client/server operation, information systems computer operations provide the server(s) to which the workstations are connected. The following procedures for this type of LAN computer system operation help ensure the safe and efficient operation of the servers and the connected network. There could be more than one such LAN computer system within the corporation.

### [B]   IT Client/Server Support

The IT computer operations help desk provides support for general computer client/server operations and will be available for local area network users with operation problems. If it cannot handle a problem, it contacts a person who can.

The LAN computer coordinator for the local area network, appointed by the workgroup management, addresses particular technical operation concerns from its work area. This person also will be responsible for communicating the group's needs to IT computer operations and/or the systems unit, and has the following responsibilities:

- Assist the IT trainer with local area network training needs
- Provide informal training to computer workstation users
- Be a knowledge source for user applications
- Be the information systems local area network contact
- Maintain a reference library of publications for the local area network

### [C]   LAN User Education

The LAN users receive information about and training for the use of its hardware and software. This will be the responsibility of the project management group installing the new system.

After the new system is operational, provisions are made for instructions for subsequent system changes. The local area network computer coordinator assists with this task.

Provisions are made for new employees using the LAN system; suggestions are self-paced learning instruments, such as:

- Computer tutorials
- Program learning manuals
- Audio instruction tapes
- VCR tapes/DVDs
- Operation manuals

The local area network computer coordinator assists with the training of new LAN computer workstation users and is, in addition, responsible for instructing the new user regarding the local area network's use of the computer system. The coordinator also informs users of pending operational changes and assists them once the changes are in place.

### [D]   Workstation Operations

Workstation operators have a responsibility to safeguard their equipment from harsh environments. The following are standard procedures for operators of terminals or workstations:

1. **Turning on the system.** To turn on the system, the operator follows the operating manual's prescribed procedures. The operator checks that the monitor display and all peripherals are operating properly. If not, the operator consults the manual and proceeds when the system is ready. If the workstation is not working properly, he/she contacts the help desk whose telephone number should be on the first page of the operating manual.

   Before contacting anyone for assistance, the operator will:
   • Write down the details of what happened.
   • Make a list of corrective measures tried.
   • When assistance is available, bring the computer system up to the place where the problem occurred.

2. **Turning off the system.** Turn off the system in the following sequence:
   a. Exit from the operating system.
   b. Turn off peripheral equipment.
   c. Turn off workstation.
   d. Remove all removable media.

3. **Daily operations.** Check hardware daily for:
   • Quality of monitor display. Adjust as needed.
   • Cleanliness of equipment. Clean equipment as needed at the start or end of each workday, and at other times of high-volume use.
     If the workstation has a printer:
   • Check paper supply in printer. Add paper as needed.
   • Check quality of printing. Replace ribbons or printer cartridges as needed.
     These actions are taken at the start or end of each workday. Some may be necessary more than once a day.

4. **Weekly housekeeping.** The administrator/user vacuums or dusts off the keyboard and wipes clean the monitor glass once a week. High-use diskette heads will be cleaned weekly. If the heads are not often used, once per month will suffice.

5. **Dust covers.** In areas with a higher than normal amount of airborne dust, dust covers are used for PCs, keyboards, monitors, and other attached devices when not in use. For very dusty areas, use special keyboard covers that can be employed while using the keyboard. Since these special covers require periodic replacement, a supply should be maintained by the PC coordinator/administrator.

6. **Removable media backup.** When data is kept on removable media and not on a hard disk, copy it for backup. Do not store both original and backup media together. The backup copy must be write-protected.

## [E] Operation Rules

The following rules apply to all persons using the computer system:

• No food or beverages on or near the hardware or software.
• No smoking near the hardware or software.

- The computer and removable media must be at least 2 ft from telephones. Keep magnetic devices away from the computer, disks, and tapes.
- No illegal copying of software is permitted.
- No hardware or software may be removed from the firm's premises without written permission.
- No personal hardware, software, or disks are permitted on the premises.
- No down- or uploading of any noncompany software or data is permitted.

## [F]  Accessories

Accessories are classified into two groups, ergonomic devices and productivity devices, which are to be purchased and coordinated by the local area network computer coordinator. (The following items are not identified by brand name.)

1. **Ergonomic devices.** Workstation ergonomic devices help the human body interact with the computer system and function with the least amount of fatigue, error, and bodily harm. The following types are available:
   - Keyboard wrist rest
   - Mouse wrist rest
   - Foot rest
   - Ergonomic keyboard
   - Arm support
   - Ergonomic adjustable chair
   - Adjustable workstations for employees with special needs
   - Radiation and/or glare monitor screen cover

### COMMENT

Remember the requirements of the Americans with Disabilities Act!

2. **Productivity aids.** The following, if used properly, can increase productivity:
   - Tilt 'n turn monitor stand
   - Copyholders
   - Copyholder and light
   - Removable media storage devices
   - Desktop print stand and/or organizer
   - PC roll-out keyboard system
   - Keyboard with mouse
   - Mouse holder
   - Keyboard labels for F keys and/or other keys

- Wastepaper container and paper shredder
- Workstations that include a drawer for personal items that can be locked
- Speaker telephone

## [G] Workgroup Newsletter

A workgroup newsletter is a great place to incorporate feedback from the help desk for systemic problems. If a large number of users are having the same problem, workarounds can be detailed here. This is a great outreach tool for proactive issues, such as pending upgrades. Remember your audience and keep the style conversational and stay away from technical jargon.

The newsletter may be published monthly, but not less than quarterly. It should announce forthcoming training programs, tell who completed what programs, announce new hardware or software availability, list hardware and software available for hands-on experience in the computer store, and list contact telephone numbers for PC or network assistance.

An information systems newsletter may take the place of a separate workgroup newsletter if it incorporates the information needs of the workgroup users.

The newsletter can be part of the company intranet or printed as hardcopy. If printed as hardcopy, the size of a newsletter should be 8½- by 11-inches: printed on 11- by 17-inch paper and folded into an 8½- by 11-inch document. If this is not possible, stapled 8½- by 11-inch paper will do. Using desktop publishing software to produce the newsletter would be ideal, but high-end word processing software also can generate a professional looking newsletter. Graphics and photos will enhance its appearance even more. The "slicker" it is, the more likely it will be read.

# 11

# IT AUDITS: CHECKING YOUR WORK

# § 11.01   MANAGEMENT OBJECTIVES AND AUDIT POLICIES

## [A]   Overview

This chapter covers the policies needed to ensure that professional information systems management objectives are maintained. These policies direct management so that resources can be properly utilized and monitored. Actions to take, identify, and implement both specific and comprehensive IT organization objectives include the following:

- Develop IT departmental policies and standards for systems, programming, operations, and users.
- Ensure prompt and continuous implementation of those policies and standards.
- Ensure projects are completed on schedule and within budget.
- Develop a cooperative attitude among IT personnel concerning users' needs.
- Develop and maintain priorities.
- Develop and maintain ongoing IT planning.
- Inform top management of the current and potential benefits of information systems.
- Maintain optimal budgeting for personnel, hardware, and software.
- Develop a departmentwide drive for accuracy.

## [B]   Management Resource Planning

IT management is responsible for the constant monitoring of the performance and output of areas under its direct control. This covers packaged applications, software development, and operating systems. End-user input should be welcomed. IT management's responsibilities for planning and directing the use of proposed resources, including personnel, hardware, and software, are defined as follows:

- Personnel requirements are a major element of resource planning. IT managers are responsible for having the requisite personnel required for current and planned needs. Planned needs will come from the strategic plans developed by the process noted in Chapter 1, Policies and Plans: Setting the Framework.
- Hardware and software planning is influenced by user justification, selection, and use of equipment resources. Requirements for change, replacement, and additions to current hardware and software are determined by the interplay of various factors. Continuous monitoring of hardware and software performance is necessary to determine the most effective course of action.
- Network resource planning is required so different computer systems can interact efficiently. The development of technology in this area is

constantly changing, requiring the attention of proactive IT management to remain current.
- A database is a volatile resource requiring constant attention to avoid misuse and to provide for the expanding demand for data.

## [C]   Strategic Planning

IT management uses either the firm's strategic business plan as a guide or its own long-range planning, taking into account long-term user needs. Short-range planning must take into consideration long-range strategic plans.

IT management also must be prepared to downsize or expand the information systems areas affected by strategic planning needs. (See § 1.05, "IT Strategic Planning Process.")

## [D]   Audit Policies

The information systems operation must satisfy the requirements of both IT audit forms: the management audit and the systems audit. The systems audit is performed by a firm's inside or outside auditors, and is mostly concerned with the system controls and audit trails. A management audit can be a self-evaluation or one performed by an outside audit firm with IT management skills.

## COMMENT

An IT operation can pass a systems audit but fail a management audit, in which case the firm pays for more than it gets. Unfortunately, not so many management audits are performed as systems audits or the turnover of IT management personnel would be greater than it is now.

It is common for a CPA firm to run a systems audit of the IT operations when it conducts an audit program. An audit policy should exist ensuring IT is able to have both systems and management audits.

*Systems audit requirement policy.* An IT operation's controls should minimize undesirable events and also alert system users to potential problems. The system controls should contain an audit trail that is maintained at all times.

*Management audit requirements policy.* Management audit policy should contain provisions enabling the system to satisfy a systems audit. They should cover the following:

1. **Management control.** Comparison of IT costs with the amount that has been budgeted. The amount budgeted must be reasonable for the level and type of service provided.

2. **Resource allocation**
   a. Maintenance of priorities in line with needs
   b. Assurance that talent is available for required projects
3. **Project management audits**
   a. Proper project controls in place
   b. Contingency planning in place for unforeseen problems
   c. Project post-implementation audit procedures in place and used
4. **Technology audit**
   a. Verification of quality of hardware and software
   b. Verification of staff's technical skills
   c. Verification that application systems have:
      • Proper documentation
      • Backup procedures
      • Acceptable programming quality
      • Standards for maintenance procedures
5. **Operations management audit to assure:**
   a. Proper machine use
   b. Acceptable recovery and security procedures
   c. Acceptable employee skills levels
   d. Maintenance of low rerun time
   e. Downtime minimums for system
   f. Cost-justified operations expenses

## [E]   The Systems Development Cycle Audit

Correct methodologies must be used so audit standards are met. The following attributes need to be assured:

1. **Preliminary analysis.** The investigatory work and analyses required for a proposed system have been done.
2. **User service request evaluation.** The current system operation, including cost to user, has been assessed. Potential tangible and intangible benefits are detailed and ultimate objectives of requested services assessed.
3. **Requirements and objectives.** Detailed definitions are assembled and descriptions of requirements and objectives are identified by the users.
4. **System design.** The design is approached in a standard manner, to satisfy the users' needs.
5. **User nomenclature.** User terminology is defined at the lowest level of required detail for the project.
6. **Manual procedure specifications.** The proper level of detail is present in all manual operations specifications that interface with the computer system.
7. **Computer programming.** Programs are prepared to process data to meet specifications of output and control. Manual inputs and outputs should be compatible with system programs.

8. **Documentation.** Operations and user manuals are current and easily understood.
9. **Implementation**
   a. Require program testing.
   b. Conduct user and operations training.
   c. Develop plan for conversion with contingency backups.
   d. Establish self-post-implementation plan for final project evaluation.

## § 11.02   MANAGEMENT PLANNING

### [A]   Overview

IT planning is becoming more important because of its impact on overall strategic planning for the business. The need for joint user and IT operations planning has increased, because the more complex systems become, the more vulnerable they are to obsolescence.

A rapidly changing outside environment increases the need for planning. State and federal regulations can impose program changes, and customer or market demands may require deploying new technology. The wise IT manager is attuned to pending changes.

In small IT departments, the IT manager may be responsible for all management planning. Large departments may have a staff assistant or a planning staff unit for most of the work.

### [B]   Develop Your IT Plan

1. **Assign responsibility.** Planning responsibility is a staff-level function. Personnel responsible report to the IT manager and should have the following qualities:
   a. Good knowledge of existing and planned applications
   b. Good knowledge of IT operations
   c. Good knowledge of the firm's operations, requiring ongoing contacts (both formal and informal) with users and users' management
   d. Good organizational, budgeting, and cost-accounting skills
   e. Good knowledge of currently used software and hardware and an awareness of pending releases by manufacturers and vendors
   f. Good technical writing skills
   g. Credibility within the firm
2. **Prepare a plan context**
   a. Obtain written record of history and success record of IT department.
   b. Maintain ongoing record of current activities and commitments—how projects fared keeping to time schedules.
   c. Know current constraints of IT department, such as:

- Budgeting status
- Status of current hardware and software
- Status of IT personnel, including good and bad points
- Users' management skill levels

  d.  Review asset management reports to establish a baseline of current technology on premises.

3. **Identify organizational goals.** Maintain list of organizational goals and users' goals. Beware of goal conflicts. Require benchmarks to determine if progress is being made toward achieving goals.

4. **Identify organizational goals for IT planning.** Ensure that planning is accomplished and budget can be justified.

5. **Identify planning priorities.** Select first those applications which will help gain IT credibility.

6. **Identify resources required**
   - Personnel
   - Hardware
   - Software
   - Vendors with credibility

## [C]  Keep Your IT Plan Current

Because of changing needs and the availability of new technology, periodic updating of IT plans is required. Perform a formal review twice a year. Do not preclude updating the plan in the event of a major change.

Along with the plan status review, perform a risk analysis to review the probability of risk for all planned projects.

**COMMENT**

Do not undertake too many risky projects at any one time.

# § 11.03  RESOURCE MANAGEMENT

## [A]  Scope

This section defines management's responsibilities for directing the use of IT resources, both expense and capital investment items. To properly manage resources, projected requirements are made for personnel, supplies, outside services, purchased software, and hardware.

## [B]  Inventory of Resources

IT management maintains an ongoing resource inventory. Monitor personnel, software, and hardware with short-term and strategic planning requirements in view. Establish an asset management system for controlling companywide computer hardware and software resources.

1. **IT personnel organization.** Maintain an organizational chart of the IT department, containing portraits of management personnel in position boxes.

   List the talent available within each unit of the IT department in a personnel skills inventory. In addition, a personnel profile needs–analysis of each unit is required, making it possible to fill current and projected needs.

   ## COMMENT

   An oil company, with its large computer services organization, found this picture-at-a-glance of organizational hierarchy helpful.

2. **Software inventory.** Maintain a listing of currently active (in-house-developed and purchased) software. The software coordinator will be responsible for making and keeping this list up to date.
   a. Purchased software information includes:
      • Dates of purchases
      • Vendor
      • Version number
      • Purchase price
      • Record of user problems
      • Type of vendor support
      • Future software needs
   b. In-house-programmed software information consists of:
      • Dates programs were written
      • Revision dates for programs
      • Author(s) of program(s)
      • Program reviser (if any)
      • A record of user problems
      • Future programming needs
3. **Hardware inventory.** A listing of current hardware is maintained and grouped as follows:
   a. Mainframe computers
   b. Peripheral devices
   c. Minicomputers
   d. PCs owned by IT department
   e. PCs owned by other users
   f. Peripheral devices owned by users
   g. Expected future purchases of hardware

### [C]   Organizational Structure of IT

The organizational structure of information systems is governed by the size and complexity of IT operations. Its distribution, whether centralized or decentralized, also affects its organizational structure.

Standardization is used throughout IT and benefits all information systems, whether centralized, decentralized, or distributed. Its organization is structured so that corresponding user levels can be identified. The three levels, with increasingly detailed procedures, are:

1.  **Policy level.** This level involves IT and user management working primarily with long-range planning. Policies are refined at this level. Procedures can then be written at lower levels executing the defined policies and agreements. The relationships at this management level are both formal and informal.

2.  **Supervisory level.** This level makes possible the enforcement of policies by ensuring that IT units develop proper procedures. The user supervisory level works with information systems ensuring that user policies are defined in written procedures. Both user and IT supervisors work on a day-to-day basis with the procedures.

    Procedures may be altered if both the supervisors and managers agree that policies are still being maintained. The relationships at this management level are both formal and informal.

3.  **Operation level.** The operations, or working, level relationships of IT personnel and users are both formal and informal. At this level IT develops the procedures that user operating personnel execute. The process steps are documented, while day-to-day contacts are less formal.

## § 11.04   IT SYSTEMS AUDIT

### [A]   Purpose

The following are information systems audit procedures ensuring that minimum standards have been established.

### [B]   Systems and Programming

Systems and programming procedures adequately meet auditing standards when the following have been accomplished:

1.  The company's application development/acquisition methodology is formalized.
2.  Written programming standards covering coding techniques, documentation, testing, acceptance, and conversion are satisfactory.
3.  The segregation of duties into application program development, cataloging of programs for production, and operating systems programming activities are established.

4. Control of program changes is maintained.
5. Program documentation library procedures are employed ensuring adherence to systems/programming standards.
6. Controls of online programming terminals are maintained.
7. Program documentation, including program changes, is complete.

### [C]  Computer Operations

Computer operations procedures adequately meet auditing standards when the following have been accomplished:

1. Compliance with computer operations standards and procedures.
2. Management uses reporting mechanisms to monitor IT operations.
3. Equipment maintenance is performed and records of equipment problems are maintained.
4. The computer center has proper physical and data security.
5. Controls are maintained over information systems hardware, files, databases, and production program libraries.
6. Proper separation of duties is maintained among input, computer operations, and output.
7. A disaster prevention and recovery plan is documented, tested, and in effect.
8. Adequate emergency power supply is in place.
9. Operating systems procedures are in effect.
   a. Duties are separated between production data file maintenance and operating systems maintenance.
   b. Documentation of the operating systems is complete.
   c. Controls are in place for changes to the operating systems.
   d. Controls are in place for utility programs, primarily those with production data or program file-altering capabilities.
10. Data controls are adequate.
    a. Evaluate control points for audit trails.
    b. Compliance exists with written procedures.
    c. Control totals generated at input are reconciled at each turnover point.
    d. There is control of negotiable or sensitive documents generated by computer.
    e. Compliance exists with data security policies for online terminals.

### [D]  Telecommunications and Networks

When telecommunications or networks are employed, audit procedures ascertain that the following are in compliance:

1. A written data security policy is in effect covering all applications employing telecommunications and/or network systems.
2. Data security activities are independent from systems and programming, computer operations, output, and data input.

3. Access to operating systems is restricted by user identification and passwords.
4. Access codes are properly protected and changed with reasonable frequency.
5. Transaction files are maintained for all transactions performed remotely.
6. Unauthorized access attempts are monitored and recorded.
7. User manuals adequately describe processing requirements.
8. Alternate processing procedures are incorporated into disaster recovery plans.
9. Antivirus tools are in place and current.

## [E]   Database Management

The database management system adequately meets audit standards when the following have been accomplished:

1. There is an appointed database administrator.
2. Written procedures are employed for maintaining a data dictionary file.
3. Transaction logs and procedures effectively allow for recovery of the database.
4. Data security measures are employed to prevent unauthorized access of data and/or changes to it.

## [F]   Personal Computers

Personal computers employed outside the IT operation adequately meet auditing standards when the following have been accomplished:

1. There exists a formal institutionwide PC policy and it is followed.
2. An assigned individual carries out the function of enforcing PC policies, maintaining an inventory of hardware and software, and assisting users in the use of the system.
3. Physical and data security are maintained.
4. A disaster recovery plan exists for PC operations.

## [G]   Workgroup Computer Systems

The client/server workgroup computer systems employed outside the IT operation adequately meet auditing standards when the following have been accomplished:

1. There exists a formal institutionwide workgroup computer policy and it is followed.
2. An assigned individual carries out the function of overseeing client/ server workgroup policies, and assisting users in the use of the system.
3. Physical and IT data security are maintained.
4. A disaster recovery plan exists and is tested for client/server workgroup computer operations.

### [H]   Contracting for Vendor Services

Vendor service contracts adequately meet auditing standards when the following have been accomplished:

1. The firm's legal authority approves contracts.
2. Vendor(s) fulfill contract requirements.
3. Applicable backup and contingency plans are in effect.
4. Vendor is financially solid.
5. Vendor's staff has confirmed credentials.

### [I]   Management Post-implementation Reviews

Determine whether the IT management maintains post-implementation reviews and continued reviews of existing systems. Reviews should adequately determine that:

1. System designs are consistent with original objectives.
2. Computer programs comply with standards.
3. Audit trails and controls are satisfactory.
4. Program and system testing plans are satisfactory.
5. Test results are satisfactory.
6. System and program documentation is adequate.
7. Program changes are properly reviewed and authorized.
8. Program changes are properly author-identified and documented.
9. Users are duly informed of changes and provided with revised user operation manuals.
10. User training is adequate and timely.
11. Source and object programs are synchronized with each other.
12. User management is satisfied with the system.

## § 11.05   IT MANAGEMENT AUDIT

### [A]   Purpose

This section provides an overview of the quality of management and supervision desirable for information systems. (The IT management function is no longer foreign to outside auditing firms. To prevent replacement by a facilities management service, IT managers should give particular attention to this section.)

### [B]   IT Organization

This section covers IT organizational structure and the procedures required to foster an effective management operation.

1. **Organization**
   a. IT and corporate organizational charts should identify:
      • Organizational structure

- IT management reporting directly to senior-level management
- Appropriate segregation of duties

  b. Key personnel biographical data is recorded and requirements for positions held are documented.
  - Qualifications required for position and credentials of individual holding position
  - Staffing-level requirements
  - Provision for management and technical successions

  c. Detailed job descriptions are written for each type of position. The job description represents the actual required work. This information is found and is accessible by anyone in current database file.

  d. Adequate continuing management and technical education are in place and monitored.

  e. An adequate compensation program is in place for attracting qualified personnel and staff retention.

2. **Planning**
   a. An active planning group including members of user community exists.
   b. Minutes are maintained of planning meetings for senior management support. The planning meeting minutes contain:
   - Dates, times, and personnel in attendance
   - Status of short- and long-range information systems plans
   - Current operating standards, including security and backup procedures
   - Status of IT budgets and current operating cost
   - Corrective actions to be taken for any present or future IT deficiencies
   - Reports or development studies that should be noted
   c. Strategic planning:
   - Documentation of current corporate strategic planning is maintained.
   - Documentation of IT strategic planning activities is maintained.
   - Future staffing level requirements by position are maintained and include positions to be created.
   - Any significant changes affecting the institution's organizational structure, hardware/software configuration, and overall IT goals are documented.

## [C]  IT Control

IT management requires controls ensuring the operation maintains adequate safeguards at all times.

1. **Management standards and procedure controls**
   a. Personnel administration has adequate segregation of duties.
   b. Systems development has sufficient audit trails.

    c.  Computer operations has adequate segregation of duties and limited access to file information. Only authorized personnel perform activities.

    d.  Telecommunications operations has proper access, with assurance that only authorized personnel access system.

    e.  Computer-stored information has limited access, only by authorized personnel.

    f.  Contingency planning procedures are current, tested, and enforced.

    g.  Disaster recovery procedures are current, published, enforced, and tested. Documentation of test efforts should be available for examination.

2.  **Effectiveness of IT reports.** Reports for senior management about IT activities indicate the effectiveness of the IT operation. These reports, also furnished to the IT steering committee, include:

    a.  Management reports providing status of software activities

    b.  Performance and problem reports prepared by user groups

    c.  Reports of systems use and planning prepared by operating managers

    d.  Internal and external audit reports of IT activities

    e.  Management audit reports

    f.  Comparable performance norms available from firms in same industry

3.  **Project performance reports.** To ensure control of projects, performance reports of selected projects are written for management. These reports compare actual performance with project plans. Reasons for any variance are determined and reported.

4.  **Follow-up documentation.** Keep documentation of management follow-up for the IT control operation. This determines whether or not management took positive action toward correcting the exceptions reported.

### [D]   IT Financial Analysis

Analyze and compare IT operating costs to that which is considered standard for the same size and type of institution. This is very important when IT has a lump-sum budget.

In analyzing financial statements and IT operating costs one must:

1.  Consider cost allocation methods used.

2.  Assure applied cost allocation methods are similar for both lump-sum budgets and user charge-back systems.

3.  Confirm units of processing are within industrial norms.

4.  Assure programs are within industrial norms.

5.  Ensure telecommunication costs of service are competitive.

6.  Affirm vendor services meet financial requirements.

**COMMENT**

When users are charged for services, these services can be compared with charges considered normal by outside vendors. Solicit competitive bids for an idea of how costs compare.

7. Obtain the name, location, and Dun & Bradstreet rating of vendor.
8. Determine that services are covered by a formal written contract.
9. Determine there is no conflict of interest between any IT employee and vendor.
10. Check vendor invoices against work done ensuring the service was rendered as billed.

**COMMENT**

Operating costs are a major concern to an IT manager. When top management looks at growing IT costs, managers may want to know the service cost if furnished by a vendor or by users performing the same procedures on their own systems.

With decreasing prices and growing capabilities of PCs, more users than ever before are considering having their own systems. This also applies to client/server workgroup systems.

## [E] IT Insurance Coverage

Insurance coverage for information systems is designed with attention to its special needs. The insurance should cover:

- Employee fidelity
- IT hardware and facilities
- Loss resulting from business interruption
- Cost of transaction errors or omissions
- Extra expense, including backup site expenses
- Reprogramming and software expense
- Transportation and living expense costs when employees work out of town

- Water damage from firefighting
- Acts of God
- Other probable risks

## [F] Public Laws

IT management must comply with a host of public laws. Its main concern is compliance with laws governing employees. These rules are from EEOC, OSHA, or the Wage and Hour Administration. Consult your human resource office periodically or when new rulings are issued.

Because of purchased software and off-the-shelf systems, copyright law is now an important consideration. Remember, the company is responsible and liable for the actions of its employees.

## COMMENT

The Wage and Hour Administration cited a large IT operation in Indiana for not paying overtime to 27 group leaders over a 5-year period. The overtime was ordered paid. In another case, the Equal Employment Opportunity Commission would not permit IT management to force a data entry operator to work on Sunday.

Information systems management and audit should not be underrated. A large Midwest company has 15 people in the information systems audit department alone. This is larger than most IT organizations. With company mergers and acquisitions, this demand should increase.

# 12

# SYSTEMS AND OPERATIONS AUDIT: VALIDATING YOUR TECHNICAL DESIGN

# § 12.01  SYSTEMS AND OPERATIONS AUDIT POLICIES

### [A]  Systems Development and Programming

Systems and operations audit policies are more technical than IT management policies. A frequent problem is when no policy is established, technicians then make decisions they are not qualified to make. Where policies have been created, a periodic audit ensures that these policies still serve the best interests of the organization.

This section covers standards and procedures applicable to the firm's systems development and programming activities. Services purchased from vendors must meet both in-house standards and the business standards the firm requires.

The procedures set forth in this chapter follow recommended standards for policies, as determined by industry norms.

### [B]  Operations Audit Policies

Operations policies cover telecommunications, data controls, and all computer operations, including user services. The procedures set forth in the operations sections are governed by industry norms. When policies affect the audit concerns of operations (data control, user services, and telecommunications), it is strongly recommended that industry norms be followed.

The size of information systems operations does not alter operations standards. Procedures should guarantee uniformity in all IT operations; this is corporate IT's responsibility.

PCs and workgroup computer systems must comply with the audit policies. Corporate IT has a dual responsibility: informing users of the policies and ensuring the policies are followed.

# § 12.02  PROGRAMMING ACTIVITIES CONTROL

### [A]  Overview

To ensure systems development and programming meet audit norms, procedures set down in this section are presented in more detail than those in other sections. Systems development and programming involvement may range in complexity from purchasing off-the-shelf software systems to developing in-house systems to purchasing turnkey systems.

### [B]  Standards for Systems Development and Programming

Standards for systems development, programming functions, systems development methodology, and program and system documentation must be adequately defined and followed. Controls should be developed and implemented for application programs and software changes. An audit of the systems development area should look for the following items:

1. Written standards for:
   a. Systems design and development
   b. Software package selection
   c. Application programming
   d. Operating systems programming
   e. Program testing
   f. Systems implementation
   g. Systems and programming documentation
   h. Program change controls
   i. Quality assurance and cataloging
2. Application systems design development standards including:
   a. Project feasibility studies
   b. Project cost-benefit analysis
   c. Predetermined progress milestones and follow-up review of progress reports
   d. Documented user approval of proposed systems design
   e. Documented user approval of program tests, user documentation, and user's final acceptance
   f. Documented post-implementation studies
3. Programming standards such as:
   a. Use of control totals, programmed audits, and validation checks of input before processing is begun
   b. Audit trails and exception reports of uncommon transactions
   c. Standardized routines and modular coding
   d. Standards for reusable coding practices
   e. Proper involvement of users in major decisions affecting input, logic flow, and output
   f. Test plans, including testing for all conceivable error conditions. Never perform tests with live database files.
   g. Completed documentation and user training before systems implementation
   h. CASE tools standards used
4. Documentation standards that include:
   a. Systems narratives
   b. Program narratives
   c. File layout schematics and output formats
   d. Database dictionary listings
   e. Descriptions of edit checking and programmed controls
   f. Current source program documentation
   g. User or operator instructions
   h. User manuals
   i. A chronological listing of program changes
   j. Documentation of maintenance changes
   k. Programming naming conventions
   l. Screen display layouts

      m.  Data element cross-references
      n.  Index of table field names
  5.  Current user manuals that are distributed to all appropriate user departments in the quantity required.

## [C]  Programming Activities Control

To control programming activities and ensure uniformity and conformity, practice the following guidelines:

1. Documents generated for new programs and after-program changes are reviewed, ensuring that documentation contains the following:
   a. Prenumbered program change control forms
   b. A description of problem or reasons for change
   c. Approval of change request by affected user management
   d. Name of programmer and date of change
   e. Signature and date of supervisor who reviewed and approved actual program change
   f. Signature and date of program librarian or quality assurance person cataloging program changes
   g. Confirmation that a copy of approval was sent to audit department
   h. Any supporting documents, as well as source listings of codes affected by a change and object listings of programs covered by the documentation, are held in the program library
2. All program modifications are reviewed and approved by the user department prior to any implementation.
3. Program documentation update must reflect that program changes are being done as soon as practical. Program documentation must be stored in the department's applications software library where it is readily accessible.
4. Changes to the operating system are subject to the same control procedures as application programs.
5. Sufficient numbers of persons with training and experience should be available to provide backup for major systems and programming functions.
6. Restrict systems programmers' access to application program libraries and documentation to assure security. (These restrictions reduce the possibility of embezzlement by the programmer.)
7. Application programmers are denied access to:
   a. Documentation and source listings for operating system
   b. Production program libraries
   c. Live data files
8. Records of temporary program changes using patches or system utilities are maintained and reviewed by supervisory personnel.
9. Replace all temporary program changes by properly authorized program changes within a reasonable time.
10. The documentation librarian's duties include:

   a.  Review of documentation during system development ensuring adherence to standards and appropriate authorization of exceptions.

   b.  Control and safeguard of documentation.

   c.  Confirmation that revised documentation reflects actual changes.

   d.  Distribution of documentation to authorized parties.

   e.  Maintenance of all documentation and standards manuals ensuring they are current.

# § 12.03  COMPUTER OPERATIONS

## [A]  Objective

The objective of this section is to provide a base of established industry norms for computer operations. This section also covers procedures for contingency and recovery planning, applicable to a wide scope of IT operation sizes, along with physical and internal controls.

## [B]  Computer Room Controls

The computer room environment must be controlled to ensure safe computer operation. The following safeguards are appropriate for a wide range of room sizes:

1. Adequate procedures are established ensuring only authorized persons are permitted in the computer room.
2. Restrict operation of computer hardware to authorized personnel only.
3. Repair of computer hardware is restricted to authorized personnel.
4. Computer room facility is adequately protected with:
   a. Procedures to minimize the accumulation of paper and other flammables in and around the computer room
   b. Heat, smoke, and water detectors
   c. Proper portable fire extinguishers
   d. A suitable fire control system
   e. Waterproof equipment covers
   f. Temperature and humidity control equipment
   g. Intrusion detection devices
   h. Alternate power supply
   i. Emergency lighting
5. Smoking, eating, drinking, and magnets are prohibited in the computer room.
6. Adequate on-call personnel are available, and maintenance agreements covering all equipment are up to date.
7. Perform preventive maintenance on a regularly scheduled basis.

### [C]   Computer Operations Management Reporting

IT management needs computer operations reporting for feedback and control. This reporting must be timely and IT management must examine it closely. Reports include, but are not limited to:

1.   Detailed hardware problem logs
2.   Computer-generated reports that include:
     a.   Proper program identification
     b.   Job processing times
     c.   Rerun times
     d.   Downtimes
     e.   Operator identification
3.   Machine utilization and performance reports
4.   Console logs or automated summaries of such logs that are reviewed for any unusual activity such as reruns, halts, unauthorized use, etc.

Reports must be produced at sufficient intervals to allow proper control and IT management review.

### [D]   Computer Operation Controls

Computer operation controls govern the personnel running the computer system. Operators should be aware of these procedures which must be enforced.

1.   Operators are cross-trained, providing backup and reducing dependence on key personnel.
2.   Operators are prohibited from:
     a.   Originating entries for processing
     b.   Correcting data exceptions, such as unposted or rejected items
     c.   Preparing any general ledger and/or subsidiary ledger entries
     d.   Performing any balancing function (reconciliation) other than run-to-run control
     e.   Running test programs against live or backup files
     f.   Executing programs from the test library during production runs
     g.   Copying source or object programs without prior approval
     h.   Controlling report generation and distribution
3.   Operators are denied access to source programs, program listings, and other documentation unnecessary for the processing of their applications.
4.   Operators' run instructions must be adequate and current.
5.   The computer center must use a formal scheduling procedure.
6.   Supervisory approval is necessary to add jobs or modify the schedule.

### [E]   Program/Data Library Controls

The computer program and data library requires its own audit readiness procedures. Site requirements may vary from location to location; therefore, the following are only core duties/procedures required for any library unit:

1. Librarians' responsibilities are prohibited to anyone with conflicting duties.
2. Enforce standard library procedures on all work shifts.
3. Only authorized personnel have library access.
4. Maintain a program and data file for all items under the jurisdiction of the library.
5. Issue data files from the library only on the basis of established run schedules or other evidence of proper authorization.
6. Use external labels to identify removable data storage media.
7. Inventory record of removable data storage media is maintained to identify:
   a. Storage location
   b. Volume serial number
   c. Creation and expiration dates
8. Maintain current copies of the operating system and application programs in the library vault for immediate backup. Maintain a second backup copy of all systems and programs off-site. All fireproof safes must meet ratings for secondary data storage requirements.
9. A machine-readable source program is maintained for each application program listed in the production object library.

## COMMENT

A major expense during the Year 2000 conversion was the lack of source code at many sites. Organizations could not find the current version of code to change and were forced into major rewrites of programs.

10. If backup copies of operating systems, application programs, transaction files, or master files are used, duplicates must be in the library or in the off-site storage location before being used by the IT production operation.
11. Periodically test backup operating system and application programs in the library.
12. Store removable data storage media in a closed, fire-resistant, and limited-access vault. The fire-resistance ratings must meet code for such items.
13. Provide controlled storage areas (on- and off-site) for workgroup programs, files, and data.
14. Provide fireproof controlled storage for blank payroll and accounts payable checks. Keep a beginning and ending control number log.
15. Program/data library area contains the following devices:
    a. Suitable fire extinguisher system
    b. Adequate air conditioning system

c.   Adequate fire alarm system
d.   Adequate intrusion alarm system
e.   Temperature and humidity recording device

# § 12.04  DATA CONTROL

## [A]  Objective

The objective of this section is to provide adequate control procedures to maintain accuracy and integrity of data, which includes input, output, and storage of data files and databases.

## [B]  Input Controls

Inputs to any computer operation must be controlled. These controls will vary depending on need. The systems and operations audit must ensure that the following procedures are followed:

1.   Reference input manuals, including examples (copies) and illustrations (drawings) of source documents, are made available for each data entry operator.
2.   All data received by the data entry unit is accompanied by prenumbered transmittal batch forms and posted control totals.
3.   Maintain a log of input received by source.
4.   Batch control documents received with the input data are retained in an orderly and logical manner for final balancing.
5.   All transactions, such as item counts, are subject to controls similar to those used for monetary transactions.
6.   Master file change requests require the following:
     a.   The request is in writing
     b.   Identification of originating personnel
     c.   Required approval from database administrator
7.   All required procedures must be in place and known by each data entry operator ensuring appropriate processing.
8.   If the data entry service is not proximate to the sending area, send source documents through a backup procedure.
9.   To ensure accuracy of critical control fields, verify input by a second data entry operator.
10.  Require monetary totals and item counts for key-to-disk and key-to-tape systems.
11.  Retain input transactions for a minimum of 24 hours in the IT computer area.
12.  Prohibit data entry personnel from originating entries for processing.
13.  Require supervisory approval for correcting entries that are:
     a.   Received by, but not charged to, the data center
     b.   Charged to, but not received by, the data center

14. Supervisory personnel regularly review exception and reconciliation items.

## COMMENT

Allowing IT-originated entries is an open invitation to theft.

## [C] Output Controls

Output controls cover CDs, printed, network-accessible, and microfiche output. The following procedures are to be enforced:

1. Review all reports for quality prior to distribution.
2. Control procedures must be established ensuring all reports are produced and delivered as scheduled.
3. Establish a systematic and orderly plan for pickup and processing of data and the delivery of output data.
4. All distribution procedures should be sufficiently organized and controlled to provide for the delivery of reports to the proper users.
5. Establish procedures for the control of signature stamps.

## [D] Database Management Controls

A database administrator, responsible for coordinating and controlling the database, follows established standards and procedures for controlling data records and files used by programmers. The following procedures apply:

1. To maintain security, the database administrator's access to live data, applications source listings, and other application program documentation is appropriately restricted.
2. The data dictionary contains detailed definitions of all data elements.
3. All changes made to the data dictionary require authorization of the database administrator.
4. Required procedures exist assuring the data dictionary remains current and accurate.
5. Written procedures covering database recovery exist in the event of hardware or software failure.
6. Transaction log is in place at all times to provide for an audit trail.
7. Report any attempts to violate database security to IT management from the database administrator in writing.
8. Client/server access controls are in place, and any violation is investigated and reported to IT management.

# § 12.05   DISASTER RECOVERY/CONTINGENCY PLANNING

## [A]   Disaster Recovery

Disaster recovery audit procedures also contain the contingency planning procedures. Proof that these are in place, combined with periodic testing, ensures proper system functioning.

Effective disaster recovery and contingency plans require maintaining proper on-site and off-site storage facilities. The disaster recovery/contingency planning audit must ensure that the following procedures are in place.

1. Off-site storage location should contain adequate storage space for:
   a. Source and object production programs
   b. Master files and transaction files to recreate the current master files
   c. System and program documentation
   d. Operating systems and utility programs
   e. Other vital records
   f. A method of transporting materials to and from the off-site storage facility with the same high level of environmental and physical security as employed at the data center.
2. Remote storage facility must contain the proper access and environmental control procedures.
3. A written emergency plan addresses:
   a. Physical security of the computer installation
   b. Actions to be taken in specific emergency situations
   c. Contingency procedures required to recover from a disaster or computer failure
4. A suitable backup procedure to:
   a. Provide backup processing for required processing in volume.
   b. Provide sufficient processing time necessary to correct the problem.
   c. Provide the documentation required so that management can adequately respond to a disaster.

## [B]   Data Center Contingency Planning

The data center disaster and recovery contingency plans should include:

1. Data files and program file backups in place.
2. Computer system backup in place.
3. A remote storage location for emergency procedures manuals.
4. An alternate input and output distribution system with a minimum time required to be operational.
5. An online network system ready for a backup if required.
6. A complete assignment of duties for reconstruction and off-site processing in the possession of all trusted personnel.

7.  A complete contingency procedure in place to recover from a disaster or computer failure.

## [C]   Systems Assurance

The following procedures provide for systems assurance:

1.  Protect data files, program libraries, and utilities by passwords and other means.
2.  Require all passwords to change periodically, using industry norms for creating passwords that are difficult to guess.
3.  Utility programs with data files or program-altering capabilities are adequately controlled.
4.  Written procedures covering the acceptance and cataloging of production programs are in place and up to date.
5.  All object code production programs are generated from the most current source code versions.
6.  Remove obsolete or unused programs from current production libraries to archive storage. Store these programs in the off-site storage area. They must be properly labeled and kept for no less than 5 years before being destroyed.

## COMMENT

Some programs are only used annually for accounting, regulatory, or budgeting purposes. Idle programs should be moved to off-line storage but hesitantly deleted. This is where your documentation library pays off.

7.  Computer center management periodically reviews and updates controls and security relating to data files and program libraries.
8.  Make proper information available to all concerned about any hardware or software system changes.
9.  Database management critical records are dumped and stored on a sufficiently frequent basis for needed backup and timely restoration purposes.
10. Maintain a procedure providing information relative to the hardware and software configuration of the backup site.
11. All outside facilities backup arrangements maintain up-to-date written agreements at all times.
12. Client/server operations employing mirrored systems are in agreement. Reconfirm at random intervals.

# § 12.06  PC SYSTEMS AND OPERATIONS AUDIT POLICIES

### [A]  Objective

The objective of this section is to establish adequate controls over the use of PCs in the organization. The degree of control necessary depends on the degree of sensitive information handled or the value of processing done by respective PCs.

### [B]  PC Standards

Standards required for the operational use of PCs, including software and hardware acquisition, apply to all PCs used in an organization. The PC audit must ensure the following standards are in place.

1.  Standards include:
    a.  Use of the output data
    b.  Restriction of access to PCs
    c.  Control of movement of software and hardware
    d.  Removal from institution of any software or hardware
    e.  Restriction on use of software and hardware to that sanctioned by organization
    f.  Restriction on personal use of PCs
    g.  Modification of hardware or software
    h.  Piracy of purchased software
    i.  Backup for all data files
    j.  Policy that approved games are to be allowed on PCs
    k.  Restriction of network access to Internet and e-mail to business use only
    l.  Review of local area network (LAN) procedures and controls
2.  Standards covering software and hardware acquisition should include the following:
    a.  Acquisition will follow standards developed for institution.
    b.  Each PC site possesses required documentation.
    c.  In-house software development is performed only by sanctioned personnel.
    d.  Software developed on firm's time and/or hardware/software is firm's property.

### [C]  PC Environment

Environments where PCs are used do not require the same degree of control needed by IT computer operations. However, their users are usually unfamiliar with IT operation requirements and must learn those that are applicable. The following are standard environment requirements:

1. **PC security**
   a. Physical security required:
      - Key locks on hardware
      - Backup data files secured in approved fireproof files or safes
      - Access areas restricted
      - Critical information backed up by IT computer operations
   b. Access controls required:
      - Use of dial-up equipment
      - Read-only attributes attached to files
      - Passwords for access
      - Encryption of classified data

2. **Housekeeping environment**
   a. No foods and liquids on same desk or tabletops containing computer hardware or secondary storage
   b. No telephones or magnetic devices closer than 2 ft from any data hardware or software
   c. No smoking in general area of PC operations
   d. Keep area dust-free

3. **Power supply**
   a. Computer hardware must not share its power outlets with any other devices.
   b. Plug all hardware into surge protectors.
   c. Areas that may have power supply problems must have uninterrupted power supply (UPS) backup supply units capable of providing power for the full time required to bring down the system.

## [D]   Inventory Control of Hardware and Software

Maintain an asset management system for all PC hardware and software. Records are kept both by the computer asset manager and also by each user area's highest level of administration. The asset manager is responsible for keeping the various inventory records in balance.

# § 12.07   WORKGROUP SYSTEMS AND OPERATIONS AUDIT POLICIES

## [A]   Objective

The objective of this section is to establish adequate controls over the use of the workgroup and client/server systems in an institution. The degree of control necessary depends on the degree of sensitive information handled or the value of processing done by the respective operations.

## [B]   Workgroup Standards

Standards applicable to all workgroups and client/server systems in an organization are required for their operational use and include those for software and hardware acquisition. The workgroup standards audit must ensure that the following standards are in place.

1.  Standards include:
    a.   Use of output data

> ### COMMENT
>
> The CIO/IT head should have a review done of the current systems and operations audit policies and procedures by the firm's outside auditors. If these auditors cannot, have them recommend a source for such a service in writing. The interval between such examinations depends on valid problem discoveries. The more problems found, the closer the review intervals should be.

    b.   Restrictions of access to workstations and terminals
    c.   Control of movement of software and hardware
    d.   Removal from institution of any software or hardware
    e.   Restriction on use of software and hardware to that sanctioned by organization
    f.   Restriction on personal use of workstations and/or terminals
    g.   Modification of hardware or software
    h.   Piracy of purchased software
    i.   Backup for all data files
    j.   Backup of server files and programs
    k.   Policy that games are not to be allowed on client/server systems
    l.   Restriction of network access to Internet and e-mail to business use only
2.  Standards covering software and hardware acquisition include the following:
    a.   Acquisition follows standards developed for organization
    b.   Each workstation and/or terminal site possesses required operation documentation
    c.   In-house software development is performed only by sanctioned personnel
    d.   Software developed on firm's time and/or hardware/software is firm's property

## [C]  Workgroup Environment

Environments of workgroup or client/server systems will not receive the same degree of control by IT computer operations as information system's own client/server systems. The users of workstations and terminals are not expected to be familiar with IT operation requirements but know those applying to them. The following are standard environment requirements:

1. **Workgroup security**
   a. Physical security required:
      - Key locks on hardware (optional)
      - Backup data files maintained
      - Access areas restricted
      - Critical information backed up by IT computer operations

---

## COMMENT

The University of North Carolina found a network server that, although missing for 4 years, had not missed a packet in all that time.

Try as they might, university administrators could not find the server. Working with Novell, IT workers tracked it down by meticulously following cable until they literally ran into a wall. Maintenance workers had mistakenly sealed the server behind drywall.

John Rendleman, *InformationWeek*

---

   b. Access controls required:
      - Read-only attributes attached to information systems files and database
      - Passwords for access
2. **Housekeeping environment**
   a. No foods and liquids on same desk or tabletops containing computer hardware or secondary storage media
   b. No telephones or magnetic devices closer than 2 ft from any hardware or software
   c. No smoking in general area of PC operations
   d. Keep area dust-free
3. **Power supply**
   a. Workstations or terminals do not share power outlets with any other devices.
   b. Areas that may have power supply problems require UPS units for a limited-time power supply.

## [D]   Inventory Control of Hardware and Software

Maintain an asset management system for all computer hardware and software. Records are kept by the computer asset manager and also by each user area's highest level of administration. The asset manager is responsible for keeping the various inventory records in balance.

# 13

# IT HUMAN RESOURCES: KEEPING PEOPLE

## § 13.01    IT PERSONNEL POLICIES

### [A]    IT Management Objectives

Policies governing IT personnel may differ from those in other departments because the nature of IT operations requires some stringency, with particular personnel needs. Therefore, we discuss specific IT personnel policies here only to augment corporate personnel policies.

The broad objectives for IT human resources management include the following:

- Develop IT personnel through training and outside education.
- Maintain an active recruitment policy.
- Develop a cooperative attitude among IT personnel concerning users' needs.
- Develop and maintain an ongoing IT personnel promotion planning system.
- Maintain a comprehensive and competitive compensation plan for each job position.
- Maintain ongoing career guidance for employee development.

## COMMENT

Computer personnel require special treatment. A *Business-Week* article, "Computer People: Yes, They Really Are Different," notes that IT people are motivated more by personal fulfillment and growth than money or job titles. Other research indicates they tend to be more loyal to their profession than to their firm.

The fact that qualified IT personnel are in high demand and job turnover above the norm indicates that retention requires extra effort. Time is required to replace a competent employee, and the replacement cannot be expected to function as well for some time. New personnel also may cost about 15 percent more than current employees; moreover, there may be a project delay.

IT employees are different from others, and IT personnel policies and procedures must accommodate these differences for the department to function at the industry norm and to minimize the turnover rate.

Unless the human resources department considers a turnover rate of 100 percent per year normal, which an IT operation in Michigan experienced, they must take the particular needs of IT personnel into account.

### [B]   Recruiting and Selection Policies

Limit recruiting and selection procedures to long-term employment. Do not hire personnel unless they are permanent. Temporary personnel are considered contract workers.

---

**COMMENT**

Firms have hired regular personnel for a project, then terminated them when the project was completed to secure "low-priced consulting services." Feeling abused, these unhappy former employees often exposed the firms' unfair employment practices, have committed sabotage before or after leaving, and have sued.

The ideal policy is recruiting and selecting the best people for the job and hiring them on a full-time basis. A wise institution attracts and pays for qualified personnel. The selection process also is a major issue. Better not to fill a position than to hire the wrong person.

---

### [C]   IT Performance Evaluation Policy

An effective IT performance evaluation system is needed. Evaluations provide both employee and firm with valuable information: Employees are interested in feedback about their performance, and the firm wants to know which employees perform well and which have promotion potential.

### [D]   Discipline and Termination Policy

Discipline and termination policies fill a special need in information systems. Discipline should not jeopardize any future relations between employees and the firm, but should be fair and acceptable.

Termination of an IT employee requires careful treatment. Procedures must be in place and followed precisely ensuring no further trouble from a departing employee.

## § 13.02   RECRUITING AND JOB SEARCH

### [A]   Overview

Recruiting and job searches are traditionally performed by the human resources department, but most need help recruiting the specific personnel required by information systems. Therefore, the involvement of IT management is crucial.

## COMMENT

More than one "fired" information systems employee has attracted negative publicity because of departing misdeeds. Keeping a firm's name out of the headlines requires some special termination procedures.

Even the U.S. government is aware of these special requirements, and uses supplemental job application forms for IT positions.

The growth of IT personnel placement firms shows the need for specialized information systems recruiting. Firms earn their employer-paid fees by delivering the IT personnel needed for the job. However, use care in choosing a placement firm. One human resources manager thought a candidate with 10 years of IT experience qualified for a systems analyst position. When the IT manager interviewed the candidate, he discovered the candidate had been a data entry supervisor for almost all of the 10 years. Better IT personnel placement firms screen out such candidates.

### [B] Methods of Recruiting

To obtain experienced personnel, the following procedures for recruiting IT candidates have been very successful when augmented with traditional forms:

1. Pay a bonus to present employees for recruiting and hiring qualified personnel. The benefits of this are:
   a. Proven personnel usually recommend qualified persons like themselves.

## COMMENT

Find a good firm and work with it. Be careful it does not place your "better" people with other firms. If it does, find another recruiting firm fast. Have the firm work with IT management, not the human resources department.

   b. The cost for the human resources department to find job candidates or to pay a recruiting firm's fee is more than the bonus paid to an employee (which should be no less than $1,000).

c.  Current personnel have a stake in finding the right person for the job. Employees can know what is needed better than human resources or the recruiting firm.
2.  Consult the person leaving, who knows the job better than anyone else, and can help define job requirements.
3.  Take the time to locate a quality recruiting firm.
4.  When a candidate is found, send his/her job application to the human resources department to confirm the credentials and work experience. Computer operations applicants, by the nature of their job, will also require a retail credit check.
5.  Avoid nepotism at all costs. Because of the controls needed for an IT operation, hiring relatives causes nothing but problems. Relatives tend not to abide by the same rules as nonrelatives. They tend to cover up more errors and have higher rates of orchestrated thefts.

## [C]  College Recruiting

College is an excellent source for entry-level IT employees, but some special effort is required to recruit the correct candidates. Graduating students can have formal training in the IT area, but a degree in computer science won't guarantee a person is qualified for entry-level IT positions. Many know coding but lack business knowledge or expertise in the particular languages used by the recruiting firm. Some of the better students may have worked as student help-desk persons. They've experienced contact with student users and can be more familiar with IT problems.

## COMMENT

One noted Midwest university computer science department did not offer any COBOL courses. Unless a company was willing to change to PASCAL, retraining was necessary if those computer science graduates were hired.

Some university teachers leave a lot to be desired. They have little, if any, background in applications programming and applications they use are mostly math oriented. Other schools or universities have teaching staffs with industrial experience so students graduate ready to fit into the industrial environment.

One company did not hire an intern, who was smart but obnoxious, from a well-known university where he served his internship. The IT manager contacted every other division in the company ensuring this intern was not hired. A candidate must mesh with the corporate culture and, more important, with the firm's IT culture. One misfit on an IT project is worse than having one less person to do the work.

Two-year technical school programs usually focus on applied industrial needs with only a limited number of liberal arts courses. Two-year graduates often cannot be placed directly into salaried positions. Here the wage and hour regulations are very restrictive. Confirm these regulations with human resources prior to hiring a job candidate from one of these programs.

No matter what level of school recruiting, make an effort to learn something about the faculty and the programs offered. When a school offers the necessary training, inform its placement office of the company's needs. Ordinarily, the school will try to place the better students first. The school may even use the company's guidelines to assist with the planning of future programs.

One program proven successful for many firms is the internship. With interns, the company gets to know the prospective candidate. The student not only has to perform, but also "fit in." If hired by the firm, they will already know the IT operation and corporate culture. A student intern program is an excellent recruiting tool. However, it must be properly managed. Unlike skilled employees, interns require a structured work situation and should not be assigned work without a mentor. Assign an intern to shadow and assist a senior worker who will take the time to explain what is happening and why.

### [D]   Environmental Influences

In employee recruitment, consider the environmental factors. The IT working environments of a programmer, a data entry operator, and a systems analyst are all different. Recruit prospective employees to fit in with the working climate. Current economic conditions and the nature of the labor market affect recruiting. Recruiting becomes difficult when the economy is overheated.

## COMMENT

There is a growing practice of importing programming talent with or without green cards. One Ohio consulting firm hired a foreign graduate student at the firm's expense, and with much effort, helped the programmer get a green card. Within a week of receiving his green card, the programmer quit and started his own competing consulting company.

Employees are poor candidates for management and systems analysis positions when they have little or no loyalty to the firm and local community. As to IT needs, the best way to use imported programming talent is to use employment firms that have talent for hire. Using these firms has worked out well, and given potential employees a chance to "earn their salt."

## COMMENT *(cont'd)*

Other factors influencing recruiting are governmental regulations, both federal and state equal employment opportunity (EEO) legislation. Human resources offices are acquainted with EEO laws and should be used as a reference regarding these regulations.

IT staff members should know they were hired because of their skills, not because of EEOC requirements. One does not need government regulations to hire qualified women, the handicapped, or minorities; it is just good business sense.

## § 13.03   SELECTION OF IT PERSONNEL

### [A]   Overview

Use the same criteria for hiring IT personnel whether from inside or outside the firm. Base the decision to promote or transfer a person to the information systems department on the person's qualifications. If the outside and inside talents are equal, the inside person may be a better choice since this encourages greater firm loyalty. Promotion or transfer of poorly qualified personnel based on company politics can create problems for IT management.

IT personnel, by the nature of their work, have many opportunities to play havoc with company information. They will have opportunities to expose personal information, company confidential information, or even steal money from the company. Whenever possible, always perform a background check prior to extending an employment offer.

### [B]   A Diagnostic Approach to Selection

IT management has to choose personnel from a list of candidates who best meet the selection criteria, while considering current environmental conditions. The size and complexity of the IT operations, its status within the firm, and technological volatility will all affect selection and attraction of the right personnel.

A second circumstance affecting the decision for IT is the current labor market. If there are many applicants, the selection decision can be complicated. If there is only one applicant, selection is relatively easy, but there is also a danger this person is unqualified. It is better to continue recruiting than select the wrong candidate. If the person is qualified, do not hesitate, because someone else may hire him or her.

## [C]    Selection Criteria

For a selection procedure to succeed, the prospective employee's immediate supervisor should specify the personal characteristics required for effective job performance. Selection techniques can be suggested and used by the experts in a firm's human resources department to uncover these defined characteristics. Selection criteria are summarized under the following categories: education, experience, personal characteristics, and future growth potential. They reflect characteristics of present employees who are happy and successful in the same position. Selection criteria should be established before reviewing anyone for a position. Criteria that is slanted toward a particular candidate will create bad feeling across the entire staff since it shows to all that the selection process was not impartial.

A major benefit of posting jobs is that it opens opportunity for all and breaks up some of the "buddy" system of promotions. If you use the "buddy" system, you open the door to a discrimination lawsuit.

## COMMENT

Managers, you get what you reward. If you reward your "friends" with promotions that their performance does not rate, then your hard-working employees will shift their efforts from IT projects to being a "buddy," since that is what you reward. Other workers will become demoralized by their exclusion from consideration and "retire on the job."

A selection is made by rating the different candidates on specified criteria, weighted according to past proven results that can be verified by bona fide documentation. These scores rank candidates. The following are part of the selection procedure:

1. **IT application form.** A separate application form (either in place of or in addition to the general company application form) is used to gather information required for filling an IT position. The IT management develops it, and the IT supervisors approve requested technical information. Before use, the form is sent to the human resources department to ensure illegal questions are not included.
2. **Formal education.** Educational criteria must be validated against job performance. The amount and type of education correlating with job effectiveness are determined for use in the selection procedure. Formal education can indicate ability, skills, and the applicant's level of accomplishment. Beware of the wage and hour rules regarding what constitutes a salaried position, which does not qualify for overtime

pay. Contact human resources to ensure that a given position warrants the salaried status. IT management should examine:

a. An official transcript sent by the school. Evaluate courses and grades.

## COMMENT

ComputerWorld publishes an annual salary survey that is one of the best. How competitive is the firm within its industry and national location by job type?

Government regulations often influence selection. One data entry operator was hired, and then terminated, because the person's religious beliefs prohibited working on Sunday. When the terminated employee filed for unemployment compensation, the government brought an EEO suit against the firm. The person was reinstated with back pay. To avoid this problem, the human resources department should be asked to help when anything unusual arises in the candidate selection process.

b. The school's catalog describing the relevant courses.
c. The kind of hardware and software used by the school.
d. Applied or theoretical orientation of the school's IT teaching staff.

3. **Experience.** Another criterion for selecting IT personnel is experience. First choice should be a person formerly successful in the same type of job. The more experience the better, to a certain point. Someone who has only programmed for 10 years would be unsuitable for a lead systems analyst position. The nature of the applicant's experience should be considered. A person working on multiple projects in a demanding environment for 4 years is usually a better selection than someone doing only payroll maintenance programming for 10 years. If the new position requires only maintenance programming skills, the latter would be the wiser selection. Ways to confirm experience are:

a. Have more than one interviewer talk with the candidate. Use interviewers with opposing technical views so the candidate is forced to be honest. Ask specific technical questions to determine their depth of understanding. It is OK if they don't know all of the answers since few technical people know every aspect of their field, but in a short time, you can determine if they are knowledgeable or not.
b. Have the candidate bring samples of written documentation. Confirm the originality of his/her work.
c. Check the candidate's references; contact former co-workers and

employers. A phone call to each produces better results than a written request.

## § 13.04  TESTING FOR IT PERSONNEL

### [A]  Overview

The human resources department should administer tests that measure skill levels, aptitude, and personality. Because of EEOC laws, tests are required to be job related and validated, i.e., that job performance correlates with the test results. There are "tests in print" measuring programming or data entry aptitude. Manual dexterity tests can be used for data entry positions. For systems analysts, analyze the desired criteria by more than one test.

Do not limit testing to entry-level personnel. A person who has been a programmer for 5 years could have been a poor programmer for 5 years. Well-organized firms recognize this.

## COMMENT

One source of tests is the book *Tests in Print,* published by Buros Inst; ISBN: 0910674515.

### [B]  Test Selection

Whichever test is selected, pretest it with current employees first. Scores correlating with the known performance records of employees can establish confidence in the tests. No one choice will be 100 percent dependable, but using validated tests is one of the best objective methods for selecting the best person for the job. Some tests are not skill tests but measure what might be expected after a person is trained. Save time and money by training the right person, not just someone who knows the right buzzwords.

## COMMENT

For example, a COBOL teacher with 2 years' teaching experience and 6 years' industry experience applied for a job as a COBOL programmer with a national company in St. Louis. She took a programming aptitude test and passed. However, not all experienced programmers can, and their work may reflect this.

# § 13.05  EMPLOYMENT INTERVIEW

## [A]  Overview

Employment interviews begin after candidates have passed the preliminary screening and testing. There are three general types: structured, semistructured, and unstructured. All three involve interaction between two or more parties: the applicant and one or more representatives of the potential employer. Do not limit the process to only one method. It is a good practice to always have two interviewers in a room with the candidate. This eliminates later accusations of impropriety against the interviewer.

## [B]  The Structured Interview

The structured interview is best for people with little or no interview experience. It is suitable, with little training, for peer or working supervisors. A list of questions is prepared in advance. Questions can be divided between the interviewers or repeated using different versions. This is an effective tool to determine the candidate's truthfulness and knowledge of information technology. Questions should be forced choice (i.e., yes or no), so the interviewer need only indicate the applicant's response on a printed form. This approach is very restricted but provides an opportunity to analyze an individual's technical skills.

## [C]  The Semistructured Interview

In a semistructured interview, only major questions are prepared in advance. Conducting this interview requires greater skill and preparation than the structured interview. It allows more flexibility than the structured approach. A skillful interviewer can probe freely into areas that merit further detail. This approach combines enough structure to ensure important information is collected. This allows for comparison with other applications and facilitates the exchange of information in a freer manner than the strictly structured interview.

## [D]  The Unstructured Interview

The unstructured interview is best left to experienced interviewers. There may be a prepared list of topics but the interviewer retains the freedom to adapt to the individual candidates. The unstructured interview's reliability may be questioned, but it does provide the manager with subjective information. This interview's results can be compared with others given to the same candidate(s) in the same fashion.

When an interview is concluded, each interviewer puts his/her objective analysis of the applicant into writing. This information is forwarded to the manager making the hiring decision. If the decision is close, the manager may call a meeting of all interviewers to discuss the merits of the applicant(s).

The analysis tends to be subjective with multiple interviewers. Each level, from peer to senior management, has its own analysis of the applicant. All peer interviewers will not only want to have someone competent, but someone who fits into the workgroup. Senior management may look for different traits that meet the current to future needs.

# § 13.06  PERFORMANCE REVIEW

## [A]  Overview

While most firms have performance review procedures, information systems may require additional reviews because performance is a function of ability as well as skill and effort. For example, a programmer who works late, comes in on weekends, and exerts great effort receives a good performance review and a raise. However, one highly skilled person who exerts less effort could possibly replace this same programmer and 10 more like him/her.

This creates a major problem in reviewing the performance of programmers and systems analysts. The systems analyst may be one of the most difficult to rate on performance. On the other hand, evaluating data entry operators presents few problems. The output less the error rate is considered the performance. IT performance determination is vulnerable to subjectivity, depending on the specific position in question.

## [B]  Computer Operations Performance Review

The operations area is less complex and more objective in analyzing a person's performance. In addition to the standard evaluation procedures, the following also are recommended:

1. **Data entry.** The volume of data input, less the error rate, ordinarily measures the data entry operator's performance. However, don't judge all data entry operators alike. The kind of source documents an operator processes affects performance. Handwritten documents that have to be coded or words requiring abbreviations slow the input rate and increase the error rate. The standard measure of keystrokes-per-minute is not a fair method of measurement and comparison.

   One efficient method is to employ a tool from the industrial engineer's domain, motion time measurement (MTM). This method analyzes the source document and the human effort required in capturing the data into computer digital form; it therefore determines a realistic standard. Some systems and procedures analysts have been trained in this technology. If no one in IT has this skill, contact the industrial engineering department. If there is no industrial engineering unit in-house, get an outside source from a technical service agency.

2. **Computer operations.** The computer operator's performance is best judged by the efficiency of running the computer operation. The control logs and system monitoring software allow evaluation of perfor-

mance. In addition, the appearance of the computer center area provides some idea of housekeeping skills. Surprise visits by management on the night and weekend shifts also provide information. That operators never know when to expect a visit helps increase efficiency.

The evaluation of operations personnel tends to be subjective. Personalities become a factor when evaluating personnel such as the computer operator, data librarian, or the data output and distribution operators. Because these evaluations could become subjective, two or more supervisors should evaluate each employee. If the operation is large enough, rotation of supervisors and/or personnel (for cross-training as well as employee evaluation) should be considered.

## [C]   Programmers Performance Review

Program development productivity is not easily measured, resulting in subjective performance reviews. Productivity of programmers rises when they know they are being observed. (This increased production is called the "Hawthorne effect.") Programming productivity can be affected by:

- Program design changes originated by customer
- Kind of language used
- Detail level of documentation
- Quality of information furnished for program(s)
- Soundness of test data
- Working environment
- Amount of supervision required

---

## COMMENT

In the 1920s researchers at the Western Electric Hawthorne Works in Chicago experimented with light levels and other factors to determine what would make the workers most productive. What they found instead was that no matter what change was made, productivity increased. The researchers concluded that productivity was increased whenever the workers felt that management was paying attention to them and their needs.

---

The above, which may affect the programmer's productivity, must be considered when reviewing performance. Avoid assessments based on lines of code per given time period or pages of documentation per month. Performance reviews may be enhanced by the following:

1. **Peer review.** Have IT peers anonymously rank each other's performance. Include programmers, systems analysts, and computer operations personnel.

2. **Time by program function.** A function is an action or activity, usually at the lowest definable level of structured programming.
   * A function has fewer than 55 coding statements.
   * A function has one entry point and one exit point. The time taken to complete a function is a better gauge of productivity than the time taken to write a specific number of lines of code. The number of functions completed in given time intervals provides information about the programming skill level of the person coding, along with their error rate.

## [D]   Systems Analyst Performance Review

Systems analysts are difficult people to review objectively. Often, the person's body language and personality can affect the appraisal. Another problem is that it takes so long to see the results of a systems analyst's efforts that appraisals may be distorted.

The number of procedures added to the firm's performance review process for systems analysts is limited. The following considerations may help:

1. Have programmers provide an anonymous appraisal ranking of each systems analyst. A preprinted form is used to collect evaluations and any remarks.
2. Have user managers appraise systems analysts who worked on terminated projects. A preprinted form for this purpose is used to collect evaluations and any remarks.
3. Use peer evaluation. Use preprinted forms to collect evaluations and any remarks.
4. Evaluate their project performance. How did he/she complete measurable task unit completion times compared to the estimated times? The project manager should provide a project evaluation of each member during and at the termination of each project. A preprinted evaluation form is used for the in-process and final evaluations.
5. Examine the status of the project after termination by the projects coordinator. Systems project managers or leaders will have no better evidence for their evaluation.

# § 13.07   EMPLOYEE TERMINATION

## [A]   Overview

To protect the company, information systems managers use special termination procedures. Departing IT employees have many opportunities for destructive activities.

Employees leaving on good terms will have an exit interview. If no provision for this exists, information systems or information technology management conducts the interview. A preprinted exit form, approved by the CIO or IT head, is used to have a structured exit interview. The human resources manager should examine the form for approval, to limit any company liability.

## [B]   Termination Procedure

Employees terminated for any reason require the following additional IT termination procedures:

1.   Notify the employee away from the work area.
2.   Remove the employee's password from the system before the notice is given.
3.   Have the employee turn in his/her IT identification and any keys or magnetic cards.
4.   Escort the employee outside the building. If the employee needs transportation to get home, provide it.
5.   Collect and box the employee's personal items. These may be picked up in the lobby or sent to the terminated employee's home address within 2 days. Require a confirmation of delivery receipt.

## [C]   Exit Interview

After giving notice, all employees should be interviewed by someone other than their own supervisor as soon as possible. This interview is to learn why the employee quit. The preprinted IT exit form provides for a structured exit interview. Data collected from departing employees may indicate an undesirable situation exists and may give management an opportunity to correct it in the future.

If the exit interview reveals the departing employee is upset, the CIO/IT head is notified immediately to review the information. The CIO/IT manager determines if the termination procedure should be enacted to prevent possible retaliation against the firm by the departing employee.

# § 13.08   EMPLOYEE DEVELOPMENT

## [A]   IT Skills Inventory

IT employees are uniquely attuned to the need to keep up with ever-changing technology. Earning a promotion requires even more effort. The better employees, if not provided educational opportunities by the firm, will pay for it themselves. They will also be less loyal because of it. They will depart at the first advantageous opportunity, leaving the firm with lesser quality employees. This education and training is necessary for IT employees and has to be provided beyond that for the rest of the firm.

A skills inventory is maintained for each employee of the information systems operation. It should be kept as current as any other file and should consist of the following:

1.   Person's name and ID number
2.   Date the person started with IT
3.   Starting salary and title
4.   Formal education received

5. Other training received
6. Certifications received
7. Current job title
8. Current supervisor
9. Start date of current position
10. Current salary and benefits
11. Promotion potential of employee:
    a. Ready for a promotion
    b. Will be ready with more training
    c. Will be ready with more experience
    d. Will be ready with more training and experience
    e. Is not ready and may never be ready
    f. Will never be ready
12. Foreign languages spoken
13. Future education plans
14. Future training plans
15. Hobbies or interests that could benefit firm
16. Next goal/promotion objective within firm
17. Status when hired by information systems:
    a. If transfer employee:
       • Date started with firm
       • Title and department of last position before joining IT
    b. Previous employer:
       • Name of firm
       • Position held
       • How long position held
       • Why he/she left former firm
    c. Student
    d. Graduated from formal education

The skills inventory file is online, with very limited access, since a person accessing the file will be able to generate a hardcopy of selected employees' records.

## [B] Replacement Order

The replacement or promotability order is depicted on an organizational chart as an inverted tree with the head or CIO of the IT organization at the top. As a systems chart, it is large enough to show the overall interrelated job positions.

Below each position's box and connected to it is another box listing the three most likely candidates for the position ranked in order of promotability. With each name is the person's title, length of time in the current position, and the code found in the skills inventory, which represents his/her promotability status.

Before this chart is produced, the IT organization must have a well-defined organizational chart with positions properly titled. For security reasons this needs to be a manual chart, produced and kept up to date by the IT head or a delegated employee.

## [C]  Continuing Education and Training

The IT operation has its own person coordinating the education and training pursuits of IT personnel. It is recommended the same person also maintain the skills inventory, since the two responsibilities are clearly related. The person writes a yearly report, before each budget request time, reporting the success of the continuing education and training program.

This person maintains records of the effectiveness of different programs. The person should be both an advisor to and an information source for those seeking education or training information. An inventory of forms is maintained for employees applying for monies for education or training, and for expense reports. Reimbursements to employees are permitted for:

- Seminars
- Vendor courses
- College tuition (for job-related or degree requirement)
- IT subscriptions to publications not currently available at firm
- Professional dues
- Attending professional events

## COMMENT

Some firms curve the tuition reimbursement to grades received; others pay a given percentage, from one-half to full tuition expense. Those curving the reimbursement to the grade pay 100 percent for a B, and books and mileage for an A. When one of the authors was with General Electric, the training was on company time if directly applicable to your job. If not, courses still could be taken, with half the time at company expense. Other education or training was on the employee's own time.

## [D]  Plan for the Future

Refer to your asset management list of hardware and software. List every hardware and software tool you use. Add to this list every critical process. Locate a copy of your department roster and build a spreadsheet. (See Exhibit 13-1 Employee/Process Matrix for an example.)

List the names down the left side of the page and the technologies across the top. Rate each employee from 1 to 5 (5 being an expert) on how skilled they are in this area. Do the same thing on a different spreadsheet for critical processes. Do you see any gaps? Are there two (preferably three) people in a high skill level for every technology or critical process? Combine this information with whatever new technologies are anticipated for the upcoming year and you have all you need to build a training plan for the upcoming year.

**EXHIBIT 13-1.** Employee/Process Matrix

**Employee/Process Matrix**

| | AS/400 | | | | | Shop Floor Systems | | | |
| | OS | | Applications | | | | | | |
| | Queue Mgmt | Admin | Order Entry | Payroll | Warehouse Sys. | VOC Tracking | Waterjet Cutter | Paint Line Robots | Tank Farm |
|---|---|---|---|---|---|---|---|---|---|
| Abraham Lincoln | | | | | | | | | |
| William McKinley | | | | | | | | | |
| Theodore Roosevelt | | | | | | | | | |

### [E]  Training and Consultants

The development or installation of a major new technology is always an exciting time in an IT department. Often, temporary technical employees (consultants) are brought in since no one in the company has experience with this technology. It is a prudent policy to always match one employee to every one or two consultants. This allows the employee to gain valuable experience with the new product and provides a path for the eventual departure of the consultants. Otherwise, the consultants could become a permanent fixture.

## COMMENT

> IT managers at a major truck manufacturer complained that their ERP consultants often cost $200 per hour, and that many were needed to support the product. When asked why they didn't train their own employees to support the product, they said that if they did, the employees would just leave to be consultants!

## § 13.09  EMPLOYEE COMMUNICATIONS

### [A]  Overview

A constant complaint from employees is that they find out more about what is happening in their own department from other groups than they hear from their managers. Use all of the tools at your disposal to push a steady stream of information to your employees. They will feel more like a team and less like isolated islands. There are many avenues for employee communications: e-mail, fax, memos, newsletters, rumor boards, telephone, voice mail, information meetings, and work meetings. (The newsletter is covered in § 9.02[E], "PC Newsletter." Meetings are covered in Chapter 5, "Project Management.") More than one method should be used to communicate important employee information.

### [B]  E-Mail, Faxes, and Memos

E-mail, faxes, and memos should be brief and to the point. Avoid personal comments and local color. Where possible, the e-mail, fax, or memo should be written so that, to save time, no reply is needed: "If no response is provided, so and so will be permitted, not permitted, or admitted by you."

### [C]  Rumor Board

Address rumors immediately. One way is by use of the "Rumor Board."

1.  A person concerned about a rumor writes it on a slip of paper and places it in a locked box attached to the department bulletin board.

2.   Management reads the slip of paper and places a response on the bulletin board.

This same idea may be used on a computer network or e-mail, which speeds up the whole process.

### [D]   IT Telephone Communications

Speak normally and clearly. Answer the telephone by the name listed: by person ("Sam Jones speaking") or by department or unit ("mailroom").

Speak at a normal speed. If you are providing information that the other person is recording, ask if a pencil is handy. When reading a list of numbers, go slowly and read the numbers in groups. For example, with the number 2379446193, repeat it as 23-79-44-61 and 93. On the telephone it is OK to break the ice with informal conversation. In fact, it is better to mix business and informal conversation.

## § 13.10   IT EMPLOYEE COMPENSATION

### [A]   Overview

IT pay is high compared with some other disciplines but can be low for several reasons. One reason might be the IT head is not making enough himself/herself, and will not have a subordinate making more. Another reason is that some industries pay more than others do, so people change to industries paying more.

Pay is not the major concern for most IT people. Depending on which survey one reads, the importance of salary varies. Some place it about fifth in what an IT person looks for in a job. Pay in one firm may be high for the industry, but company benefits may be meager. However, if the pay is not approximately the market rate, then the better people will be hired away, and only the dregs will remain.

## COMMENT

Many years ago, one of the authors worked at a large company in Kansas City. The managers complained that the programmers did not stay with the company for more than 2 years. Most people that left moved to higher paying jobs. When asked why they did not pay their people more, the manager said, "Why? They'll just leave anyhow." Soon after, the author left for a higher paying job. The moral is, some companies are a place to which people migrate and some are places from which people migrate. At which type of company do you work?

## [B]   Determining IT Pay

There is a universal procedure for performing wage surveys. A consultant in IT wage studies is retained. This avoids internal conflicts known to occur with IT salary surveys. Consultants render unbiased reports. They have the credibility to support their findings. Also, have the consultant collect data on cost-of-benefits packages.

Before calling the consultant, have all job descriptions well defined and titled properly. This saves time and money. Do not provide any current salary or benefit information. The consultants should provide the firm with comparable salaries for all jobs within the IT organization. The organizational structure and staffing levels are needed to assist with the IT management salaries. The consultant should be familiar with the hardware complexity and total staff working within IT. When the study is completed, it is then safe to reveal the internal pay and benefit scale of IT. Another reason for not providing the information at the start is to convince top management that the information did not influence the consultants' findings. This information will help the consultants rectify any major pay difference in any of the job positions.

The next step is determining what percentile level is agreeable to top management. To be competitive, the pay scale should not be any lower than the upper third for the geographic region. This is recommended in IT supplemental personnel policies, and is a top management decision. It may not be resolved until after planning for the next budget year. If funds are available, problem areas may require attention now.

## [C]   IT Benefits Package

The consultant's report provides the benefit amounts paid by other firms. The IT supplemental personnel policies' recommended amount is for the average benefits, spousal and family, to be within the upper third of the region. This is a top management decision. Benefits may be more of a problem than salary, because benefit programs are designed for the company as a whole.

One solution is outsourcing the IT operation to implement an attractive salary and compensation package. Another approach is for the company to implement a cafeteria-style benefits program. The information systems unit could easily have the larger dollar amount needed without any problems. The other solution would be to raise the salaries even more so that the two together would be what is needed.

The ultimate solution is having a cafeteria plan. It provides an equal amount of money for each employee at the same job level. Employees select what is best for them:

- Life insurance
- Medical plan with options for dental and optical
- Company-matching 401k plan
- Stock purchase options
- Subsidized child care
- Profit sharing

- Paid membership in clubs or organizations
- Extra vacation days
- Tuition reimbursement
- Paid book and publication subscriptions

# § 13.11   IT EMPLOYEE BURNOUT

## [A]   Responsibility

No employee should suffer from burnout. Any supervisor responsible for pressure and time demands resulting in an employee's experiencing burnout is subject to a reprimand. The details for the reprimand are placed in the supervisor's folder. This will also include project managers or project leaders.

## [B]   Company Assistance

The management of information systems will do whatever is needed for the employee's recovery. The company pays for any medical and therapy assistance. Information systems will also arrange for the employee to have one week's vacation to recuperate. This will not be counted against the employee's accrued vacation time. Non-IT company employees will be granted the same privilege at IT expense. At the first signs of impending burnout, management must take steps to prevent it.

The following are suggestions to combat the problem:

- Encourage the person to take a seminar someplace that will reduce the strain and include a weekend "on the house" for some fun time. He/she may include his/her family in this weekend. No contact between company and employee will be allowed during this time.
- Periodically rotate IT tasks.
- Allow for telecommuting and more flexible work hours.
- Limit overtime.
- Limit on-call demands.
- Reassign workloads.
- Encourage feedback.
- Schedule social group activities for meeting project milestones.

## [C]   Signs of Burnout

IT management should be aware of any signs of impending burnout. Symptoms of burnout are:

- Extreme dissatisfaction with their work
- Notice of heavy drinking or substance abuse during lunch or after work
- Reduced productivity
- Panic attacks
- Marital problems

- Problems working with co-workers
- Persistent eating, sleeping, and fatigue disorders
- Noticeable signs of depression

# § 13.12    IT EMPLOYEE PRODUCTIVITY

## [A]    Overview

The first consideration of worker productivity is what management does about it. The buck stops at the manager's desk. The United States has some of the world's best and worst management. An MBA doesn't guarantee a person has management and leadership skills required for IT management. IT productivity requires both management and leadership skills.

## [B]    IT Management Productivity

There are several indicators of good management: low employee turnover and absenteeism, no employee sabotage, good productivity, and a reliable employee suggestion system. The signs may look good but must be confirmed. Some ways to confirm this in information systems are:

- Projects are finished when planned.
- Completed projects are finished within budget.
- End users have faith in information system reports.
- Most IT job promotions are filled from within the company.

IT managers must actively work outside their offices. Do not depend on memos and the telephone to understand IT productivity. The following suggestions can help management actively promote IT production:

- Encourage participatory management.
- Ask what can be done about problems, and listen.
- Set realistic norms and goals.
- Use real quality circles.
- Employ time management.
- Delegate and follow up.
- Learn when to say no.
- Set deadlines.
- Finish what is started.
- Do difficult jobs during the more productive time of day.
- Make a daily timetable.
- Do unpleasant things first.
- Realize employee behavior may be due to weak supervisors.

Management requires feedback to gauge productivity results. One way is the question and suggestion box. Also, praise managers who deliver results. Inform them if they are meeting your goals as the project moves along, not a month later.

### [C]   IT Employee Productivity

It is more difficult measuring IT personnel's productivity than production jobs. Areas hard to monitor are systems and programming. Programmers are too often measured on how hard and long they work, and how many lines of code they write. The ignored programmer is often the one who could do the same program in much less time with half the lines of code and no test data errors. He/she will not get the credit or salary increase but will leave the firm.

To discover the level of a programmer's productivity, survey other programmers about how they would rank their colleague's skills. Do this at employee review time. The feedback could be informative. Other ways to get feedback are:

- End users speak well of the help desk and other IT assistance by programs and systems. The flip side of this is when users specifically ask that you not send a certain person to their department again.
- Use work simplification studies for programmers and systems people.
- Compare performance with other projects and tasks.
- Have all projects' work effort ranked regarding each member's contribution to the project's completion.
- Have a programming contest. Identify your best programmers. This may also confirm management's suspicions.
- What course grades are received?
- Notice who is the most helpful and who people go to for help.
- Review how systems conversions are made. Are the end users satisfied with the assistance, training, help-desk response, and the presence of project members during and after the conversion?

## § 13.13   REMOVING PROBLEM IT EMPLOYEES

### [A]   Overview

There will be times when an employee has to be removed from his/her job. The person may also be a problem with other IT or end-user employees; therefore, the only solution is removal. This may be required from time to time. This procedure must be in place before it's needed.

### [B]   Firing Problem IT Employees

Firing an employee for reasons other than stealing, sabotage, or physically assaulting a co-worker requires some documentation. The following should be practiced before terminating an employee:

- Provide honest feedback on areas requiring improvement and document the information.
- Don't expect things to improve—report incidents when they occur, and document the time and date of what was said.

- Present the information during evaluations, and have the employee sign that he/she has received the information.
- Be very clear about standards governing the person's responsibility.
- Prepare for the termination quietly. Have all his/her computer access cut off at a given time. Have him/her return anything that he/she may have removed from the company site.
- Inform the individual that he/she is a good employee but not suited for his/her job.
- Provide any assistance in planning his/her next career move. Consider using outplacement professionals for assistance with the transition process.
- Inform him/her that his/her personal items will be packed that night and sent to his/her home. Any company property (e.g., books or training material) must be returned.
- Have the employee escorted to his/her car. If he/she does not have a car, call a cab and have the company pay for it.
- Let the employee know he/she can feel free to use the company as a reference.

# § 13.14    IT MANAGEMENT COMPETENCIES

## [A]    Overview

It is not enough having technical knowledge, skills, and experience to be successful in an IT management position. As technology becomes integrated with every aspect of a business, the business community expects solutions from IT management. Technology solutions reduce the complexity of business processes, cut costs, and help manage independent work activities. General management skills rather than the traditional technical management skills help make an effective IT manager.

## [B]    Seven Key Competencies

IT management is much more than implementing, supporting, and maintaining systems. It is working closely with business line management and end users to best understand their needs and requirements. It is working as a member of a cross-functional team designing new systems. Change does not happen when a new system is implemented and new policies are established. IT management needs to influence behavior change to support the new system. Once upon a time the IT function focused on knowing how to use machines; now it is focused on how people use information.

There are seven key competencies that are needed for the successful IT manager.

1. **Business knowledge.** This involves having an overall knowledge of how business works, including understanding policies, practices, and trends affecting the industry and the organization. It also includes

identifying current and future competitors and the strategies and tactics making them successful. The IT manager should be able to discuss IT issues in the context of finance, sales, marketing, logistics, and distribution to evaluate the best business technology solutions. With this knowledge, the IT manager becomes a better business partner, aware of the issues, priorities, and concerns of their internal customers. IT management moves from a functional focus to a big picture focus.

With the big picture view, the IT manager enables the company to best benefit from technology as a business resource. Today e-commerce alone is changing how organizations do business. An example is the emergence of Amazon.com, which is challenging the methods of other booksellers such as Borders and Barnes & Noble.

2. **Communication.** For the IT manager to be a true business partner in the organization, he/she will need to communicate his/her knowledge and perspective related to technology and the business. This message has to be communicated with the audience perspective in mind. Not all business partners are literate in IT terminology; therefore, choose words wisely to communicate effectively. A skilled communicator expresses his/her thoughts clearly, concisely, and in a manner appropriate to the audience.

Organize communications so the main point of the message is clear. Messages that are too wordy, have grammatical or usage errors, or are disorganized are ineffective and present a poor image of the IT function.

Knowing when to communicate is as important as knowing how to communicate. When in doubt about communicating an issue, inform the appropriate parties. Very rarely are internal customers complaining that an issue has been overcommunicated.

3. **Customer-focused.** The first step in providing excellent customer service is knowing the customers, their needs, and their expectations. This information should be received firsthand from the customer, not what the IT manager believes the customer needs are. Customer contact involves regular communications to keep up to date on changing needs and expectations. Once customer information is gathered, decisions should be made with the customer perspective in mind.

## COMMENT

Remember that IT is a service organization that only exists to serve the users. If the service is poor, then the service needs to be replaced.

IT management must be committed to providing exceptional customer service. IT management's role is to identify and remove any barriers to providing top-notch service. Some of these barriers include excessive paperwork, acceptance of the status quo, or front-line workers lacking decisionmaking authority. The IT manager also seeks feedback from the customer. The IT manager has to handle criticism, complaints, and special requests. This is all part of improving customer service.

Some organizations have established "Service Level Agreements" with their internal customers. These agreements specify and measure the services IT provides to its internal customers. These are often established with a team of IT professionals and representatives from the business units to benchmark current service levels and to negotiate future needs and service levels.

4.  **Interpersonal skills.** At all levels inside and outside the organization, interpersonal skills are critical in building effective teams and in meeting organizational goals and productivity levels. Interpersonal skills involve treating people fairly and with respect, being approachable, showing a personal interest in others, being positive in all interactions, using diplomacy and tact in volatile situations, and developing a more accepting view of others' strengths and weaknesses.

    The IT function is sometimes seen as being more interested in technology than in people. To overcome this stereotype, it is important that IT management is visible in the organization and increases contact with those outside their own department.

5.  **Project management.** A project is often defined as a problem with a defined schedule for a solution. Project management is different from general management, which involves managing repetitive activities. Project management involves defining, planning, and meeting project objectives. These objectives include performance levels, time commitments, and cost issues.

    Effective project management skills rely on the ability to organize resources and activities. Problem-solving skills are as important as organizational skills. Use problem-solving skills to simplify complex processes and identify opportunities for synergy and integration. A strong knowledge of the business and organizational culture helps identify the best solution when problem solving.

    Because project management skills involve coordinating people, excellent interpersonal and communication skills are key. Many projects use team members from different functions in the organization, which means the project manager has no direct authorization over these individuals. Strong communication and interpersonal skills are helpful in dealing with issues that may occur because of this situation.

6.  **Strategic outlook.** With technology constantly changing, strategic thinking is paramount in any IT organization. A strategic outlook requires anticipating future trends and consequences and envisioning credible possibilities for the future success of the organization. The person with a strategic outlook displays curiosity, flexibility, and breadth of knowledge and interests. The person must have critical, conceptual, creative, and intuitive thinking skills. The higher his/her role in the organization, the more strategically focused the individual must become.

7. **Team builder.** Much of the work in the IT arena involves teams. Teams are established when implementing new financial software, developing a Web site, or identifying business requirements for a new marketing system.

   A team builder establishes a common cause and shared mindset among team members. This person also creates a strong sense of morale and team spirit that supports open dialogue and open lines of communication between team members. The skilled team builder knows the best teams comprise a variety of skills and abilities, and brings out the best from each team member. The effective team builder recognizes that success or failure of the project depends on each team member fulfilling his/her role.

## [C]   Methods for Developing Competencies

Once key competencies are identified, the IT organization begins assessing the skill level of its current and future management population. Skill assessments, supervisor and peer observations, and feedback from customers are effective skill assessment tools. Once skill levels are assessed, establish a development plan. Few individuals fully demonstrate the above-mentioned skills, but people can develop these skills if properly trained. Just as technical skills can be learned and practiced, so can the competencies listed above. Here are several methods to develop the skills discussed earlier.

1. **Job rotation.** Job rotation ranges from a complete job change temporarily to acting as a project manager for a small assignment. It can include filling an IT position or performing general management responsibilities temporarily.

2. **Memberships.** Use associations to gain and share information about products, best practices, and the newest developments in technology. Associations exist at the national, regional, and local level for those in the IT industry from CIO to IT professional. Below is information on four IT trade associations:
   • Society for Information Management; Phone: (312) 527-6734 Fax: (312) 245-1081 Web site: *www.simnet.org*
   • Association of Information Technology Professionals; Phone: (800) 224-9371 Fax: (312) 245-1070 Web site: *www.aitp.org*
   • The Conference Board and the Information Management Center; Phone: (212) 759-0900 Fax: (212) 980-7014 Web site: *www.conference-board.org*
   • The Information Management Forum; Phone: (770) 455-0070 Fax: (770) 455-0082 Web site: *www.infomgmtforum.com*

3. **Mentoring.** A mentor helps a junior person identify areas for improvement, develops an action plan, provides feedback, and holds the person accountable for improving his/her performance and skill level. Mentors also seek out opportunities for the mentored to attend or make presentations at upper management meetings they would not normally attend. These events provide an excellent opportunity for

upper management to notice the mentored. Mentoring is an effective tool, especially helpful in learning to navigate a company's culture and politics.

The mentor also gains from the relationship. The mentor develops his/her management skill, and is often credited for the mentored's success.

Some mentoring programs are formal, including policies, training for mentors, and a defined process for matching mentor and mentored. Less formal programs rely on the mentor and mentored making their own contact.

4. **Reading.** There are many IT magazines and books, but to understand general business issues and strategic thinking skills, use other books and publications. Check *Forbes, Fortune, Wall Street Journal, Harvard Business Review, Wired, Fast Company*, and *Strategy and Leadership*, a publication of the Strategic Leadership Forum.

5. **Training.** Use both internal organizational training programs and outside sources. Large organizations have complete curriculums for developing the competencies discussed earlier. Colleges and universities across the country have executive education programs focusing on management skills. Some include the University of Pennsylvania's Wharton School, Stanford Continuing Education Executive Programs, and The Ohio State University Fisher College of Business. Other training sources include the American Management Association and the Center for Creative Leadership.

## § 13.15   IT TELECOMMUTING POLICY

Telecommuting is a growing alternative to the traditional office-bound work practice. Telecommuting benefits both the employee and the employer. Improperly implemented, however, due to poor policies and procedures, it can be disastrous. Require a formalized policy to develop program procedures. If a program already exists, examine it carefully to determine if appropriate modifications are required. If none, then the firm's policy may be adapted. If modifications are required, add them as "riders" applied to existing policies.

Before a policy is adopted, establish the telecommuting definitions. The policy can apply to any forms of telecommuting. The definition and taxonomy are the following:

- Telecommuting is providing telecommunications hardware and software to an employee working out of the house. Most often this work is done from, but not limited to, an employee's home.
- A full-time telecommuter is an employee whose work is performed offsite. At times, the employee will have to be away from his/her place of work. This can be for staff meetings, seminars, etc. If this is not possible for the employed telecommuter, other arrangements will be required. The definition of full-time is that 100 percent of the work effort is done 100 percent of the time as a telecommuter. The employee is not re-

quired to be a full-time employee, and the hours of work can be defined, not defined, or flex-time. (See § 13.17, "IT Flex-time Policy.")

- A part-time telecommuter works part time at his/her company site and the rest of the time as a telecommuter. This can be a part-time or full-time position. It can even be a job-shared arrangement (see § 13.16, "IT Job-sharing Policy") or flex-time (see § 13.17, "IT Flex-time Policy").
- Extended workday telecommuters are employees extending their full-time workday. This can be for days normally off, and include after-hours telecommuting. Limit this form of telecommuting to salaried personnel.

There could be problems with hourly workers' time records and overtime problems, but none with salaried personnel. Provide human resources management with policies and procedures for telecommuting IT employees. The human resources manager will approve the policy in writing. Human resources can assist the development of the program and can provide formal follow-up feedback as to the program's success.

Telecommuting has gained popularity over the last few years. There will soon be over 10 million telecommuters in the United States. Information technology is a natural for this work arrangement. With the shortage of available IT personnel, this can be an attractive option for attracting new employees. With the advent of cable modems, DSL, and other broadband connections, the speed of telecommunications has far exceeded the telephone line modem for Web site and e-mail access. Some of the documented benefits have been:

- Marked employee productivity
- Greater job satisfaction
- Less job turnover
- Lower absenteeism
- Lower company worksite expense due to:
  - Annual office floor space cost
  - Reduced employee parking requirements
  - Reduced janitorial service costs
  - Less need for utilities

Some workers with physical challenges would prefer to work at home. Others could work from remote sites or even out of the country. Employees could benefit from the following:

- Lower day care costs
- Lower transportation costs
- Less travel time and fighting traffic
- Less time spent getting ready for work
- Reduced eating-out costs
- Reduced wardrobe investment
- Less need for a second car
- More flexible lifestyle
- Can have the radio on

Test the feasibility with a pilot test program, limited to a given area of information systems. When the program has been in operation for 6 or more months with success, proceed with a more permanent operation plan. Both programs will require budget requests.

Contract service personnel can provide telecommuting services. The arrangement would be on a test basis before signing a formal final contract. All contracts require the corporate legal advisor's approval before any commitment in writing.

Set up a budgeted account for this operation's expense and capital expenditures. The budgeted expenditures are classified as the following:

1. Capital expense
   - PC system and software
   - Office furniture
   - Power backup, UPS and/or generator
2. Telecommuter operational expense
   - Utilities allowance
   - Hardware maintenance contract
   - Help-desk contract/service
   - Computer and office supplies
   - Replacement parts
   - Software updates
3. Administrative expense
   - Off-site insurance
   - Training remote workers
   - Employee off-site insurance
4. Off-site supervisory expense

## COMMENT

One company had a highly productive employee who left the company to spend more time with her newborn baby. She had extensive knowledge of accounting data systems that no one else in the department possessed. They retained her as a part-time telecommuting worker, and removed everything from her workload except the accounting support.

## § 13.16   IT JOB-SHARING POLICY

Job sharing can benefit both parties. Two different skill levels, not necessarily equal, can fill one full-time position. They may share the same IT talent or not, but could share the same office facilities. It does not require each have half of the job. Divide this position as flex-time responsibilities or even tele-commuting. Flexibility can attract higher skilled talent than more traditional routes for IT specialties. Fill the position with salaried employees.

Pay for job-shared positions will not require equal pay for equal time. The employee benefits package may not be the same for both parties. The cafeteria benefit plan provides for a more equitable distribution of benefits. Paid vaca-tion time as part of the benefit program should resolve the vacation question. Policy about taking unpaid vacation time should be determined in advance for this arrangement.

This policy attracts better talent to the IT opportunities with the firm. It assures a backup is available. It is better to lose a half-person specialty than a whole, if that position is the only one IT has. This provides for safer backup than that talent being vested in one person. Depending on the re-sponsibility, the job sharing may be done by related people, as long as one of the people, upon giving notice of leaving the firm, would not affect the other member, too.

## § 13.17  IT FLEX-TIME POLICY

Flex-time has been tried successfully in many firms. Flex-time is defined as when the IT staff has open windows of time to arrive or leave work provided an 8-hour day is completed. This also applies to telecommuting and job-sharing positions. The job may be hourly or salaried depending on the position.

There will be core time when all employees are required to be present: for meetings, training, etc. This will be no less than a 3-hour window. Core time is at the discretion of the CIO/IT head. The flex-time window will be no more than 4 hours on each side of the core time. Anyone abusing this will be placed back on standard work hours the IT operation maintains.

# 14

# IT TRAINING: BUILDING THE TEAM

# § 14.01 IT TRAINING POLICIES

Information technology training begins with the orientation of new personnel and continues to help employees meet changing technology skill requirements. Computer personnel realize their skills can quickly become obsolete. This is one of the reasons they move on to jobs providing opportunities to learn new skills.

An IT training policy provides the opportunity for ongoing education and training of IT employees and information systems users. An IT department functions effectively only if its personnel and users are properly trained.

Conduct an evaluation after each training course or program is completed. A second evaluation follows 3 to 6 months after.

# § 14.02 MANAGING IT TRAINING

## [A]  Overview

Traditionally, training responsibility has come under the jurisdiction of computer operations managers. IT training is not limited to information systems personnel, but extends to all system users; therefore, the training manager for IT should control the training function and report to the manager of IT.

The scope of IT training covers areas from new employee orientation to retraining current employees in new technologies. Employees should be able to draw on a host of training opportunities, because no one single device serves all needs.

## COMMENT

IT training costs exceed $10 billion a year in the United States, but in fact, direct training expense is normally far less than the cost of the employee's time during the training.

## [B]  Keeping Records of Training

Each IT employee file contains education and training information, including training the employee brings to the department and recommendations for future training. All additional training received is posted to a file that is part of the IT skill inventory. (See § 13.08, "Employee Development" for more procedure information.) Starting a file is simple; keeping it up to date is a more challenging task. Don't neglect this.

IT employee training files contain the following information.

1.  **Education and training before joining the IT department**
    a.  Degrees received, courses taken, dates, and grades
    b.  Dates of noncredit courses taken

     c.   Type of work-related material read

     d.   Dates of certifications received

     e.   Listing of professional memberships and any offices held

     f.   The hardware type and software used if the employee owns a personal computer

2. **Future education and training benefiting the employee.** Establish the training needs of each employee. This information can justify a training program and give the people on record first choice. Priority is as follows:

     a.   Training or education that helps develop personnel for current positions:

        • Areas of weakness

        • Areas that require training to stay current with new technology

     b.   Training or education needed for promotion

3. **New education or training received**

     a.   Upon completion of training not provided in-house, each employee forwards to the IT department a memo containing the following to be included in the employee's file:

        • What training was received

        • Who provided the training

        • What grade was received, if any

        • When the training was received

     b.   Upon completion of in-house programs, the overseer of IT training programs forwards the necessary information for inclusion in the training record files. For non-IT people, a memo will be sent to each supervisor listing which of their employees have completed the training and indicating the following:

        • What training was received

        • When the training was conducted

        • Personnel who are to receive credit for completing the program

## [C]   Employee Recognition

When an employee completes an in-house course, his/her supervisor should present a certificate for course completion. Certificate forms are available from most office supply firms and should be completed and signed by the manager of training and also the IT manager.

## [D]   Education Information Booklet

The IT education unit provides an "education information booklet" to all new IT employees as part of an orientation package. Revised editions are distributed to all current IT employees. It should contain the following information:

1. **IT outside education policy and procedures.** Outline the type of support the firm provides for outside education and training, and the procedures required to apply for sanctioned education outside the firm. Copies of any required reimbursement forms are included.

2. **Scheduled courses offered by the training unit.** Detail the

courses offered, including dates and times, requirements for admission, and procedure for enrolling in courses and/or programs.

3. **A list of self-paced training packages available.** This list is available from the IT training unit and includes videotapes, self-teaching texts, and PC self-instruction programs. Include an explanation of how to request this material.

4. **Publications available.** A list of books and journals should be available in the IT training department and/or computer store.

## [E]   Non-IT Employee Training

The need for computer operation training is not limited to the IT department. Make companywide training available to all computer users. This not only provides needed training, but also helps to create goodwill between IT and the rest of the firm. The charge-back for these services depends on corporate cost accounting procedures.

Request for training may be initiated by a user or an IT project leader. A user's request should be in the form of a memo from the user's management, directed to the IT trainer. If a project leader desires the service, make it part of the formal project effort.

Furnish a list of users completing each course to the employee's supervisor(s) by a memo from the manager of the IT training unit. All persons completing the program receive certificates of completion forwarded to the employee's supervisor for presentation.

## [F]   Outsourced Training

Because not all information systems departments have resources available for in-house IT training, it is common to use outsourcing firms for professional IT training at the firm's location. (See Chapter 15, Vendors: Getting the Goods, for more information.)

Recordkeeping of outsourcing personnel training is still done by the IT department for IT personnel. A person delegated by the manager of IT provides user training. Costs will be paid from the IT training budget. User training can be charged back to the user's budget and prorated if need be. This is all dependent on the internal accounting practice of the company.

Training evaluation is performed by a person from the IT department at the end of the course or program. Payment may be governed by the results of the evaluation. If so, inform accounts payable of this procedure before the outside firm bills for the service. The follow-up 3- to 6-month evaluation, also performed by the IT training department, is particularly important to alter future training if needed. The evaluation also is an effective way to judge the provider of the outsourced training.

## [G]   Annual Reporting

The IT training unit should submit an annual report of activities, including cost.

> ## COMMENT
>
> Cost justification (relating dollars to return on investment) of training dollars spent can be a problem because most of the returns are intangible. Any input from user management can help. However, intangible items contribute to the company's bottom line and should be listed in the annual report. There is a worldwide fast-food chain known for its training programs and even more for its success story.

Time required to produce instruction packages is often more than anticipated. Preparation time rule of thumb for a lecture presentation with simple slides can be as much as 15 hours for each lecture hour. Producing a 30-minute video presentation can take up to 200 hours. General planning, setup, reporting, and equipment repair will consume time. All these hours are reported. Treat each new program as a project with individual cost of materials and time cost reported. Compute time cost as hourly cost plus benefits.

> ## COMMENT
>
> Be aware that training and education evaluations can be subjective. People tend to give higher appraisals when they are entertained.

Both students' and trainers' time is a cost factor. With new technology, training and preparation time can be reduced. Therefore, the training department should house an array of software and hardware tools to be effective. Drop ineffective resources. Include plans for the coming year, as well as current year results, in the annual report. The report also should contain activities of the training unit for the year. The following items are reported:

- Number and size of classes conducted
- Number of self-study programs completed
- Number and purpose of new programs developed
- Total number of people served by training unit
- List of participant evaluation comments with any supervisor's comments or memo information

# § 14.03   NEW EMPLOYEE ORIENTATION

## [A]   First Impressions

First impressions are lasting, and in time, those employees reacting negatively may depart for another firm. To create a positive, lasting impression during the employee's first few days, the IT department follows two simple procedures. First, designate a mentor. Second, give the employee a welcome education package.

> ### COMMENT
>
> An insurance company in Ohio thinks so highly of this training that they developed and carefully follow a detailed procedure for new employee indoctrination and education.

## [B]   IT Orientation Package

This package is a compilation of useful information for the new IT employee. It should contain the following information:

1. **Organization description.** At a minimum, the organization description includes an explanation of each unit's function and identifies those in charge. An organizational chart is useful for large departments.

   Include a short chronological history of the information systems operation. This provides the new employee with information about promotion tracks, areas of vested interest, and fast-track employees. Note IT's position within the organization.

2. **Equipment and facilities.** List all the hardware in use and its locations. Identify personnel authorized to use the equipment.

   A facilities map should include the locations of the restrooms, dining areas, and restricted facility areas.

3. **Telephone numbers.** Provide an up-to-date telephone directory of the firm. Include a supplementary list of numbers for frequently called IT units, personnel, and services.

4. **E-mail listing.** Indicate the proper way to address e-mail to other employees.

5. **Mail.** Note when and how the employee will receive his/her mail. This covers both interoffice and outside mail (U.S. Postal Service, UPS, FedEx, etc.).

6. **Forms.** Include a listing of all important forms required by IT personnel, providing the name and number of each form, its source and destination(s), purpose, and any other special information.

Include samples used by the new employee's unit. The needs of computer operators are not the same as systems analysts, so packages for new employees may contain different forms.

7. **Schedules.** Include schedules of operations in the procedure package. These can be daily, weekly, or monthly. For daily schedules include begin and end times of normal activities, such as breaks and lunch hours.

The weekly, monthly, and annual schedules contain paydays, holidays, vacation scheduling, and meetings. Some IT departments publish monthly listings of employees' birthdays.

8. **Glossary and practices.** This section contains a list of common terms and acronyms used by IT and the firm. Note practices that are extremely important or different from the industry norm.

9. **Unit procedures.** This section contains a listing of all IT procedures and where they are explained. Use a check-off list for each type of IT procedure. Check off and date as new employees read the material.

## COMMENT

A firm in Michigan, for its own reasons, does not run a slash through the character zero. They place the slash through the alpha character O. There were problems because a new programmer was unaware of this practice. Emphasize unusual department practices to minimize difficulties.

10. **IT project descriptions.** New programmers, systems analysts, and other staff personnel should be provided a list of current and pending IT projects. Note a short description of the objective, as well as target dates, along with the project managers' names.

### [C]   Mentor Assignment

Joining a company can be a personally traumatic situation. New employees feel disoreinted since they do not know where basic services in the facility are located or how to make requests for simple support. At the same time, they are striving to make a good first impression on the new co-workers.

New IT personnel require a "personal touch." Each new employee is assigned a mentor, someone to give a permanent positive impression of the firm. The selected mentor should be personable, someone who the new employee feels comfortable about asking questions concerning procedures. The mentor must also be patient. Often a simple question answered calmly by a mentor is critical for a new employee. The mentor should not be condescending, which only makes the new IT employee nervous and doubtful about his/her future. A mentor program allows new employees to become productive much more quickly since all of the new employee's questions can be answered directly.

The mentor is responsible for ensuring that the new employee is given a tour of the facility to see where basic services are located, and is properly introduced to his/her co-workers. The mentor ensures that a work area is ready when the employee arrives for the first day of work. The work area should include a telephone, a workstation, a desk containing basic office supplies, log-on passwords, voice-mail password, and in some cases, their new business cards.

Remember that first impressions are lasting. A new IT employee joins the department with high hopes, and a mentor's positive attitude can become infectious, reinforcing these high expectations. Make them feel welcome and a member of the team.

# § 14.04  EMPLOYEE TRAINING

## [A]  Determining Training Needs and Objectives

This section does not attempt to address the detailed, day-to-day procedures of running a training unit, which are up to the manager of training. IT managers should have a grasp of what to expect.

The first step is determining the objectives of the training. Next, make an instructional assessment of each person involved in the learning project. What does each need to learn? All IT training or educational projects should contain this information in their "training project" documentation.

Determine the kind of learning to be accomplished. There are three basic classifications of learning, each requiring different training instruments. They are:

1. **Cognitive domain.** Cognitive learning requires intellectual activity of some sort, such as making judgments, synthesizing information, applying learned information, interpreting information, and recalling information. This is the most common form of learning in IT training.
2. **Psychomotor domain.** Psychomotor learning requires muscle coordination and includes hearing and eye movement. Traditionally this has been associated with IT keyboard data entry, but with the advent of PCs the need for these skills has expanded.
3. **Affective domain.** Affective learning involves values and attitudes. It includes changing undesirable attitudes and may be required in training users with values or attitudes affecting productivity or the success of projects and operations.

Select the training instrument after determining instructional needs. At the same time, develop evaluation criteria determining when the learning objective has been met. This evaluation may be an exam—written answers to questions, performance of a task or procedure, or execution of a response to a given condition.

Exams can be written confirming that the desirable learning level has been met. This is criterion-referenced testing. People who master a test at the level required by the learning criteria then pass. If a whole group does not meet the criteria, the learning project has failed. This is a better evaluation than a subjective evaluation by employees upon completing training.

### [B]  Types of IT Training

Training can be provided in a formal manner for groups or informally for individuals. Formal IT training can be divided into two types: instructor-based and self-paced. Instructor-based training includes seminars, classroom workshops, and one-on-one instruction.

One-on-one instruction may be the best training, but is the most expensive. Classroom instruction is less expensive, but the cost of the students' time must also be considered. Sending employees away for vendor class instruction can be expensive if employees are out of town overnight.

There can be problems with classroom workshops and seminars. All personnel involved may not be available at the same time. More than one group may have to be scheduled at a time, and even then there can be scheduling conflicts.

For these reasons, self-paced instruction has gained popularity in information technology. The training is available to fit schedules and people can work at their own pace.

Self-paced instruction is not only reading manuals and other vendor-furnished materials. It includes PCs, audiocassettes, video, and Internet-based training. When selecting a training approach, the trainer ensures it is appropriate for the learning domain needed. Validate that the hardware and/or software meets the training objectives before any commitment to buy or lease.

For informal education/training of both user and IT personnel, have reading material available. Computer journals and magazines are a good source of up-to-date information. The average systems analyst should spend at least 7 to 8 hours a week just reading. IT management personnel have been known to do even more.

## § 14.05   PRESENTATION METHODOLOGIES

### [A]  Overview

Successful training presentations require a capable presenter, supported with instructional tools and a proper learning environment. It is management's responsibility to supply these. The instructor has the final responsibility for the learning presentation. Preparation can average 15 hours for each hour of delivery. The more frequent the presentation, the more preparation can be justified. A good 30-minute slide production can take 200 or more hours to produce.

Thanks to TV, today's students recognize quality media productions. The presentation can run from a few minutes to an extended program of many hours.

There are several good publications covering industrial instruction and presentations, with some of the better ones free. One recommended publication is *Presentations,* published monthly by Bill Communications Human Performance Group, 50 South Ninth St., Minneapolis, MN 55402. National organizations, including Toastmasters International and industrial training groups, help people develop presentation skills. Reference material for both organizations and publications is available in the public library.

One of the best, if not the best, training facility in the world is McDonald's® Hamburger University in the Chicago area. McDonald's would not be successful today without its training program. Not only is training conducted using state-of-the-art technology, but it is also cost-justified and administered by qualified management. This training is not limited to Hamburger University but incorporated at every level of McDonald's operations.

## [B]   Presentation Room

Conduct the presentation in a room adequate for presenting instructional materials. It should be large enough to comfortably house learners without distractions, with enough light for note-taking. The temperature should be between 68 and 72 degrees.

Rooms can be rented off-site, if need be, when adequate rooms are unavailable or to get the people away from work distractions. The instructor should be familiar with the room before he/she commits to using it.

Conveniences enhancing the presentation are:

- Lights controllable by the presenter
- Power outlets in locations needed
- A whiteboard for writing or projection
- A lectern
- Restrooms close by
- Place for learners to hang their coats
- Tables with comfortable chairs
- A ceiling-mounted screen that can be tilted to be perpendicular to a projector

## [C]   Presentation Devices

The trainer selection of presentation aids is limited only by his/her budget. Operation of training devices may be augmented by the vendor and by demonstrations. The company's own training department may also help. Before using any new device, the trainer should be familiar enough with its operation to concentrate on the presentation, not the device.

Consider both audience size and composition before preparing a media presentation. Time allotted will determine the amount of information presented and consumed. The location, importance of the presentation, and time limits all influence the choice of presentation materials.

- The importance of the presentation determines the cost, time, and effort expended. Will the presentation require several types of visuals and can the cost be justified?
- The purpose of the presentation determines which visual materials are employed. If mainly to inform, PowerPoint presentation software may best be chosen. If explaining complicated information, such as new procedures, systems, concepts, or numerical information, chart and graph overheads might be employed so the presenter faces the audience.
- Consider audience education level and corporate status when making the visuals.
- Do not assume the audience's technical knowledge. If possible, do some research. Better to understate technical complication than overstate it.
- Remember, whatever visuals are used in a presentation are to enhance what is said, not replace or detract from it.

Effective visuals are designed for simplicity, clarity, and visibility. The following suggestions should be helpful when constructing these aids:

- Proofread before presenting. Look for misspellings and information errors. Have someone else verify the materials for you. Set the presentation aside for a day or two, then give it a final look.
- If there is too much information to fit on the visuals, make handouts.
- Never have more than 6 to 8 words per line on the screen.
- Use only key words or phrases in the visual. This gives the presenter something to say.
- Never read the visual information for the audience.
- Add colored backgrounds and colored lettering for impact.
- Do not show lots of numbers. Information is better visualized by employing graphs or charts.
- Do not overuse computer-generated clip art.
- Remember KISS: Keep It Simple and Short. Show each visual briefly, less than a minute. Don't overload it with information.

1. **Flip charts.** Flip charts endure because they are simple to use, quick to prepare, and inexpensive. They are bulky to carry, but many conference rooms still have them. There are portable versions easier to carry in their cases. Smaller ones may be used for up to 15 or 20 people; larger ones are good for groups of 30 or more. Following are recommendations that can improve the presentation when using a flip chart:
   a. **Easel**
      - Consider using more than one easel.
      - When using more than one, position each so it can be seen by everyone.
      - Make sure the easel is tall enough so that all can see the bottom of the pads.
      - Use sturdy easels with a lip to hold different colored marking pens.

b.  **Easel pads**
    - Not all pads have the same spaced mounting. Make sure all easels and pad holes match up.
    - Use perforated pads because it is easier to remove pages from them.
    - Writing on white pad paper shows up more clearly than on colored paper.
    - Using lined pads makes writing before an audience neater.
    - If more than one easel is used, try different lightly colored pads. They may help the delivery.
    - Use paper heavy enough that the audience cannot see pages under the one being used or shown.

c.  **Marking pens**
    - Use wide felt-tip, watercolor markers. Permanent markers bleed through the paper and cannot be used on the whiteboards.
    - Multicolored markers add variety to the presentation.
    - Have a systematic method for employing colors, such as using green for page headings and items needing attention, and black for other items.
    - When not using the pen, place it on the easel lip.
    - When the pen starts to squeak, it is running out of ink. Discard it.
    - Have a good supply of colored pens.
    - Avoid using light-red pens as red is difficult to read from a distance. In addition, about 12 percent of men are color blind, and the most common color they have a problem with is red.

d.  **Prepared pages.** There are advantages to preparing flip charts in advance. For one, the printing will be neater and more legible. Class time will not be wasted writing. In addition, notes can be prewritten in pencil, unseen by the audience until the presenter goes over them with a felt-tip pen. If some pages are prepared in advance, a second easel is recommended for writing during the presentation. The following are suggested to enhance the prepared pages presentation:
    - Have a computer printer produce flip charts in color. If your firm does not own a printer for the size needed, find a graphics firm or large copy shop that does.
    - When traveling, place the rolled-up charts in a large cardboard mailing tube.
    - Insert blank pages between thin pages so the audience cannot read what comes next.
    - If using a large number of prepared pages use extra easels.

e.  **Use of flip charts.** First visualize, then write an outline (on $8\frac{1}{2}$-by 11-inch lined paper) of the presentation. After the outline is complete, highlight key points to be printed on the flip charts. The outline and any other notes can later be penciled on the edges of the flip chart pages. Do this after the pages have been lettered.

If there is only one easel available, place blank pages between the lettered ones for writing on. Notes can still be written on these blank pages. The following are suggestions that should help improve the presentation:

- Print the block letters 1 to 1½ inches high.
- Use wide felt-tip markers.
- Use the colors in some consistent fashion.
- Limit the number of lines of information to 10 if the audience is small, and to 8 if the group is large (over 25 ft away).
- Write key points in a shortened form. Abbreviations and acronyms are OK.
- When writing during the presentation, pencil in the words beforehand.
- Allow 20 to 30 seconds after writing before flipping the page. Give audience members time for any note-taking and thinking.
- Never stand in front of the easel after you have just completed writing.
- Minimize loss of audience eye contact except when writing.
- Practice your presentation a few days before in the designated room. If presentations are new to you and/or if this is a presentation important for your career, practice it a week in advance in the designated room and have it videotaped. You do not need anyone to run the camcorder. Just put it on a tripod.

2. **Overhead projectors.** Overhead projectors have been popular for presentations for some time. Low price makes them attractive; laser and inkjet printers can produce appealing color overheads. Although not as widely used as in the past, many presentation rooms are still equipped with an overhead projector.

There have been other improvements to the old design. Portable, compact overhead projectors are available. Automatic transparency feeders are also available. The continuous roll-feeding device provides a source of blank film to write on, freeing the presenter from standing next to the projector.

Additional information and advice about this device follows:

a. **Overhead projector concerns**
- Always have a spare bulb.
- Make sure the screen is usable.
- Lower room light level to enhance the projected image, but keep it high enough so people can take notes.
- Have heavy-duty extension cords available when needed.

b. **Ways to produce transparencies**
- Color inkjet printers
- Laser printer
- Copy machine
- Heat transfer
- Write-on
- Continuous-roll transparencies

c. **Resources for transparency material**
   - PowerPoint software
   - Digital cameras
   - Clip art
   - Scanners to input slides or photographs and hardcopy to a PC for producing overhead transparency output

d. **Markers**
   - Overhead color projection pens
   - Permanent color markers
   - Extra markers or pens

e. **Using the overhead projector**
   - Write on the whiteboard with erasable projection pens. This allows the presenter to add to what is projected on the board.
   - Look at the audience while reading.
   - The size of the printing should be large enough to read when it is lying at your feet while you are standing.
   - Allow 20 to 30 seconds at the end of each overhead for note-taking.
   - Do not crowd the overhead with copy.
   - Use color pens and transparencies to enhance the presentation.
   - Face the audience while operating the computer keyboard and/or overhead projector.
   - Never leave the light or screen for any length of time without a transparency in the projector.
   - Use graphics to enhance a presentation. Computer presentation software is available with alternatives to the use of a bullet chart. (You are reading a bullet chart now.)
   - Using transparency overlays adds impact to the overhead presentation. Overlays allow the presenter to build and reveal concepts, focusing the audience's attention on the evolving subject. As an example, a bullet chart can be built by superimposing lines of information, adding one bulleted line or section at a time, from succeeding layers of transparencies. In this instance, the pages are hinged so they will be in the proper position when overlaid and projected onto the screen.
   - Carrying the transparencies can become a problem, as static electricity can stick them together. A simple solution is placing them in transparency frames, which makes handling easier. Using a frame blocks out any unwanted light from around the edge during the projection. In addition, the edge of the frame provides space for presentation notes.

f. **LCD overhead projector.** This device is used either stand-alone or with an overhead projector and allows PC-generated information to be presented on the screen. With the proper hardware and software tools, it can greatly enhance the overhead presentation. The same presentation considerations apply to this as to the overhead projection method.

**COMMENT**

PowerPoint from Microsoft is probably the most popular program for creating slide presentations to be used with an LCD overhead projector. Microsoft can be reached at *www.microsoft.com.*

Visual information can be imported from other sources. Digital still cameras can photograph artwork that can be inputted to the system for display on the screen. Live photos, in color, can be taken of subjects or even of people in the audience and projected on the screen during the presentation.

g. **Digital program presentations.** With the availability of digital video cameras, even motion pictures can be inputted, along with digital stills on CDs, to the PC and displayed on the screen. If seriously considering digital video, look into digital projectors. It simplifies the hardware requirements for projecting still and moving images. If using this type of presentation material often, consider a multimedia PC system.

Digital CD PC programs can be developed for a group screen presentation or a self-paced PC learning package. Depending on the need, it can be a supporting instruction tool or a self-contained stand-alone package.

These software program applications are commonly referred to as "digital CD-slide show programs," even though they may contain "film clips." The orchestrated visuals, sound, transitions, and titles result in professional outputs. The DVD is the newest technology for final digital outputs that training units can now afford to use.

**COMMENT**

There are software packages available for all levels of expertise. Adobe Premiere, Ulead Video Studio, and Videoware are some of the many available. Your available supporting hardware and time to learn the skills needed to put programs together should dictate how professional your software should be.

h. **Slide projectors.** Although software programs such as PowerPoint have supplanted slide projectors for most presentations,

35mm slide projectors are still used today by some organizations. It provides better quality presentations than digital images for large groups. Slide projectors with sound added make for excellent, large-scale multimedia presentations.

For small groups, the easy-to-carry Caramate in its self-contained box can be placed at the end of a conference table and the slides projected on the wall, on a pull-down screen, or rear-projected onto its own 12- by 12-foot screen. With its self-contained sound tape system, it is an excellent teaching instrument, well suited to a self-paced learning program.

3. **Other devices**
   a. Sound presentation is useful, for example, in walking a person through a set of instructions for a particular procedure. The person can hear the instructions and, with hands and eyes free, take notes or perform the indicated actions.
   b. Video (digital and analog) productions are even more involved than slide sound or CD productions. Any presenter for limited applications can use video, but any major effort should be left to people with the skill and editing equipment needed.
   c. Showing VCR tapes for information and instruction is an increasingly available way of presenting programs. Some computer vendors have training videos. There are also videos for all kinds of PC instruction. If you can, preview before you buy.
   d. A computer can deliver a program via floppy disk, CD, or network that can be available for a group to view at its convenience or for a single-person tutorial. The program can employ text, graphics, stills, motion pictures, simulations, or interactive learning.

# 15

# VENDORS: GETTING THE GOODS

# § 15.01  VENDOR POLICIES

## [A]  Overview

The size of information systems operations and the uneven demand for IT services influence the type and amount of outside services required. In addition, available funds must be balanced with need: the two are seldom in accord. Outside service vendors can be management consultants, application service providers, Web hosting providers, and outsourcing and contract personnel.

The best policy for dealing with outside vendors is exercising good business practices based on sound moral and ethical codes. Depending on its dealings with vendors, the firm can lose or gain respect from other vendors, employees, and the industry at large. Remember that you need the vendor as a reliable partner and supplier; and the supplier needs you as a good customer.

## [B]  Vendor Selection

How does one select a firm that will actually deliver what is wanted, when it is wanted, and at the agreed price? The two major participants in this scenario are the firm providing the service and the firm purchasing the service.

Vendor service contracts should be signed based on the optimal solution for the IT department, not just on price. To avoid any form of possible collusion, there must not be any family or close personal relationships between a vendor and personnel with selection authority in a firm.

## COMMENT

Once airborne, cynical military transport pilots like to remind their passengers that their aircraft was built by the lowest bidder.

All agreements between a firm and the vendor must be in writing. The contract agent of each organization is the person signing; or else a designated person is specified in the agreement. Both parties signing must have the authority to represent their respective firms. Each contract should have a cancellation and a performance clause included.

Unfortunately, there are charlatans who are only in business to make a fast buck and some firms that overrate their services. Steering the company through the minefield of vendor incompetence is only half the challenge; the other is understanding one's own firm. An unrealistic internal cultural assessment can spell disaster for any undertaking even when employing the most competent service organization.

Be careful not to develop enemies when negotiating vendor services. Information systems personnel are mobile; their paths cross in unexpected ways. Interaction with a past vendor may be required in job searches. Attempt to steer clear of problem situations, but, in business as in marriage, many discoveries are made after the contract is signed.

## [C] Outside Services

The computer field is too complex to master all of its facets, let alone the technology necessary to deal effectively with outside services. For this reason, services of the firm's purchasing unit and/or legal staff might be requested. If the firm is too small to have in-house experts, rely on an outside service for this expertise.

The purchasing department provides information about vendors with which the company deals. For instance, it is advisable to know, when possible, if a vendor will still be in business next year. Part of the purchasing department's responsibility is knowing the financial status and reputation of vendors as well as the quality of their merchandise. This is information an IT department head should have before beginning negotiations.

The legal department reviews any contract with a vendor before large sums of the firm's capital are committed. There are a growing number of attorneys with this type of expertise who may be of assistance. The firm's attorneys should include a penalty clause in the event the vendor does not perform according to the agreement.

Most firms have a procedure to confirm upon receipt that an item meets purchase order requirements and to start the payment process for the invoice or bill received. This is usually not the case when purchasing outside services. Therefore, the IT manager must contact the accounts payable department before the bill arrives to ensure only services stipulated in the contract are paid. In addition, a delay of payment can be used to force an obstinate vendor to be cooperative in meeting contract obligations.

## [D] IT Outsourcing Policies

IT outsourcing is not the same as out-tasking. Out-tasking is traditional supplemental staffing for peak activity periods, while outsourcing is identified as a noncore function or one that is not directly involved with the major money-making areas of the firm.

The area for the outsourcing operation(s) is budgeted annually. Vendor contracts that expire within the next budget year require a new contract proposal one month before the cut-off for budget considerations. If the current vendor's performance or new proposal is unsatisfactory, a request for proposal (RFP) is sent to no fewer than two other vendors.

IT management must have a clear set of long-term goals and objectives for outsourcing efforts. Outsourcing should be used:

- For operations difficult to manage and staff
- To supply talent/resources unavailable in the organization
- To reduce internal operation costs

- To free resources for other efforts
- To bring improvements and benefits on board faster

To assist in the refinement of policy and strategy for outsourcing acquisition, The Outsourcing Institute may be contacted at (516) 681-0066 or at its Web site at *www.outsourcing.com.*

## § 15.02  CONSULTING SERVICE CONTRACTING

### [A]  Overview

Consulting services are often justified because in-house skills are unavailable, extra workerpower is required, or the firm is seeking an unbiased, objective opinion. Consulting firms have a variety of talented personnel with special skills who justifiably may not be employed in a corporate IT operation. Because work is usually divided into projects and accomplished at that level, these specialists are valuable for specific undertakings. Many of these personnel are well-paid, ambitious individuals who enjoy the variety of challenging assignments that only a consulting firm offers.

Projects and conversions can require more workerpower than normally available within the organization. Hiring extra people for such undertakings, then terminating them after completion of a task creates morale problems. Because consultants are temporary, they are ideal for these situations.

Outside consultants can be totally objective because they are not embroiled in the organization's political struggles. Therefore, they should be able to render excellent professional judgments. Unfortunately, whoever hired the consultant may sometimes have influenced the selection of a "cooperative" consultant, thereby losing objectivity.

### [B]  Kinds of Consulting Organizations

Consulting firms provide a wide array of skills. Some are part of an accounting firm while others are separate entities; the services provided can and do vary widely.

Some firms are computer-related. Feasibility studies and/or total systems design and implementation may be their specialty. They may also provide specialized skills in the areas of database systems, communication networks, IT audits, and related functions. Use these consultants on a temporary basis for a specific project or to troubleshoot a given problem.

Other firms may provide software development services and programming talent. These services require a great range of skills from coding to systems analysis and have a wide range of prices. There must be assurance that skill levels are commensurate with costs and that promises are kept. Some firms have been known to promise more than they deliver.

Accounting firms offering IT consulting services are expensive because of their interest in high-revenue contracts. Their area of expertise tends to center on financial and accounting systems. If there is a need for assistance in this area, contact a firm's own CPA first.

In the final analysis, the area of the country and metropolitan density determine what is available. A good source of information is other local IT management who required such services. There is nothing wrong with trying out a new firm; however, test performance with small "safe" projects before entrusting a major undertaking and a critical completion date. Include a time contingency when establishing due dates. The time needed will vary based on proven skills of the consultant and the importance of the finish date.

## COMMENT

The wise IT manager uses caution when hiring because consulting can be an avenue for gaining instant professional status with very little money or education. In one case, a student who failed a systems analysis course and dropped out of college later became a computer systems analysis consultant with a record of failures. No official board certifies or regulates computer consultants, and no codification of standard skills and procedures exists.

### [C]   Consultant Relationship Procedures

Consultants can be valuable assets if a proper relationship is established. They can be effectively employed or acquired for all the wrong reasons. Therefore, it is imperative that proper conditions are maintained maximizing the benefits a consultant provides while minimizing the cost. There are several procedures to follow when acquiring the services of an outside consultant.

1.  **Have defined goals.** The more nebulous the goal, the more time and money are spent on the project. Since consultants charge hourly, the more defined the goal, the less cost in time and money. The area should be well defined to narrow the scope of the project. In addition, do not acquire a consultant for any of the wrong reasons, such as:
    a.  To let the consultant be the bearer of bad news for projects in trouble.
    b.  To have the consultant as a political ally, the outside "expert" with credibility to justify decisions already made. This is an expensive practice.
    c.  Being impressed with the out-of-town expert. There sometimes seems to be a correlation among price, the distance traveled, and perception of the expert's skills. Management may be unduly impressed with a consultant's title, especially one who travels from afar and has "Ph.D." after his/her name.

    d.   Consultants often come up with solutions gleaned from present employees. There is really nothing wrong with this because a good consultant explores all possible solutions. It does, however, irritate competent in-house personnel.

    e.   To be a surrogate. A weak project manager may require a consultant to make decisions. However, a consultant serves at the staff level and should never take management responsibility. If this is needed, a "facilities management" service should be contracted. It is the less expensive route to take and creates fewer problems.

2.  **Define specifications and scope.** This gives the consultant a clear understanding of what to do and what to avoid. Make very clear what is expected as far as specifications and have this confirmed in writing. A major mistake in managing consulting services is to hire the consultant before clear specifications are developed and then complain about the cost.

    Any wasted effort will be included in the bill even if the firm does not get what it wanted. The IT manager should manage consultants just as any other employee—except that they should be used for the expertise for which they were hired. Do not drop them in a desk and walk away without instructions or you find a bill for a lot of wasted time!

    Because of the high turnover in the computer field, personnel may be here today and gone tomorrow. This also applies to new small consulting firms.

3.  **Required documentation.** The documentation left behind after the completion of a project may be the only source of reference when the job is finished. Proper documentation must also be provided for the consultant ensuring the consultant knows what is expected. Documentation is expensive and is all too often ignored to save time or money. Saving in this way will create more expenses later. When defining documentation requirements make sure the consultant and firm's standards are indistinguishable using the firm's format.

4.  **Monitoring the consultant's progress.** Agree to a monitoring procedure for the consultant in writing before signing a contract. Obtain feedback on the status of the consultant's work at predetermined time intervals by defining efforts in the smallest measurable units and relating them to percentages of the total. As progress is reported, the cumulated percent of progress completed can be compared to the cumulated dollars spent. These two values should be in accord to assure dollars budgeted would not be depleted before the project is completed. The effectiveness, or lack thereof, of the consultant's performance should not be a surprise at the end. As a visual monitor use a Gantt chart comparing the percent of units completed to the percent of funds billed by the consultant to date.

    Consultants are self-directed persons; they must be to survive in the profession. However, they may be sidetracked by extending their scope or may misinterpret directions received from more than one source. As with any newly employed personnel, consultants should

not be left alone for long periods. Nor should there be any misunderstanding as to the status of an in-process project. This should be well
documented in clear and understandably written, dated, and signed
reports.

5. **Always pair a consultant with an employee for development
   projects.** If the consultant has worked alone, the consultant walking
   out of the door when the project is completed has all of the project
   knowledge in their head. True, there may be system documentation
   but experience provides so much more. By pairing an employee to
   work alongside the consultant, you build in-house expertise for supporting the new project. It is also a good way to infuse a different
   technical perspective into your staff. A negligent IT manager ignores
   this step and then is forced to rehire the consultant for a high fee to
   provide ongoing system maintenance.

6. **Know who you're hiring.** When hiring consultants, you either hire
   a company's services or you hire the services of a specific individual.
   - When hiring a specific individual, it is easier to estimate the time
     and cost for a project based on their proven expertise. However,
     you must ensure that the specific person is available when they are
     needed. This is difficult if the purchasing paperwork is held up by
     budget politics.
   - When hiring the services of a company, interview each consultant
     before accepting them into your project. Large projects may require
     a number of consultants to complete it on time. A written "job
     description" prior to meeting with them will help to establish the
     appropriate billing rate for each level of expertise.
   - Whoever works on your project, ensure that they will remain on
     it for its duration. Do not allow the consulting company to change
     personnel assignments without your approval.

# § 15.03   CONTRACT PERSONNEL

## [A]   Overview

There may be reasons for using additional labor for a project or for conversion
to a new system. In these cases, use talented temporary personnel, not consultants, working in-house. These individuals vary in skills and include data entry
personnel, clerks, trainers, coders, programmers, and systems analysts. Length
of stay varies depending on when they are needed for a project. These people
will be paid through the accounts payable system like any other outside service.

This talent can be obtained in a number of ways. Although consultants
might provide some of these services, they can be an expensive choice. Many
temporary employment agencies can provide these types of people.

Some vendors may also provide systems and/or programming services.
Smaller firms tend to make this choice when acquiring a new computer system. Even mainframe vendors may have personnel available at an hourly rate
that also may be negotiable depending on the competitive climate.

## [B]   Justifying Contract Personnel

Many of the reasons for acquiring contract personnel are the same as for contracting a consultant. However, contract personnel are less expensive than consultants, and there may be other benefits to the company. Consider the following when deciding to go with this arrangement:

1.  **Contract personnel staffing.** Other than being paid through the accounts payable unit, contract personnel are treated like the firm's own personnel. They should be assigned work like regular employees, with the understanding there is no long-range commitment. Assignments can run from a few hours to an almost ongoing basis. Some years ago contract workers were thought of as semiskilled at best. Today they are found at the technical or management level.

2.  **Adjunct status.** Employees on a contract basis are "adjunct" to the project. Their connection is to the project or task, not the firm. A set sum of money is budgeted for a project with a given number of billable hours. To avoid the assumption of ongoing employment status, inform contract personnel of the given number of hours budgeted for the project. If his or her work is monitored, poor performance can be detected early and an inadequate person replaced by someone else more competent before the money runs out.

3.  **Monitoring performance.** When a contract person is finished with a project, his/her performance level should be established and recorded. If the same person is used in the future, that performance level can be used to compute a reasonably accurate schedule. It is a good practice to try out personnel on small tasks before making long-range commitments.

4.  **Specialization availability.** For a one-time effort, it is often cheaper to hire a contract person than incurring the expense of in-house training (even assuming that in-house personnel are available to concentrate their energies on acquiring a new skill). A specialist, who constantly uses a talent, continually honing it, can perform at a higher skill level than anyone trained in-house for just one project.

5.  **Maintaining employer reputation.** When large projects or parallel operations occur without contract personnel, the question arises as to what will happen to surplus personnel after the demand is over. Whether or not job security doubts are justified, employees will begin to notice other job opportunities. The most valuable are the candidates who can most easily find opportunities elsewhere. This can leave the firm with less qualified employees to run the operation after conversion.

    Because employers compete in a market for skilled talents, it is best not to earn the reputation of hiring, then firing skilled personnel. As the firm compares job candidates when hiring, people seeking employment compare the merits of different firms. One of the major reasons for job candidates not accepting a firm's offer is its unstable employment profile. This is one reason it is a good practice to contract skilled workers when demands fluctuate.

On the other hand, there are some valid reasons for not contracting personnel. One involves the learning curve, the time needed to master the job or learn about a firm. This is not so much of a problem with lower-level jobs.

Another reason is that part-timers are less loyal. While this is a valid concern, many contract workers are comfortable with temporary employment and commit to the task at hand.

The more professional the responsibility, the greater the loyalty that person will exhibit to the profession than to the firm. This may account, in part, for the turnover of skilled personnel who feel their firms are not giving them opportunities to gain professional maturity.

In addition, contract people might make work for themselves to extend their employment, another reason for monitoring their work effort. The old saying that good contract people must be dragged kicking and screaming from the building isn't too far off the mark. Always document their exit plan before hiring contract workers.

## [C]   Contract Personnel Source Procedures

Vendors may be a good, but not the only, source for obtaining contract personnel. Often the hardware vendor does not have the staff or the price is too high.

Use the Yellow Pages when looking for contract personnel. If an area has limited resources, the local library can provide the Yellow Pages from cities in the general area. These services may be listed under more than one category. Check "computer services" or "information systems contracting firms." Computer service firms usually limit the available talent to programming and computer systems personnel.

Data entry firms may have a wide selection of data entry or clerical personnel available. For training needs, look under "training" or "education services" and see what computer service firms offer.

There are also self-employed and third-party-employed contracting personnel. Their skills and dependability vary widely. Be careful when using a new firm without an established track record. There have been reported cases of contract programmers planting "time bombs" in their programs to ensure they are fairly paid. Delay of payment to confirm all goes well might also be a problem because many new firms are undercapitalized. Dealing with such firms is the same as sailing uncharted waters: it may yield surprises.

Think carefully before hiring any contract personnel. When there are delays finding temporary people, managers tend to lower their standards. Therefore, time is required to prove the worth of contract people on the job. More caution is necessary than for regular personnel because contract people are not loyal to the firm and can create havoc when working with a firm's regular employees in established departments.

With all this in mind, the following procedures for contract acquisition should be followed:

1. **Referral contacts.** Try to find a contracting service firm through contacts with other firms. Referrals are the best way to find proven personnel contractors. Maintain memberships in IT professional organizations to provide these contacts.

2.  **Internet.** If referrals do not provide satisfactory results, the Internet can be used to find firms in your area. It also can be used to advertise for companies to bid for the work.
3.  **Yellow Pages.** The Yellow Pages are always a last resort. Check your area's first. If there are not more than three or four contracting services listed, check the local library for out-of-town telephone books. Be sure to contact no fewer than three or four firms for comparison.
4.  **Competency verification.** When the selection has been narrowed down to no fewer than three vendors, verify past performance. Ask each vendor for three or more customer references to be contacted by telephone and of whom you can ask the following questions:
    a.  Would you seek the firm's services in the future?
    b.  Did the vendor complete the project in the agreed time?
    c.  Was the cost of the service within the bounds expected?
    d.  Did the talent offered come up to expectations?
    e.  Did the vendor leave behind sufficient documentation?
    f.  Did the vendor's employee get along with your firm's users and IT people?
    g.  Were the contract employees available after the project for clearing up any problems?
    h.  Did the contract employees follow your standards for procedures and documentation?
5.  **Purchasing department's role.** After selecting possible contract candidates, contact the purchasing department, which should be involved with the request for bids. Many lack experience here; however, they have the resources to help avoid selecting the wrong firm. Purchasing should, as a minimum, do the following:
    a.  Confirm the Dun & Bradstreet ratings of each firm selected.
    b.  Have the firms checked out as to their business status in their community.
    c.  Submit the requests for bids.
    d.  Establish contacts with the bidding firms.
    e.  Play their usual role in purchasing. They are trained to say no to vendors.
    f.  Submit in writing the status and ranking of firms asked for bids.
    g.  Assist in drawing up the contract. Depending on its nature, it would be wise to have purchasing ask the legal department to review anything that is to be signed, before legally committing the firm.
6.  **Reviewing bid offers.** All bid offers should be reviewed with the help of the legal and purchasing departments. After approval, inform all parties in writing as soon as possible. Include those not getting an offer; they may be needed in the future.
7.  **Contract outline.** The contract should contain no less than the following:
    a.  The start and finish dates.
    b.  The names of people assigned to the project. A copy of each person's resume should be included if not previously received.
    c.  Number of hours that will be expected for each person assigned to the project.

    d.  The ground rules:
- Contract employees' office space
- Tools that will be made available
- Vendor contact person
- Contact person for contract employees
- What procedure is required to remove a contract person from a project
- The hours of the day they are expected to be present
- How they will be paid
- What penalty fees will be charged for being late with a project
- What rewards will be allowed for completing the project early
- What constitutes a completed job
- The level of competency that each position requires

# § 15.04   IT OPERATION SERVICES

## [A]   Overview

Information systems may need expertise best provided by outside operation services. These can be hardware, technical, or management skills and can be provided on an ongoing basis or in a project mode.

## [B]   Hardware/Software Needs

Outside technical services may be appropriate when an application is too large or too specialized for the in-house IT operation. A service bureau or application service provider (ASP) is an economical alternative if the application is not performed frequently enough to justify a hardware purchase. If on-site I/O is preferred, a time-sharing service or ASP is a reasonably priced alternative. For one-of-a-kind or seldom-used complex applications, time-sharing is appropriate.

There are also turnkey services available that can be designed for specific applications. These provide the hardware and operating systems software, along with the applications software. In either case, the company is billed for hardware, running time, and any special software rentals.

The company can supplement its computer services through the use of full-service bureaus, public databases, and backup system services.

    1.  **Service bureaus and application service providers.** Service bureaus solve a number of problems by providing data entry services, various computer services, or machine-time rental. Full-service bureaus provide a wide range of services tailored to the specific needs of a customer. These range from providing a turnkey operation at the customer's site to performing the functions part of a systems operation at the service bureau's location. Subscription service bureaus and ASPs provide opportunities to share a computer application system with other subscribers. The reports produced can be specialized, but the programs and the basic system are the same.

This shared computer application system has very specialized applications and is often used for a specific system or procedure. Reasons for considering this service are twofold. First, the specialized service has a higher level of expertise than an in-house computer operation. Second, the cost is substantially lower than performing the same procedure in-house. Billing or providing mailing labels is a sample of what may be offered.

Following are some major reasons for seeking assistance from a service bureau or ASP:

- To add capacity to an overtaxed in-house computer system
- To reduce in-house computer demands by farming out some computer applications during peak load periods
- To convert a mass of hardcopy data to a captured computer form, or convert one kind of computer data file to another
- To provide a reliable source of computer hardware backup
- To assist with parallel testing of a new system before the actual acquisition of the new hardware

The procedure for acquiring the services of service bureau firms is fairly simple. Most firms have a price list for services. However, the business is very competitive, and should your company require anything other than normal procedures, you should receive several bids.

Following is the procedure for seeking the services of an IT service bureau or ASP:

a. Seek someone in the IT profession able to provide referrals.
b. If unable to locate three or more firms by referrals, use the local Yellow Pages. If these provide fewer than three firms, consult the local library for out-of-town phone books.
c. Confirm competency by asking for current customer referrals, and ask those customers the following questions:
    - Would they recommend service firm to others?
    - Did service firm complete work as promised?
    - Did cost of services match agreed upon cost?
    - What kind of relations did employees have with firm?
    - What is best thing about the service?
    - What is worst thing about the service?
d. Contact the purchasing department after selecting two or more firms. It should:
    - Confirm Dun & Bradstreet ratings of each firm.
    - Have firms checked out as to business status in their community.
    - Have firms submit requests for bids.
    - Establish contact person to deal directly with bidding firms.
    - Have contractors submit bids in writing.
e. Review received bids and issue a purchase requisition to the purchasing department for the company selected. Notify the chosen firm. Also, notify the firms not selected, explain why, and thank them.
f. Set up a payment method and notify accounts payable about forthcoming billings. Approve invoices prior to payment.

2. **Public databases.** Public database services are less expensive than having this same service provided in-house. Neither public database nor time-sharing systems are commonly provided in-house because performing these services is beyond the financial limits of most firms.

   Public database information systems are available to the general public, and the types of customers utilizing these services range from large firms to single persons working in home offices. The service may be thought of as a dial-up computerized reference library.

   There are four major types of vendors of public database services:

   a. Commercial services containing one or more databases. The Dow Jones and The New York Times are two examples.

   b. Commercial services offering access to numerous databases produced by other firms or publishers but that may also contain vendor-produced databases. The information provided can range from scientific to business and financial. The hourly access rate usually varies from one database to another within the same vendor's service. Dialog, Lexis, Nexus, and VU/TEXT are some firms providing such services.

   c. Government and nonprofit organizations. ERIC is a nonprofit public database service providing an educational research database. The federal government offers several services, including the National Library of Medicine with online medical data.

   d. The Internet, which provides for a host of worldwide accessible databases.

3. **Backup system services.** If one of today's interactive online computer systems goes down, severe problems can occur. A large, multisite IT operation can provide its own online backup. A UPS is also required, ensuring that service is accessible in the advent of a power failure.

However, small companies often cannot afford to own backup hardware. Luckily, backup services are available to be used only in the event that a system fails or if the backup system needs to be tested. It is not a service that provides extra computer power for peak load periods. This service is an expensive off-site backup with a monthly standby fee plus additional use charges. The switchover can be performed so that online users detect no interruption in service.

## [C]   Outsource Management

Traditionally facilities management services have been contracted to replace the management of IT computer operations. Today, outsourcing is often used instead. Contract outsourcing services for a wide range of IT operations include:

- Help-desk services
- Maintenance
- Training
- Programming
- Systems analysis
- Database operations
- Network operations
- Web site operations
- IT computer operations
- End-user computing

## COMMENT

One large, well-known corporation contracted all of its IT responsibilities. Accounting-oriented people developed a multimillion-dollar manufacturing system that turned into a multimillion-dollar disaster. Make sure the outsourcing organization has the skills needed for the area in question. Also, beware of the bait-and-switch routine. Some well-known consulting accounting firms have been known to pull this. Remember the saying, "caveat emptor" (buyer beware).

Facilities management/outsourcing of computer operations does not provide new hardware or software; it utilizes what is in place. This does not mean that an existing operation will not be changed at a later date. Existing operating personnel may be replaced with more competent people if necessary. Personnel may be terminated if there is an overstaffing problem.

Facilities management/outsourcing of computer operations might be considered for the following reasons:

1.   To reduce operating cost through better management. Outside management with no internal loyalties may be needed to make necessary staffing changes.
2.   To start up an operation. Once a professional facilities management service starts up an operation, the department can be turned over to internal operations management. The outside service can stay on temporarily to ensure everything is up and running, while permanent personnel have a chance to develop skills necessary to run the department.
3.   To avoid unionization or break a union shop. Using an outside management service or outsourcing converts the facilities to a nonunion operation without going through a difficult decertification process.
4.   To provide services where no in-house talent is available.

There are some problems with using a facilities management/outsourcing service operation: The operating responsibility shifts away from the firm's own controlled management, and the outside management may not understand the firm's particular needs.

There is also a morale issue involved when acquiring a facilities management/outsourcing service. Information systems personnel may resent reporting to an "outsider." This can be a greater problem when there is an expected reduction in the workforce. The problem could escalate to sabotage.

Never enter into this sort of agreement without an agreed upon exit plan for the contractor. Relationships can sour over time and once your contractor has all of the expertise in their control, they may be very expensive or difficult to get rid of. The contract should allow that at a minimum, you can hire the contractor's on-site employees for no penalty.

## COMMENT

> In one company, a major outsource service provider also provided mainframe database licenses at a reduced price (due to their special relationship with the supplier). If the contract company were sent away, the company would be forced to purchase the licenses from the supplier at full price!

## § 15.05   SELECTION PROCESS

### [A]   Overview

Selecting vendors for outside services and hardware requires the application of stringent evaluation procedures. Note that off-the-shelf software selection does not require this same procedure. Evaluate this software before making vendor selection. In this case, the item selected determines the vendor.

## COMMENT

> In the final analysis, computer operations has to do the job asked of it—and do it while being price-competitive. Often a facilities management arrangement provides the fastest route for accomplishing these goals.

### [B]   Request for Proposal

When IT management is ready to receive vendor proposals, a formal request for proposal (RFP) letter will be sent to all possible candidates. The RFP defines the format of the proposal, ensuring a responding vendor can be evaluated and compared with others.

Such a request for service is different from that for hardware. (Service RFPs include outsource RFPs.)

1. **Proposal for specific hardware/system.** This request approach specifies the hardware or hardware configuration. The item is clearly identified, and the RFP basically asks for a price quotation. The RFP

can be open-ended, allowing the vendor to offer newer or different technology for a given price.

2. **Proposal for system operation.** This request approach defines the desired system and asks the vendor to translate the performance objective into a hardware configuration. The system operation requirements must be well-defined, including:
   - System design defining documentation
   - Security required
   - Types of user access
   - I/O volume
   - Network requirements
   - Method of system installation
   - Evaluation criteria/benchmarks for measurement
   - Vendor maintenance, training, and operation support
   - Reliability level required
   - System expandability
   - Current and future database requirements
   - Computational and process time requirements
   - Off-line data-storage requirements
   - Hardcopy output requirements
   - Price/budget constraints
   - Current installations running with proposed system
   - Current users of vendor's systems
   - IT contact person
   - Vendor contact person

3. **Proposal for outsourcing/service.** This request for proposal is for an ongoing service contract with a given time limit. Either party not wanting to renew gives written notice to the other party 3 months before the end of the contract. Renegotiate before this 3-month period.

The service is billed monthly at a flat rate or prorated by volume. A method for recording service provided and cost should be in place. No invoice should be paid until this information is confirmed.

A detailed description of the service to be provided is required for the RFP. Any terms not used by the information technology industry will be identified in the RFP. The following items should be considered:

- System operation documentation
- Security required
- Service volume
- Reliability level required
- Performance evaluation criteria
- Service volume expandability
- Hours and days of service
- Facilities required by vendor
- Identification of vendor's employees
- IT contact person
- Vendor contact person
- Clients of vendor's service
- Contacts for confirming vendor's credibility

- Length of time vendor has been performing this service
- Principal owners/officers of vendor's firm

4. **Proposal for one-time service.** This request for proposal is for a one-time service contract. This can be for a project that runs over a given time or an operational task. The service is billed monthly or upon completion. Benchmarks are required ensuring that service billed was rendered. The invoice should not be paid until this is confirmed.

A detailed description of the service to be provided is required for the RFP. Any terms not used by the IT industry will be identified in the RFP. The following items should be considered:

- System operation documentation
- Security required
- Service volume
- Reliability level required
- Performance evaluation criteria
- Service expendability
- Hours and days of service
- Facilities required by vendor
- Identification of vendor's employees by task
- One-page resume for each consulting employee
- Amount of time to be spent on tasks by each employee
- IT contact person
- Vendor contact person
- Former clients of vendor's service
- Contacts for confirming vendor's credibility
- Length of time vendor has been performing this kind of service
- Principal owners/officers of vendor's firm

## [C]  Evaluating Vendor Proposals

Analyze all proposals received. The elements to be compared should be in the same sequence on each proposal. Give copies to each evaluator, with a date and time selected to meet and discuss them.

Vendors who provide clear and complete information asked for in the RFP and meet preliminary evaluation standards are selected for more detailed analysis. Those who do not will be removed from further consideration.

Vendors' proposals should address the specification elements noted in the RFP. The vendor should make clear statements about the items addressed, including:

1. **Hardware**
   - Hardware configuration
   - Size of primary memory
   - Execution time
   - Cache memory
   - Transfer rates
   - Performance measurements
   - Mean time between failures
   - Maintenance provisions
   - Parts availability
   - Backup system options

- Disk capacity and access time
- Maximum I/O channels
- Brand and model numbers
- Functional descriptions
- UPS provisions
- Operation manuals quality
- Published evaluation information
- Benchmark by actual workload samples

2. **Software.** This covers contract programming, custom software service, source code of available software, and off-the-shelf software.
   - Documentation clarity and completeness
   - Program maintenance or updates availability
   - Customer support available
   - Software guaranteed virus-free
   - Customer training resources available
   - Next expected release
   - Compatible operating systems
   - Language software was written in
   - Amount of primary memory required
   - Best operation at determined level of primary memory
   - Published evaluation information
   - Benchmark by actual workload samples

3. **Service/outsourcing.** Base your evaluation of service or outsourcing on the reputation of the chosen firm. Its past and current service quality should be investigated carefully.

## COMMENT

It is a common practice for some firms to showcase their best people to get the contract signed, and afterward send in their third string. Even worse, you are charged for the first-rate talent. Reserve for your company the control over who works on the project and prohibit the replacement of people by the contract company. If they must remove someone from the project, interview and approve the replacement, and charge the contractor a 2-week orientation fee since no one walks in the door and is immediately productive. The replacement needs time for "new employee" orientation just like anyone else. This practice is not limited to unknown firms. Some of the "better" nationally known firms do it, too.

Some things that can assist in the selection of a service firm are:
- Confirm credentials.
- Make certain names of specific people and the amount of time they will spend on the project are in the contract.
- Ask for former and current customer references.

4. **Contact with vendor's customers.** Make a final evaluation before signing any contract. Make telephone calls to a vendor's customers with a similar operation. Ask if they would recommend the vendor's product or service. If they do, set up a site visit. Be sure to talk to the project manager who would be familiar with the details—not the upper executives who do not hear about the routine problems.

Visit the operation and observe anything reflecting the vendor's accomplishment. Since most people are reluctant to offer negative information, ask the following:

a. Would you use the same vendor again? If so, why? What has been the major problem with the vendor? Do you know other users of the vendor's product? Are they generally happy? If so, why? Who are the other users? What are their names and telephone numbers?

b. How long does it take for a vendor's response? Are the people who respond knowledgeable and friendly? Has the vendor ever lied? Has the vendor had the resources to resolve your problem(s)?

c. Does the hardware/software satisfy your needs? Follow up with questions about how long they have had the system and how often it has gone down. Ask about its expandability and upgrading possibilities.

d. Do the users like the system or service? Ask to talk to users and confirm this. Ask users their likes and dislikes about the system or service and why.

e. Ask how long it took to put the hardware/software into operation. Did they receive adequate training? Are the operator's manuals easy to understand and follow?

f. Is the operation or service provided better than what they could do themselves, and why? Is the service worth the cost?

g. Were there any unexpected or hidden costs? What was the nature of these costs? Were the costs reasonable? Was the vendor confronted? If so, what was the reaction?

h. Were the vendor's employees easy to work with? Did their salesperson follow up after the sale? Does the vendor exhibit a genuine interest in the success of the service or product?

i. If you were starting all over, what would you do differently?

## [D] Vendor Selection

Final selection is based on more than one factor. To make the process more objective, set up a weighted matrix to compare vendors by selection factors, with the weight of any one factor a percentage of the whole. An example may be seen in Exhibit 15-1. The nature of the item being requested by an RFP determines the factors and their weights. Determine the factors and prepare the matrix parameters before the request for proposal is mailed out to avoid a subjectively weighted matrix.

In the sample presented in Exhibit 15-1, a consultant is being chosen to install a client/server database. Exhibit 15-2 presents selection factors for a firm manufacturing secondary storage devices. Note each chart contains different weighted factors, chosen for the particular need.

**EXHIBIT 15-1.**   Vendor Selection Matrix 1

**Date 11/28/2002**
**Consultant to Install a Client/Server Database**

| *Factor* | *Weight* | *Vendor A* | *Vendor B* | *Vendor C* |
|---|---|---|---|---|
| How long in business | .1 | | | |
| Quality of staff | .4 | | | |
| Track record | .4 | | | |
| D and B rating | .1 | | | |
| Total | | | | |

**EXHIBIT 15-2.**   Vendor Selection Matrix 2

## Date 11/28/2002
## Manufacture Secondary Storage Devices

| Factor | Weight | Vendor A | Vendor B | Vendor C |
|---|---|---|---|---|
| How long in business | .2 | | | |
| Sales personnel | .2 | | | |
| Track record | .4 | | | |
| D and B rating | .2 | | | |
| Total | | | | |

Compilation of the weighted factors is best done using the Delphi method. Have seven or nine people familiar with the proposal needs independently list those factors and their corresponding weights each considers important for the vendor to possess. Send the lists to a person not involved with the selection to compile. This person makes a list of all the factors and returns this new list to the participants. They will once again go through these factors, choosing and weighting their choices. Again, the papers are sent to the person not involved with the selection who groups together the factors (together with their weights) most prevalent. He/she discards those assigned low-weight values or mentioned only once. The possible combinations are then placed on one sheet of paper and copies are distributed to all contributors for reselection. This process is repeated until a general consensus is reached.

Vendors passing the preliminary selection process are rated from one to ten by the same seven- or nine-person panel or by a new panel. An example of this rating system is shown in Exhibit 15-3. Each rating (from 1 to 10) is then multiplied by its weighted factor to get a vendor rating value. Vendor then totals these values. The one with the highest total is rated first, as shown in Exhibit 15-4.

The vendor rated number one is chosen to receive the contract and will then submit, usually, a standard contract, which of course will be in his/her favor. The vendor's representative will be invited to discuss this offered contract in the information systems head's office.

At this meeting the IT head could be drinking coffee out of the vendor's competitor's cup. This, believe it or not, has helped negotiate a more favorable contract. If not a coffee cup, some other sign of a competitor's presence can give the same message.

The vendor's representative and IT management will negotiate contract terms. Training, documentation, conversion, performance, and acceptance are all included in the bargaining process. Some items in general to consider are:

- Delivery or start dates
- Finish or completion dates
- Vendor versus customer responsibilities
- Pricing methods for purchase, lease, or rent
- How and when vendor will bill
- Removing vendor's disclaimers
- Provisions for equipment, software, and personnel backup
- Emergency and preventive maintenance
- Provision for detailed specifications for hardware, software, or service performance
- Contract for outsourcing on a job-by-job basis
- Realistic launch dates for implementations
- Using only one vendor at a time to avoid conflict in the working environment
- Avoiding long-term contracts with new or unproven vendors
- Any contract includes performance clauses and penalties for nonperformance or late delivery times. After negotiation, the company's legal representative examines the final contract before it is signed.

**EXHIBIT 15-3.**   Vendor Selection Matrix 3

### Date 11/28/2002
### Manufacture Secondary Storage Devices

| Factor | Weight | Vendor A | Vendor B | Vendor C |
|---|---|---|---|---|
| How long in business | .2 | 10 | 5 | 1 |
| Sales personnel | .2 | 3 | 5 | 9 |
| Track record | .4 | 2 | 6 | 8 |
| D and B rating | .2 | 8 | 9 | 7 |
| Total | | | | |

**EXHIBIT 15-4.**   Vendor Selection Matrix 4

**Date 11/28/2002**
**Manufacture Secondary Storage Devices**

| Factor | Weight | Vendor A | Vendor B | Vendor C |
|--------|--------|----------|----------|----------|
| How long in business | .2 | 10 x .2 = 2.0 | 5 x .2 = 1.0 | 1 x .2 = 0.2 |
| Sales personnel | .2 | 3 x .2 = 0.6 | 5 x .2 = 1.0 | 9 x .2 = 1.8 |
| Track record | .4 | 2 x .4 = 0.8 | 6 x .4 = 2.4 | 8 x .4 = 3.2 |
| D and B rating | .2 | 8 x .2 = 1.6 | 9 x .2 = 1.8 | 7 x .2 = 1.4 |
| Total | | 5.0 | 6.2 | 6.6 |
| Vendor Ranking | | 3 | 2 | 1 |

# 16

# MOBILE DEVICES: BUSINESS TO GO

# § 16.01   MOBILE DEVICE POLICY AND SCOPE

## [A]   Overview

Mobile device policy formalizes standards for how Personal Digital Assistants (PDAs), wearable computers, single and two-way pagers, browser-enabled mobile phones, and related portable devices are used and managed within the organization. This policy applies whether the mobile devices are used on or off company property and mandates the endorsement and support by the CEO/head of the organization.

This policy covers all mobile devices not traditionally considered computers, but that store and/or collect information that is in some way connected to the organization. It covers all data and information from the input of raw data to the disposition of output documents and/or data. All raw source material and stored data is company property and may be used only for company-approved activities. Examples of covered items include customer lists, company directories, schedule information, etc.

## [B]   Operation Policy

The information technologies (IT) department is responsible for maintaining and enforcing a companywide operation program for all mobile devices. The information systems manager assigns the responsibility to an IT unit to coordinate usage of mobile devices. An end-user committee is formed, containing no more than seven or fewer than three end users. Include a purchasing department representative on the committee. A representative of the IT unit chairs the committee. The committee follows management's policy and defines it for companywide policies and procedures.

All user department managers will comply fully with the policies. There will be enforcement procedures in place. Each department manager is provided with a policy and procedures manual, which includes a recommended equipment and software list. Refer to the approved equipment list for all acquisitions. In cases of mobile needs not on the approved list, a request memo is sent to the committee chairperson. The committee may grant a waiver.

Personally owned mobile devices and other equipment of any kind are not allowed on company property without special permission from the policy committee.

# § 16.02   MOBILE DEVICE INVENTORY

## [A]   Responsibility

The chief information officer assigns the mobile device inventory responsibility to the IT manager. If there is no inventory- or equipment-tracking system in place, the IT asset manager will establish one.

## [B] Tagging Mobile Devices

Devise a coding method before the tagging of equipment begins. Tag devices upon receipt with a sequential numbering system. The numbering of mobile devices employs a two-character preface, followed by a space and a sequential number. The two-character preface identifies the type of mobile device being tagged.

After the inventory system is in place, an agent of the asset manager tags new devices upon receipt. The device and packing slip is compared with a copy of the purchase order confirming that what was received was ordered. Supply items received are checked with the packing slip and a copy of the purchase order. If the purchase is by a blanket purchase order, the quantity received each time is added to the total received to date and the quantity compared with the original blanket-ordered quantity.

Use a bar-coded tag along with a visually identified number posted on the tag. New mobile devices received will have tags made and attached to the item. After the tag is secured to the device, it is used as its identification number during inventory checks, and when the device is moved to a new location, repaired, or disposed of.

## [C] Mobile Device Inventory System

A computer inventory system is maintained for each type of mobile device. The following file record information will be maintained for each mobile device:

- Tag number, prefix, and sequential number
- Date of purchase
- Original cost
- Manufacturer's code number
- Vendor from which device was obtained
- Purchase, lease, or free-trial code identification
- Last date of preventive maintenance
- Last date of repair service
- Last date of warranty service
- Maintenance code

Provide a telephone number for end users needing maintenance. This number can be an IT service unit's number doing preventive or repair maintenance, or the vendor's number.

Annual reports are run by type of equipment, department assigned, department total, and grand total by type of equipment. Amount of usage is also reported when such records can be provided. When equipment is acquired, moved, or disposed of, the information will be used to update the information database files.

# § 16.03 MOBILE DEVICE MAINTENANCE

## [A] Overview

The information systems manager assigns the mobile device maintenance support to the IT service unit. The IT service unit head compares maintenance service with vendor and in-house service for quality and cost. The service may be a mix of vendors and in-house service. The maintenance service should be reviewed annually because of changing technology, availability of in-house vendor service personnel, and the needs of the company.

## [B]   In-house Maintenance Control

The IT service unit performing in-house maintenance will perform whatever mobile device repairs and preventive maintenance they can. Cost and in-house availability is a determining factor regarding who performs what service. A service telephone number is available for people needing service. Larger organizations might have a separate service desk for these items. The service desk assists the end user by telephone about a device problem. If the problem cannot be resolved by telephone, the service desk informs the caller he/she will be called back. The service desk person then contacts an in-house service person or the vendor with the service contract.

The service desk has vendor warranty or repair service information. The end user is informed when he/she may expect the service person to arrive. At no time should the end user send a device directly to a retail service center to be repaired. These centers usually replace the device rather than perform repairs, so that sensitive corporate data is now potentially available to others outside the organization. The service desk will re-image or erase any data on the mobile device before sending it off-site for repairs.

In smaller operations, the help desk and the service desk may be combined into the same job. These smaller operations may also have the IT PC services unit people perform some of the mobile equipment maintenance. There is also the value of having well-trained power users available to perform minor maintenance. It broadens the scope of their job and provides for a level of care not requiring a skilled technician's attention. The extra training is well worth the investment. With this, smaller operations may not require a full-time help desk.

## [C]   Service Budgeting

Budgeting for in-house maintenance control and the service desk comes from the IT service unit's lump-sum budget. Although the item purchased may come from a department's budget, the IT service support cost may or may not be charged to the department. This charge will depend on the company's accounting policy.

All service maintenance done by the IT service unit is reported on a daily service log. The completed work log sheets are turned in daily to the IT service unit's manager. The log report contains the following information:

- Service person's name
- Machine number serviced
- Time spent on service call
- Type of call: service, preventive maintenance, or operator problem
- Any replacement parts used

Departments purchasing their own mobile devices with their own budget require funds to obtain their own maintenance service. The departments have to request funds for this maintenance service in their budgets. Some leased items may come with a provided service agreement.

The IT service unit reports all service performed by the in-house IT service unit or vendor. The IT service people provide their daily report to the IT service unit manager. The service desk records any service provided by an outside vendor. The vendor code number and device number are reported. The vendor's service document is turned over to the help desk. Each day the service report is given to the unit head along with the vendor's service document—a copy is made for the IT unit head and the original is sent to the department head. A request for vendor service may come in one of the following forms:

- Time and parts
- Blanket maintenance contract
- Warranty service call

## [D]   Maintenance Service Report

Vendor maintenance is reported by the device types that each vendor has a contract to repair. The kind of vendor maintenance service reported is shown as warranty, preventive, or service maintenance. Time and replacement parts service charges are listed.

The monthly maintenance service reports will list the devices and locations that were serviced. The report provides the following information:

- What type of device was serviced
- Who performed the service
- Estimated cost for the service
- The kind of in-house service performed
- The kind of vendor service performed
- What kind of service was performed
- What kind of service was performed on the device the last time it received a service call
- When the last service call date was and what the current service call date is
- A total monthly expense by device type and a monthly grand total—there will be a year-to-date cost by device type and a year-to-date grand total

A second report (IT and Vendor Maintenance Cost Report) is printed with information by vendor and the IT service unit. The report will list who provided what service to which devices. The report lists the subtotal cost for the month. The service provider lists year-to-date costs and a grand total year-to-date sum is given.

## [E]   Vendor Maintenance Contracting

The IT unit manager, the asset manager, and a purchasing department representative will work together to solicit vendor contract bids. The same purchasing department representative should be used from year to year. It would be beneficial if the same purchasing agent is also responsible for mobile supplies and computer supplies.

After IT has identified which items they cannot do or service because they lack the required people, a list is composed of the devices requiring vendors' maintenance bids. A form letter is used listing all the items for which bids are requested. Vendors can provide an offer for any one item, any number, or the entire lot of items listed.

The list of vendors to contact can come from the IT service unit's manager, the IT asset manager, and the purchasing department's representative. It is the purchasing department representative's responsibility to evaluate each vendor before they are sent the letter. The purchasing agent can use information his/her department may already have. Contacts with other firms' purchasing departments may be a source of information along with the firm's Dun & Bradstreet rating.

When composing the request for bids letter, provide as much information as possible. A vendor company contact person is provided in the letter. Any site visits are arranged through the company's contact person. The letter furnishes the name and telephone number of the contact person, and the last day the bids will be received. The following information will be furnished in the vendor letter or attachment to the letter:

- A list of unit types that the bid calls for servicing
- The number of units for each unit type
- The age and condition of each device
- Units that are under current warranties, and when those warranties expire

If a particular vendor's bid is selected, would they be willing to provide a help-desk telephone number? This allows for company employees to contact them for information or a service call. Will there be a charge for this service if it is available?

Vendor selection is based on several variables. Each variable is weighted before the request for bid letters are dispatched. Vendor analysis is based on this matrix. See Chapter 15, Vendors: Getting the Goods, for information about setting up a weighted matrix. Short-term contracts may be considered for yet unproven vendors. Before any contract is signed, contact the firm's legal representative, who has the last word before the firm's authorized representative signs it.

# § 16.04  OPERATION OF MOBILE DEVICES

## [A]  Overview

Mobile devices cover a wide range of applications and complexities. The total investment in mobile devices can be difficult to track and is not known in most companies. More important, the data kept on mobile devices is difficult to track and control.

Meanwhile, most mobile devices operate without a central sense of direction. Without the orchestration and guidance of information systems, their costs continue to grow while their efficiency diminishes. A major part of controlling mobile devices is the procedures set forth by an IT unit of information systems.

## COMMENT

According to a 2002 report by ComScore Media Metrix, 10 million Internet users go online via a cell phone or PDA; 5 million report accessing the Internet via a PDA, and 6 million go online with a cell phone.

Information systems is responsible for maintaining and enforcing a companywide software application policy for all mobile devices. The acceptable application software list is maintained in the asset management software database, and is updated monthly by the information systems software committee. Installation of unauthorized application software is not permitted. Help-desk support is not provided for unauthorized application software.

Most mobile devices are configured by default to power on with no security. If supported by the mobile device, a password must be entered when the device is powered on. The password should be the same as the password used by the user when logging into their personal computer or corporate network domain.

### [B]  Personal Data Assistants

A PDA is a small hand-held computer used to write notes, track appointments, contacts, and otherwise keep your life in order. Early PDAs required data to be input using a keypad with keys the size of Chiclets, but other models (e.g., the Palm Pilot or Palm PC) use a combination of pen-based input and character recognition software to accept user input. Many can also be used to send and receive e-mail and browse the Internet. Information in the PDA can be synchronized with data in a PC-based application such as Microsoft Outlook.

Information systems is responsible for determining the manufacturers and models of PDAs that will be supported. At no time will personally purchased PDAs be allowed to be used and supported due to security concerns.

Information systems is responsible for maintaining and enforcing a companywide synchronization policy for all mobile devices. A standard synchronization package should be selected that supports all the different PDAs in use at the company. The applications and data to be synchronized must also be determined. It is desirable to use synchronization software that can be administered from a single server to control what is being transferred to and from the PDA. Other items to consider include:

**Filtering of data**—Information systems must determine what subset of data records is to be synchronized with the PDA. Filter setting can protect sensitive data that should not be synchronized and can be used to save time by transferring only data that is actually needed.

---

## COMMENT

The popularity of PDAs can prove a headache for corporate IS departments. Palm and Windows CE have long targeted enterprise customers, touting the benefits of employees connecting remotely to corporate databases of information via their hand-held computers. According to Ken Dulaney, vice president at Gartner Group, the influx of new products, designs, and technologies will add 10 percent in technical support costs.

---

**Field mapping**—This is used to map fields from the PC application to the PDA application. Information systems must create standards for which data fields can be synchronized and where they map between the PC and the PDA.

**Conflict resolution**—Data kept on both a PC and a PDA have conflicts when data is changed in one or both places. Establish policies to resolve these conflicts.

**Control at the server**—Some synchronization products allow settings to be controlled at a central server. This also makes it possible to synchronize over the LAN without being connected to a PC.

The use of PDAs makes good data backup procedures even more critical, as there are more opportunities for data to be changed inadvertently. Verified backups before the first synchronization are very important.

PDA users are notified that the data on the PDA is valuable and sensitive company information, and must be protected. All PDAs should be password-enabled to prevent unauthorized access to the data if the PDA is lost or stolen.

### [C]   Internet-enabled Cellular Phones

An Internet-enabled cellular phone allows users to access the Internet using their cell phones. Information systems is responsible for maintaining and enforcing a companywide usage policy for all cell phones. Use should be monitored periodically to ensure the phones are used for business-related purposes.

---

## COMMENT

Intellisync from Puma Technology synchronizes data from all Windows-powered Pocket PCs, hand-held PCs, and Palm devices with a broad number of PC-based PIM, contact management, and groupware applications using advanced features like conflict resolution, filtering, and field mapping. Intellisync supports Microsoft Outlook 97/98/2000, Microsoft Schedule+ 7.0/7.0a/7.5, Lotus Notes 4.5/4.6, Lotus Organizer 2.12/97/GS/4.1/5.0, Novell GroupWise 5.2/5.5, Symantec ACT! 3.08/4.0/4.01/4.02, GoldMine 3.2/4.0, Meeting Maker 5.0.3/5.5, and other PC-based PIMs.

---

Cellular phone users are notified that the data on the cell phone is valuable and sensitive company information, and must be protected. All cell phones should be password-enabled (if possible) to prevent unauthorized access to the data if the cell phone is lost or stolen.

### [D]    Wearable Computers

A wearable computer is a computer used by those who must be mobile. The system is normally worn on a belt, with optional peripherals including a wrist-mounted touch-screen display, voice-enabled headset, and a head-mounted monitor. Information systems is responsible for maintaining and enforcing a companywide use policy for all wearable computers.

Wearable computer users are notified that the data on the wearable computer is valuable and sensitive company information, and must be protected. All wearable computers should be password-enabled to prevent unauthorized access to the data if the wearable computer is lost or stolen.

Information systems is responsible for setting up processes for backing up data on all wearable computers. Procedures include standards for use of docking stations, connections to the LAN, and backing up data to a server. A directory on a server that is regularly backed up is created for storing data and applications from the wearable computer. Instructions for backing up data and applications are created by information systems and provided to all users of wearable computers.

## COMMENT

IBM's Almaden Research Center is working on personal area network (PAN) technology, which uses the natural electrical conductivity of the human body to transmit electronic data. In the future, a user of PAN technology will be able to transfer information via touch rather than issuing typed commands or pressing buttons. For example, your computer might recognize you as you if you simply touch the keyboard. This capability could yield significant benefits in the area of access control and data privacy.

### [E]  Power Users

A power user is a person using a particular device on a regular basis (usually daily), who becomes very knowledgeable about its operation. This person usually enjoys sharing information about using the device with others in the organization. Ask power users if they could be contacted if a new user needs assistance. If they agree, their names should be listed as power users with the instructions given to new users.

A power user should be able to operate and perform minor device adjustments. He/she knows how to replenish its expendable stock items, and perform standard housekeeping and preventive maintenance procedures. A power user can be walked through some of the malfunctions by the service desk or a maintenance person over the telephone. At the service desk will be a power user's location book with the power user's name, telephone number, and location listed. A second listing will be by location with the power user's name and telephone number listed. This is used to contact another power user who is close by for assistance when the nearer power user is not available.

### [F]  Mobile Device Operations Procedures

These are the operating procedures furnished to all device users. The IT service unit or the systems and procedures unit furnishes the operator procedure manuals. The manuals will provide operator instructions, minor maintenance instruction, backup procedures, and procedures for troubleshooting. Minor preventive maintenance procedures are provided. If practical, the manual should be provided on the company's intranet site.

The procedure manuals contain any manufacturer's furnished material helpful to clarify the device's operation. The illustrations used by the manufacturer could be beneficial to the operator. Close-up and wide-view photographs would be helpful if included in the operator procedure manuals.

A prototype manual is developed and tested before it enters service. Use an unskilled person for the test. This should be done with more than one subject. Avoid the brightest person in the area and any experienced operator for debugging the procedure manual.

## [G]  Supply Requisitions

Use the standard supply requisitions that the firm has in place. If the form is outdated or there is no form, one will be designed by the IT systems and procedures unit.

A central supply location is placed to limit the travel time involved. This prevents unnecessary travel for the person seeking supplies. The supply center could also function as supply distribution location for the end-user computer operations supplies. Supplies that are not too large can be delivered by inter-office mail. A requisition system is employed to obtain supplies. The unit manager approves the requisition after all the items are listed with their respective quantities. A line is drawn across the lines not used by the person before signing the requisition. Depending on company accounting practice, supplies are charged to the unit receiving them or from a lump-sum company budget. Spot-checks on usages for units that employ a lump-sum budget are recommended. The loss on supply items can be costly to a company. The supply area is locked when unattended. Supplies stored in operating units are locked at the end of the day or locked at all times if the area is not easily visible.

## [H]  Service Desk Assistance

Help desks, along with service desks, cannot solve all user problems. It requires other assistance to service the user's special needs. Some operations, such as mobile phones, are better off with vendor-supplied service. Vendor help and service desks for special systems can provide much better service than an in-house service. If the company is willing to provide an in-house service desk and support it, there are still vendor services providing better assistance. They will do it better, and the equipment will be up and running faster.

The asset manager publishes an approved mobile device acquisition list for new mobile device purchases. This covers what is in-house, currently operating, and found on the mobile device inventory property list, but not on the approved mobile device acquisition list. The mobile device inventory property list is company property, identified and tagged. The approved mobile device acquisition list is a list of items that the IT service unit can repair or for which the service desk has a vendor contact. The service desk also has the mobile device inventory property list and the source of service for each item. Some items were company property before the service desk assistance program was established.

Some devices either have a long life span and never need to be replaced, or are no longer manufactured—they can be replaced only with used equipment. The help desk will have a special number to call to have the item serviced. In cases of this kind, it is best to have a power user trained to do most of the repairs and preventive maintenance. Contact the vendor service person only if the problem is beyond the scope of a power user or one is unavailable. Some of the items may not use the English measuring system and may require special tools to repair the equipment, or the manufacturer may be the only one making the tool.

The service desk does not have to be covered at the company site any more than the help desk. This is why many vendor help desks are not found at company sites. This may be more difficult when having the vendor provide full-service desk coverage. If coverage is needed past normal working hours, service desk personnel can be on call at their homes for specific time periods. This can also apply to help desk personnel. These two jobs can be combined into one in smaller firms. There would be one number to call in the event of a problem. There is also the possibility that the problem may be related to both the help desk and the service desk. The help desk and service desk person should be able to have at home the current information he/she has at work. Have it installed in a notebook computer.

# § 16.05   USER AND IT SUPPORT TRAINING

## [A]   Overview

The provision for training covers a wide area of needs. The technology skill levels required for each mobile device will be multilevel. Vendor-contracted mobile device service will not require so many levels of skills as an in-house service program. The service desk has the skill level available for each device listed in the mobile device inventory property list. Depending on the nature of the problem, a skill level is determined to resolve the problem. The item listed will have posted to it the persons who can perform a given level of skill. A person with a higher level of skill can perform a lower level of skill task, but a lower-level skilled person should not perform a higher-level skill task. The training certifies a level at which the service person can perform a task.

The training provided is for certain skill levels. This training is for vendor- and company-serviced equipment.

## [B]   User Training

The user should learn the basic operation of the device to produce the desired results: the more complex, the more to learn. Changing batteries would be considered a task level expected of a user. Loading applications into a PDA is much more complex, but still a user's job. Provide user training in more than one form:

1.  **New user training.** When a new mobile device is to be used, conduct the training in class. The vendor or a power user conducts the classes. The vendor provides handouts. The company instructor provides any additional handouts needed. A video or slide presentation is helpful along with any hands-on training.

    Compile a list of the people attending the meeting. Anyone missing the class is notified they should attend the next class offered. If the classes are over, they take the individual training provided to new employees later.

2. **New employee training.** Anyone missing class will take the self-paced individual training. New employees having no experience with the device receive self-paced individual training. They are credited with receiving the instruction for the new device. Part of the instruction is provided to the user as on-the-job training (OJT) instruction.

## [C]   Power User Training

The power user training is given for all users desiring recognition as power users. Training can be from more than one source. The IT service unit holds classes for power users or OJT instruction for devices they maintain. The power users receive manuals from the IT service unit.

Vendor training programs are provided at the company site or the vendor's place of instruction. The vendors provide manuals. The IT unit provides power user procedure manuals. The vendor provides some sort of certificate showing the person is now a certified power user for the given mobile device.

The power user should be able to provide OJT to new device users. They should be able to operate the device, make adjustments to its operation, and perform some light preventive maintenance. They are the key contact persons in the area for users, service desk, vendor service people, and the IT service personnel.

## [D]   IT Service Unit Training

Each IT service person has a list of devices they service for their own records, along with the service desk and the IT unit manager. Training comes from one of the following sources:

- OJT
- A self-paced learning program provided by vendor
- Attending vendor's classes
- Passing a qualifying exam for equipment
- Taking correspondence course from vendor or private correspondence program

## [E]   Service Desk Training

Effective service desk people are often individuals with some IT service experience. Their training can come from the areas where the IT service person receives his/her training—as a power user and from operator training. It helps a new service desk operator to work with an experienced worker, which is a form of OJT learning. On days when the workload is light, they may try working at the service desk.

Service desk personnel are expected to work overtime and be on call at their homes. The unit has one or two laptop computers that service people can take home with them when on call. They are expected to have no less knowledge than a power user about each device and a general knowledge about vendor-maintained devices. They should have enough knowledge to assist a user and communicate with a service person working for the company or vendor. They should be able to assign service people effectively. They can reduce maintenance costs with the proper assignments and the ability to walk users through problems.

# § 16.06   MOBILE DEVICE ACQUISITION PROCEDURES

### [A]   Budgeting Procedures

Budgeting can come from a corporate lump-sum budget or department budgets or both.

Each department submits its expected needs for the following year's budget. This is based on the last year's budget plus inflation, replacement of old equipment, and new needs. It is supported by the use of the current equipment and forecasted use for the next budget year.

Budgets will be needed for supplies and replacement of current equipment. Departments with their own hardware for one-of-a-kind use will require a budget for maintaining the equipment.

The information systems IT service unit needs a budget for its operation. The unit needs a budget for capital expenses benefiting the whole company plus a replacement parts budget. In addition, a vendor service budget is required.

### [B]   Requisition Procedures

Budgeted items can have a requisition issued. The requisition goes to the IT asset manager to confirm it meets standards or requires a standards waiver.

The requisition is approved and sent on to the budgeting department so it can adjust the records. It is then sent on to the purchasing department.

### [C]   Purchasing Procedures

Purchasing receives the approved purchase requisition. If needed, they will take care of the competitive bids for the item. After the purchase order is sent to the vendor, a copy is sent to receiving and accounts payable.

### [D]   Receiving Procedures

The agent for the asset manager or a special order item representative inspects the item for approval. After it is approved, a receiving notice is sent to accounts payable.

The asset manager's agent affixes a tag to the device and records the information. The information is sent to the asset manager.

# 17

# THE INTERNET:
# MAKING IT PRODUCTIVE

# § 17.01   PURPOSE OF THE INTERNET AND E-MAIL POLICY

## [A]   Overview

Internet and e-mail policy formalizes standards for how the company connects to the outside world through the Internet and e-mail. While the Internet provides access to a wealth of valuable information and facilitates communication, it also opens the potential for others to access the company's valuable proprietary information. Internet access and e-mail are valuable and costly corporate resources and must be used only for company business. Irresponsible use reduces their availability for critical business operations, compromises corporate security and network integrity, and leaves the company open to potentially damaging litigation. This policy mandates the endorsement and support by the CEO/head of the organization.

## [B]   Scope

The Internet and e-mail policy covers all types of connections to the outside world through the Internet. The types of connections include:

- Individual computer using a plain old telephone service (POTS) connection through a modem
- Workgroup server using a dedicated dial-up POTS connection through a modem
- Workgroup server using an ISDN, DSL, T1, or cable modem connection

The policy also covers all activities performed while using the Internet, including but not limited to browsing (viewing Web pages), using e-mail, Instant Messaging, and transferring files using file transfer protocol (FTP).

## [C]   Policy Objectives

This policy provides guidelines ensuring the secure, proper, and reliable use of the Internet. Policy objectives should be flexible enough to cover new methods of Internet connectivity as they become available.

The company's Internet and e-mail use policy are part of the new employee orientation process. All new or existing employees sign an acknowledgment that they have received a copy of this policy and that they will abide by it. The Internet and e-mail use policy also appears in the employee handbook. An online message, appearing when the user logs onto e-mail or the Internet, is helpful to remind employees of this policy. The company should offer training sessions on proper Internet and e-mail usage.

> **COMMENT**
>
> An analysis of a survey of more than 9,000 MSNBC.com readers found one in five men and one in eight women admitted using their work computers as their primary lifeline to access sexually explicit material online. Other studies have revealed that 70 percent of e-porn traffic occurs between 9 AM and 5 PM on weekdays.

# § 17.02   METHODS OF INTERNET ACCESS

## [A]   Overview

There are several methods to connect to the Internet from an individual workstation. Each individual workstation might have its own connection to an Internet Service Provider (ISP), or be connected through the workgroup or corporate LAN. The connection itself can be on-demand or continuously connected to the Internet. Each method has its own set of advantages and disadvantages.

## [B]   Individual Access

The technically simplest method to connect to the Internet is for each individual PC to connect directly to an ISP using a modem and a POTS line. The user's PC connects to the local ISP using dial-up networking (if using Microsoft Windows) and uses a browser to view content on the World Wide Web.

The IT technical support unit develops the procedure for connecting to the Internet through individual PCs. The procedure will be distributed to users requiring individual Internet access. The IT technical-support unit also determines the browser software used and may need to install the browser on the user's PC if not preinstalled.

An advantage of this method is there is less direct exposure of the LAN to the outside world if any existing LAN connection is unplugged. Another is the user's PC is exposed for only the time he or she is connected. This gives hackers less opportunity to gain access to the user's PC. Personal firewall software should be used as a form of protection while connected to the Internet.

A disadvantage of individual connections to the Internet is the lack of centralized monitoring or control. Usage standards cannot easily be enforced, and virus protection is left up to the user. Speed is severely limited when using a modem and POTS line. Anytime you have a connection to the Internet, the machine with which you connect and any subsequent machine behind it are subject to unauthorized access.

When using the Internet via an individual connection, the following procedures must be followed:

- Personal firewall software must be installed and active.
- Any LAN connections must be unplugged.
- Virus-scanning software must be installed and active.

## COMMENT

Examples of personal firewall software include ZoneAlarm and WinProxy. ZoneAlarm from Zone Labs costs less than $20; see their Web site at *www.zonelabs.com* for the latest information. WinProxy 3.0 from Ositis is a personal firewall and proxy product. They can be reached at *www.winproxy. com.*

### [C]  Corporate/Networked Internet Access

In most cases employees have access to the Internet and e-mail from their workstations through the corporate or workgroup LAN. The LAN is connected to the Internet through a router and/or proxy server; this acts as a firewall to protect the LAN from unauthorized access. The user's PC uses a browser to view content on the World Wide Web.

The IT technical support unit develops the procedure for connecting to the Internet through the corporate or workgroup LAN. The procedure is distributed to users requiring Internet access. The IT technical support unit also determines the browser software used and may need to install the browser on the user's PC if not preinstalled.

An advantage of this method is Internet use can be centrally monitored and controlled. Also, a centralized firewall (either software or hardware) is used to protect the LAN from unauthorized access. Virus software is centrally installed and kept up to date.

A disadvantage of Internet access through the corporate or workgroup LAN is there is a single point of failure protecting the LAN from the outside world. The connection is normally up 24/7, which gives hackers more opportunity to test your protection. Anytime you have a connection to the Internet, the machine with which you connect and any subsequent machines behind it are subject to unauthorized access.

When using the Internet via the corporate or workgroup LAN, the following procedures must be followed:

- Firewall software or hardware is installed at the point of connection to the Internet, and updated daily.
- Virus-scanning software is installed and updated daily. All downloaded files and e-mails are scanned for viruses.
- The IT technical support unit generates a weekly report. The report shows the most frequently visited Web sites and total time connected to the Internet for each user.

# COMMENT

Losses related to Distributed Denial of Services (DDOS) attacks in early 2000 that shut down several popular Web sites could easily come to more than $1.2 billion, according to a report from the Yankee Group.

## § 17.03   INTERNET SECURITY POLICY

### [A]   Responsibility

The chief information officer assigns the responsibility for Internet security to the IT manager. Internet security policies are critical for protecting corporate systems while connected to the Internet. The IT unit responsible for the corporate Internet connection develops and enforces security procedures protecting corporate systems while connected to the Internet.

A connection to the Internet not only connects a computer to systems all over the world, but also with all computers it may be connected to over a LAN. The Internet was not designed to be very secure, as open access for research purposes was a major consideration. Other factors making an Internet connection a possible security problem include:

- **Vulnerable TCP/IP services.** A number of the TCP/IP services are not secure and can be compromised by knowledgeable intruders; services used in the local area networking environment for improving network management are especially vulnerable.
- **Ease of spying and spoofing.** The majority of Internet traffic is unencrypted; e-mail, passwords, and file transfers can be monitored and captured using readily available software. Intruders can then reuse passwords to break into systems.
- **Lack of policy.** Many sites are configured unintentionally for wide-open Internet access without regard for the potential for abuse from the Internet; many sites permit more TCP/IP services than they require for their operations and do not attempt to limit access to information about their computers that could prove valuable to intruders.
- **Complexity of configuration.** Host security access controls are often complex to configure and monitor; controls that are accidentally incorrectly configured often result in unauthorized access.

### [B]   Firewall Usage

A firewall is a system providing security to a network. A firewall includes a number of items such as policy, network arrangement, and technical controls and procedures. The firewall protects the network from probing by unauthorized users and allows only authorized access to the system.

Management first defines the type and level of security desired for the Internet connection for the protection of company information resources. Issues to consider include:

- Dial-in policy
- SLIP and PPP connections
- Which Internet services the organization plans to use (Telnet, FTP, etc.)
- Assumptions about security versus usability (When does a service become too risky to use?)
- Access to internal resources from the Internet
- Restriction of access to approved sites only or restrict only certain sites
- Use of chat programs such as mIRC and ICQ
- Use of streaming audio and video

There are two types of access control—explicit denial or explicit approval. Explicit approval restricts access to approved sites only and denies all other services by default. This is the more secure method, but more difficult to implement and maintain. Explicit denial restricts only certain sites and is easier on users, but new services that become available may expose the network to security problems.

The firewall installed should have the following features:

- The firewall should be able to support a "deny all services except those specifically permitted" design policy, even if not the policy used.
- The firewall should support the company's security policy, not impose one.
- The firewall should be flexible; it should be able to accommodate new services and needs if the security policy of the organization changes.
- The firewall contains advanced authentication measures or contains the software hooks for installing advanced authentication measures.
- The firewall employs filtering techniques to permit or deny services to specified host systems as needed.
- The IP filtering language should be flexible, user-friendly to program, and should filter on as many attributes as possible, including source and destination IP address, protocol type, source and destination TCP/UDP port, user, and inbound and outbound interface.
- The firewall uses proxy services for Internet services such as FTP and Telnet, so advanced authentication measures can be employed and centralized at the firewall. If services such as NNTP, http, or gopher are required, the firewall contains the corresponding proxy services.
- The firewall contains the ability to centralize SMTP access, to reduce direct SMTP connections between site and remote systems. This results in centralized handling of site e-mail.
- The firewall accommodates public access to the site, so public information servers can be protected by the firewall but segregated from site systems not requiring the public access.

- The firewall should contain the ability to concentrate and filter dial-in access.
- The firewall contains mechanisms for logging traffic and suspicious activity and contains mechanisms for log reduction so logs are readable and understandable. Mechanisms for alerting someone when suspicious activity occurs are also important.
- If the firewall requires an operating system such as Unix, a secured version of the operating system is part of the firewall, with other security tools as necessary ensuring firewall host integrity. The operating system should have all security patches installed.
- The firewall is developed so its strength and correctness are verifiable. It should be simple in design so that it can be understood and maintained.
- The firewall and any corresponding operating system are updated with patches and other bug fixes in a timely manner.

## § 17.04   INTERNET USE POLICY

### [A]   Overview

The company encourages the use of the Internet and e-mail to make business and communication more effective. However, Internet service and e-mail are valuable, costly corporate resources and their purpose is to facilitate company business. Irresponsible use reduces their availability for critical business operations, compromises corporate security and network integrity, and leaves the company open to potentially damaging litigation.

---

### COMMENT

According to a 2002 study by ComScore Networks as reported in *The Wall Street Journal,* online shopping jumps noticeably about 10 AM and builds up through noon; online buying then drops noticeably between noon and 1 PM, then rises again between 3 PM and 5 PM as the workday concludes. Visitors to auction sites spend about 2½ hours a month surfing the Internet from the office.

---

### [B]   Tracking Internet Usage

The company tracks all Internet transactions by employees. The purpose is simply to enable the company to manage its Internet and e-mail resources in a cost-effective and efficient manner and to plan more efficiently for future technology expansion. Please note that the company does not currently intend to examine the content of communications over the Internet, whether in e-mail, chat, or any other medium. The intention is to monitor the existence of the traffic being generated, much like a telephone bill tracks the calls made, the numbers called, the time of the calls, but not the content. In this manner the company will be aware of how its resources are being used, where they are needed, where new capacity is required, and other infrastructure management issues. Additionally, because of the vulnerability to litigation over inappropriate conduct in the workplace environment, it is the company's responsibility to ensure that company resources do not support inappropriate activities.

## COMMENT

Software from Fatline Corp. allows users to monitor their own Internet usage, which some firms have found to be an effective way to reduce non-work-related Internet use.

### [C]   Internet and E-mail Use Guidelines

To ensure all employees understand their responsibilities, the following guidelines are established for using company e-mail and Internet access. Any improper use of the Internet or e-mail jeopardizes the company's legal standing and will not be tolerated.

1. **Acceptable uses of company e-mail and Internet access.** The company provides Internet and e-mail access for business use. Every staff member has the responsibility to maintain and enhance the company's public image and to use company e-mail and access to the Internet in a manner that reflects well on the company. The company recognizes there will be occasional personal use on lunch breaks and during nonworking hours (with the approval of management), but this shall not be excessive nor unreasonable.

2. **Unacceptable uses of company e-mail and Internet access.** The company e-mail and Internet access may not be used for transmitting, retrieving, or storage of any communications of a discriminatory or harassing nature or materials that are obscene or "X-rated." Harassment of any kind is prohibited. No messages with derogatory or inflammatory remarks about an individual's race, age, disability, religion, national origin, physical attributes, or sexual preference shall be transmitted. No excessively abusive, profane, or offensive language is to be transmitted through the company's e-mail or Internet system.

   Electronic media also may not be used for any purpose that is illegal, against company policy, or contrary to the company's best interests. Solicitation of noncompany business, or any use of the company e-mail or Internet for personal gain, is prohibited. The use of streaming audio or video for noncompany purposes is prohibited.

3. **Communications.** Each employee is responsible for the content of all text, audio, or images that he/she places or sends over the company's e-mail and Internet system. No e-mail or other electronic communications may be sent hiding the identity of the sender or representing the sender as someone else or someone from another company. All messages communicated on the company's e-mail and Internet system should contain the employee's name.

   Any messages or information sent by an employee to another individual outside the company via an electronic network (e.g., bulletin board, online service, or Internet) are statements that reflect on the company. While some users include personal "disclaimers" in electronic messages, there is still a connection to the company, and the statements may legally be tied to the company. Therefore, the company requires all communications sent by employees via the company's e-mail and Internet system comply with all company policies and do not disclose any confidential or proprietary company information.

4. **Software.** To prevent computer viruses being transmitted through the company's e-mail and Internet system, there is no downloading of any unauthorized software. All software downloaded is registered to the company. Employees should contact IT if they have any questions.

5. **Copyright issues.** Employees on the company's e-mail and Internet system may not transmit copyrighted materials belonging to entities other than the company. Note that failure to adhere to this policy puts the company in serious legal jeopardy, opening up the company to significant lawsuits and public embarrassment. All employees obtaining access to other companies' or individuals' materials must respect all copyrights and may not copy, retrieve, modify, or forward copyrighted materials, except with permission. Failure to observe copyright or license agreements may result in disciplinary action including termination. If an employee has questions about any legal issues, he/she speaks with their manager or IT before proceeding.

6. **Security.** The company routinely monitors use patterns in its e-mail and Internet communications. Reasons for monitoring are many, including cost analysis, security, bandwidth allocation, and the general management of the company's gateway to the Internet. All messages created, sent, or retrieved over the company's e-mail and the Internet are the property of the company and should be considered public information.

   Notwithstanding previous comments regarding the company's current intention not to monitor content, the company reserves the right to access and monitor the content of all messages and files on the company's e-mail and Internet system any time in the future with or without notice. Employees should not assume electronic communications are totally private and should transmit highly confidential data in other ways. E-mail messages regarding sensitive matters should warn that such communications are not intended to be secure or confidential. This is good business sense.

7. **Violations.** Any employee who abuses the privilege of company-facilitated access to e-mail or the Internet can be subject to corrective action including termination. If necessary, the company reserves the right to advise appropriate legal officials of any illegal violations.

## COMMENT

One source of Internet use monitoring software is Sequel Technology. Their product supports all major Internet platforms. The software reports usage, volume, and protocol information, as well as cost allocation. They can be reached at *www.sequeltech.com*.

### [D]   E-mail Etiquette

As e-mail has not only replaced paper-based communication but has also become a substitute for having a conversation, the proper use of e-mail etiquette has become increasingly important. Communication received in an e-mail does not easily convey the mood and emotions of the communicator. Most messages come across harsher than intended. The following are useful guidelines for communicating by e-mail.

1. **Be brief.** E-mail messages should be concise and to the point. It is helpful to think of your e-mail as a telephone conversation, except you are typing instead of speaking. You should also make your main point as quickly as possible. Many software programs used for reading e-mail allow for a preview mode, where only the first few sentences are displayed. Many people receive hundreds of e-mails a day and use this preview mode to determine which e-mails they will read completely.

## COMMENT

Thank you for sending me a copy of your book—I'll waste no time reading it.

                              Moses Hadas (1900–1966), book reviewer.

2. **Use the subject line wisely.** An accurate subject line is helpful for determining which e-mails merit closer attention by those who receive mountains of e-mail, but be careful not to earn a reputation for over-

hyping your message in the subject line; your really important messages may not get read.

3. **Use grammar and punctuation correctly.** Poor grammar and punctuation reflect poorly on the sender. Don't overuse exclamation points (sometimes called "bangs") in an attempt to emphasize the importance of your message. If something is important, it should be reflected in your text, not in your punctuation.

4. **Use special formatting sparingly.** Avoid the use of fancy formatting. What looks great using your e-mail client software may look like gibberish to the recipient. Stick to commonly available fonts, and realize that the spacing as displayed by the recipient may be different from that in which the message was sent, especially when displaying columnar data.

5. **Abbreviations.** Abbreviation use is rampant with e-mail. In the quest to save keystrokes, users have traded clarity for confusion (unless you understand the abbreviations). Avoid using abbreviations that you would not normally use in a paper-based communication. Some of the more common abbreviations follow.

| This: | Means this: |
| --- | --- |
| BCNU | be seeing you |
| BTW | by the way |
| FAQ | frequently asked questions |
| FWIW | for what it's worth |
| FYI | for your information |
| HTH | hope this helps |
| IIRC | if I recall correctly |
| IMHO | in my humble opinion |
| LOL | laughing out loud or lots of luck |
| OBO | or best offer |
| ROTFLOL | rolling on the floor laughing out loud |
| RTFM | read the funny manual |
| TNSTAAFL | there's no such thing as a free lunch |
| TTFN | ta ta for now |
| TTYL | talk to you later |
| <G> | grinning |
| <J> | joking |
| <L> | laughing |
| <S> | smiling |

6. **Smilies or emoticons.** Smilies or emoticons (emotional icons) are used to compensate for the inability of written communication to express the emotions, facial expressions, and gestures seen in a verbal or face-to-face communication. Emoticons can be useful in avoiding misunderstandings of the writer's intentions. Most emoticons are designed to resemble what a person's face would look like if rotated 90 degrees counterclockwise. The most commonly used emoticon is the smiley face :) or :-), which resembles a person smiling. Following are some more examples:

| **This:** | **Means this:** |
|---|---|
| : ( or :-( | unhappy |
| ;-) | light sarcasm |
| ;-> | heavy sarcasm |
| :-\| | indifference |
| :-/ or :-\ | undecided |
| :-0 | surprise |
| :-p | tongue sticking out |
| :-S | loss of words |

Emoticons are typically found at the end of sentences and usually refer back to the prior statement. Use them sparingly, as their meanings are not universal.

7. **Salutations.** Each situation will be different, but in general, use what you would in a business letter. Some form of salutation should be included in every e-mail as a common courtesy.

8. **Signatures.** Do not rely on your e-mail address to inform the recipient who sent the e-mail. You should sign your e-mail just as you would a business letter. Include your full name, title, company name, and telephone number. You may want to also include your e-mail address, because it can sometimes be difficult to locate your e-mail address within the e-mail. Avoid using quotes or images at the end of your e-mail.

9. **Printing e-mail.** Avoid printing a paper copy of e-mails received unless absolutely necessary. Most e-mail systems allow you to create folders for storing old e-mails if you need to save a copy.

# COMMENT

According to an American Management Association survey published in *The Wall Street Journal*, 27 percent of major corporations surveyed in 1999 monitored employee e-mail; 84 percent of those told employees that their e-mail was being monitored.

10. **Privacy.** Remember, e-mails are not private. The company reserves the right to monitor e-mail content ensuring that the e-mail system is used for appropriate purposes. Also, no security is 100-percent hacker-proof; someone outside the company may intercept and read your e-mail. Routing of e-mail is not without errors; someone other than the intended recipient may receive your e-mail. Do not send anything by e-mail that you would not place on the company bulletin board.

11. **Other.** Remember, all recipients may not read your e-mail immediately. While your e-mail usually arrives quickly, this is not always the

case. E-mail is not designed for immediacy (that's why you have a tele-phone); it's designed for convenience. Do not use e-mail to schedule a meeting the same day or for anything requiring an immediate re-sponse.

Avoid using e-mail to deliver bad news. You cannot answer ques-tions when a person reads the e-mail.

## COMMENT

The consequences of e-mail content were highlighted in the Microsoft antitrust trial, where the government used e-mails written by Microsoft executives to undermine their credibility. Statements made by executives in e-mails con-tradicted their public statements.

If you receive an e-mail causing you to have a strong negative reaction, avoid responding immediately by e-mail. Use the telephone to clear up any possible misunderstanding.

Using all capital letters in an e-mail is the equivalent of SHOUTING.

When replying to an e-mail, either leave the old message as part of the new one or clearly reference your response. Do not assume the reader knows exactly what you are talking about.

### [E]   Instant Messaging

Instant Messaging is one of the most popular and most interactive services on the Internet. Using an Instant Messaging program such as Trillian or mIRC, you can chat instantly with anyone anywhere in the world. Many companies find instant messaging to be a useful tool for communicating with co-workers and customers. If you are on the phone, a message can be sent that pops up instantly on your screen. But the capability to interrupt concentration—such as a ringing telephone—makes Instant Messaging very disruptive in the office. Many Instant Messaging programs won't work through a firewall and can be difficult to monitor. The use of external servers to distribute the messages can present a security issue. Information systems is responsible for developing poli-cies and procedures for using Instant Messaging programs.

## COMMENT

According to Media Metrix, over 29 million home users and about 7 million business users use Instant Messaging.

### [F]   Internet Training

Training for connecting to the Internet and for using the e-mail system is provided by the information system's IT training unit. If the site does not have an IT training unit, training material is made available by the local training unit. If unavailable, the company information systems organization provides the training material.

Internet connection and e-mail system use training is available as individualized training. The material is loaned to the user, and then returned to the unit providing the material. The training provided will be in one of the following forms:

1.  **Tutorial.** The user will learn via a tutorial. The user—at his/her own pace and as time is available—learns how to connect to the Internet and use the e-mail system. The user is provided with a learning guide with step-by-step instructions that assumes basic knowledge of the computer's operating system. After the user has completed all items in the learning guide, he/she returns the tutorial to the training unit.
2.  **On-the-job training.** An experienced Internet user provides on-the-job training (OJT). The OJT instructor has a learning guide provided by the information systems organization. The IT organization provides the user with a copy of the learning guide via the instructor.

    The OJT instructor follows the learning guide when working with the student. They proceed as time and the student's learning skills permit. A skill test is provided with the learning guide to ensure the student's mastery of the material.

# § 17.05   ACCEPTABLE USE AGREEMENT

### [A]   Overview

An acceptable use agreement is put in place ensuring all employees understand and agree to the company's Internet use policies. The employee's immediate supervisor reviews the policy with the employee ensuring the employee understands the seriousness of the policy.

### [B]   Sample Acceptable Use Agreement

Exhibit 17-1 is a sample e-mail and Internet user agreement that is signed by all existing employees and by all new employees at orientation. The employee receives a copy, and another copy is placed in the employee's personnel file.

**EXHIBIT 17-1.**   E-Mail/Internet User Agreement

Employee Agreement:

I have received a copy of XYZ Company's E-Mail and Internet Acceptable Use Policy #_____, dated _____. I recognize and understand that the company's e-mail and Internet systems are to be used for conducting the company's business only. I understand that use of this equipment for private purposes is strictly prohibited.

As part of the XYZ organization and use of XYZ's gateway to the Internet and e-mail system, I understand that this Acceptable Use Policy applies to me. I have read the aforementioned document and agree to follow all policies and procedures that are set forth herein. I further agree to abide by the standards set in the document for the duration of my employment with XYZ Company. I understand that e-mail and Internet usage may be monitored by the company to ensure compliance with the Acceptable Use Policy.

I am aware that violations of this Acceptable Use Policy may subject me to disciplinary action, up to and including discharge from employment. I further understand that my communications on the Internet and e-mail reflect XYZ Company worldwide to our competitors, consumers, customers, and suppliers. Furthermore, I understand that this document can be amended at any time.


_____          _____

Employee's Signature                               Date


_____

Employee's Printed Name


_____

Manager's Signature

# § 17.06   USE OF APPLICATION SERVICE PROVIDERS

## [A]   Overview

Application service provider (ASP) policy formalizes standards for how ASPs are used and managed within the organization. With the increasing shortage of skilled workers to operate systems in-house, more companies turn to ASPs to manage and maintain their system infrastructure. It is critical that the information systems group manage the selection and use of ASPs ensuring the company receives the value the ASP was hired to provide. This policy mandates the endorsement and support by the CEO/head of the organization.

## [B]   Definition

An ASP is a supplier who makes applications available on a subscription basis. The ASP model works similarly to the time-sharing systems used in the 1960s and 1970s. ASPs typically provide access to the following types of applications:

- Supply chain management
- Accounting
- E-purchasing
- Human resources
- Recruiting
- E-mail
- Document and workflow management
- Customer relationship management
- Group scheduling
- Help desk
- Secure collaboration communities

An ASP combines service offerings traditionally not offered by one company. The four primary ingredients are the following:

1.   **Packaged software applications.** Licenses to products developed by ISVs are sold for a sizable up-front fee or on a per-use basis.
2.   **Data centers and connectivity.** Data-center services are offered by hosting companies (e.g., Jumpline), hardware companies (e.g., IBM), and telecom providers (e.g., Qwest). Telecom and business Internet service providers (ISPs) provide connectivity.
3.   **Application monitoring and ongoing support.** Firms such as AmQUEST, Digex, and Jumpline typically offer application monitoring. Ongoing support is typically offered at the first level by firms such as Support Technologies. SIs or ISVs typically provide second-level support.
4.   **Systems implementation and integration.** Systems integrators (SIs) or the service arms of ISVs traditionally offer these services.

The ASP is used to provide access to a single application or can be used to replace the entire user desktop.

**COMMENT**

Over one-third of information technology and development managers at large corporations expected to rent applications from application service providers in 2000, according to a study conducted by Evans Marketing Services (EMS).

## [C]   Application Outsourcing Policies

Corporate and IT management must have a clear set of long-term goals and objectives for the outsourcing of applications. ASPs should be used:

- For operations difficult to manage and staff. ASPs can reduce headcount needs.
- To avoid hardware and software obsolescence.
- To improve focus on core competencies. Most companies do not include IT as part of their core competency.
- To supply talent and/or resources unavailable in the organization.
- To reduce internal operation costs.
- To make applications available to a mobile, distributed workforce.
- For their ability to scale rapidly.
- To make IT cost more predictable.
- For turnkey solutions. The role of general technology contractor shifts from the company to the ASP.
- To free resources for other efforts.
- To bring systems up and running faster. ASPs can generally deliver software to a customer more rapidly than in-house resources or an external software developer can.

The areas for which an ASP is used are budgeted annually. ASP contracts that expire within the next budget year require a new contract proposal 3 months before the cutoff for budget consideration. If the current ASP's performance or new proposal is not satisfactory, an RFP will be sent to no fewer than two other vendors.

**COMMENT**

A recent report from Deloitte Consulting estimates the entire United States market for ASPs, Web hosting, and application outsourcing at close to $10 billion. It is projected to grow to more than $50 billion by 2003.

# § 17.07   ASP VENDOR SELECTION PROCESS

## [A]   Overview

Selecting a vendor to provide application services requires the use of stringent evaluation procedures. Not only must the applications themselves be evaluated, but hosting facilities, bandwidth, and support capabilities must also be carefully considered. The relative newness of the ASP market and the volatility of the stock market upon which they rely for funding make the selection of the right ASP extremely important. Betting your organization's technology infrastructure on a company that may experience a sharp drop in its stock price may cause you trouble. If its stock price drops, the company may not have the money to invest in research and development, which may impact your ability to service your customers.

In addition to technical considerations, constantly reevaluate with whom you do business. Have a companywide agreement on the criteria for choosing a technology vendor. Get involved in a professional network of chief technology officers (CTOs) who you can talk to on a regular basis about technology providers' performance. Bet your infrastructure on a combination of established and newer companies. The best dot-com companies, and the ones most likely to stay in business, are those that have formed a technology and business alliance with an established company such as IBM, Microsoft, or Oracle. These more established companies have done their own evaluation of technology providers and found them credible partners. A small sample of ASPs are listed below:

| **ASP** | **Product** | **Web Site** |
|---|---|---|
| Success Factors.com | PerformanceManager | *www.successfactors.com* |
| BlueStar Solutions | SAP R/3 | *www.bluestarsolutions.com* |
| Great Plains Software | eEnterprise | *www.greatplains.com/hosting* |
| Smart Online, Inc. | Small business software | *www.smartonline.com* |
| TeleComputing | Microsoft BackOffice | *www.telecomputing.no* |
| USIS | Health/medical applications | *www.usishealth.com* |

## [B]   ASP Request for Proposal

When IS management is ready to receive vendor proposals, a formal request for proposal (RFP) letter is sent to all possible candidates. The RFP defines the format of the proposal ensuring that a responding vendor can be evaluated and compared easily with others. The RFP should cover the following items:

- Type of applications to be outsourced
- Minimum performance requirements and evaluation criteria
- Reliability level required
- Level of integration with other systems required
- Any required reporting capabilities
- Service volume expandability
- Vendor contact person

- IS contact person
- Vendor maintenance, training, and operation support
- Current users of the ASP's systems

This request for proposal is for an ongoing service contract, with a given time limit. The service is billed monthly at a flat rate or prorated by transaction or user volume.

All items in the contract with the ASP are negotiable. A 3- to 5-year contract is typical. Standard support is usually 12/5 (12 hours a day, 5 days a week) with 24/7 support available at an additional cost. Systems with a small number of users are typically placed on a shared server with other customers of the ASP. Dedicated servers are available for an additional cost. The base fee per user normally covers the infrastructure at the ASP (but not the cost to connect) and any software licenses required. A fixed amount of hard-disk storage space is usually included, with 100MB per user typical. Carefully evaluate what your users need and try to ensure as much as possible is covered in the standard agreement. As with any major purchase, add-ons can significantly add to the cost of the service.

The method by which you will connect to the ASP is also an important consideration. A dedicated frame relay connection to the ASP is the most secure and reliable, but usually more expensive than connecting over the Internet. A connection over the Internet can be much less reliable, as overall Internet traffic can impact your performance. Using a dedicated frame connection, a good rule of thumb is 10 users for a 64K line, 20 users on a 128K line, and 50 to 60 users on a full T1 connection. For the same connection over the Internet, about one-half to two-thirds as many users can be supported as on the frame connection. For each vendor selected to receive a copy of the RFP, assign an internal IS person the task of being the liaison between that vendor and the company. That person's job is to manage the communication between the vendor and the company and to encourage the vendor to provide its best response to the RFP. Encourage the vendor to put the maximum effort into its response, especially if the vendor suspects that another vendor may have an advantage. Even if another vendor is selected, any attractive items in the losing vendors' proposals can be used as negotiating points with the vendor ultimately selected.

## [C]    Evaluating ASP Vendors' Proposals

All proposals received are analyzed using a predetermined set of criteria. The elements compared should be in the same sequence on each proposal. Copies are given to each evaluator, and a date and time are selected to meet and discuss them.

Vendors providing clear and complete information requested in the RFP and meeting preliminary evaluation standards are selected for more detailed analysis. Those who do not will be removed from further consideration.

The vendors' proposals should address the specification elements noted in the RFP. Clear statements should be made by the vendor to address the following items:

- Credentials of firm
- Former and current customer references
- Documentation clarity and completeness
- User-training and implementation resources available
- Process to ensure data security and availability
- Reliability of service
- Scalability of service
- Availability of support
- Quality of support (credentials of staff, average length of service, etc.)
- Security of connection
- Physical security of data center
- Next expected release of software
- Types of reports issued detailing application access and use statistics
- Management of software upgrade process
- Dedicated or shared server
- Storage space available per user and cost
- Backup and redundancy resources available
- Customization options available, if any

Current and former customers are contacted to discuss their experiences with the vendor. The following questions are helpful for obtaining useful information:

1. Would you use the same vendor again? If so, why? What has been the major problem with the vendor? Do you know other users of the vendor's product? Are they generally happy? If so, why? Who are the other users? What are their names and telephone numbers?
2. How long does it take for the vendor to respond to problems? Are the people who respond knowledgeable and friendly? Has the vendor ever lied? Has the vendor had the resources to resolve your problem(s)?
3. Does the application satisfy your needs? Follow up with questions about how long they have had the system and how often it has gone down. Ask about its expendability and upgrading possibilities.
4. Do the users like the service? Ask to talk to users and confirm this. Ask users what they liked and disliked about the service and why.
5. Ask how long it took to put the application into operation. Did they receive adequate training? Are the user manuals easy to understand and follow?
6. Is the service provided better than they could do themselves, and why? Is the service worth the cost?
7. Were there any unexpected or hidden costs? What was the nature of these costs? Were the costs reasonable? Was the vendor confronted about this? If so, what was the reaction?
8. Were the vendor's employees easy to work with? Did their salesperson follow up after the sale was made? Does the vendor seem to have a genuine interest in the success of the service?
9. If you were starting all over, what would you do differently?

# § 17.08   ASP VENDOR MANAGEMENT

## [A]   Overview

Managing a long-term ASP project is not an easy task. Some of the reasons for difficulty include:

- Pricing and service levels established at the beginning of the contract do not contain meaningful methods for measurement and improvement of service.
- Expectations and assumptions of both parties change over time. Most contracts cannot anticipate changes in technology, personnel, business processes, etc.
- Cultural differences between the two companies can cause misunderstandings and mistrust.
- Differences in the goals and objectives of the two companies can cause problems.
- Lack of management oversight may cause priorities to become out of sync with the reasons for entering into the contract in the first place.

## [B]   Service Level Agreement

Information services and affected business units must work together to determine the service level requirements for the applications that are outsourced to the ASP. These service levels are determined at the outset of the agreement, and used to measure and monitor the supplier's performance. The service levels are written in a contract called a Service Level Agreement (SLA). The SLA defines the consequences for failing to meet one or more service levels.

The SLA should include the following sections:

- A precise definition of key terms
- Specific service levels for all key categories (system availability, help-desk responsiveness, security administration, change management, etc.)
- Frequency of service level measurement (usually monthly)
- Weighting by importance of key service levels
- Calculation of credits for missing service levels
- Calculation of credits for frequency of missing service levels. Increased frequency of missed service levels might increase the service credit by some predetermined factor. The performance factors specified in the SLA not only provide an objective measure of the vendor's performance, but can serve as a basis for termination of the service if threshold service levels cannot be met. Other nonkey performance levels can be specified to add to the case for termination if warranted.

Typical credit for failure to meet routine service levels ranges from 5 to 15 percent, with penalties for severe service failures reaching 20 to 25 percent. Force majeure clauses excuse a party's failure to perform if the failure resulted from an act of nature such as an earthquake or other natural disaster beyond the party's control. The ASP vendor will attempt to include as much as possible in this category; define it as narrowly as possible. Under no circumstances should a force majeure absolve the vendor completely from its responsibilities.

The SLA might also include provisions for rewarding the vendor for extra value-added services provided. Make sure these services will really add value before agreeing to payment.

Negotiating and designing an SLA is difficult and time-consuming, but a fair and comprehensive SLA is critical for a successful ASP relationship. During the negotiation, both parties learn a lot about how their future partner approaches various aspects of their relationship.

# 18

# END-USER IT DEVELOPMENT: EVERYONE'S A PROGRAMMER

## § 18.01   END-USER IT DEVELOPMENT POLICY

End-user IT development policy focuses on autonomous individual and work-group operations. However, this autonomy does not allow disregarding normal industry development practices. End users who manage their own IT resources are expected to follow the policies and procedures as recorded in this document.

End-user development has a liaison relationship with corporate IT if no other relationship is defined, which provides information and guidelines used to develop its systems. These guidelines are established to avoid corporate lawsuits and public embarrassment on the part of end-user system development.

## COMMENT

Every day more tools become available for end users to develop their own custom applications. Tools from Microsoft are especially popular; FrontPage allows users to create their own Web pages; Access is used to create database applications; and even Word can interface with back-end systems using Smart Tags to create custom applications.

End-user management is fully responsible for any employees not abiding by the information and guidelines provided by corporate information systems. Repercussions resulting from noncompliance will be dealt with accordingly. The procedures offered here apply only to information and guidelines for end-user IT development.

## § 18.02   END-USER IT PROJECT DEVELOPMENT

### [A]   Overview

End-user IT project development focuses on individual and workgroup operations. These activities can cover the following:

- Analyze end-user requirements
- Analyze end-user workflows
- Evaluate turnkey systems
- Develop user applications from available software packages
- Write user application programs using sanctioned software
- Conduct feasibility studies
- Conduct procedure analyses
- Perform end-user systems design
- Implement end-user systems

Project development will include the following phases of project methodology:

- Identify problem
- Define scope of problem
- Conduct feasibility study
- Assess results of feasibility study
- Conduct procedure analyses
- Analyze procedure
- Select or develop solution
- Implement solution
- Evaluate results
- Document operation for further implementation

## [B]  End-user IT Project Team

The concept of a project team has long been used by corporate IT which has involved users in a largely secondary role, if any. The end-user IT project team does not require corporate IT, but, depending on need, may request corporate IT systems' assistance. The relationship of corporate IT and end-user project efforts depends more on their individual cultures than on technology.

The end-user IT project team is mostly representative of a single area of the company which, whether it be a division, department, or section, has user management with a vested interest in the project. This interest is more than budgetary. The project team members are mostly from this same area of the company.

The team is formed to resolve problems identified within its own area. End-user management appoints a project leader, who is informed about the scope of the problem, and requests a feasibility study.

The project leader conducts a feasibility study on his/her own. If assistance is required, it may be drawn from the area being studied. After the feasibility study results are assessed and accepted by user management, the project undertaking starts. The selection of the end-user IT project team is up to the project leader. All members of the project team, including the leader, continue the duties of their primary jobs.

The job profile of the team members varies with the needs of the project. The following are possible team member titles and the respective skills required:

1. **Project leader**
   a. **Maturity.** The person must be recognized for his/her maturity in handling political situations.
   b. **Administrator.** The person must be able to routinely perform day-to-day part-time administrative activities, such as reporting, requisitioning, memo writing, etc. This includes the ability to set and follow schedules, meet deadlines, and handle resources and any budgets. A proactive administrator is more desirable than a reactive administrator.
   c. **IT skills.** The project leader must have the technical skills to gain the respect of the user staff and management.

   d.   **Company knowledge.** The person should know the formal or-
        ganization chart, but more important must understand the infor-
        mal organization to help the project progress smoothly.
   e.   **Delegator.** The person must delegate and recognize that when
        a project team member is successful, that member gets all the
        credit. When the member fails, the project leader shares this fail-
        ure.
   f.   **Communicator.** The project leader keeps the project team,
        management, and others with vested interests in the project well
        informed. This includes informal day-to-day oral communication,
        written communication, formal presentations, teaching, and
        chairing meetings.
   g.   **Innovator.** The project leader is not limited to traditional solu-
        tions. He/she must be innovative and encourage others to be the
        same.
   h.   **Leader.** The project team must be able to lead through the most
        trying times. The leader must be able to work under pressure, re-
        main calm, keep the project objective in focus, and still be sensi-
        tive to the team and others.
   i.   **Maintain two jobs.** The leader still has the responsibility of an-
        other job. The other position may be related to the users' IT opera-
        tion or not.
2. **Project team members.** These people must possess skills needed for
   the project to be successful. They are available part-time for the dura-
   tion of the project, but still retain their other primary responsibilities.
   The people could have the following project titles:
   • Programmer (Visual Basic, SASS, etc.)
   • Project librarian
   • Project secretary
   • Forms designer
   • Data entry operator
   • Corporate IT personnel on loan
     These personnel can be loaned for the user project for given time
   limits. They can act as consultants and/or project workers. They have
   talents normally not found in an end-user operation.
   • Systems analysts
   • Systems and procedure analysts
   • Analyst programmers
   • Forms designers
   • Database designers
   • Senior programmers
   • Network specialists

## [C]   End-user IT Project Formulation

After people have been selected by the project leader and approved by management, they meet to formalize and plan the project. The leader assigns tasks
and develops a schedule with the team.

To complete an end-user project requires various skills and knowledge. At times the project may require the assistance of the corporate IT systems department which may be free or charged back to the user's budget. Tasks involved can be to:

- Use project management software packages
- Perform feasibility studies
- Document data flows and procedures
- Design data collection tools
- Conduct analysis interviews
- Perform observations of current operations
- Perform statistical analyses
- Perform cost-benefit analyses
- Design software application programs
- Conduct software package evaluations
- Write application programs
- Design operator-supporting materials
- Sell users on the merits of alternative systems
- Train users for the operation of systems

The project planning and formalizing effort will:

- Determine project scope and tasks
- Confirm team has needed skills
- Confirm members have time for their duties
- Determine what kind of assistance is needed from corporate IT and how much
- Finalize planning tasks
- Reassess member talent and required time available
- Assign specific project tasks
- Assign vendor contact person

## § 18.03  SYSTEM DOCUMENTATION

### [A]  Overview

It is essential to understand the current system employed in the user's area before a new system can be devised to replace it. The current system must be completely documented.

This documentation requires the analyst to make personal contact with user operational personnel, giving him/her an opportunity to develop a rapport and establish a relationship based on trust with the current operators of the system. This is necessary to ensure positive attitudes toward the pending new system. In addition, the higher the level of cooperation, the better the data collected will be.

Current system documentation activities should include the following:

- Define documentation scope
- Study current published procedure
- Study actual process
- Document actual procedure
- Confirm documentation
- Redefine scope
- Complete documentation of analysis

## [B]   Current System Documentation

Before any effort is expended on the development of an end-user system, a thorough understanding of the current system and a required needs analysis are prerequisites. This study helps avoid repeating the mistakes of the past.

- **Define documentation scope.** The boundaries of any proposed system are defined before any effort is spent to delineate the scope of the operational activities used by the end-user information system.

  The scope of an end-user information system seldom extends beyond the boundaries of any one department or area of operation. Information collected for the defined area of scope may reveal what is expected is not possible. The scope of the study often shifts, expands, or even contracts from its original definition.

  It is important to identify key employees involved in the analysis. It is also important to reveal the critical operations and their priorities. Interpersonal, political, and microculture elements can alter the project scope. Deal with these carefully because the project requires the collaboration of all involved people to be successful.

- **Study current published procedures.** The formal, published procedures are studied before examining the actual procedures to provide information about those originally developed. Later, when studying the actual procedures, investigate deviations. Read existing documentation with a general overview. This includes looking at organizational charts, annual reports, mission statements, former budgets, and the policies and procedures manual.

  As the study becomes more involved, more specific aspects of the current operation are examined, including such items as any former procedure analyses, cost studies, systems planning information, current forms, and personnel staffing reports. The person doing this study will want to have his/her own file, so some documents will need to be copied.

- **Study actual process.** To understand the actual current process, follow the actual procedure through from beginning to end. This investigation also covers the unstructured processes of the area under study. When a change from the prescribed procedure is discovered, note the reason for it. If there is no formal documentation of these processes, the analyst doing the study has to record these findings in the project report and complete the needed documentation.

- **Document actual procedure.** The collected information is documented in the form of flowcharts, forms, and written information. The actual procedure information is collected in the form of worker interviews, observations, work sampling, and questionnaires.
- **Confirm documentation.** The analyst verifies the flowcharted procedures; while doing so he/she notes any problems because of user management preferences, worker attitudes, and the department's culture. The political and social environments as well as worker personalities are critical to the development of the end-user system.
- **Redefine scope.** After collecting all the data, redefine the scope of the project if necessary. This information is then presented to the highest level of management within the department or division, i.e., the person responsible for the project approval and budget. This person has the final responsibility for the scope, which can change during the course of the project.
- **Complete documentation of analysis.** Completing the documentation and assembling it for the feasibility study shortens the project delivery date.

## [C]   Information Collecting Techniques

Information is collected when a system is reengineered or created. The proposed operation may be a simple, short procedure or a complex end-user system application. However, whatever the end project, information is required for its design.

Members of the project team or IT personnel are responsible for gathering this information. The following are techniques that make it possible to obtain the most current information needed to design an end-user system.

1.  **Document review.** Collect printed materials used to operate a manual or computer system. Analyze them to provide as much information as possible about the operation: cost, job requirements, and detailed process information. The documents are grouped by type:
    a.  General documents
        - Organization charts
        - Annual reports
        - Department budgets
        - Policy manual
        - Job descriptions
    b.  Procedure operations
        - Procedural manuals
        - Process flowcharts
        - Former procedure studies
        - Work measurement studies
        - Work sampling studies
        - Internal and external forms

2. **Current computer system**
   - System flowcharts
   - Dataflow diagrams
   - Document flowcharts
   - Data dictionary
   - Programming flowcharts
   - Monitor displays
   - Operation logs
   - Operation manuals
3. **Operational personnel interviews.** Conduct interviews in the same manner as presented in § 3.03[D], "Information Gathering Interviews" and §3.03[E], "Document the Interviews."
4. **Work sampling studies.** Work sampling is covered in Chapter 3.
5. **Current operating costs.** Collect cost information for the operating department including cost per measurable unit of output. Break down cost information as follows:
   a. **Direct labor cost.** This includes direct labor for the operating department, including per-unit cost (the cost of processing one unit through the operation). Examples would be the cost per purchase order processed, or the cost to complete a customer order. Costs also will note employee benefit expense.
   b. **Indirect labor cost.** This includes management, training, support, and corporate prorated indirect cost. Compute the cost for the operating department. Compute per-unit indirect labor cost.
   c. **Direct material cost.** This is the direct material cost per unit processed.
   d. **Indirect material cost.** This is the cost of supply items:
      i. Paper clips
      ii. Paper
      iii. Printer toner and ribbons
      iv. Expensed work aids
      v. Expensed computer software
      vi. Computer disks
      vii. Other general expensed office items

      Indirect material cost is reported as the total cost and also prorated to show the per-unit cost of output.
   e. **Space cost.** This is the standard charge per square foot for the department's office space and utilities. This is reported as the total cost and also as the prorated per-unit cost of output.
   f. **Capital depreciation cost.** This is the annual capital depreciation cost to the department and the prorated per-unit cost of output.
   g. **Other costs.** This includes all costs not already covered. (Examples are employee bonding costs, software and hardware leased, etc.) This is reported as the total unit cost and also as the prorated per-unit cost of output.
6. **Data dictionary.** If there is an existing computer system in place, the data dictionary is brought up to date.

# § 18.04   END-USER IT FEASIBILITY STUDY

## [A]   Purpose

The end-user IT feasibility study is conducted to determine the feasibility of proceeding with the innovation considered for the end-user workgroup or stand-alone computer system. The information collected by the end-user project team is a major input to this analysis.

To justify a new end-user system, it must satisfy three feasibility requirements:

1. **Economic feasibility.** Economic feasibility analysis determines if the solution meets measurements of cost effectiveness. This is justified on the basis of cost/benefit analyses.
2. **Technical feasibility.** Technical feasibility analysis determines if the solution is technically practical: Is the technology available and can the end user and the facilities accommodate the solution?
3. **Operational feasibility.** Operational feasibility analysis determines if the solution meets end-user requirements: Does the solution fit into the end-user operational environment and meet the requirements of an acceptable time schedule? It also ascertains if human factor requirements will be met for the users, and if it fits into the social work scene.

## [B]   End-user Feasibility Study File

When starting the feasibility study, a feasibility file folder is labeled with the title of the study and will accumulate the following:

- An accumulated table of contents
- All memos related to study
- E-mail documentation
- Vendor correspondence
- Vendor literature
- Accumulated costs data for feasibility study
- A log listing calendar days and hours worked on feasibility study
- Documentation of all meetings
- A telephone log regarding all phone calls made and attempted
- A copy of final report

## [C]   Feasibility Study Report Requirements

Format the feasibility study report in the following manner:

- Cover page, containing project title, author, and date
- Overview of request
- Rationale for initiating information systems project, or for changing an existing system
- Body of final report providing details of project

- Exhibits
- Summary, containing recommendations, estimated costs, estimated calendar time needed, and estimated worker-hours of all persons involved in project

## [D]  Economic Feasibility Analysis

The economic feasibility analysis determines if the solution can be justified on the basis of cost and benefits studied separately—if possible, by two different people—then compared. The decision is affected by this cost-benefit analysis that looks at the payback calculations.

1. **Cost identification.** Costs are classified as:
   a. **Development costs.** There are one-time costs incurred while the system is being developed. Personnel time, including fringe benefits, is stated in dollars. Development costs can contain:
      - Personnel costs
      - Hardware purchased
      - Software development or purchase
      - Document preparation
      - Site preparation
      - Furniture and fixtures
      - End-user training costs
   b. **Operating costs.** Operating costs are ongoing costs incurred while the system is in operation.
      - Operation personnel costs, plus benefits
      - Lease of hardware and software
      - Consumable supplies
      - Communication expense
      - Ongoing hardware and software upgrades and maintenance
      - Ongoing training
   c. **Variable costs.** These are costs based on production volume and include costs for such items as:
      - Supplies based on workload
      - Telephone and WAN line charges
      - Utilities used
      - Maintenance costs
      - Overtime costs
   d. **Intangible costs.** Intangible costs are those not easily converted into a dollar value. These come in many forms; some examples are:
      - Customer dissatisfaction
      - Time lost for learning new system
      - Learning errors incurred
      - Duties expanded due to creeping enlargement of scope
2. **Benefit identification.** Benefits for end-user information systems come in various forms and must be totaled for a complete cost/benefit analysis. They can be classified as:

a. **Tangible benefits**
   - Personnel dollars saved
   - Intangible benefits
   - Morale improvement

## COMMENT

There is often a misconception about computing personnel dollars saved. One might think if a new software package saves each company secretary one hour a week of work, then the 40 secretaries the company has will provide a savings equal to one secretary. Wrong!

The company will most likely keep all 40 secretaries and the cost will still be the same; therefore, no direct savings. However, if the secretaries are paid for overtime work, and overtime can be reduced, this can be credited as a savings.

b. **Cost-displacement benefits.** Cost-displacement benefits occur when the end-user information system provides for more efficient task performance. This, in effect, makes the end user more productive by saving time or money.

   An example is the use of a spreadsheet software package in the cost accounting department. If enough of these cost-displacement benefits assist the department, one or more cost accountants could be eliminated. Alternatively, if a person left the department, he/she would not have to be replaced.

c. **Value-added benefits.** These benefits occur when the end user increases his/her effectiveness. Value-added benefits are long-term results based on short-term operation costs. One example is when operation cost remains the same but customer billing is increased. Cost of new technology subtracted from benefits over time can produce a dollar savings. This technology also attracts new business because of the organization's enhanced status. Value-added benefits are often realized with professional and managerial personnel. A good example is the laptop computers (short-term cost) used by attorneys in courtrooms (long-term results: elimination of time to transcribe notes, among others).

   Value-added benefits can be obtained by:
   - Providing more time for reviewing designs, proposals, or alternatives
   - Reducing calendar time needed for designs, analysis, research, or planning

- Reducing effort required for administrative duties
- Permitting more opportunities for professional collaboration among colleagues in workgroup efforts

3. **Cost/benefit analysis.** After the total costs and benefits are computed and verified, begin the cost-benefit analysis. Use one or more of the many techniques available to do this.

   Because of the short life spans of hardware and software, don't use lengthy payback periods. A timeframe of 3 to 5 years is still reasonable. Whichever cost-benefit technique is employed, the analysis should be unbiased. The payback time should not be extended simply to justify the need, because maintenance costs can grow exponentially.

   a. **Payback analysis.** Payback analysis or cost/benefit comparison helps determine the time it will take for the proposed system to pay off the cost of developing and installing the new system. To compute the number of years necessary to recover costs:
   - Compute dollar total of expected benefits.
   - Compute dollar total of expected operation costs.
   - Subtract expected operating costs from expected dollar benefits.
   - Divide total development costs by average net annual expected benefit.

   This gives the number of years or payback period expected to recover this cost. The expected recovery cost is a one-time cost for the system development.

   b. **Operational benefits.** This is the estimated cost savings accrued during routine administrative operations of the proposed system.

   c. **Time-valued payback.** Time-valued payback is the discount rate found in a present value table, which represents anticipated interest earning, inflation depreciation, etc., over a given time. An up-to-date present value table is essential to find the factor needed to determine the time-valued payback (or a good financial calculator). The longer the payback, the less the return on investment because the dollar's buying power becomes deflated because of interest revenue lost.

   d. **Net present value.** Knowing the net present value allows the analyst to compute the time value of money and compare different investment opportunities that may have different costs, discount rates, and benefits.

   Determine the costs and benefits for each given year of the system's life span. The yearly adjusted costs and benefits are compared to the current dollar value of the investment. Compare these figures with the adjusted costs and benefits to arrive at a final new present value, which can be positive or negative. A positive net present value indicates that the return exceeds the comparison rate, while a negative indicates that the proposed project return is less than the value of a comparative investment. A zero net present value indicates that either investment would yield the same.

## [E]   Technical Feasibility

The technical feasibility of the proposed solution is the practicality of its adapting to the technology available. The technology can seldom, if ever, be altered for the sole convenience of the solution. This study must address all five of the following items:

1.  **Availability of technology.** Information technology changes at a rapid rate. Many technical obstacles existing a few years ago have now been overcome. If a technology problem does exist, shelve the proposal for a while until the technology is further developed.

    The technology needed to make a proposed innovation feasible may be waiting in the wings. By working with an informal information network and developing a good vendor relationship, a member of the end-user project may discover this knowledge. This is one of the reasons some organizations use to justify becoming a beta site.

    Both hardware and software are upgraded frequently, bringing new technology to the market daily. The project leader should follow these developments closely.

2.  **Practicality.** The hardware and software technology needed to implement the proposed project may be available, but it must also be practical. Many questions must be asked:
    *   Is it affordable?
    *   Will the vendor be in business next year?
    *   Can the item be modified?
    *   Has the item been proved over time?
    *   What is its track record with users?
    *   Is the source code available?
    *   What about vendor support and documentation?

3.  **Availability of technical skills.** The necessary end-user talent also must be available. If there is no in-house talent, the training cost and/ or time required may or may not be justifiable. Outside assistance may or may not be practical.

4.  **Project delivery schedule.** The project delivery schedule must be practical. When working back from a required finish date, the start date might have already passed. Or the vendor's promised delivery date might be too late to use the technology when needed.

5.  **Obsolescence problem.** It is important to make certain, if possible, that the proposed process performs as desired. Deliverable technology can become obsolete before the system is installed or too soon after installation. If so, the payback time might not be completed because of this obsolescence.

    Many hardware manufacturers no longer stock replacement parts because of shortening product life cycles. Some supply items might also no longer be available.

## [F]   Operational Feasibility

Operational feasibility analysis determines if end-user IT requirements are feasible. These operational concerns cover the end user's individual and group process and political needs. The proposed system or innovation needs to satisfy these requirements.

1. **Is the problem worth correcting?** Will the new innovation be worth the effort for correcting the problem?

## COMMENT

A large Midwest teaching hospital installed an online laboratory information system. One of the supposed benefits was having the billing information downloaded to the business computer, thereby reducing billing time and data entry cost. However, laboratory technicians and medical doctors were entering the data. This resulted in a higher error rate than before, as well as lost time for key personnel.

2. **What is the users' attitude?** The management is sold the new system and approves its creation, but the users are the ones operating it. Because the new end-user system affects their daily work efforts and relationships and their traditional ways of working, gaining users' acceptance can become a challenge.

   Introducing new technology or a new system can create outright resistance, hostility, and even worker sabotage. This may be because it lowers a worker's importance within a group, diminishing the power and status that the former job provided. End-user workgroups may lose their power, status, and credibility within the company.

   This attitude can destroy a new system. The problem can be noticed during the interviewing phase of the systems analysis. Blind workgroup questionnaires are also informative. Once attitudes surface, make plans to alter them. Some suggestions are:

   - Have user management show strong visible support.
   - Provide end-user education.
   - Encourage end-user design involvement.
   - Reevaluate worker job descriptions, presenting more opportunities.
   - Provide new worker status symbols.
   - Upgrade job titles.
   - Present the total picture to workers.
   - Inform them of their new job responsibilities and the increased status, as well as value to the company, that the jobs will give them.
   - Improve worker environment.
   - Have an open house to show off the new system.
   - Provide news coverage about the workers and their new system in the company newspaper.
   - To be effective, it is recommended that two or more of these suggestions be followed.

3.  **What is the political environment?** A stable political environment provides a better opportunity base for end-user IT development than one in transition or that is volatile. One major advantage of end-user IT development over corporate IT development is end-user developers have a far better understanding of user political problems.

    If there are political problems between departments, having two independent end-user IT operations may make more sense than a corporate-sponsored integrated system involving both. Corporate IT should stay clear of warring departments.

4.  **Are there end-user skill problems?** There can be end-user skill level problems. Senior management personnel cannot always be expected to have keyboard skills. Workers who traditionally operated at lower-level clerical positions can be intimidated by a computer system. The terminology, the mystique, and the lack of skills can present a challenge to any group of workers.

    Meet this challenge by providing a hands-on opportunity for all personnel to play with the computer. They can begin by playing simple games. There is far less apprehension when a user can beat the computer in a game.

    The next step is presenting a slowly paced training program, beginning with formal classes and proceeding to self-paced program learning, with tutorials last. A trainer should be available to work closely with these people. Some may not master the skills needed as fast as desired, but a skills handicap is like a physical handicap in that provisions must be made to circumvent it. Once these people master the needed skills, they generally become dedicated employees.

# § 18.05   END-USER PROCEDURE ANALYSIS

## [A]   Overview

After the feasibility study has been completed, end-user management must make a decision. The choices are:

*   Abandon the project.
*   Proceed with the installation (less complex undertakings or prototypes).
*   Proceed with procedure analysis and systems design.

This section is concerned with the third possible decision: end-user procedure analysis. When designing a new system, the proposed output should be the same as the old system or better, incorporating features that the current system does not provide. To deliver the desired new system, the elements of the current system must be analyzed in detail.

Simple projects that do not have involved elements do not require a procedure analysis to begin. More complex projects, however, will use a prototype operation to expedite the process and correct any systems problems during the shakedown operation.

## [B]  Detail Process Documentation

The process is studied in detail from the input point to the finalization of the process within the scope of the project. For a current manual operation a detailed Procedure Flowchart is drawn of the process elements. (See the "Procedure Flowchart" in § 2.08[E] for the process.) For a current computer operation, a dataflow diagram is drawn down to the lowest detail level to show the process elements. (See the "Dataflow Diagrams" in § 2.08[F] for the process.)

Drawn flowcharts are examined by the employees performing each task to confirm their authenticity and are examined by all operational people involved. Data information held in files also should be confirmed.

## [C]  Procedure Data Analysis

The procedure data analysis covers current user opinions, operating costs, operations, and the actual procedures that drive the present system. While the end user's opinions may be subjective, other collected data is objective and correct but might not be totally representative.

Take care to ensure that enough information is available when analyzing the collected data.

1. **Value of current operation.** Address the effective points of the current operation. How well does it actually perform?
   - Does it satisfy current end-user management?
   - Are costs within reason?
   - How well does it meet output needs?

### COMMENT

For one particular system, the data collected noted a weekly volume of 720 units processed. So the new system was designed to handle 750 units per week. After the system was operational, it was discovered that of the average 720 units processed in a week, 303 had to be processed on Mondays. The system could handle only 125 a day (750/5 days). The information collected was correct, but was not all the information needed.

2. **Cause of problems**
   - What are causes of problems?
   - Can problems be corrected in new system?
3. **Achievability of project goals**
   - Will proposed technology achieve goals?
   - Can goals be reached within cost estimated?

4. **Enhancement opportunities.** How can the proposed system best add benefits to the present operation? These benefits will often be items that are not considered by current end users and their management. In fact, enhancements may be a byproduct of the proposed technology.

## [D]    Recording Analysis Information

The information collected is recorded and placed in the project folder for future reference. A copy is given to each project member and the project-sponsoring management.

It will be documented in the following format:

1. **Title page.** This contains the project name, date, and project team members with their project and normal work titles.
2. **Summary introduction.** This is a one-page introduction and project summary report. It should note the end-user IT project objectives.
3. **Body of report.** This will contain the detailed information collected and the analyzed results. Unfamiliar terms will be defined.
4. **Appendices**
   • Sample of forms collected
   • Vendor literature
   • Flowcharts
   • Sample of any questionnaires used
   • Sample of any work sampling forms used

If the report reveals any major items of concern, an information meeting is held with end-user management and all members of the project team. The project leader delivers an oral presentation covering the report and any concerns.

In preparing for the meeting, the project leader should:

• Obtain a room.
• Send meeting notices, choosing the time based on management availability.
• Prepare a presentation outline.
• Prepare visual aids. (See "Presentation Devices" in § 14.05[C].)
• Rehearse the presentation in the room provided.
• Confirm that all invited management will attend.

After the meeting, resolve the issues discussed. Send out memos to this effect. If required, schedule a follow-up meeting.

# § 18.06    END-USER IT DESIGN

## [A]    Overview

After the detailed analysis is completed and no problems remain, the end-user IT project team may start the design phase. The designers do not have total freedom for developing an optimal design. One or more factors beyond their control may influence the final design:

- Inflexibility of off-the-shelf software
- No source code available for purchased software
- Corporate policy constants
- End-user political problems
- Corporate IT's end-user policy
- Budget reduction for proposed system

The design process begins after identifying the design scope and constants. One of the major design constraints is the software driving the proposed system. The required software will come in one of the following forms:

- Off-the-shelf software
- Purchased software, object code only
- Purchased software, object and source code
- Program(s) to be written

Know this information before the end-user IT design starts. The design tasks follow a given sequence as indicated.

## [B]  Design Phase

Begin the design process with a general design overview. The general design evolves through successive iterations into a detail design level suitable for being turned into computer program instructions and/or manual procedure operations.

1. **General logical system design.** The general logical design concentrates on content components and the data handling operation of the system without regard to hardware or software needs. The logical concept is first drawn at the context level of a dataflow diagram. (See "Dataflow Diagram" in § 2.08[F].)
2. **General physical system design.** This next step includes the instruments needed to perform the tasks. Dataflow diagram, level 0, is used. Hardware, software, and people needs of the evolving system come into consideration at this level.
3. **Detail operation design.** This next level uses level one of the dataflow diagram. It defines which procedures will be followed by end-user operational personnel and which program modules will be required.
4. **Program design level.** Construct the monitor screen displays at this level. Format output documents. Use the same illustrations as required for the Input-Output Prototype. (See the "Types of Prototyping Methods" in § 3.05[C].)

    This prototype does not have an operating program. The program design level also has no coded programs but has the detailed information needed to write them. At this level the monitor screen displays and output forms can receive final approval or be altered so that the next step, program implementation, can be started.

5. **System programming.** Complete the programming tasks at this level. This can consist of a written program or a purchased program with the source code provided. Do whatever customizing is necessary and possible with off-the-shelf software. All program documentation is completed and placed in a program project folder.

## [C] Human Factor Considerations

Much has been written about human factor problems in end-user application systems. These problems are valid and occur when the system designers do not take human needs into consideration. One major concern is that all people do not have the same size, weight, or environmental requirements.

1. **Workstation ergonomics.** Adding a keyboard to the standard desk height, which is higher than a typing table, can cause problems. To be ergonomically correct (most comfortable for a user) the keyboard should rest on an adjustable tabletop. The tabletop should be movable to place the keyboard keys from about 25 to 32 inches from the floor.

   The chair is the most important item of furniture at the workstation. The chair seat should adjust from about 15 to 21 inches from the floor. The backrest should also adjust both up and down, and back and forward. The seat width and depth should be available in more than one size. Four or more casters support the chair.

   The monitor has an adjustable support so that the viewing screen can be set horizontal to the eye height. The light display should be adjustable for both output and contrast.

   The desk or workstation provides enough top space to spread out items needed to work and store them. There is a lockable area for personal items.

2. **Office area.** The general office area is clean and neat. There are sufficient electric outlets because computer outlets are not shared with other electrical items. Power surge protectors and a UPS may be considered, too.

   Lighting is important when working all day at a workstation. The ambient light is a fluorescent or indirect tungsten bulb. Window light can be a problem if the light does not come from the north. To reduce glare, windows not facing north should be to the left or right of the user at a monitor screen.

   With laser and inkjet printers, office noise is less of a problem today than previously. Use drapes and other noise-control devices to reduce or mask noise if it is present.

3. **Monitor screen display.** It is still more difficult to read a monitor screen than a newspaper, and laptop computers are even worse. Better and bigger monitors reducing some of the problems are appearing on the market.

   However, screen glare and reflection from current monitors results in discomfort and eyestrain. There is also a tendency for screens to be clearer in the middle than at the margins. Screen image sharpness leaves something to be desired. Contrast can be adjusted and a selection of three or four colored monitor screen covers may provide a solution for this.

4. **Keyboard.** There are increasing numbers of different keyboards appearing on the market. There are also a number using ergonomic-related design. More laptop keyboards provide for wrist rests and have built-in pointing devices.

5. **Screen output display.** Screens, as well as input documents and output hardcopy, require ergonomic considerations. People in the United States still read from left to right and top to bottom, whether it be hardcopy or screen displays.

   When designing the screen display, keep the following in mind:

   - Avoid red and black combinations because of the number of color-blind people who cannot see red as a distinct color.
   - Know the users and their needs.
   - Keep instructions for use simple.
   - Optimize operations, using touch-screen menus, pointers, etc.
   - Keep screen commands simple.
   - Be consistent with all systems.
   - Place most often used items on the screen at the top left side.

## [D]   Project Completion and Acceptance

After the design effort has been completed, the project should be wrapped up with the following:

1. **Documentation.** The design and operation documentation is completed. The operator's instruction manual is completed and tested by a random selection of no less than 20 percent of the operating personnel. The documentation of the detail system design and programming is accurate and complete, presenting no problems with maintenance later.

2. **Training.** Training is provided to all operations personnel. Independent learning instructions are provided to new employees. Provisions are in place for independent learning of later modifications to the system.

3. **End-user management presentation.** The completed end-user IT design is presented to end-user management for final acceptance and support before implementation.

4. **End-user operations presentation.** This is a presentation for all end users. Encourage end-user management to be present to give its support to the new system.

   a. **Introduction.** The senior end-user manager makes the introduction, explaining why the project was started. He/she makes it clear that end-user management wanted and supported the project and its objective from the beginning.

b. **General overview of the system.** The project leader introduces all the project team members. He/she gives a general overview of the system and its benefits.

The following will be stressed during the presentation:

- It is the end users' system.
- There was a need for it.
- It will be better for all concerned if everyone provides 100 percent support for the implementation and operation of the system.
- There can be problems expected with any new system, but the project team will be there to help. Users should not be afraid to ask questions or ask for help. There also is a need to learn the operations manual.

c. **Close of the presentation.** Just before the meeting ends, open it to questions.

## § 18.07   EXTERNAL END-USER ASSISTANCE

### [A]   Overview

External assistance can be available either from within or outside the company. Depending on corporate policy, the corporate IT organization can freely provide this service or it can be charged back to the requesting department. If not charged back and the corporate IT organization is capable of giving assistance in the timeframe needed, use its services. If there is a charge, obtain a cost estimate.

If the corporate IT department is unable to supply the needed service, cannot within an acceptable timeframe, or does not have the expertise required, issue outside service bids. If the IT service is billable and available, outside bids should be issued to determine the least expensive source.

The service from an outside source can be consulting or contract services. See Chapter 15, Vendors: Getting the Goods, for policies and procedures.

### [B]   Software Vendors

With the growth of end-user IT software, vendors are encouraged to market vertical software produced for a restricted market of common users. An example would be Solomon Software of Findlay, Ohio, which produces and markets accounting software limited to accounting end users. Vertical market software is found for the following areas (among others):

- Accounting
- Human resource management
- Car body repair shops
- Manufacturing
- Purchasing
- Engineering
- Construction
- Billing
- Scheduling
- Publications
- Drafting
- Statistical analysis
- Photography

Another kind of software for general end-user applications is horizontal software. Horizontal software are applications used widely throughout companies. The three common types are word processing, spreadsheet, and database applications. This software has a supplemental use by many company end users, but often has a primary use within some departments. Examples would be word processing for the administrative staff and spreadsheets for the cost-estimating department.

Demand for off-the-shelf software increases as more PCs are used. More vendors develop end-user software and provide services, such as both free and billable help-desk assistance, for their customers.

One of the best sources of vertical software vendors is professional publications where many ads target end-user applications. Horizontal software ads appear primarily in computer literature; however, they also appear in publications ranging from the daily *Wall Street Journal* to the weekly *US News and World Report*.

## [C]   Vendor Assistance

Because end-user computing is found in a variety of user areas, assistance for such end users is often beyond the resources of the corporate IT department. However, it can be found in the vendor market.

1. **Full-service consulting vendors.** These are nationwide firms providing a wide array of consulting services for the end-user IT project.
2. **Specialty end-user vendors.** These are consultants or service providers with the skills for given areas of end-user applications.
3. **Contract vendors.** These vendors provide services across such different end-user applications as:
   - Contract programming
   - Networking
   - Database
   - Client/server
4. **Turnkey vendors.** These vendors provide the total system package, which may contain the following:
   - Hardware
   - All the software
   - Network system
   - Database system
   - Training
   - Operational manuals
   - Help desk
5. **Outsourcing vendors.** These vendors install and/or operate end-user IT operations. These vendors are more involved in the operation than turnkey package vendors because they also operate the system.
6. **Application service providers.** These vendors provide standardized software such as accounting packages, CRM software, etc., hosted at their location and accessed over the Internet or a dedicated connection.

Finding vendors is easier because of the growth of this industry. Local vendors advertise in the Yellow Pages, while national vendors advertise in national publications. Local vendors are a good source for a single-site operation; national firms are better for multisite operations.

National professional consulting societies and members of national professional societies are both sources for finding vendors. Another source is published directories of consultants. The local library may also be helpful.

### [D]  Vendor Contacting

One way to contact a vendor is with a request for information letter (RFI). This gives the vendor an opportunity to analyze the client's needs and match them with what he/she offers. The RFI provides the following information:

- The nature of the end-user IT application
- The time window within which it is to be developed
- The current resources available to the end user
- The expected goal of the project
- The company contact person's name, phone number, and e-mail address

If the end user has firmed up plans and is seeking a vendor for a given service, a request for proposal (RFP) is sent to vendors. This is a detailed document specifying the needed services, which might be a consulting service to provide contract services. See Chapter 15, Vendors: Getting the Goods, for more information.

## § 18.08   END-USER IT IMPLEMENTATION

### [A]  Overview

Implementation is the startup of the end-user IT system. This is scheduled at a lull (or slow) time in the end user's cycle of operation. Present the new system to the end users in a positive light.

The process is like launching a newly constructed ship; it will either float or sink. A lot depends on the attitude of the end users, which profoundly affects the success of the system.

## COMMENT

> One of the authors worked on a project where the end users wanted the system to work at all costs. It had to be shut down because of design problems. The users did not want to give up their system. They were upset and wanted to keep on trying.

### [B]  Types of Implementations

The implementation can be carried out in any one of four ways, each having pros and cons.

1. **Parallel implementation.** This is a popular and safe way of implementing a new system, definitely recommended for critical applications. It is safe because the old system is not unplugged until the new system has proved itself. Both the new and the old are operated in parallel. A learning curve is allowed for end users to be brought up to the needed skill level before the conversion is made.

   Parallel implementation also costs more than the other types. Extra people need to be recruited, trained, used, then let go. In this situation, extra contract workers are the best solution.

   However, implementation during lull time reduces the number of contract workers needed and, in some cases, the entire process might be handled using only overtime.

2. **Phased implementation.** Phased implementation occurs when the new system is placed into operation in phases. This reduces the load carried by the end users. There is less to learn at one time, and the new system can be pulled back if needed. This transition can proceed at the rate best suited to the situation.

   However, not all end-user systems lend themselves to this type of conversion; it can also prolong conversion.

3. **Pilot/prototype implementation.** This form involves choosing a developmental site that offers the best chance of success with the new system. Then, if the system works, it can be implemented at other sites. Using a single site first is a safer procedure. The effort to train the end-user operations people is extensive. In this situation, the workers are screened to obtain those attributes needed for a successful conversion. The pilot/prototype is refined until operating at the desired level of efficiency.

   However, success at a pilot/prototype development site in Salt Lake City does not guarantee the same success in New York City. People, local culture, and operations are not always the same. Sometimes the process to convert all other sites at once takes more resources than available, so this is the only option.

4. **Direct cut-over implementation.** This type requires that operations be cut over to the new system at the same time the old system is terminated. Some applications can be handled only in this manner. It is a fast way of starting a new end-user IT system, and less costly than the other methods of conversion, especially parallel implementation.

   Any failure made public, however, can be a disaster. While provisions to return to the old system are in place, the credibility of the new system can be undermined.

## COMMENT

There was a company in Michigan that attempted a direct cut-over implementation that did not work too well. The system was such a failure that a correct inventory could not even be provided for the firm's bankruptcy auction.

## [C]   Implementation Requirements

A combination of factors and attitudes is required for the implementation to be successful. Some factors are recognized as important long before the conversion is executed, but they are most effective if all work in concert from the very beginning.

They are:

1. **Systems design.** The quality of the final product has all the earmarks of excellence. The project team, the end users, and management are elated about the delivery system; their attitudes alone will impact the success of the conversion.

    The performance and reliability level of the system satisfies the users' requirements. The users look forward to using the new system, because it will do something for them.

2. **User involvement.** End users are very much a part of the new system because of their involvement in the analysis and design. Their input is recognized as important to the success of the implementation and operation of the new system. It is this *esprit de corps* that supplies the momentum essential to the undertaking; the end users believe their system will not fail.

3. **User-management commitment.** Management commitment provides the resources needed for the end-user project team. However, resources alone will not guarantee success. Management must demonstrate its eagerness for the success of the project. It must set the tone for the workers.

4. **Resources/value.** Resources committed to the project reflect the value of the project to the company. Cost-benefit analysis can confirm this value and the resources committed. There should be a direct correlation between the two: the greater the value, the more resources can be committed.

## [D]   Implementation Success Factors

There are universal factors that affect the success of a project, including end-user IT projects:

1. **Project size.** Project size directly affects the level of risk. The larger the project, the more calendar time required. The longer the calendar time, the more the opportunity for requirements to change. The more requirements change, the less likely the implemented system will succeed because the need is no longer the same.

    The larger the project size, the more members required for the project team. The more members on the project team, the greater the communication problems. The greater the communication problems, the more the opportunities for project errors and project delays.

    It is better to have several smaller projects than one large one. The efficiency rates and success rates are much higher for smaller projects.

2. **Complexity risk.** The more complex the project, the greater the risk for implementation. There are just too many interdependent things that can go wrong.

    Dividing a complex project into smaller ones seldom is possible. Using a pilot/prototype implementation would enhance the success of this type of project.

3. **Technology risk.** The newer and more complex the technology, the greater the risks. The first release of a given software package usually has more bugs than the third release.

    A pilot/prototype is a good candidate for implementation. Indeed, the direct cut-over implementation of a risky project has been called a kamikaze implementation.

## [E]  Implementation Follow-up

All end-user IT implementations are required to have a follow-up evaluation to answer a number of questions:

- Is the system operating as planned?
- Are the end users happy with the system?
- What parts of the system are not working?
- Was the system oversold?
- Was the cost-benefit analysis correct?
- What else needs to be done?

The list can continue. No one point in time is the best time to begin implementation follow-up. Data is collected as an ongoing process. Different problems happen at different time intervals and new corrective actions create new items to evaluate.

Reports of the follow-up findings are given monthly until the operation is fine-tuned. Later, as the system becomes obsolete, the entire analysis and design process begins again.

End-user IT evaluation should include the following:

1. **Evaluation items.** The items to be evaluated come from end-user management, the project leader, project members, and corporate IT systems. The basic questions may address the evaluation of the total system and its parts.

2. **Evaluation criteria.** The same people who established the evaluation items provide the criteria used. The criteria must be objective. Industry norms may assist in the criteria selection.

3. **Evaluation instruments.** Evaluation instruments are measurements such as turnaround time, benchmark comparisons, errors per unit of process, ratio of customer complaints, worker overtime, etc.

4. **Evaluation data.** Collect data from the following sources: the help desk, system performance logs, operator questionnaires, error logs, customer complaints recorded, etc.

5. **Analyze collected data.** Analyze the data using past performance information and industry standards.

6. **Design corrective action.** Corrective action will be designed and documented. The documentation is sent, with a cover memo, to the end-user manager. On receipt of this document, end-user management, the project leader, other project members involved, and any outside persons who were involved will meet to design corrective action for resolution of any problems. The end-user manager has to approve any designated corrective action.

7. **Carry out the corrective action.** The corrective action is executed. At a given predetermined date, unless there is an emergency, the process is evaluated again.

# 19

# END-USER IT COMPUTER OPERATIONS: END-USER SELF SUPPORT

# § 19.01   END-USER POLICIES

## [A]   Overview

End-user IT policies cover end-user IT workgroups and end-user stand-alone PCs autonomous from the corporate systems. However, autonomy does not allow end-user operations to disregard normal industry operation practices. They must follow the policies and procedures as recorded in this document. They have a liaison relationship with corporate IT if no other relation is defined. Corporate IT provides information and guidelines used to operate end-user information systems. These guidelines are established to avoid corporate lawsuits and any public embarrassment.

End-user management is fully responsible for any employees who do not abide by the information and guidelines provided by corporate information systems. Any repercussions resulting from noncompliance will be dealt with accordingly. The procedures offered here apply only to information and guidelines for end-user computer operations.

## [B]   End-user Computer Workgroups

"End-user" computer workgroups as part of information systems can be somewhat autonomous. However, the more the group relies on information systems for assistance, the less autonomy it has. Even with "total" autonomy, it needs to comply with universal standards for hardware and software use.

An end-user workgroup system can be a client/server operation employing an information systems server, or an autonomous workgroup with its own end-user server system. It can be a closed system or provided with a gateway for external network access. The hardware configuration of the end-user workgroup is not restricted as long as the equipment is justified by end-user management.

The company is responsible for complying with certain industry practices. Responsibility for assuring these practices are followed by the end-user workgroup is delegated by end-user management.

## [C]   End-user PC Policies

Information systems controls site-licensed software. The user pays the cost of software with charges based on quantity.

Departments may purchase their own software. However, if not on the list of software the information systems department supports, they cannot expect user support for that particular choice.

## [D]   Personal Hardware and Software

No personal hardware or software is allowed. All hardware and software, including in-house-developed programs, is the sole property of the firm. This policy is enforced to reduce problems with equipment, software failure, damage to data files, and the introduction of viruses. To restrict access to the firm's data and/or programs and prevent virus transmission, disks or tapes belonging to the firm are not to be used in personal home computers.

### [E]   Backup Hardware and Software

End-user IT is responsible for maintaining backup hardware and software. Arrangements with the corporate computer service group are made by end-user management for the availability of hardware backup as needed, on a loan basis, to end users.

### [F]   End-user Training

The information systems department is responsible for coordinating and providing PC training for end users. This consists of both formal classes and individual, self-paced instruction.

# § 19.02   END-USER WORKGROUP OPERATIONS

### [A]   Overview

End-user workgroup computer systems can vary in configuration and process from one area to another within the same corporation. However, the end-user workgroup operations procedures applicable to "common procedures" are to be followed by all groups in the corporation. When operation needs expand beyond the common procedures, procedure documentation conforms to the requirements set by information systems.

### [B]   General Operations

This subsection covers general operations followed by the end-user workgroup when operating the computer system. Each group has a person appointed as the unit's computer coordinator (full- or part-time duty).

1. **Computer coordinator's responsibilities**
   - Anticipate possible hardware needs
   - Anticipate new software needs
   - Provide information and service for users
   - Provide for informal and formal training
   - Oversee operation policies
   - Be a source for operation documentation
   - Disseminate new operating information
   - Be liaison between end-user workgroup computer operation and corporate information systems
   - Be knowledge source for user applications
   - Perform hardware maintenance
   - Perform software updates

- Perform backup of files and database
- Maintain supply inventory
- Be facilitator for disaster recovery
- Be on call for after-hours problems
- Maintain computer security procedures
- Police system for unauthorized software
- Maintain operation performance problem log
- Write monthly exception report to end-user unit manager

2. **End-user workstation operations.** Each workstation is provided with a current operations manual. Other manuals supplied by vendors or written in-house may supplement this manual.

There are standard workstation operating procedures applicable to all workstations:
- Turning on workstation
- Daily housekeeping operations
- Weekly housekeeping
- Turning off workstation

3. **End-user operation rules and procedures.** When providing rules and procedures to be followed by all end users, the computer coordinator explains the rationale behind them.
- No food or beverages close to workstation area
- No smoking near software or hardware
- No telephones near computer disks
- No illegal copying of software
- No personal software allowed
- No personal use of a company computer
- No personal disks allowed
- No hardware may be removed from department

End-user operators should inform the coordinator of any need for ergonomic devices. The devices available include:
- Keyboard wrist rest
- Mouse wrist rest
- Foot rest
- Ergonomic keyboard
- Arm support
- Ergonomic adjustable chair
- Adjustable workstations for employees with special needs
- Radiation and/or glare monitor screen cover
- Special telephone needs

## COMMENT

Remember the requirements of the Americans with Disabilities Act!

# § 19.03   CLIENT/SERVER PROCEDURES

## [A]   Overview

In an end-user workgroup client/server operation, information systems computer operations typically provide the server. The following procedures for this end-user workgroup computer system operation help ensure the safety of the IT computer operation. There could be more than one end-user workgroup computer system within the corporation.

## [B]   IT Client/Server Support

The IT computer operations help desk provides support for general computer client/server operations. It is available for end-user workgroup users with operation problems. If help-desk employees cannot handle a problem, they contact someone who can help.

A person from its end-user work area addresses the end-user workgroup's particular technical operation concerns. This person is appointed by the workgroup management and will be identified as the computer coordinator. This person is also responsible for communicating the workgroup needs to IT computer operations and/or the systems unit.

The coordinator's responsibilities are to:

- Assist IT trainer with end-user workgroup training needs
- Provide informal training to computer workstation users
- Be knowledge source for user applications
- Be information systems' end-user workgroup contact
- Maintain reference library of publications for end-user workgroup

## [C]   End-user Workgroup Education

The end-user workgroup receives information about and training for using its hardware and software. This is the responsibility of the IT project management group installing the new system.

After it is operational, provisions must be made for instructions for subsequent system changes. The coordinator assists with this task.

Provisions are made for new employees using the end-user workgroup system. There are self-paced learning instruments, such as:

- CD-ROM tutorials
- Program learning manuals
- Audio instruction tapes
- VCR tapes
- Operation manuals

The coordinator assists with the training of new end-user workgroup computer workstation users and is responsible for instructing the new end user regarding the workgroup's use of the computer system. The coordinator also informs end users of pending operational changes and assists them once changes are in place.

## [D]   Workstation Operations

There are standard operating procedures for users of terminals or workstations:

1. **Turning on the system.** To turn on the system, the user follows the operating manual procedures checking to see that the monitor display and all peripherals are operating properly. If not, the user consults the manual and proceeds when the system is ready. If the workstation is not working, contact the help desk. Put its telephone number on the first page of the manual.

   Before contacting anyone for assistance, the user will:
   • Write down details of what happened
   • Make list of what corrective measures were tried
   • When assistance is available, bring computer system up to place where problem occurred.

2. **Turning off the system.** Turn off the system in the following sequence:
   a.   Remove all removable media
   b.   Exit from operating system
   c.   Turn off peripheral equipment
   d.   Turn off workstation

3. **Daily operations.** Check hardware daily for:
   a.   Quality of monitor display; adjust as needed.
   b.   Cleanliness of equipment; clean equipment as needed at start or end of each workday, and at other times when there is high-volume use. If the workstation has a printer, do the following:
   c.   Check paper supply in printer; add paper as needed.
   d.   Check quality of printing; replace ribbons or printer cartridges as needed.

4. **Weekly housekeeping.** The end-user administrator/user vacuums or dusts off the keyboard and wipes clean the monitor glass once a week. Clean high-use diskette heads weekly. If the heads are not often used, a once-per-month cleaning will suffice.

5. **Dust covers.** In areas with a higher than normal amount of airborne dust, use dust covers for PCs, keyboards, monitors, and other attached devices when not in use. For very dusty areas, use special keyboard covers that can be employed while using the keyboard. These require periodic replacement; therefore, the coordinator should maintain a supply.

6. **Removable media backup.** When data is kept on removable media, make a copy of the backup. Do not store both copies, original and backup, together. The backup copy must be write-protected.

## [E]   Operation Rules

The following rules apply to all persons using the end-user workgroup computer system:

• No food or beverage on or near hardware or software
• No smoking near hardware or software
• Computer and disks are at least 2 ft from telephones. Keep other magnetic devices away from computer, disks, and tapes

- No illegal copying of software
- No hardware or software may be removed from firm's premises without written permission.
- No personal hardware, software, or disk is permitted.
- No down- or uploading of any noncompany software or data will be permitted.

### [F]    Workstation Accessories

Accessories are classified into two groups: ergonomic devices and productivity aids. The devices are to be purchased by the end-user workgroup department. The coordinator is responsible for arranging this effort. (The following items are not identified by brand name.)

1. **Ergonomic devices.** Workstation ergonomic devices help the human body interact with the computer system and function with the least amount of fatigue, error, and bodily harm. The following types are available:
   - Keyboard wrist rest
   - Mouse wrist rest
   - Foot rest
   - Ergonomic keyboard
   - Arm support
   - Ergonomic adjustable chair
   - Adjustable workstations for special employees
   - Radiation and/or glare monitor screen cover

2. **Productivity aids.** The following, if used properly, have been known to increase end-user productivity:
   - Tilt 'n turn monitor stand
   - Copy holders
   - Copy holder light
   - Diskette storage devices
   - Desktop print stand and/or organizer
   - PC roll-out keyboard system
   - Keyboard cover
   - Mouse holder
   - Keyboard labels for F keys and/or other keys
   - Wastepaper container and paper shredder
   - Workstations that include a drawer for personal items which can be locked
   - Speaker telephone

## § 19.04    END-USER PC COORDINATOR

### [A]    Overview

The end-user PC coordinator's duties and responsibilities vary from one location to another, depending on needs. The actual title of coordinator may also vary, but whatever the title, this person ensures that PC policies are enforced.

## [B]   Responsibilities of the PC Coordinator

Following are the responsibilities of the person assigned to the coordinator position:

- Process requests for new hardware and software
- Keep abreast of end-user hardware and software needs
- Provide an ongoing hardware and software troubleshooting service for end users to handle day-to-day operating problems
- Provide informal and formal training assistance for PC users
- Enforce policies regarding PC hardware and software operations
- Disseminate new hardware/software information
- Provide backup service for PC hardware and software
- Provide PC LAN service and/or supervision
- Maintain a Web site for end users' concerns

## [C]   In-house Consulting Service

The coordinator acts as an in-house consultant for end users of approved PC equipment and software. The PCs can be desktop, laptop, or hand-held machines. Assessing present and future needs of these machines is one of the services provided. The consulting service also covers the areas of PC communications and networking. The coordinator is responsible for maintaining a compatible standard for PC and LAN or WAN communications. He/she also works with personnel responsible for communications to ensure continuity and compatibility of the PC systems. The PC coordinator's consulting role includes advising end users on the true capabilities of equipment and helping them match business needs to the proper, cost-effective equipment.

PC access to mainframe databases requires approval by the coordinator before any contact with the database administrator and/or data manager. Be careful to reduce the amount of replicated data not properly labeled as to age or origin. Database access often requires the owner's permission.

The coordinator maintains a daily log that is the data source for monthly reports of his/her activities. The daily log records time spent on the following items (travel time also will be included):

- PC hardware troubleshooting
- PC software troubleshooting
- Informal and formal training assistance
- User consulting service

The coordinator's indirect (administrative cost) time is kept in the following categories:

- Reading and other education methods used to keep up with current technology
- Communication network services
- Web site use and maintenance
- User education and training preparation when not charged to a given department
- General administration duties, etc.

## [D]   PC Training

The coordinator is the training provider for end-user PC and computer work-station users and may enlist the services of the IT training unit or the firm's training department in carrying out this responsibility. Training is provided on a group or individual basis. Charges for this service will follow established cost-accounting practices. There is no service charge for the loan of text material, the use of self-paced instruction programs, or the loan of instructional hardware.

---

### COMMENT

Outside training providers are sometimes an efficient way to provide PC training. Use them and release them as required.

---

The coordinator maintains an up-to-date library of reading material and self-instruction programs available. Include the latest versions of operating hardware and software manuals.

Instructional programs are developed in-house, contracted for with outside developers, and purchased off the shelf. Unless developed or purchased for given departments, the cost is applied to the indirect administrative training budget.

The coordinator requires a work area to house his/her office and training development effort. The whole area will be:

- Secured when not in use
- Air conditioned and air purified
- Equipped with furniture and storage facilities
- Equipped with a classroom that can double as a meeting room

A required minimum of capital equipment is needed for a PC training operation. Most items are stationary, but some are portable and loaned to users. Have on hand more than one of each item to be loaned. The following PC training equipment is considered the minimum needed:

- Whiteboard (Many whiteboards can double as projection screens.)
- Table-top lectern
- Portable overhead projector or LCD projector
- Flip chart (floor model)
- VCR and color monitor
- Supply items: nonpermanent color markers, overhead transparencies (both write-on and laser printable), spare projection bulbs, flip chart paper, and erasers

# § 19.05   PC ACQUISITION

## [A]   Overview

The coordinator is responsible for the inventory control of all PC hardware (desktop, laptop, and hand-held) and software acquisitions, and should be attuned to PC users' expected needs. He/she also assists users with any future hardware and software requirements.

Purchase requisitions for PC hardware, software, and service or consulting contracts are forwarded to the coordinator who approves the purchase requisitions and forwards them to the end-user manager, who in turn approves them and forwards them to the purchasing department. Use purchase requisitions only for approved budgeted expenditures.

## [B]   Hardware Acquisition

The procedures for hardware acquisition are as follows:

1. **Approved hardware purchases.** Departments with budget approval for hardware expenditures complete a purchase requisition and forward it to the coordinator, who checks the capital expense budget listing and confirms the purchase can be approved.

    If the purchase is not on the approved list, the requisition is returned with a memo explaining why. If it is on the approved list, the coordinator dates and signs the purchase requisition and forwards it to the end-user manager for his/her approval. It is then forwarded to the purchasing department.

2. **Hardware loans.** End users requesting a loan of hardware from the coordinator provide the following information:
    - What is to be loaned? Include a checklist of accessories, such as cables and power supplies that must be returned with the unit. Otherwise there will be a delay in loaning it again.
    - Expected length of time for loan. A firm return date is critical.
    - Reason for loan.
    - Department and person requesting loan.
    - Where equipment will be used.
    - Person who will be using equipment.

    When the equipment is released, an "out card" with the date, time, equipment loaned, serial number, and to whom it is loaned is completed and signed by the person receiving the equipment. The card is filed, by date, until the item is returned when it will again be signed and dated by the person returning the item.

    The "out card" file is reviewed once per month. Contact delinquent borrowers about returning the equipment. Cards for returned items are held on file for one year.

    If the item is damaged, it is noted on the card, and the card becomes the source for a damage memo report to be completed by the coordinator. This memo is sent to the end-user department head of the borrower. Arrangements are made to repair or replace the piece of equipment at a cost to be decided by the coordinator. That amount is reported to the end-user head. Ensure they have removed their data, and reload the system's standard configuration promptly on its return before shelving it.

3. **New hardware acquisition.** The coordinator serves as an information source for future hardware acquisitions and maintains a published list of "approved" hardware, i.e., sanctioned for purchase. If the desired hardware is listed, the user need only provide budgeted funds to acquire the equipment.

   The purchase of hardware not sanctioned requires a request either for a one-time purchase or for the item to be placed on the approved list. For either action, write a memo to the coordinator explaining the special request and containing the following information:
   
   • Item's name, vendor's name and address
   • Cost of item
   • Quantity required
   • Reason special item is required
   • What happens if item is not approved
   • Personnel responsible for item's maintenance
   • Personnel responsible for training and operation support

   If required, a meeting is held with the party interested in the new hardware and the coordinator. If an alternate piece of approved hardware is not acceptable to the user, and the request is not resolved, the coordinator contacts the head of information systems for resolution of the problem.

   The information systems manager will inform the requesting party by memo of his/her decision. If the equipment acquisition is still not approved, the user may appeal in writing to the PC advisory panel whose decision is final.

## [C]   Software Acquisition

Software may be developed in-house or acquired from an outside source. In-house software development is pursued only if no commercially available software is available for less than the in-house cost. Also, consider the availability of in-house programming end-user personnel. The coordinator makes arrangements for any in-house-developed software. The actual programming effort is done in-house by end-user personnel or the corporate IT programming unit, or contracted out by the coordinator. The cost requires the end-user manager's approval because it is charged to that department's budget.

Software can be purchased for multiple users or a single user. Most software is purchased from vendors, with some only available for an annual fee. In addition, upgrades are generally available for a single user or multiple users. Purchased off-the-shelf software is available in two forms: one is for the horizontal market, for widespread use by many different kinds of firms (word processing or spreadsheet software); the other is for the vertical market, for applications pertaining to given industries. Vertical market software may be more flexible because sometimes the source code is available. This makes it possible to alter the program to meet the user's own needs.

The coordinator maintains a published list of approved PC software to be continually updated with newly approved equipment. It is the duty of the coordinator to continually seek and respond to needs for newer and better software. Only approved software may be used. In the event that the coordinator will not approve requested software, the requesting party may appeal in writing to the corporate PC advisory panel whose decision is final.

Software acquisition procedures are as follows:

1. **Specially developed software.** When a user requires software not available by purchase, the coordinator works with the user to define the needs and assigns the project to an end-user programmer. If one is unavailable, the coordinator submits a memo to the person responsible for corporate PC programming systems and provides enough information so a project proposal can be developed.

    Review project proposal information with the user requesting the program. If time and money are available, a formal request in writing is issued by the end-user management.

    Program development is handled using the same standard procedures as for information systems program development. As long as no security problem exists, the new software is made available to other PC users.

2. **Purchased software.** The user sends a memo to the coordinator requesting the approved software. The coordinator reviews the request and, if in order, sends the software to the party requesting it. If need be, an internal charge is made to the requesting department's account.

    If the software is not in stock, the coordinator issues a purchase requisition on behalf of the requesting department and sends it to the end-user head for approval.

    Since this software is from the approved list, hold a training class. Send a copy of the class schedule along with the software. If no local classes are available, see if local community colleges offer continuing education classes and pass on the schedule and registration forms.

    It is critical that the PC coordinator maintain software licenses in a fireproof file cabinet, preferably off-site. In the event of a disaster, you may be able to use copies of software without repurchasing the software (often the manufacturer will even send a "gold" disk if you have adequate documentation). This is a primary company defense in case of a software audit. From a cost prospective, it is evidence for buying upgrades instead of purchasing new software.

3. **Software registration.** All software registration is completed and mailed by the coordinator in the company's name.

4. **Software library.** Copies of all in-house-developed PC programs and the original licensed software, as well as backup copies of other purchased software, are maintained in the end-user software library under the control of the coordinator. Encourage users with one-of-a-

kind software to have backup copies housed here as well. All library software is the most current version in use.

5. **Software demo disks.** Software demo disks are provided to users requesting them and will not be charged to the user's account. They can be provided by vendors or developed in-house.

## COMMENT

The software library provides an opportunity for potential users to try software before obtaining their own. The library contains proper documentation and user instructions to test software. The coordinator may be called on to demonstrate software or demo programs to potential users.

### [D] Communications Acquisition

PC communication systems require some planning on the part of the potential user and the coordinator. The coordinator acts as a resource person for PC communications acquisitions; this requires the maintenance of an information file of LAN (and to a lesser degree, of WAN) hardware and software to be used when considering future acquisitions or upgrading. There are a variety of LAN systems today, including wired or wireless. There is even one that employs power supply lines as the transmitting media. Remote network users (working from mobile or home offices) use modems to link with LAN systems or the Internet.

For modem acquisitions a user-request memo signed by the user's manager and defining the modem needs is sent to the coordinator. The user is supplied with an "approved" modem with the required (or a higher) transmission rate. The appropriate hardware and software are supplied and installed by the coordinator.

PC network communication acquisitions may require approval of the person responsible for corporate communications. This is true with WAN system interfacing or when linking two or more LAN systems. The gateway and modem selection also requires the approval of the organizational communication person. If not, the coordinator is fully responsible for installing the micro-LAN communication hookup. Users are provided with the required instructions and operations manuals for the online communication systems by the coordinator.

LAN-based e-mail has mostly replaced information systems host-based systems. Some major reasons for this move are: lower prices, availability of Windows support of LAN-based e-mail, and emerging mail-enabled applications.

Acquisitions of LAN-based e-mail systems, as well as their maintenance, upgrading, and support, are the ongoing responsibility of the coordinator.

### [E]   Database Access Acquisition

PC users requiring access to a mainframe database consult the coordinator who then contacts the IT PC manager regarding their needs. The manager reviews these and contacts the database administrator for user access. If the organization has a data administrator, this person is also informed of the user's needs. Both administrators' approvals are required for the user to access the information systems database. If the database is another user's (in the same end-user workgroup), or part of a network of PCs, the coordinator contacts the data administrator for written approval. If there is none, the coordinator resolves the problem and sends a requesting memo to the database administrator for access.

The coordinator makes arrangements for new PC users to access the database and provides training and an operations manual.

## § 19.06   PC OPERATIONS

### [A]   Overview

PC (desktop, laptop, and hand-held) operations use recommended manufacturers' standards as outlined in the manufacturers' manuals supplemented by those provided by the information systems PC manager. The supplemented manuals are both purchased and written in-house if unavailable from outside sources.

## COMMENT

> Because manufacturers' manuals are often written to meet deadlines and need correction after use, publishers have responded with some that are easier to understand.

Today's technology encourages the use of the PC as a user information and learning instrument with the aid of self-paced tutorials or even the HELP key. The person responsible for the organization's PCs should not overlook this technology.

Various operations within the company may have differing degrees of autonomy, but the PC policies, enforced by the coordinator, apply to all PC users.

### [B]   PC Security

Desktop or any stationary PCs are located in a safe environment. The person assigned a mobile PC assumes full responsibility for the safekeeping of both the hardware and the software. Preventing unauthorized access of any PC system is of utmost concern to all employees. The following items address the PC security issue:

1. **Physical location.** The room where the computers are kept is locked when not in use. If not possible, seriously consider employing a cable lock to deter any removal of the desktop computer hardware. Any mobile computers are kept in a safe place at all times, including the time the hardware is in transit. All portable computers must be handled as "carry-on luggage" while in public transit. When PCs are being transported for a special event and cannot be carried individually, permission must be requested in writing from the coordinator. Approval is granted in writing, along with the special one-time procedures to be followed for the event.

   If a desktop PC is moved to a new permanent location within an area under the jurisdiction of the coordinator, he/she will be informed in writing within 24 hours of the move. In the event that the new location is not under the jurisdiction of the current coordinator, he/she must approve the move before it takes place and then inform both the asset manager and the new area's coordinator of the move.

2. **Access security.** Stationary PCs with a modem or network and/or hard drives with any restricted information are required to have one of the following:
   - A lock
   - An access security board with a lock-slot, so the board can use a cable security system
   - Personal access code software in the event the PC does not have an available slot for an access security board
   - An access security board with a motion alarm (In the event a building alarm is available, and the situation warrants, an external connection to the building alarm system should be made. The alarm may be set to notify IT operations, and the firm's own security force, or an outside security service.)

3. **Software and data security.** Software media are stored in a locked place. Data disks and backup tapes and disks are stored in a PC media safe or other such comparable device if so warranted by the data administrator or coordinator.

## [C]   Daily Operating Procedures

There are standard operating procedures that apply to all PC operations:

1. **Turning on the system.** To turn on the system, the operator follows the manufacturer's procedures.

## COMMENT

Approved power backup hardware is recommended in the event of a power failure. If no such device is connected to the system, take care not to use the machines when a power failure is likely.

The operator checks to see that the monitor display and all peripherals are operating properly and, if not, consults the operating manual. He/she then proceeds when the system is ready.

Mobile computers having access to AC power supply are checked for battery status. If they require recharging (or to prolong battery life), use the available AC power supply. If the user is outside of the United States, be sure the power supply is compatible with your hardware requirements.

2.  **Turning off the system.** When turning off the system:
    -   Remove any removable media disks
    -   Exit from operating system
    -   Turn off peripheral equipment
    -   Turn off computer
    -   Turn off surge protect switch
    -   Check battery-powered PCs for recharging needs, and when necessary, recharge batteries as soon as possible

3.  **Daily operations.** Systems are checked daily (by the administrator/user) for:
    -   Paper supply in printer; add paper as needed.
    -   Quality of printing; replace ribbons or printer cartridges as needed.
    -   Quality of monitor display; adjust as needed.
    -   Cleanliness of computer equipment. Cleaning equipment as needed may be done at the start or end of each workday, and at other times during the day when there is high-volume use.

4.  **Weekly housekeeping.** The administrator/user vacuums or dusts off the keyboard and wipes clean the monitor glass once a week. Clean high-use diskette heads weekly. If the heads are not often used, a once-per-month cleaning will suffice.

5.  **Dust covers.** In areas with a higher than normal amount of airborne dust, dust covers should be used for PCs, keyboards, monitors, and other attached devices when not in use. For very dusty areas, use special keyboard covers that can be employed while using the keyboard. These require periodic replacement; therefore, the coordinator/key operator should maintain a supply.

## [D]   Operation Rules and Procedures

The following rules and procedures apply to the operation of all PCs:

1.  No food or beverage on or near hardware or software.
2.  No smoking near hardware or software.
3.  A clean, cool, and dry air working environment is recommended for computer.
4.  Computer disks and reading heads are at least 2 ft from telephones. Keep other magnetic devices away from computer, disks, and tapes.
5.  Plug all computers and peripherals into a surge protection unit. Don't plug noncomputer electric devices into surge protection outlet or into same wall plug with surge protection device. Use only grounded electrical outlets.

6. No illegal copying of software.
7. No hardware or software may be removed from firm's premises without written permission, for each occasion, from coordinator. Portable computer systems used away from workplace require a permission letter or ID card signed by coordinator to be kept with system at all times. Permission letter/ID card identifies who has permission to use and carry authorized equipment and software. It will also contain serial numbers of units authorized and identifies software contained in system.
8. No personal hardware, software, or disk is allowed.
9. No hardware or software (including portable equipment) will be loaned to noncompany persons.
10. Removable media labels will be marked with permanent marker before being applied to media.
11. Removable media are kept in disk containers or storage unit when not in use.

### [E]  Backup Procedures

Backup procedures may vary depending on the area of use within the company. Not all data and software have the same value (although it is better to be safe if not sure). The following backup procedures are recommended:

1. **New software.** New purchased software is backed up in accordance with the software manufacturer's specifications. If only one copy can be made, the backed-up copy is sent to the coordinator for the software library. After being copied, the new software is tested. Contact the coordinator if a problem is found. All copied software disks and tapes will be write-protected.
2. **Hard drive backup procedures.** The following is recommended for hard drive backup procedures:
   a. At the end of each workday, all new data should be backed up onto disks or tape. Some active transactions (such as word processing, billing, etc.) will need to be backed up more often.
   b. A backup copy of the hard drive software is maintained on disk or tape.
3. **Removable media data.** When data is kept on removable media (floppies, Zip disks, CDs, etc.) and not on a hard drive, copy the disk for backup. Do not store the two copies of the disks together. It is recommended that the backup copy be write-protected if applicable.

### [F]  PC System Crash

In the event of a PC system crash, the operator turns off the power, records what occurred just prior to the crash, as well as the time, and contacts the coordinator or administrator for assistance. Post a sign on the computer stating that the system has crashed and the equipment is not to be used. Portable computers should be taken to the coordinator.

## [G]  Hardware Problems

For hardware problems, the operator refers to the operating manual. If the problem cannot be corrected, the problem and its effect on the hardware are noted, and the coordinator or administrator is contacted. Place a sign on the (desktop) PC indicating it is not working and not to be used. If a peripheral does not work, place a sign on the device noting it is out of order and indicating whether or not the computer is usable.

## [H]  Software Problems

For software problems, the operator contacts the help desk. If the help desk cannot resolve the problem, the operator contacts the coordinator.
    Before contacting anyone for assistance, however, the operator will:

- Write down details of what happened
- Make a list of what corrective measures were tried
- When assistance becomes available, bring software up on computer at place where problem occurred

## [I]  Accessories and Supplies

PC accessories can improve productivity, reduce fatigue, and improve morale. These accessories and supply items are on a "recommended or approved list" provided by the coordinator and carried by the corporate computer store. Other items not stocked will be listed, with their vendors, in the computer store. This information helps when ordering through the purchasing department. The approved list of items is published, updated, and distributed by the coordinator.
    The items are purchased from the user's department petty cash fund or with a budget requisition. Accessories are classified as production aids or ergonomic devices. Supply items are requisitioned from the unit responsible for office or computer supplies. The standard operating procedure for requisitioning office supplies or computer supplies is followed.
    Accessories come in two groups: ergonomic devices and productivity aids. (The following items are not identified by brand name.)

1.  **Ergonomic devices.** PC ergonomic devices help the human body interact with the PC system and function with the least amount of fatigue, error, and bodily harm. The following types are available on the "recommended list":
    - Keyboard wrist rest
    - Mouse wrist rest
    - Foot rest
    - Ergonomic keyboard
    - Arm support
    - Ergonomic adjustable chair
    - Adjustable workstations for employees with special needs
    - Radiation and/or glare monitor screen

2. **Productivity aids.** The following, if used properly, have been known to increase productivity:
   - Tilt 'n turn monitor stand
   - Copy holders (flex arm, attachable, or standard)
   - Copy holder light
   - Diskette storage devices
   - Cartridge storage devices
   - Desktop print stand and/or organizer
   - PC roll-out keyboard system
   - Keyboard cover
   - Mouse holder
   - Keyboard labels for F keys and/or other keys
   - Wastepaper container and paper shredder
   - Workstations that include a drawer which can be locked for personal items
   - Speaker telephone

## § 19.07   END-USER ASSET MANAGEMENT

### [A]   Overview

Developing, installing, and operating an asset management system is complex. The development and installation is handled as an end-user asset management project, and the installation provides a well-documented, operating end-user asset management system.

---

**COMMENT**

The computer asset manager should contact the Business Software Alliance at 1150 18th Street NW, Ste. 700, Washington, DC 20036 or call 1-888-NOPIRACY for current PC and client/server software piracy information. A copy of the Alliance's latest newsletter is available on the Internet at *www.bsa.org*, and antipiracy information is available through its home page. It provides information, software, and membership opportunities.

---

A project leader is appointed who, in addition to having the qualities and skills of a good project leader, is familiar with end-user PC hardware and software, and understands software licenses and copyrights.

## [B]   Developing the Asset Management Plan

The project leader and the corporate computer asset manager develop the asset management plan, with the approval of the end-user manager. The plan should contain the following:

1. **Asset management project team.** An asset management project team is formed, the size to be determined by the end-user head.
2. **Preplanning survey.** The project team develops a hardware and software asset management plan. Before the plan is completed, a survey is conducted as to current:
   - Internal hardware controls
   - Internal software controls
   - Acquisition procedures for hardware and software
   - PC data and software protection
   - Software license compliance
   - Unauthorized PC hardware
       This information defines the current status used as a control. It also provides information on how the asset management system can be installed with a minimum of conflict and effort.
3. **Asset management plan.** The plan uses the information from the preplanning survey to:
   - Define components of proposed asset management system
   - Draft project timetable
   - Plan selection of standard software
   - Plan for communication and implementation
   - Plan for needed controls
   - Select user test area for system
   - Determine project and operation costs

## [C]   Plan Implementation

The implementation of the plan is a major part of the asset management project. Following are its major areas:

- Selecting and obtaining delivery of software
- Installing software
- Testing software
- Training operational personnel
- Setting up help desk
- Preparing for system audit
- Asset tagging hardware and making inventory of software
- Establishing proof of purchase
- Taking corrective actions
- Developing continual audit program
- Putting in place an operating hardware/software acquisition system
- Maintaining PC users' education program
- Installing and maintaining disaster recovery system
- Providing network security and virus-protection system

## [D]   Implementation and Operation

The implementation starts in a prototype area, preferably one offering the best opportunity to debug the system. After a particular area is operational, the system can be implemented in additional areas. Following are steps to be followed to implement and operate the new asset management system:

1. **Inventory of hardware.** Take the inventory in the shortest calendar time possible. After each unit has been inventoried, an update procedure—augmented by random inventory spot-checks—should be established to maintain a current inventory.

   Tag each hardware item with a bar-coded inventory tag placed on the equipment in the same location for each type of hardware.

   Each new acquisition of hardware must be tagged before the system is operational. The cost, department, and employee-assigned ownership of the hardware are input to the PC inventory system.

2. **Physical inventory of software.** Take the inventory of PC software at the same time as the hardware inventory or later. This depends on the system software selected. The software on each PC and file server is identified and logged in. Unauthorized software is purged and recorded in order to identify to what degree, for each area and user, software violations have occurred.

   This software data, by each PC (desktop, laptop, and hand-held system) and person responsible for that computer, is input to the PC inventory system. Cost, department, and employee-assigned ownership information relating to new PC software added later will also be input to the system.

3. **PC inventory system.** Departments and employees within departments use the PC inventory system to maintain an ongoing PC hardware and software inventory. The system will generate a physical inventory report by department after the first and each of the subsequent inventories. The report is also run at the end of each fiscal year and upon demand by the software coordinator. A copy of the department report is sent to the department head and to the software coordinator. It lists the following:
   - Department name
   - Date physical inventory was taken
   - Name, total quantity, and total cost of each software type
   - Total cost of department's software inventory
   - Number of each kind of software removed

   A detailed listing of each employee and his/her assigned PCs is also produced. A copy of this Department Users Report is sent to the coordinator and the department head, and is available for the software coordinator, if requested. It contains the department name and the date of the inventory. This report also lists the following by each employee:
   - Hardware assigned
   - Software on each computer after inventory

- Unauthorized software removed, by computer
- Total cost of hardware
- Total cost of software
- Total cost of both hardware and software

A Department Hardware Inventory Report is run after the Department Users Report for each department. A copy is sent to the department head, to the coordinator, and to the corporate computer asset manager. It lists:

- Department name
- Date report was run
- Hardware type, quantity, and total cost of each type
- Total cost of department's hardware inventory

A Total Hardware/Software Asset Report is run, listing the hardware/software assets by department. There are four columns across each page: department name, number of PCs, total original investment for hardware/software, and average age of department PCs. The bottom line indicates totals of the same information for the whole company. This report is run at the end of the fiscal year and upon demand. It is sent to the manager of information systems, the controller, and the corporate computer asset manager.

# 20

# PERIPHERAL AND NON-PC SYSTEMS: ALL THE LITTLE STUFF

§ 20.06   PERIPHERAL DEVICES AND SUPPLY ACQUISITION PROCEDURES
    [A]   Budgeting Procedures
    [B]   Requisition Procedures
    [C]   Purchasing Procedures
    [D]   Receiving Procedures

# § 20.01   CORPORATE POSITION

## [A]   Overview

The information systems unit provides central computer operations for the firm along with the responsibilities for corporate LAN, WAN, and voice communications. The control and standardization responsibility of end-user stand-alone and workgroup PCs is also the responsibility of information systems. The remaining natural area left that would be an inherent extension of the information systems unit's responsibility would be corporate peripheral service devices. The importance of policy concerning peripheral and non-PC systems mandates the endorsement and support of top management of the organization.

Peripheral service devices are information-processing devices used by the company to conduct day-to-day business office operations. Traditionally, these devices are used in office areas and other company areas requiring information processing for customer service or products. Having these devices standardized and controlled by information systems reduces their total cost of operation and improves the overall service to the company. This may be accomplished at a local operating firm or at multiple sites a company may have.

## [B]   Scope

The devices can be stand-alone, used in workgroups, or systems that cross workgroup boundaries. The scope of this area of information systems corporate responsibility can cover, but is not limited to, the following company-owned, rented, leased, or loaned peripheral service devices:

- Fax machines
- Copy machines
- Micrographic systems
- Wireless networks
- Digital audio-visual equipment
- Multimedia PC systems
- Nonlinear video editing systems
- Digital photo editing systems
- Video duplication machines
- In-house video communications systems
- Library CD information systems
- Other related devices

## [C]   Policy Objectives

Policy objectives are standardization, data logging, controlling, and inventorying these devices. The objective is to also optimize the use of these devices. This responsibility includes the maintenance, the provision for procedural operating instructions, operator training, and equipment placement for optimum use. Supplies are purchased at the best cost for companywide control and standards use. Purchasing works in concert with the information systems to obtain uniform products and supplies at the best price.

# § 20.02   INVENTORY OF PERIPHERAL SUPPORT EQUIPMENT

## [A]   Responsibility

The information systems unit manager assigns the peripheral support systems inventory responsibility to the IT manager. If there is no inventory or equipment system in place, the IT asset manager establishes one.

## [B]   Tagging Peripheral Support Equipment

Devise a coding method before tagging equipment. Tag peripheral hardware upon receipt by a sequential numbering system. Use a two-number prefix followed by a space and a sequential number on the tag.

The prefix number identifies the type of peripheral support equipment. After the inventory system is in place, an agent of the asset manager does the tagging upon receipt. The equipment and packing slip is compared with a copy of the purchase order confirming that what was received was ordered. Supply items received will be checked with the packing slip and a copy of the purchase order. If the purchase is by a blanket purchase order, the quantity received each time is added to the total received to date and the quantity compared with the original blanket-ordered quantity. Either use a bar-coded tag, along with visually identified numbers posted on the tag, or a scanner to ensure the correct identification number is read. New hardware items received have tags made and attached to the item. After the tag is secured to the equipment, it is used as its identification number (during inventory checks, when it is moved to a new location, repaired, or disposed).

## [C]   Peripheral Support Equipment Inventory

A computer inventory system will be maintained for each type of peripheral support equipment. The following file record information will be maintained for each unit of hardware:

- Tag number, prefix, and sequential number
- Date of purchase
- Original cost
- Manufacturer's code number
- Vendor purchased or leased from
- Purchase, lease, or free-trial code identification
- Last date of preventive maintenance service
- Last date of maintenance service

- Last date of warranty service
- Maintenance code

A telephone number is provided for the organization doing the maintenance. This number can be the IT service unit's telephone number doing the preventive or repair maintenance. Each vendor can perform warranty service, preventive maintenance, or repair service.

Annual reports are run by type of equipment, department assigned, department total, and grand total by type of equipment. The usage will also be reported when such records can be provided. When equipment is acquired, moved, or disposed of, the information is used to update the information database files.

# § 20.03  MAINTENANCE OF PERIPHERAL SUPPORT EQUIPMENT

## [A]  Responsibility

The information systems unit manager assigns the peripheral equipment maintenance support to the IT service unit. The IT service unit manager compares maintenance service with vendor and in-house service for quality and cost. The service may be in the form of a mix of vendors and in-house service. The maintenance service is reviewed annually because of the changing technology, availability of in-house and vendor service personnel, and the company's needs.

## [B]  In-house Maintenance Control

The IT service unit performing in-house maintenance (service desk) performs whatever peripheral equipment repairs and preventive maintenance possible. Cost and in-house availability are determining factors as to who performs what service. A service telephone number is available for people needing service.

The service desk assists the person with a problem by telephone. If the problem cannot be resolved by telephone, the service desk asks the caller to place an out-of-order sign on the machine. The help desk informs the caller they will be called back. The service desk then contacts an in-house service person or the vendor with the service contract.

The vendor is contacted for a warranty or repair service call. The service desk has that information. The person contacting the service desk is informed when the service person is expected to arrive, and asked to write the information on the out-of-order sign posted on the inoperative machine. In smaller operations, the help desk and the service desk are combined into the same job. These smaller operations may also have the IT PC services unit people perform some of the peripheral support equipment maintenance. This is the value of having well-trained power users. It broadens the scope of their job, and provides for a level of care not requiring a skilled technician's attention.

The extra training is well worth the investment. With this, smaller operations may not require a full-time help desk.

## [C]   Service Budgeting

Budgeting for in-house maintenance control and the service desk comes from the IT service unit's lump-sum budget. Although the item purchased may come from a department's budget, the IT service support cost may or may not be charged to the department. This charge depends on the company's accounting policy. All service maintenance done by the IT service unit is reported on a daily service log. The completed work log sheets are turned in daily to the IT service unit's manager. The log report contains the following information:

- Service person's name
- Machine number serviced
- Time spent on the service call
- Type of call: service, preventive maintenance, or operator problem
- Any replacement parts used

Departments purchasing their own equipment with their own budget require funds to obtain their own maintenance service. The departments request funds for this maintenance service in their budgets. Some leased items may come with a provided service agreement. All service performed, whether performed by the in-house IT service unit or an outside vendor, is reported by the IT service unit. The IT service people provide their daily report to the IT service unit manager. The service desk records vendor service. The vendor code number and machine number are reported. The vendor's service document is turned over to the help desk. Each day the service report is given to the unit manager along with the vendor's service document—a copy is made for the IT unit manager and the original copy sent to the department manager. A request for vendor service may come in one of the following forms:

- Time and parts
- Blanket maintenance contract
- Warranty service call

## [D]   Maintenance Service Report

Each contracted machine type reports vendor maintenance. Vendor maintenance service reported is shown as warranty, preventive, or service maintenance. List time and replacement parts service charges.

The monthly maintenance service reports lists the machines and locations serviced. The report provides the following information:

- What type of equipment was serviced
- Who performed service
- Estimated cost for service
- Kind of in-house service performed

- Kind of vendor service performed
- Kind of service performed (preventive maintenance, repair)

What kind of service was performed on the machine the last time it received a service call? When was the last service call date and what was the current service call date?

There is a total monthly expense by machine type and a monthly grand total. There is a year-to-date cost by machine type, and a year-to-date grand total.

A second report (IT and Vendor Maintenance Cost Report) is printed with information by vendor and the IT service unit. The report lists the name of the company that serviced each machine. The report lists the subtotal cost for the month. The service provider lists year-to-date costs and a grand total year-to-date sum.

## [E]  Vendor Maintenance Contracting

The IT unit's manager, the asset manager, and a purchasing department's representative work together to solicit vendor contract bids. Use the same purchasing department's representative from year to year. It is helpful if the same purchasing agent is also responsible for peripheral supplies and computer supplies.

After IT has identified which items they cannot do or will not be able to service because of lacking the required people, a list is composed of the equipment requiring vendor's maintenance bids. A form letter is used listing all items up for bid. Vendors can bid on any one item, any number, or the entire lot of items listed.

The list of vendors solicited can come from the IT service unit's manager, the IT asset manager, and the purchasing department's representative. It is the purchasing department representative's responsibility to check each vendor before it is sent the letter. The purchasing agent can use information his/her department already has. Contacts with other firms' purchasing departments are a source of information along with the firm's Dun and Bradstreet rating. When composing the request for bids letter, provide as much information as can be given. A vendor company contact person is provided in the letter. Any site visits are arranged through the company's contact person. The letter furnishes the name and telephone number of the contact person, and the last day bids will be received. The following information is furnished in the vendor letter or attachment to the letter:

- A list of unit types the bid calls for servicing
- Number of units for each unit type
- Age and condition of each
- Units under current warranties, and when they expire

If a particular vendor's bid is selected, would they be willing to provide a help-desk telephone number? This allows company employees to contact them for information or a service call. Will there be a charge for this service if available?

Vendor selection is based on several variables. Each variable is weighted before sending the request for bid letters. Vendor analysis is based on a matrix. See § 15.01[B], "Vendor Selection" for information about setting up a weighted matrix. Short-term contracts may be considered for yet unproven vendors. Before signing any contract, contact the firm's legal representative, who has the last word before the firm's authorized representative signs it.

## [F] Outsourcing Legal Ramifications

Outsourcing different applications from companies has provided mixed results, some good, and some bad. Be careful when using independent contractors that the IRS will not consider them an employee. The IRS has defined rules to classify a person as an employee. IRC 530 of the Revenue Act of 1978 provides relief from some consequences of misclassification of employees as independent contractors. There are 20 guidelines presented in Rev. Rule 87-41, along with other IRS data. Some of the key guidelines of Rev. Rule 87-41 are:

1.  **Working on the employer's premises,** especially when the work could be done elsewhere. This is indicative of an employer/employee relationship.
2.  **Method of payment.** Payment by the hour, week, or month generally is indicative of an employer/employee relationship. Payment by the job generally indicates that the person is an independent contractor. A lump sum may be computed by the number of hours required to do a job at a certain rate per hour.
3.  **Furnishing tools and/or materials.** An independent contractor ordinarily furnishes his/her own tools and materials.
4.  **Working for more than one firm.** The service provider's ability to work for more than one service recipient at the same time is indicative of an independent contractor.
5.  **Service available to the general public.** That a service provider makes his/her services available to the general public is indicative of an independent contractor. A business telephone listing is supportive of this guideline.
6.  **Business investment.** The investment by a service provider in facilities is a factor tending to indicate an independent contractor. The investment must be significant and essential. The investment must be essential to the contractor. The investment by the service provider in facilities adequate to perform the services contracted for indicates the status of an independent contractor.

There may be other legal ramifications with labor unions and the contract. Here, a good labor relations attorney is a wise investment. If programming outsourcing results are used in classified software development for the government, it could be a major problem. Outsourcing to parts of the world using prison labor can also be problem. Outsourcing to discharge employees over the age of 40 years also could spell trouble with the EEOC.

# § 20.04   PERIPHERAL OPERATION PROCEDURES

## [A]   Overview

Peripherals cover a wide range of applications and complexities. Most companies do not always know the total investment. Meanwhile, most peripherals operate without a central sense of direction. Without the orchestration and guidance of information systems, costs will grow while efficiency diminishes. A major part of controlling this operation is the peripheral operation procedures set forth by an IT unit of information systems.

## [B]   Posted Device Operations

Less complex operating peripheral devices require only a simple set of posted operation instructions. If possible, the operating instructions are placed on or near the device. Lettering size should be bold enough to be seen and read in a minute or less.

   The operator instructions should refer to a separate document of troubleshooting instructions. At the end of the troubleshooting instructions a contact person—not the operator—should be identified if there is a problem with the machine. This could be the area administrator or a person known to be a heavy user of the equipment. If none of these are listed or are unavailable, post the service desk phone number.

## [C]   Support Operator Responsibility

This is a person responsible for turning on the machine in the morning and turning it off before closing for the day. His/her name is posted as the support operator to be contacted if the machine needs attention or operator assistance. When turning on the machine in the morning, check its running condition and that it is supplied with its needed supplies. The support operator is able to operate and perform minor machine adjustments. He/she will know how to replenish its expendable stock items, and perform standard housekeeping and preventive maintenance procedures. The support operator can be walked through some of the malfunctions by the service desk or a maintenance person by telephone. At the service desk is a support operator's location book with the support operator's name, telephone number, and location listed. A second listing is by location with the support operator's name and telephone number listed. This is used to contact another support operator who is close by the unit for assistance when a unit's support operator is unavailable.

## [D]   Machine Operator Procedures

These are the operating procedures furnished to support operators and stand-alone peripheral machine operators. The IT service unit or the systems and procedures unit furnishes the operator procedure manuals. The manuals provide operator instructions, minor maintenance instruction, and procedures for troubleshooting. Minor preventive maintenance procedures are provided. The procedure manuals contain any manufacturers' furnished material helpful to clarify the machine's operation. Illustrations used by the manufacturer could be beneficial to the operator. Close-up and wide-view photographs are helpful if included in the operator procedure manuals. A prototype manual is developed and tested before being placed into service. Use an unskilled person for the test. Do this with more than one subject. Avoid the brightest person in the area and any experienced operator for debugging the procedure manual.

## [E]   Supply Requisitions

Use the firm's standard supply requisitions form. If the form is outdated or there is none, the IT systems and procedures unit will design one.

Place a central supply location to limit the travel time involved. This prevents unnecessary travel by the person seeking supplies. The supply center could also function as supply distribution location for the end-user computer operations supplies. Supplies small enough can be delivered by interoffice mail. Other items too large for interoffice mail will require a daily run to be delivered.

Employ a requisition system to obtain supplies. The administrator or unit manager approves requisitions after all the items are listed with their respective quantities. A line will by drawn across the lines not used by the person before signing the requisition. Depending on company accounting practice, supplies will be charged to the unit receiving them or from a lump-sum company budget. Spot-check usage employing a lump-sum budget. The loss on supply items can be costly. The supply area is locked when unattended. Supplies stored in operating units are locked at the end of the day or locked at all times if the area is out of view.

## [F]   Service Desk Assistance

Help desks, along with service desks, cannot solve all user problems. It requires other assistance to cover the user's special needs. Some operations, such as turnkey systems, are better off with vendor-supplied service. Vendor help desks and service desks for special systems can sometimes provide better service than in-house service. If the company is willing to provide for an in-house service desk and support it, there are still vendor services that can provide better assistance. They do it better, and the equipment will be up and running faster.

The asset manager publishes an approved peripheral acquisition list for new peripheral purchases. This covers what is in-house, currently operating, and found on the peripheral inventory property list, but not on the approved peripheral acquisition list. Peripheral inventory property list is company property, identified and tagged. The approved peripheral acquisition list is a list of items the IT service unit can repair or for which the service desk has a vendor contact. The service desk also has the peripheral inventory property list and the source of service for each item. Some items were company property before the service desk assistance program was established.

Some items either have long life spans and never need to be replaced or the item is no longer manufactured—it can be replaced only with used equipment. The help desk has a special number to call to have the item serviced.

In these cases, have the power user trained to do most of the repairs and preventive maintenance. Contact the vendor service person only if the problem is beyond the scope of the power user or one is unavailable. Some items may not use the English measuring system and may require special tools to repair the equipment, or the manufacturer may be the only one that makes the tool.

The service desk does not have to be covered at the company site any more than the help desk. This is why so many vendor help desks are not found at company sites. This may be more difficult than having the vendor provide full-service desk coverage. If coverage is needed past normal working hours, service desk personnel can be on call at home for specific time periods. This can also apply to help-desk personnel. These two jobs are combined into one in smaller firms. There is one number to call in case of a problem. There is also the possibility the problem may be related to both the help desk and the service desk. The help-desk and service desk person should have at home the current information that he/she has at work. Install it in a notebook computer.

## § 20.05  OPERATOR AND SERVICE TECHNICIAN TRAINING

### [A]  Overview

The provision for training covers a wide area of needs. The technology skill levels required for each service item will be one or more levels. Vendor-contracted peripheral service will not require so many levels as an in-house service program. The service desk has the levels of skill available for each item in the peripheral inventory property list. Depending on the problem, a skill level is determined to resolve it. The item listed has posted to it the persons who can perform a given level of skill. A person with a higher level of skill can perform a lower level of skill task. However, a lower-level skilled person should not perform a higher-level skill task. The training will certify a level at which the service person can perform a task.

The training provided is for certain skill levels. This training is for vendor- and company-serviced equipment.

### [B]  Operator Training

The operator should learn the basic operation of the device to produce the desired results. The more complex the device, the more the operator will be required to learn. The job of putting paper into a copy machine is considered a task level expected of an operator. Video editing is more complex, but also an operator's job.

Operator training is provided in more than one form:

1. **New device operator training.** When a new peripheral device is introduced, conduct the training in class. The vendor or the administrator conducts the classes. The vendor provides handouts. The com-

pany instructor provides any additional handouts needed. Have a video or slide presentation along with any hands-on training.

Compile a list of the people attending the meeting. Notify anyone missing the class that he/she should attend the next class offered. If the classes are over, have the person who missed the class take the individual training provided to new employees later.

2. **New employee training.** Anyone missing class takes the self-paced individual training. New employees with no experience with the equipment receive the self-paced individual training. They are credited with receiving the instruction for the new equipment. Part of the instruction is provided by the operator as OJT instruction.

## [C]   Support Operator Training

Support operator training is given for all devices in his/her job area that merits the attention of a support operator. Training can be from more than one source. The IT service unit holds classes for support operators or OJT instruction for their devices. Support operators receive operator manuals from the IT service unit.

Vendor training programs are provided at the company site or at the vendor's place of instruction. The vendors provide manuals. The IT unit also provides operators' procedure manuals. The vendor will provide a certificate showing the person is now a certified support operator for the given machine. The support operator should provide OJT to new device operators. They are able to clean the machine, make adjustments to its operation, and perform some light preventive maintenance. They are the key contact persons in the area for operators, service desk, vendor service people, and the IT service personnel.

## [D]   IT Service Unit Training

Each IT service person has a list of equipment he/she services for his/her own records, along with the service desk and the IT unit manager.

Training will come from one of the following sources:

- OJT
- A self-paced learning program provided by vendor
- Attending vendor's classes
- Passing a qualifying exam for equipment
- Taking Internet-based course from vendor or a private Internet-based course

## [E]   Service Desk Training

Effective service desk people are often individuals with some experience as IT service persons. Their training can come from the same areas the IT service person receives his/her training—as the support operator and from operator training. Have new service desk operators work with experienced workers, which is a form of OJT learning. On days when the workload is light, have them try their skills at staffing the service desk.

Service desk personnel are expected to work overtime and be on call at their homes. The unit has one or two laptop computers that service people may take home when on call.

They are expected to have no less knowledge than a support operator does about each device and a general knowledge about vendor-maintained devices. They should have enough knowledge to assist an operator and communicate with a service person working for the company or vendor. They are able to assign service people to be used most effectively and best serve the company's needs. They can reduce maintenance costs with the proper assignments and the ability to walk operators through problems.

# § 20.06  PERIPHERAL DEVICES AND SUPPLY ACQUISITION PROCEDURES

### [A]  Budgeting Procedures

Budgeting can come from a corporate lump-sum budget, department budgets, or both. Each department submits its expected needs for the following year's budget. This is based on last year's budget plus any inflation, replacement of old equipment, and new needs. It is supported by the use of the current equipment and forecasted use for the next budget year. Budgets are needed for the department's use of supplies and replacement of current equipment. Departments with their own hardware for their one-of-a-kind use require a budget. The information systems IT service unit needs a budget for its operation. They need a budget for capital expenses that benefit the whole company plus a replacement parts budget. Also, a vendor service budget is required.

### [B]  Requisition Procedures

Budgeted items have a requisition issued. The requisition goes to the IT asset manager who confirms it meets standards or requires a standards waiver.

The requisition is approved and sent to the budget department to adjust their records, then sent on to the purchasing department.

### [C]  Purchasing Procedures

Purchasing receives the approved purchase requisition. If needed, they take care of the competitive bids for the item. After the purchase order is sent to the vendor, a copy is sent to the receiving department and accounts payable.

### [D]  Receiving Procedures

The agent for the asset manager or a special order item representative inspects the item. After it is approved, a receiving notice is sent to accounts payable.

The asset manager's agent affixes a tag to the machine and records the information. The information is sent to the asset manager.

# 21

# BUSINESS CONTINUITY PLANNING: STAYING IN BUSINESS

## § 21.01  PURPOSE AND SCOPE

Business continuity planning (BCP) is a lot like car insurance. If you don't have it when you need it, then it is too late to get it. Most executives are optimists by nature. There are so many urgent, exciting, or challenging things to work on that it is hard to find time for something as doom-and-gloom as BCP.

> ## COMMENT
>
> It should be a policy in your company that every critical business tool and process has a written business continuity plan and that the plan is tested at least annually. The exercise of writing this plan will reap major business benefits as it forces managers to examine their processes and drive out their weak links.

Over the years, business continuity planning has evolved as our business environment has changed. Thirty years ago, we were primarily concerned with disaster recovery planning (DRP). DRP was focused on major problems such as how to rebuild a flattened facility. It contained its own dirty little secret that it was sometimes easier and cheaper to take the insurance check and close the business rather than rebuild the facility. Examples of this might be a department store roof collapse, a factory fire, or even an accusation of selling less-than-wholesome foods.

Disaster recovery planning was mandated by the government for financial institutions under the assumption that it held assets belonging to others and closing up was not an option. Hospitals also had tested plans since a major crisis could open them to a slew of major lawsuits. The DRPs of other companies were confined to their data processing operations.

A major problem with DRP was testing the adequacy of the plans. A test was expensive and company funds are always under pressure to address today's issues rather than a pessimistic future that may never happen. Testing, if ever done, usually occurred when the crisis was at hand with no time left to repair flaws in the plan. Still, the DRP concept survived.

Eventually disaster recovery planners recognized how important a company's customers and suppliers were to long-term recovery. What good was recovering a facility if in the process, you neglected suppliers and customer relationships have gone? This led to adding business recovery planning (BRP) as a layer around disaster recovery. It detailed how to address customer concerns and explain to them any delays in their orders. It might also include explaining to your customers where to find other suppliers in the interim. Suppliers were asked to help by taking inventories that could not be immediately used and kept informed as the recovery progressed. BRP made these two critical groups participants in the recovery efforts.

Time marches on and companies recognize the huge expense of holding materials inventories and large queues of work-in-process material. Impressed by the results from Japanese automakers, many companies around the world introduced lean production practices. Under the previous model, a factory might hold a 30-day supply (safety stock) of a key material to protect against interruptions to the supply chain. Under this business model, the carrying of extra inventory was assumed necessary to protect the continuous flow of goods down the production lines. Multiply this carrying cost across all materials companywide and the facility is paying a lot of money to buy, store, and handle safety stock.

Under lean production methods, the company realized this was really not a necessary cost and drastically cut its safety stock. In return, companies became dependent on the reliability of their suppliers to consistently deliver quality goods on demand. Many customers now rate their suppliers on the credibility of delivery promises. Late goods may idle their own factory. On the other hand, keeping delivery promises in the face of adversity can be a major competitive weapon!

Taking this on-demand requirement even further, the Internet has made most companies 24/7 (24 hours a day, 7 days a week) sales centers. If your operations are interrupted due to internal issues, your customers will simply cancel their orders and go to someone else. Every company has charts that show the longer their customers must wait for their goods, the more the cancellation rate increases. Few companies can afford this.

So out of lean production and the around-the-clock world arose a need for business continuity planning (BCP). BCP acts as the outer shell of disaster recovery planning. It addresses not only major tragedies such as burned warehouses but also the occasional major crisis such as natural disasters, infrastructure disasters, and even loss of a key machine. It is more than a set of dusty plans; it is a way of planning business processes to drive out problems and keep running.

Can you think of any ways that you apply business continuity in your daily life? Consider your car. You identify a risk that you may be in an accident. In this case, you transfer the risk of loss to someone else (insurance company). This could be similar to disaster recovery if the insurance money was needed to buy another car. If your car was severely damaged and you had difficulties making the journey to work every day on time until the repair shop was finished, you are using business recovery planning by informing your employer, your family, and any other outside parties. If you used a small, inexpensive "commuter car" for driving to work and a larger car for family outings, then your business continuity plan is to drive the larger car to work until your commuter car is repaired. The concepts are not new; they just need to be transferred from your own life to your business.

Business continuity planning is a major topic unto itself. Our goal here is to provide some ideas for assembling a basic plan you can use in your business. If you stop with what we have here, then your plan is off to a good start. If you want the full benefits, then you should write a full plan. If you are unsure how to do this, hire a professional business continuity planning consultant to help you develop it.

**EXHIBIT 21-1.** Planning Scope Relationships

There is an even more important reason for you to develop a business continuity plan—keeping your job. Companies without plans waste time fighting crisis after crisis and never seem to run smoothly. This translates into higher cost of goods through overtime pay, air freight for critical materials, and delayed customer shipments. Perhaps some people enjoy the chaos. These companies are costly to operate and gradually fall by the wayside.

## § 21.02 WHAT SHOULD A PLAN LOOK LIKE?

### [A] Overview

A BCP is not a know-all book of how to recover from any potential problem. Such a tome would be far too large to be useful. Instead, it will consist of a series of smaller plans that address specific risks your company faces. Has your building ever lost electrical power or telephone service? Have you ever run your factory with half your employees because the other half was trapped by a major snowstorm? You made it through these problems, so a lot of the plan is in the collective memory of your managers and work force. ***Write it down!***

A plan should explain the basic steps to take while you wait for your key support staff to arrive. It will explain immediate steps to take (similar to the concept of First Aid) that will address most of the common problems or to stop the spread of the damage.

### [B] Basic Planning Assumptions

The following is a list of assumptions that should be covered in your plan:

1.  **Problems arise in their own good time.** It could be in the middle of the day or in the dead of night on a holiday weekend. If a problem arises while your key staff is on-site, the issues will be handed directly to them. However, if it occurs in the middle of the night, or while they are away on business, would anyone have something to which they could refer? What if these people have resigned?
2.  **A major problem is characterized by chaos.** Imagine the confusion caused by a loss of electricity in your building. Hopefully your support staff would know what to do, but just the loss of lights is enough to bring work to a standstill. Since their workstations are dead, they will shuffle off to break rooms or congregate anywhere there is light. This reaction is normal.
3.  **People are prone to inaction.** When problems arise, most people will just sit down to await the arrival of the "experts" as if there is nothing to do until they restore operations to normal. Is that what you want them to do? Is it really true that they are helpless?

### [C] The Local Expert

Companies tend to have two types of disaster plans—formal and informal. The formal plans rot on a dusty shelf while the real plan is whatever is cobbled together at the time. Most departments have someone that everyone turns to when there are serious problems—and it is rarely their boss. The "local expert" is often a long-time employee who has seen or worked through the most common forms of problems that arise in the department. Whatever happens, this person is always consulted immediately.

The problem with the local expert approach is that everyone is sitting around until the expert appears on the scene. In addition, despite their air of confidence, the local expert's experience tends to be spotty and often their solution is something that others in the staff could have pulled together. Still, this is how things have always been done—until now.

There are many problems with the local expert approach.

- What will you do if they are not available?
- It assumes this person is "all knowing" of your business processes and technologies, including the latest ones.
- It makes your staff (*and you*) dependent on one person.

If you were to watch the local expert in action, you would witness someone with his or her own informal continuity plan. They would have telephone numbers for vendors, help sheets for resolving problems (perhaps given to them by the original developers), and their own notes from over the years for what to do. What the local expert has is a mental index of where to find these fragments of information. A cynic would say that the local expert keeps the information dispersed to protect their status as the department's "wise one."

Rather than bet your company and your own job on this person, begin your plan by moving all of this information out of their drawers, off of the "sticky notes," and into a central department filing system. This still is not a plan, but at least you have something to start with.

# § 21.03 BUSINESS CONTINUITY PLANNING BASICS

## [A] Overview

Basic business continuity planning involves three steps:

1. Identifying what is critical to your organization
2. Identifying what risks (threats) it faces
3. Developing action plans to reduce these risks

## [B] Identify What Is Critical

What are the essential elements of your business? For some companies, delivering a high level of customer service is critical. For an electrical supplier, it might be a high level of service. For a factory, it may be the on-time shipment of promised material to customers. Identify those critical few things your facility provides. In other words, what is your reason for being?

Your critical elements are the foundation of your plan. They are what you are trying to protect. Any functions that do not directly support these activities should still have a plan but are secondary in a recovery. It is typically an executive management responsibility to identify these critical few. If any critical function is having problems, then you must expend whatever effort is necessary to resolve the problem.

---

## COMMENT

> The authors have worked for companies whose critical functions were, "To build, ship and invoice product on time." Another company's vital few functions were, "To maintain 24 by 7 customer service, the ability to receive orders and the timely shipment of goods."

---

### [C]   Identify Risks (Threats)

Every day our critical few functions are challenged by a series of risks. Our second step is to examine these threats so we build defenses against the right ones. To evaluate risk, we build a spreadsheet to sift through the threats and help us identify the key ones to address.

A risk, or threat, is the potential that something may happen. Typically, it is something that has gone wrong. Risks have many dimensions. Risks can be examined based on how badly your facility will be damaged if it occurred. For example, if a meteor hit your building it would be severely damaged. This leads to the second dimension of risk—likelihood.

There are many horrible things that could happen, but what is their likelihood? If this is judged to be very, very small, then it can be ignored. Yes, the sun might quit shining tomorrow, but its likelihood is too small to address. What is the likelihood that a crazed employee with a gun will rampage through your offices? What is the likelihood that severe weather will shut your facility down?

The third dimension of risk is the impact to your operations if that event occurred. For example, if you lived in Minnesota, the likelihood of a severe snowstorm is high. The impact of the storm can be high due to problems of shipping raw materials in and finished goods out. The higher the risk, the more likely that its restoration time can be reduced through experience.

Contrast the snowstorm with a department store fire where the fire damage is magnified by the smell of smoke on all of the remaining goods in the store. Recovery time to clean out all the smoke-damaged clothes and refill the building with fresh goods can be long.

A bank has a risk for robbery. The impact is high but the recovery is quick. The police are usually finished within a day and with a fresh stock of money the bank can reopen.

Refer to Exhibit 21-2 for some ideas of risks you should consider. Use this

**EXHIBIT 21-2.** Risk Assessment Form

| Date: | | Likelihood | Impact | Restoration Time | Score |
|---|---|---|---|---|---|
| **Grouping** | **Risk** | **0 - 10** | **0 - 10** | **1 - 10** | |
| **Natural Disasters** | | | | | |
| | Earthquakes | | | | 0 |
| | Tornadoes | | | | 0 |
| | Severe thunderstorms | | | | 0 |
| | Hail | | | | 0 |
| | Snow / Ice / Blizzard | | | | 0 |
| | Extreme temperatures | | | | 0 |
| | Floods / Tidal surges | | | | 0 |
| | Forest/Brush fires | | | | 0 |
| | Land slides | | | | 0 |
| | Sink holes | | | | 0 |
| | Sand storms | | | | 0 |
| | | | | | |
| **Man-Made Risks** | | | | | |
| | Highway access | | | | 0 |
| | Railroad | | | | 0 |
| | Pipelines | | | | 0 |
| | Airports | | | | 0 |
| | Harbors / Industrial areas | | | | 0 |
| | Chemical users | | | | 0 |
| | Dams | | | | 0 |
| | Rivers | | | | 0 |
| | | | | | |
| **Civil Issues** | | | | | |
| | Riot | | | | 0 |
| | Labor stoppage / Picketing | | | | 0 |
| | | | | | |
| **Key Suppliers** | | | | | |
| | (list your suppliers here) | | | | 0 |
| | | | | | 0 |
| | | | | | 0 |

example just to get you started. Change it according to your local situation. Replace the section on natural risk with the ones in your area. Carry on with this throughout the chart. Then working with other managers, assign scores (1 through 10) for likelihood (10 means almost certain), impact, and restoration time. Multiply the scores together and sort them with the highest scores on top. These are your top risks that must be addressed. At some point, draw a line across and ignore anything below it.

As you look at the risks, you see that some of them would have the same recovery actions, such as a fire that flattened a building or if a tornado wiped it away. Two different risks, but one recovery plan.

## [D]   Other Risks Considerations

Some risks are very localized. In the previous example of the bank, the office that was robbed will be out of service for the day but the rest of the banking company is still operational. A bad day for that one branch office but the company as a whole experienced no disruption. Another localized risk is a tornado—terrible where it hits but generally, the rest of the area is fine.

The opposite of a local risk is a wide area risk, such as the snowstorm in Minnesota. This risk may close roads across several counties, keep employees away, and prevent the flow of materials on the highways. The factory is intact and may still be churning out goods but nothing is moving outside the facility's four walls. No fresh materials come in and no finished goods flow out until the highways are reopened. Other wide area risks to consider are floods, hurricanes, and earthquakes.

Man-made threats come in many forms. There could be a terrorist threat against your company, a truck carrying toxic chemicals could crash outside of your facility and force evacuation, or an angry person with a gun could be looking for victims. Man-made threats tend to be localized.

Infrastructure threats would include problems with the things your company needs to continue operating. Electrical power is an essential part of any company. Without it, there are no lights for your offices, your desktop workstations fall dark, and the heat and air conditioning stop. We have all experienced electrical outages. Another infrastructure threat is to the telecommunications lines outside your building. These lines also carry your data traffic so this risk is a double whammy.

Possible subsets to the previously mentioned infrastructure risks are associated with your facilities. This includes roof collapses, interior electrical failures, etc. Many things can cause leaking water pipes and water damages spread quickly.

A very common risk that companies face involves the security of their assets and employees. Computers make attractive theft targets as do a wide number of things within a company's walls. The risk to this can be high as the PC stolen may be full of company secrets, confidential legal files, or the only copies of accounting records. A good internal security program is a key part of any business continuity plan.

It is a rare company that doesn't have at least one disgruntled employee. As an insider, this person knows your company processes and what would hurt you the most if it was damaged. Employee sabotage may be difficult to stop. Alongside of this is employee theft. Sometimes a thief will try to cover their crime by setting a fire to destroy evidence. All of this can be addressed by your company's security practices.

It is very important that you carry on with the risk analysis through the specific process threats within your facility. These threats will occur most often. Consider your critical few activities to protect and determine the specific threat to them.

## [E]   Develop Action Plans to Reduce These Risks

Now that we have spread enough "doom and gloom" to depress the brightest optimist, let's begin fighting back. Once we have stripped away the element of surprise from these risks, we can take steps to address them. There are three basic actions to consider:

1.  **Avoidance.** Are there any steps that can be taken to avoid the risk? If hurricanes bother you, could the company move to Wisconsin? This move should successfully avoid the threat to your company from hurricanes. Avoidance actions often introduce new threats to your company.
2.  **Mitigation.** Steps to reduce the likelihood or impact of a threat. These are all around. Consider the fire sprinkler system in your offices. A sprinkler does not stop a fire from starting. It takes the heat from a fire to activate it. A fire sprinkler contains and douses the fire—reducing the damage it can cause. To reduce the likelihood of a flood, locate your business on a hilltop, far above the flood plane.
3.  **Transference.** After trying to avoid and mitigate a problem, you can transfer the risk to someone else. This is usually done through insurance policies. For example, product liability insurance can protect you in case someone was hurt using your product. Since you cannot easily protect yourself from stupid people misusing your product, the risk can be transferred to an insurance policy. Insurance rates can be reduced through the introduction of well-written and tested business continuity plans. Insurance companies will often help you write your plan since it reduces their risk.

If you cannot avoid the threat, then take steps to mitigate its impact. If you cannot mitigate the threat, transfer the risk of loss to someone else. Using these three strategies, reexamine the list of threats to your company and see which strategy is best suited to each threat. The steps required to carry these out become your first continuity planning action items. You may find some of these steps have already been taken, such as fire sprinklers. You may identify simple actions that could mitigate some of your risks.

This third step of planning includes the development of specific plans to address threats to your critical few company activities. This is where you can pick back up the folder you built from information from your local expert. Compare it to your list of risks and see which ones are covered and which ones are not. You will find some risks specific to business processes in this folder.

As we build out the plan we will constantly ask ourselves:

- What are my critical assets and critical processes?
- What threatens them?
- How can I reduce the likelihood of threat becoming reality?
- How can I minimize the damage if it does occur?
- What does the team do if this occurs?
- Where can I find more information on this?

## COMMENT

If you cannot describe what you are doing as a process, you don't know what you're doing.

W. Edwards Deming

## § 21.04 PLANNING—THE NEXT STEP

### [A] Use What Is Already Available

Before writing the plan, check around to see what information is already available. Writing a plan can be time-consuming and yet much of what you need isn't that far away. With a few calls and a notebook, you can pull together a basic continuity plan. In most crises you will need three keys—key people, keys to the doors, and key support contract information. Be sure to label the origin of any information collected, as you may need to go back for further clarification later.

1. **Start with the basics—who do I call.** Obtain a current organization chart for your facility. This will at least show who works in what areas. Now get an organization chart for your entire company—specifically the key technical areas and executives. In a crisis, you may need their help. For example, if you had a severe crisis with your data network, you could call on the network experts from sister companies to come in and help for a few days.

2. **With these names in hand, match them to three telephone numbers.** This is very important for people directly supporting your facility and less so for people at other sites. For each person, find their:
   - Office telephone number
   - Home telephone number
   - Cellular telephone number

3. **Check with security staff to see if they have a key to every**

**door in a secure key locker.** Keys have a habit of being copied by people who don't need them so if possible, get a report on who has access to which doors protected by electronic locks. A part of this step is the ongoing identification of doors you need access to.

4. **Build a spreadsheet of service contract information.** The sheet should indicate who to call for which items, the terms of service (24/7, Monday through Friday, etc.), how to call for help, and the contract expiration date. This could be a long list. A copy should go to your help desk.

5. **Build a vendor list of anyone who supplies critical material.** In IT, this could be the company that prints your special forms (such as invoices and checks), the place from which you buy backup media, etc. Also on this list will be every company you have service contracts with.

6. **Take a walk around asset inventory.** Take your time and note every major piece of equipment and what room it is in. Which device is critical to your operation? Which device must always be available? Compare the asset list to the service contract list. Is the service contract coverage adequate?

7. **Talk to your systems programmers and make a list of software assets.** This includes purchased software as well as homegrown code. Do the purchased packages have service support agreements? Are they included on the service contract list?

8. **Identify the various business functions that your department supports.** Make a list of them and then fill in the technologies that are necessary to support them. Big list? Are you seeing the power of building this plan yet?

9. **Establish a list of restoration priorities.** This is based on the list of business functions. Later on, review this list with your executive management so your efforts coincide with their expectations.

10. **Build an employee skills matrix for your IT department.** This will give you some idea of who to call on for emergency backup on a specific technology. It can also be matched against your critical equipment list and software asset lists to develop a staff training plan. Identify the skills gaps now and begin training your people!

So with these ten basic steps, you probably spent a couple of days pulling the information together but now have a lot of information which can be provided to the help desk and other key people in your organization. This will also form the nucleus of your formal plan.

One way to see how ready your staff is (and to uncover any more hidden caches of information) is to make an unannounced visit to your support people and ask for their critical information. Some will reference the "sticky notes" that encircle their monitor; some will dig deep back into an address book for bypass codes, and some will bring out the "cheat sheets." Others will give you a condescending blank stare. Imagine the ball of energy they would become fumbling for this same information in a real emergency! Be sure to copy all of this information into your files, as it will be useful later.

After organizing what you have collected so far, begin validating it with people other than those who provided the information. As you cross-check the accuracy, you will begin to see who was better organized than others. It is especially important if the notes you copied were rather old and you believe the system has been updated since then. All information should be neatly typed (or copied) and placed in a three-ring binder, broken down by subjects with tabs to make the sections. In an emergency, the tabs allow you to quickly access just what you need to know without fumbling through a lot of pages.

Be sure to mark the binder and all sheets as "company confidential." If you haven't already, you will soon be stepping through some information that would be useful to mischievous people.

## [B]   Distributing Copies

You now have enough of a plan to make copies and distribute them to key people. This is an important step as your project has now progressed from a one-worker show to a team. Ask each of these people to help improve the book by filling in the gaps and commenting on what has been collected so far.

- Keep one copy of the book at your office desk. Use this when problems arise.
- Take one copy home so you can better address problem calls when they come in—and in case something happens to the copy on your desk.
- Provide one copy to the IT manager.
- Provide one copy to the IT help desk.

At this stage it is best to keep the number of copies in circulation to a minimum since there will be many updates as you flesh out the plan. You might skip the IT manager's copy and the help desk's copy by storing the document as a read-only file on the LAN.

## [C]   Adding to Your Plan—More Contact Information

In Step 1 of our plan development, we obtained an organization chart for your facility and other sister companies. In Step 2, we gathered telephone numbers for key people. There are reasons for this.

During normal work hours, you know where to find people when problems arise. Rather than chase them down, obtain a facility telephone directory. You can get one from your telephone technician. Now you know at what number people can be reached—during the day. Emergencies have a habit of arising in the middle of the night, on holiday weekends, etc. So using your telephone list, make a note of the key managers in your facility who you may need to call after hours. Ask these people for their home telephone and cell phone numbers. In many cases, you probably already have the information in your notes.

These numbers are important so you can advise them of IT problems during off hours; so when they come into work in an emergency, they are prepared for the situation. This might be to inform the material manager that the warehouse system has failed and will take many hours to repair. By calling them in the wee hours of the night, they can decide if their staff needs to come in early and work around the problem. The same situation holds for about every department, accounting, payroll, human resources, engineering, etc.

Respect the personal privacy of these home telephone numbers and never give them out to anyone. While we are at it, draft a brief policy explaining the circumstances that are severe enough to call someone at home and when to let him or her find out when they come into the office.

## [D]  Keys!

An important step in business continuity planning is keeping people away from your critical equipment. Some people are curious, like to push buttons, and see what happens. There is the occasional discontented person who wants to express their outrage by turning off a server or unplugging a network hub. It could be almost anything. So wherever possible, limit the ability of anyone to disturb the operation of your equipment. Keep critical equipment in locked closets, hard wired into the electrical outlet, and away from the wondering masses.

Now that we have kept everybody else out, make sure you can get in! Problems can happen at any hour of the day or night. If you are called in to work on something, could you get in? If you have a security force at your company, they should have a copy of the key to every door. If not, then you should establish your own key cabinet. A key cabinet is used to hold one copy of every key to everything to which you need access. Be sure to attach a label to every key because in a small pile, they all look alike!

Some people are certain that the world is out to get them, and they will attach their own locks to doors and tool lockers. They typically forget to pass a copy to the key locker. Fortunately, a well-stocked key locker includes a master key named "Mr. Bolt Cutter." Whenever you encounter someone's personal lock on one of your equipment room doors, introduce that lock to Mr. Bolt Cutter. If you don't do this, valuable time will be lost in a crisis looking for someone to open a lock that should not have been used.

## COMMENT

If you do not already have one, introduce a policy that only company locks are allowed to be used (except on personal lockers) and that security will be immediately provided with a spare key or a correct combination. Include in that policy a directive to the security staff to remove any non-company locks they find. Usually by publicizing this policy, the times you will need to cut locks will be few.

A major problem with physical keys is that they can be copied without anyone else knowing it. You can never know for sure how many copies of a particular key are floating around. So always sign out keys to people so they can at least be retrieved when they leave the company. Otherwise, they will be given away to people who should not have them.

Physical keys can effectively keep out most people, but by far the best approach is the use of electronic locks. You have seen them in hotels. Instead of turning a key, an electronic key checks the database to see if they should have entry through that door. It also maintains a log of who unlocked what door, and when. In addition, if the door is propped open, you can see who did it.

Electronic keys allow you to grant or remove access easily. Over time, some people forget their pass card and ask for a "temporary" one for the day. Then they forget to turn it back in. Some people will go through this frequently. I doubt they lose their car keys so often! When issuing a temporary card, always limit its access to one day. Otherwise, it is like the copies of physical keys floating around. You never know who is walking through what door and what they might be carrying out!

Passwords are the logical keys to your equipment. Just like a master key, a system administrator password is the golden pass to anywhere and anything on a computer system. Such a password must be closely guarded and never left in a place where it can be stolen. The problem here is that in a crisis, you may need specific passwords to shut down or restart servers, mainframes, computers, etc. Establish a secure place to store them so they are available in an emergency.

## [E]   Service Contracts—HELP!

Your company probably pays a princely sum every month for someone to be on call to repair your vital equipment. This is a common practice. However, paying someone to come in at any hour to fix something is useless if you don't know how to contact them! Take the time to pull information on **all** of your service contracts and put it in your book. This is important information for the help desk to have too.

Ask everyone in the department for a copy of their service contract information. This would include:

- **Vendor's name**
- **What is covered.** Sometimes equipment is covered by serial number, sometimes the agreement is for everything on the premises.
- **Hours of coverage.** Your company pays one rate for service to cover normal working hours, and a higher rate for around-the-clock coverage. If you pay for 24-hour coverage do not let the service company off the hook if they try to defer until morning. Around-the-clock coverage is double the cost of normal service.
- **Who to call during normal working hours and after hours.** You need the telephone numbers to call for help! Most service companies have a 24-hour number. Try to get an after-hour telephone number

even for the companies you only have 8 to 5 service with. You'll pay a lot to get them in on a Saturday to help with a repair but it might be worth it.

- **When the contract expires.** This information should go on a calendar so you can make a decision before the contract expires. You should consider the importance of that piece of equipment, its incidence of repair, and whether the service should be bumped up to 24/7 or all the way down to time and materials.

- **Any limitations or extra cost provisions.** Sometimes the agreement covers parts and labor, sometimes it only covers the labor cost of "best effort."

- **Contract number.** The larger companies will check to see if you have been paying your bills before they send anyone out. They will look up your contract number in their database to see if the item in question is covered. In some cases, they want the unit serial number instead.

- **Company-appointed contact person.** Usually, one or two people are designated the company's identified person(s) who can make the call. It helps to know who they are. Often, these are people who know how to make minor adjustments to the equipment and avoid service calls.

- **Guaranteed response time.** How long before they show up. Usually this is something like 4 hours or 8 hours. If they don't show up on time, start escalating your requests!

There are five basic types of service agreements. You should select the one that best suits that piece of equipment's failure rate, the degree of criticality of the equipment, and the availability of alternate devices until that machine is repaired.

1. **Call for service.** This is where your fingers do the walking through the phone book and find someone to come out. The result will be a long service call since they know nothing about your site or its equipment. They may also take several days to get around to coming out.

2. **Time and materials.** The service vendor will come out for a set rate per hour and work until the machine is repaired. They will also charge you for the parts. Although the hourly rate is expensive, this may be cheaper than a service contract. This approach is good for equipment that rarely breaks and for equipment where you have on-site spares. Under the time and materials arrangement, there is an existing business arrangement so the service company should be somewhat familiar with your equipment and how your company does business.

3. **Normal working hours.** This is usually 8:00 AM until 5:00 PM. Under this agreement they will do what they can during these hours. If the job runs a little past 5:00 PM, they will stay and fix it. Otherwise, the repairperson will go home and pick up where they left off during the next business day.

4. **Full service.** This is 24/7 service. Unlimited calls at any time of day,

for any day of the week. The contract includes all costs. Always use this type of service contract for mission critical equipment.

5. **Exchange.** This is a good approach for smaller items like scanner guns. Keep your own spares on-site and send in the broken ones for repair—usually at a set rate. However, this may take weeks to get the device back.

With this service contract information in hand, walk around and look at all of your critical equipment. Is it covered on your service contract list? Did someone forget to tell you something or is there a gap in your service agreements? Does each critical device have the best level of coverage? Business needs change and often the service contracts do not keep up with them.

After collecting all of this information into a spreadsheet, provide a copy to everyone who has your BCP book. The help desk will find this all very handy.

To ensure that everyone knows what to do, make up small cards with the service contract information on them. Attach them to the major devices like large printers, servers, etc. If possible, put it somewhere inside the machine where they are easy to find, such as under the dust cover of a printer. Be sure to remove any old service information you find. If there is a lot of equipment in a room, just post the collective information on the wall.

## [F]   Vendor Contacts

Like your service contracts, you need to know who to call for a particular service or material. This is not an all-inclusive list. It should only include current vendors or someone you might need to contact in an emergency. This list will do more than help you in a major crisis; it can help with the more mundane emergencies that pop up everyday. Did you ever have an off-brand printer that ran out of toner at a critical business time? Knowing who to call could get the ball rolling. Calling your usual suppliers could delay delivery for many days.

A vendor list also provides a single point of contact for everyone in the department who needs materials. (Of course they would still need to work through the usual approval process.) Often, cost estimates must be gathered for users to build project proposals and this list will make it easier.

Information about each vendor on the list should include their company name, account manager's name, daytime and after-hours telephone number, fax number, e-mail address, the company's address, and a description of what you buy from them. The vendor list should also contain everyone on the service contract list.

When drafting the list, remember your "other" vendors; list the electric company, telephone company, water company, rubbish removal service, local ambulance, etc. These numbers may become very handy in a crisis.

## [G]   Walk Around Asset Inventory

Grab a pad and pencil and begin a walk around of your company area. Begin in the IT department. Make a note of every major item you find, like a server, network hub, major printer, etc. Don't try to do this from memory. In particular, look for equipment that has popped up in user departments. Indicate which of these items support critical company processes. Walk everywhere. You will be surprised what you will find. Be curious and open cabinets.

## COMMENT

In a large factory, one of the authors found modems connected to antifreeze coolant tanks so someone could remotely monitor the contents, old 8088-based PCs used to monitor PLCs, a copper pipe bender that used 8-inch floppy disks, some IBM controllers who used a 5¼-inch floppy for storage—a floppy so worn you could almost see through it! More 8088-based PCs turned up, but these had a custom circuit board in them for communicating with PDP-11s, etc. No, this wasn't 15 years ago, it was in 1999—and that was just one end of the plant! (Most old equipment was replaced due to Year 2000 software issues.)

As you walk through, note the location of disconnected equipment that can be recovered, cleaned up, and reissued. You will probably uncover some pockets of new equipment that someone keeps as their personal emergency spare parts stash. Check every closet! Arrange to have all of this collected into one spot and lock it up. Repair and reissue the good material and scrap the broken ones.

Compare your asset inventory to your service contracts. Is the level of coverage adequate? Are all the critical devices covered? Sometimes the machine itself will have a sticker saying who to call for service. When in doubt, ask the operators who they call with questions.

Include special equipment on your list that enables other devices to work. This might be an uninterruptible power supply or critical air conditioning unit. It may also include electronic time clocks or electronic door lock servers.

### [H]   Software Asset List

With the easy part out of the way, we move on to backup copies of software and data. Look around and you will see a vast proliferation of computers; from departmental servers, to special client software that interfaces with other companies, to shop floor equipment controllers. Inside each of these is valuable and potentially irreplaceable software and data. You must ensure that a backup (or safety copy) of this is regularly made.

For each critical piece of equipment, make a list of its critical software. You will probably find replacing the hardware a much easier chore than replacing the software. Some software is unique and almost all software has settings to customize it to the situation. The scariest machines are the ones that no one will shut off since they are not sure if they will ever start again.

Ensure that every device has more than one backup copy and that they are stored separately. If possible, make a copy of the disk for the IT department. You know the users will beat on your door to save them if the equipment ever expires.

### [I]    Identify Your Few Key Critical Business Functions

The anchor that drives your business continuity plans is a clear identification of the primary business functions at your site. These few items will require many things to support them, but provide a clear idea of what to repair first in a crisis. In this case, the squeaky wheel does not get greased first!

An example might be to ensure that the around-the-clock service center in your facility is always up. The implied tasks of this would include their primary tools, such as PCs, databases, the servers that run the database, the telephones, etc. It does not include the coffee machine (gasp!), the print room, or other areas.

Executive management normally identifies the critical few things for which your facility exists. There are usually five or less things, and when they are listed, you will find these were the areas that you probably have closely supported all along. This formal identification relieves you from other duties whenever they are threatened. By verifying this with your executives, you will ensure that what you perceive to be important is what they want you to, and IT only exists to serve its executive customers!

### [J]    Restoration Priorities

With the list of the critical few processes in hand, the next logical step is to develop restoration priorities for specific technical systems around the facility. This list might be kept in the help-desk area so that they know which problem to dispatch a technician to first. It can be discussed during departmental meetings so everyone knows what is expected.

A valuable use for this list is to identify ways to keep these systems running even in the face of adversity. It might mean adding small UPS units to departmental servers. Another possibility is installing stand-by servers next to the active ones. If the software is preloaded, then once it pulls in the current data table, off it goes.

It may also be used to identify areas where manual workaround instructions are needed until the equipment can be restored to service. Recovery from manual processing (which usually involves keying in all the data that was not captured) can be tedious but the facility can keep moving forward!

### [K]    Toxic Material Storage

For safety's sake, everyone on your staff should know where potentially toxic materials are stored and used within your facility. If someone is called in to repair some equipment, they should take extra precautions in case whatever damaged the equipment also damaged the toxic materials containers.

This becomes a future planning item to isolate or move the equipment far away from the toxic storage area.

### [L]   Employee Skills Matrix

If your key support person is on vacation in India, who are you going to call to fix your problems? You can guess or you can ask around, but in the meantime, the problem is simmering and so is the boss. Save time by building an employee skills matrix before problems arise.

Begin with a list of the critical processes you support. Identify who has worked on them before. You could even tag them as basic, intermediate, or expert. Add to this list (or make another one) for technologies. On this list, include every hardware and software item you support (don't be ridiculous, but do be thorough). Again, list each person.

You can add a few more columns to this list, such as who is emergency medical technician (EMT) qualified, who is a volunteer firefighter, etc. As an important added benefit, this list can be used to identify people for training over the upcoming year.

## § 21.05   WRITING YOUR PLANS

### [A]   Overview

Some people are reluctant to write recovery plans because they don't know where to start. Starting a plan is easy. It is the same as carefully explaining to someone what they should do. The difference is that instead of speaking the instructions, you are writing them down. Writing a plan is as simple as stating the basics of any story: who, what, where, when, why, and how. Your format is based on what to do first, what to do second, etc. If your plan addresses these basic points, then it should be sufficient.

If you have a good risk analysis, then you have an idea of the various things that could go wrong. No one can predict exactly what will happen but you can generalize the actions required in most situations. As you work through your risk analysis, you see that most plans contain the same details. Recovering a destroyed office is the same whether it was burned out in a fire or a snow-packed roof collapsed.

A plan is not a complete set of instructions to completely rebuild something. Typically, they are specific actions to repair something or contain the spread of damage to your operations. Full recovery plans will be developed while the containment effort is still underway. When writing, always remember your target audience. Emergencies affect people in different ways. Emergencies are characterized by chaos. A good plan reduces this chaos by providing directions on what to do. Once the team is working on the problem, they will feel more in control and the chaos will gradually disappear.

## [B]   What to Write About

Every department should have a plan that addresses natural and infrastructure risks. People shouldn't sit helplessly waiting for things to happen, they should be participants in forcing the results they want. All department processes depend on some basic infrastructure support to be in place for them to be successful. This includes electricity, telecommunications, data communications, and data systems. Therefore, your facilitywide continuity plans should begin with supporting these areas.

Each plan should include three major sections:

1.  **First Aid.** The first section is the "first aid" to be applied by the technician on the spot. These "immediate actions" would include things like shutting off the sprinkler valve once the fire is out to minimize the amount of water damage to clean up. Another immediate action is to use employees' cell phones for communications during a telephone system outage. Many things can be done if thought out in advance.
2.  **Containment.** The next section describes containment actions to reduce the spread of the damage until the primary support people arrive. This is not busy work. These are usually the same steps the "experts" would take when they arrive. In the fire sprinkler example, it would be containing the water on the floor, picking up items from the floor to minimize water damage, etc.
3.  **Establish minimal service levels.** The third major section of the plan contains the actions to return the process to a minimal level of service. Your company cannot sit idle until a full recovery is completed. This could be establishing a temporary office, shifting this process to a different company site, etc.

With these three sections in mind, we can begin to formulate a basic plan format. In this way, all plans at your facility will have a similar "look and feel."

## [C]   Contents of a Typical Plan

Let's return to the target audience for your plan. Your terminology and level of explanation is based on the assumed audience. These plans are not targeted at the process expert who might use the plan to gather some ideas in the midst of chaos but typically they just act. The plans are written for execution by others in the department who were either on-site during the emergency or were the first ones in.

Begin with how obvious the problem is. A building hit by a tornado is obvious. Magnetic damage to backup tapes is not. Hard to detect problems require detailed step-by-step instructions.

How much warning do you have before a problem hits? Some natural disasters, such as a hurricane, provide extensive warnings before they hit. Other disasters, like a lightning strike or blue smoke wafting from the back of a computer provide little advance warning. Emergencies that have a warning time can trigger containment actions before they begin. Again, a hurricane is an excellent example of an emergency where actions can be taken to prepare. This can be from covering all of the windows with wood to testing the emergency power generator.

Your second consideration in writing a plan is how long the reader must hold out before expert help arrives. If they are fighting to contain a problem, can the expert be on-site within an hour, 2 hours? They will need enough information to contain the problem and fight it until the expert arrives.

Finally, if a key process is dead, is there anything that can be done to keep the facility running? Can employees use their cell phones until the telephone system comes back online? Can the factory manually do the processes that the dead machine used to accomplish? Can the warehouse receive material into a separate area until it can be properly received?

So in each plan, remember:

- The target audience
- How obvious the problem is
- How much warning you will have
- How long until expert help arrives
- Are there any manual workarounds?

## [D]   What Processes Need a Plan?

It is not practical to write a plan to cover every eventuality for every item. A plan is only required for critical processes. The facilities department should have a plan to address all natural disasters and man-made disasters (as described in the previous risk analysis section). Other departments are also involved in these areas, such as human resources.

All infrastructure risks should also have a plan. This includes electrical service, data processing, and telecommunications. This is the point at which most companies stop, and if your company has plans this far then they are in pretty good shape—if testing has validated the plans.

Most companies have a few other critical processes outside of the infrastructure area for which they should also plan. It might be an expensive and unique machine in the factory. It might be special equipment to route incoming calls to individual salespersons or even a very old but reliable machine that manages your inventory of finished goods. Whatever your specific critical processes are, they need a plan.

## COMMENT

Even in our mechanical world, there are still some critical processes that are entirely manual. They need recovery plans too!

A caveat to this is when a critical device needs something else to make it work. Let's go back a minute to the inbound telephone call routing equipment. This machine may be fine but the device that feeds it or that it connects into may be at fault. The plan must encompass all of the devices that together make up a process, not just the central item.

## [E]    More Tips for The Plan

Write the plan as if you were explaining it to someone. In your mind's eye, select someone who might be called on after hours to react to the emergency and imagine yourself explaining it to them. Perhaps begin with a short overview paragraph that explains what the business purpose of the process is and essentially how it accomplishes it. Another way is to imagine yourself in the room during the emergency and you could not move, only speak. How would you direct the people to take mitigation actions?

Sometimes, a picture is worth a thousand words. Include pictures of hard to describe locations or drawings of how the major pieces work together. Digital cameras are common in companies so it is easy to include some photos in your plan. Pictures can also shorten your narrative since who has time to read more than two pages in a crisis?

## COMMENT

Business continuity planning can be a time-consuming process. This overview can get you started but if you want a complete plan, contact a business continuity planning professional.

# 22

# TECHNOLOGY RELOCATION: SUCCESSFULLY MOVING YOUR IT OPERATIONS

# § 22.01  PURPOSE AND SCOPE

Relocating a modern office is fraught with challenges. The infrastructure that supports the modern office worker is usually built up over a long period of time. Many firms have not relocated their offices for 10 or 20 years, which means that most of the technology being used in the office has been added over that period. Since the office was first established, new workstations have been purchased, new servers installed, network and communication cabling is ran and reran, and phone systems are installed and upgraded as the technology improves.

In an ideal world, each new addition or modification to the office infrastructure would be clearly documented. Each new system or upgrade would be seamlessly integrated with the existing technology. Unfortunately, what we normally end up with is a collection of technologies that are jury-rigged together and poorly documented. As long as the technology works, no one pays much attention to it, and as time goes on, the person who implemented the system moves on to another firm. This can happen with network configurations, server configurations, cable routing, etc. Worse yet, even the configuration information that is part of your computer infrastructure is not always backed up as part of your backup process, and is many times not documented elsewhere.

Adding to the challenge of office relocation is the infrequency of such a project. Since moves are so infrequent, the firm rarely has someone on staff that has been through the entire process.

A relocation project has a lot in common with the activation of a disaster recovery plan—just with usually more notice. Both are a major disruption in the operation of your business, consist of hundreds of small tasks that must be done properly, and involve operating your systems at a second location; neither normally give you the amount of time you would like. This new location is permanent in a move; it is hopefully temporary in a disaster. A relocation plan can just be a modified version of your disaster recovery plan, and is an excellent opportunity to test your disaster recovery plan. If you do not have a disaster recovery plan (DRP) (shame on you!), then a relocation project is an opportunity to collect the information necessary to prepare a DRP.

# § 22.02  BUSINESS ISSUES

## [A]  Overview

When faced with a technology relocation project, there are several issues to consider:

1. **Resources.** What resources do you currently have within the organization that can be used on this project? Will you have enough people to perform all the tasks required leading up to and including moving day?

2. **Experience.** What level of experience do people within the organization have with a project of this type?

3. **Downtime.** A relocation project will be disruptive to your operations. What are your vital processes and how long can you afford to have them unavailable?

4. **Cost.** There are numerous costs to be considered in a relocation project. In addition to the cost of the physical move, don't forget to include costs for outside resources, temporary furniture, last-minute glitches, etc.

Exhibit 22-1 is a questionnaire you can use to help begin the planning process for your relocation project. The questionnaire is useful for determining the readiness of the organization for the move, as well as helping to highlight areas where you may need outside support.

## [B]   What Can Go Wrong

Like most projects, a relocation project consists of many small tasks, most of which must be done correctly if the project is to be successful. You will of course want to have help in physically moving the furniture and equipment, but what else do you need to worry about? As you begin your planning for this project, think about the following aspects of the relocation process:

1. **Disruption of ongoing business.** A move is going to be extremely disruptive to your ongoing operations. Your users will have to pack their stuff, and then unpack it when it arrives at the new location. Someone has to plan for the infrastructure requirements such as telephones, local area network, connectivity to the outside world, etc.

2. **Relocation learning curve.** You have probably never managed a relocation project before, so you will be learning as you go along. The learning curve can be steeper than it looks.

3. **Downtime costs.** Just what are the costs you will incur if users are down after the move? What if they can't use their workstations, or there's no connection to the Internet, or the telephones don't work and your customers can't reach you? What is the cost to your organization if one or all of these problems occur?

4. **Day-to-day stuff.** While you are planning for the move, users still have their day-to-day work to do. Do your IT people have extra time to plan for the connectivity required at the new location, and to work with all the vendors involved?

5. **Things that can go wrong.** Many things can go wrong during the relocation. Some things to consider include:
   - Phones not working the Monday after the move—customers can't reach you
   - Elevators not accessible over the weekend—movers are being paid by the hour
   - Phone vendor cancels install order—they thought is was complete

**EXHIBIT 22-1.** Relocation Information Questionnaire

# Relocation Information Questionnaire

1. What is the impact of this project to the success of the organization?

   ☐ Mission critical
   ☐ Very important
   ☐ Somewhat important
   ☐ Not very important

2. What is the reason the company is considering the move?

   ☐ Current facility too big
   ☐ Current facility too small
   ☐ Consolidation of facilities
   ☐ End of lease
   ☐ Improved location
   ☐ Cost reduction
   ☐ Acquisition
   ☐ Other

3. Are you moving or renovating into the following:

   ☐ Constructing a new building
   ☐ Existing site with no renovation
   ☐ Existing site with renovation
   ☐ Renovation of current site

4. Location information if moving:

   **Moving from:**

   Address: _____

   _____

   Sq. footage: _____

   **Moving to:**

   Address: _____

   Sq. footage: _____

5. Will this relocation affect daily operations?

   ☐ Yes
   ☐ No

6. Will this relocation affect critical projects?

   ☐ Yes
   ☐ No

7. Will this relocation affect the company's computer technology?

   ☐ Yes
      ☐ Workstations
      ☐ Servers
      ☐ Infrastructure
      ☐ Internet connectivity
      ☐ Other
   ☐ No

8. Will other technologies be affected by this relocation?

   ☐ Yes
      ☐ Telephones
      ☐ Building security
      ☐ Time clocks
      ☐ Other
   ☐ No

9. What dependencies exist?

   ☐ Construction schedule
   ☐ Equipment schedule
   ☐ Lease expiration
   ☐ Personnel resources
   ☐ Communications connectivity
   ☐ Utilities connectivity
   ☐ Other

10. Has a budget been established?

    ☐ Yes
    ☐ No

**EXHIBIT 22-1.** *(Continued)* Relocation Information Questionnaire

## Relocation Information Questionnaire

11. Has a schedule been established?

☐ Yes
Start date: _____

End date: _____

☐ No

12. Who is responsible for coordinating the move?

Name: _____

Title: _____

Phone: _____

13. Has a project team been created?

☐ Yes
☐ No

14. How are current IT needs supported?

☐ Internally
☐ No support currently maintained
☐ Outsourced to a third party

Who: _____

15. Do you have internal staff to provide follow-up support after the move?

☐ Yes
☐ No

16. Do you have people on staff experienced in managing relocation vendors (construction/utility/movers, etc)?

☐ Yes
☐ No

17. Have you addressed any of the following?

☐ Choosing vendors
☐ Vendor management
☐ Communication to employees
☐ Establishing timelines
☐ Allocating resources
☐ Preparing the project plan
☐ Identifying the risks
☐ Controlling the budget
☐ No decisions have been made

18. Is the documentation of all the company's technologies current and complete?

☐ Yes
☐ No

- Payroll not being sent—someone forgot to order the modem line
- Workstations cannot be installed—improper installation of furniture, carpet, cabling, no electricity—pick your poison

## [C]  Benefits of Outsourcing

There are many reasons why you may want to consider outsourcing the management of a technology relocation project. A relocation expert can have the following advantages:

1. **Ability to focus on task.** As a project manager at your organization, you probably have multiple projects that you are responsible for at any one time. An outside person can focus 100 percent of their time on your project, without the distractions of other activities within the organization.

2. **Availability as needed for project.** An outside project manager can more easily dedicate time to your project. Your project managers still have other project responsibilities, and may have trouble dedicating the required time. Like a lot of projects, a technology relocation can take more time than originally estimated.

3. **Vendor connections.** Does any one person within your organization have connections will all of the vendors required to successfully complete the move? These vendors may include:
   - Movers
   - Security/safety
   - Property manager
   - Technical furniture/cabinets
   - Equipment disposal
   - Temporary office space
   - Cabling
   - Utilities
   - ISPs
   - Construction
   - Architects
   - Off-site storage
   - Office furniture
   - Hazardous waste removal

4. **Availability of qualified resources.** Do you have the necessary people in-house to assist with the relocation? You will probably need to work with multiple outside vendors for many of the required tasks, and it helps to have experience working with these vendors.

5. **Can scale to meet needs of the project.** When it comes time to make the move, an outside vendor can bring needed extra resources to help complete the project on time.

6. **Past experience.** Your organization does not move very often (hopefully), so it is not likely you will have someone on staff with recent experience with a project of this type.

## COMMENT

Firms that specialize in technology relocation are usually a division of a moving company or a technology consulting company. If using outside help, make sure they specialize in technology relocation.

### [D]   Relocation Project Coordinator

One of the most important tasks of a relocation project is the selection of a relocation project coordinator. This should be someone with a broad knowledge of your operations. Even if an outside vendor will perform most of the relocation effort, you must have an internal person responsible for making sure the firm's objectives for this project are achieved. If this job is relegated to a person with low status within the organization, then the relocation is guaranteed to be plagued with problems. The relocation project coordinator should be someone who can gain the willing cooperation of the team members and their supervisors. Who you select to lead this project will signal to everyone else in your facility how serious you are about the relocation project.

The relocation project coordinator should be publicly assigned to this task with management's unqualified support. This is essential to overcome internal politics and to let everyone know their assistance is important and required. As the project moves forward, regular public displays of support are required if the project is to result in a smooth and trouble-free relocation.

The relocation project coordinator should be someone with good analytical, communications, and leadership skills that can keep the project focused. Except in the smallest of shops, no one person knows all aspects of the operation. Supporting the relocation project coordinator will be a team of representatives from the various departments within the organization. Building a viable relocation plan is based on these people contributing information about their area of specialty. Therefore, the relocation project coordinator must be a skilled negotiator, able to reach consensus with the various company departments to gain the use of their key people. To a great degree a team's success will depend on who is selected as the relocation project coordinator and how well they work with their team.

The relocation project coordinator has the following responsibilities:

1. **Accepts total responsibility for the relocation.** Someone has to be in charge of the project. This should be their main responsibility for the duration of the project.
2. **Creates documentation.** It is critical to document every aspect of the project. If the current environment is not well documented, then the relocation project coordinator must lead the effort to get it updated. The layout of the new facility must then be documented, as well as the move from the current facility to the new one.

3. **Maintains vendor relations.** Working closely with all the various vendors is critical. This might be simply working with the outside relocation vendor, or managing all the individual vendors if the project is managed in-house. A good rapport must be established with each vendor to ensure their cooperation as the project progresses. You never know when you will need one of them to put out some extra effort to get something completed on time or to accommodate last-minute changes.

4. **Central point of contact for all communications.** The relocation project coordinator is the central source for information concerning the project. A relocation project requires the coordination of the services of multiple vendors and task requirements with the organization.

5. **Provides leadership and direction.** The relocation project coordinator must keep everyone involved focused on the successful completion of their tasks.

6. **Authority to make quick decisions.** No matter how complete the planning and attention to detail, many tasks will require last-minute adjustments or change orders. The relocation project coordinator must have the task and budget authority to get these things done in a timely manner to keep the project on schedule.

## [E]   Partners

Few companies will have all of the resources required to successfully complete a relocation project. Most will require the assistance of several different vendors that specialize in some aspect of the project. As much as possible, try to find vendors that have experience with technology relocation projects. Moving servers and other delicate equipment is not the same as moving household furniture. These vendors may include:

1. **Movers.** No matter how modern and sophisticated the technology, there will still be plenty of heavy lifting that needs to be done. These people have the skill, training, and muscle to get your equipment moved to the new location with a minimum amount of damage.

2. **Security/safety.** Make sure the vendors have security plans in place to ensure that your equipment arrives safely, and is not damaged or compromised during the move. You want to ensure that access to corporate data is not compromised due to poor security during the relocation.

3. **Technical furniture/cabinets.** You may need new furniture and equipment cabinets due to differences in the layout of the new facility from how the old facility was structured.

4. **Equipment disposal.** A relocation is the perfect time to dispose of equipment that is no longer being used. Many areas now have restrictions on placing old computers and monitors into the normal trash due to the high concentrations of toxic material within this equipment.

5. **Temporary office space.** If all new construction is not completed when the move date arrives, you will need temporary office space for those affected personnel.
6. **Cabling.** Your new office will of course need network cabling installed to your specifications. You may have engineers that have the talent to run new cable, but do they have the time and workerpower needed?
7. **Utilities.** You've got to have electricity, water, heating, cooling, etc., to operate a modern office. Separate contractors, whose work will require someone to coordinate their efforts, install most of these items.
8. **ISPs.** You most likely have a corporate or department connection to the Internet that will need to be up and available on day one. You also may have dedicated connections to an application service provider if you are using software applications delivered in this manner.
9. **Construction.** Your construction team will need to work closely with many of the other vendors to ensure that everyone can complete their tasks.
10. **Architects.** If your new location requires extensive remodeling, an architect will be required to ensure that the new facility is designed properly.
11. **Off-site storage.** You may need off-site storage for certain equipment that cannot be installed right away in the new facility.
12. **Office furniture.** Now is a great time to get rid of old, worn furniture rather than move it.

# § 22.03  RELOCATION PROCESS

## [A]  Benefits of Planning

Just like any other major project, a relocation benefits greatly when it is well planned. Some of the benefits of planning include:

- Resource needs are known ahead of time
- Problem areas are identified
- Lower follow-up support costs
- Environmental problems are identified and cleaned up
- Consolidation of other resource-intensive projects
- Asset management can be initiated
- After hours and weekends worked without exhausting current personnel
- Efficient project management
- Disaster recovery/site guide can be developed

The results of not planning and instead trying to fly by the seat of your pants can include the following problems:

- Lack of testing
- Longer project duration
- Possibility of theft
- Poor use of personnel
- Reduced time for daily support and other business projects while on relocation project

Numerous things can go wrong on this kind of project before, during, and after the move. Most if not all of them can be prevented with careful planning. Some things that can go wrong before the move begins can include:

- Forgetting to arrange copier move
- Not having updated floor plans
- Not having accurate inventory of furniture
- Non-networked equipment not accounted for
- Inventory of all networked equipment incomplete

During the move, problems that may crop up include:

- No power at new location
- No access to elevators
- Telecommunications lines not installed
- Unorganized activities can make work very inefficient

After the move is complete, some problems that may occur include:

- Basic supplies missing
- PCs can't connect to network
- Old telecommunications lines not cancelled
- No coffee in new facility
- Fax machine won't dial out
- Pictures need hanging

A well-planned relocation project managed by an experienced project manager will take much less time and resources than a relocation managed by someone without that experience. Exhibit 22-2 shows the results of research performed by Franklin Technology Relocation Group (FTRG), a technology relocation firm, comparing moves managed by experienced versus inexperienced project managers. FTRG's research shows that although the experienced manager spends a little more time up front, this planning time pays big dividends later in the project. The small shaded area on the left side of the chart in Exhibit 22-2 shows the extra time spent by the experienced manager. However, the shaded areas at the top and right portion of the chart show a dramatic increase in the amount of hours spent by the inexperienced manager versus the experienced one. Proper planning allows the experienced project manager to complete the project more quickly, with fewer fires to fight after the move has taken place.

**EXHIBIT 22-2.**   Experienced vs. Inexperienced Coordinator

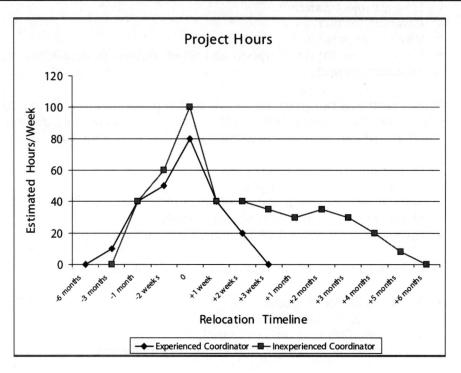

## [B]   Design Phase Activities

Once the initial planning is completed, you can begin designing the logistics of the relocation project. This consists of performing the following steps:

1. **Select tracking tools.** Determine what tools and software you will need for project tracking, budget tracking, and for implementing your communications plan.
2. **Create a communications plan.** This will include a central repository for communications such as meeting minutes, budget status, and scheduled items for both internal and external contacts to refer to. A good communications plan will reduce miscommunication and reduces the workload of the project coordinator.
3. **Develop a budget.** You must have the necessary budget resources to complete the project effectively. Make sure you have a contingency fund for unexpected items that pop up at the last minute. This fund should be approximately 10 percent of your total budget.
4. **Collect data.** You will need lots of data about many areas of your organization in order to get it moved to the new location. Look for office diagrams, review floor plans, and develop checklists to make sure you have covered everything. Some areas requiring special attention include:
   a. **General**
      * Room dimensions
      * Electrical requirements
      * HVAC
      * Security
      * Floor coverings
      * Dedicated spaces for technical equipment
      * Backup batteries for computer and phone equipment
   b. **Local Area Networks**
      * Document and assess current network architecture and applications
      * Review technology standards, policies, and procedures
      * Interview affected user groups
      * Create list of reusable equipment
      * Determine budget for new local area network
      * Develop new local area network architecture design
      * Issue RFPs if outside vendors are required
      * Review RFP responses and provide recommendations
   c. **Wide Area Networks**
      * Document and assess current network architecture and applications
      * Review technology standards, policies, and procedures
      * Interview affected user groups
      * Create list of reusable equipment
      * Determine budget for new wide area network
      * Develop new wide area network architecture design

- Coordinate with network service providers
- Issue RFPs if outside vendors are required
- Review RFP responses and provide recommendations

d. **Voice Systems**
- Document and assess current voice communications architecture
- Review technology standards, policies, and procedures
- Interview affected user groups
- Determine budget for voice system
- Develop new voice network plan and specifications
- Issue RFPs if outside vendors are required
- Review RFP responses and provide recommendations

e. **Data Center**
- Audit existing equipment to determine what can be used at new location
- Define equipment layout and cabling floor plan
- Issue RFPs if outside vendors are required
- Review RFP responses and provide recommendations

f. **Business Continuity Plan**
- Develop a business continuity plan for move
- Determine possible points of failure and develop prevention and restoration plans
- Coordinate design of all systems to ensure connectivity
- Develop technology delivery schedule for new location

5. **Confirm lead times.** Many of the tasks that will be performed for the relocation must be done in a specific order. For example, you cannot complete the construction of any new walls until all new cabling is done.

6. **Review new space.** You will want to walk through the new facility and compare what you see to the diagrams you were given. Pay special attention to wiring, door locations and swing, size of furniture, and how the furniture will be delivered. Make sure the doorways are wide enough for your equipment, and for the moving equipment that you will use. In addition, do not forget about the hallways, elevators, etc.

7. **Identify resources required.** Different types of resources will be required during the relocation project. Without having the required resources levels and skill levels available, the project will suffer.

8. **Finalize employee locations.** It is critical to know where everyone will end up at the new location and what infrastructure requirements they have. When planning for network drops, plan to have extra drops in case there are last-minute changes.

9. **Develop timeline.** Work your way back from the relocation date to make sure you have enough time to get the project done.

Other items you will need to account for in your project plan include:

- Business cards
- Letterhead and envelopes

- Marketing materials. Use up old stuff before the move; have new stuff delivered to new location.
- Notify business contacts—customers, vendors, partners
- Have calls automatically transferred to new number

If new construction is involved, work closely with the contractor. Be available to answer questions at any time during the project.

## COMMENT

Rarely is a new cabling job 100 percent correct. If at all possible, test the cabling at the new location before the move. You can test the new cabling using a laptop, a server, and a switch. Plug in the server and switch, then take the laptop to each location and see if you can log in.

### [C]   Implementation Phase Activities

Once you have planned and designed how you will perform the relocation, you are ready to begin implementing your plan. The following are some of the tasks performed during the implementation phase:

- Develop project plan and schedule
- Manage purchase, delivery, integration, installation, and configuration of equipment
- Define labeling standards for new building

## COMMENT

The importance of labeling cannot be overstressed. Label computers, peripherals, boxes, binders, etc., with some kind of identification of the new location.

- Review network and telecommunications plans
- Manage inventory-tracking system
- Manage change management system
- Manage project budgets
- Create acceptance test plan
- Conduct quality audits
- Facilitate project status meetings

Other things to consider during this phase include:

- Pack nonessential items early and identify temporary storage locations
- Make sure plenty of moving material is available—boxes, packing material, etc.
- Check employee vacation schedules and other reasons to be out

## COMMENT

It is a good idea to give every user a large plastic zip lock bag for all the smaller items, such as cables, mouse, etc. Have them label the bag and their equipment with the location of their new desk.

### [D]  Relocation Phase Activities

Finally, you are ready for the move. The following tasks are performed during the relocation phase:

- Develop final relocation plan
- Develop relocation contingency plan
- Establish relocation help desk
- Manage and coordinate relocation of systems
- Conduct acceptance testing of new and relocated systems
- Complete final documentation of new facility

Follow-up support after the move is critical to success. No matter how well-planned the relocation, minor issues are sure to pop up that will need your attention. Quick resolution of these items will ensure that everyone affected by the relocation is back at work and productive as soon as possible.

## COMMENT

Do not forget to have phone services, T1 lines, etc., disconnected at the old location after the move is completed. Forgetting to do so simply wastes money.

# GLOSSARY OF IT TERMS

**ABORT** To cancel, or terminate, a program, command, or operation while in process.

**ACCESS** To retrieve data or program instructions from "secondary storage" (hard disk, floppy disk, CD or tape) or another online computer device.

**ACCESS CODE** An identification code or password used to gain access to a computer system.

**ADDRESS** A unique identifier associated with a station, line, path, or unit. Addresses of main memory are for instructions or data locations. LAN addresses are assigned for each device on the network. Random access storage requires an address locator to find the actual location address of the record sought. For example, finding John Smith's record in storage would require matching "John Smith" to the address location that holds the record.

**AFTERMARKET** The market for peripherals or software created by the sale of large numbers of a specific brand of computer. For example, sales of the IBM AS/400 computer have created a market for software or hardware peripherals developed by companies other than IBM.

**ALGORITHM** A specific set of mathematical and logical procedures that a computer can follow to solve a problem.

**ALPHANUMERIC CHARACTERS** Character letters (A to Z), numbers (0 to 9), punctuation, and special symbols.

**AMERICAN NATIONAL STANDARDS INSTITUTE (ANSI)** Organization devoted to the voluntary development of standards. It has worked with the computer industry to develop standards for languages such as FORTRAN and COBOL.

**ANALOG** A continuously varying electrical signal with an infinite number of amplitudes.

**ANSI SCREEN CONTROL** A set of standards developed by ANSI to control the information display of computer monitor screens.

**API (Application Program Interface)** A method of allowing an application to interact directly with certain functions of an operating system or another application.

**APL (A Programming Language)** A high-level language used for programming scientific or mathematical applications.

**APPLICATION** A term referring to a software program that accomplishes a certain task.

**APPLICATION LAYER** The layer of the OSI model concerned with application programs such as electronic mail, database management, and file server software.

**APPROVED LIST** A list of computer software and/or hardware for which the IT department provides user support.

**ARCHITECTURE** A system's architecture is described by the type of components, interfaces, and protocols it uses and how these elements fit together.

**ARCHIVAL BACKUP** A procedure to back up or copy files in secondary storage onto another secondary storage device.

**ARPANET** A wide area network developed by the Defense Advanced Research Projects Agency that primarily connects universities and government agencies on the Internet.

**ASCII (American Standard Code for Information Interchange)** A standard for encoding characters (including the upper- and lowercase alphabet, numerals, punctuation, and control characters) using seven bits. The standard set is 128 characters; IBM expanded this to 256 by adding an eighth bit to each existing character. This expanded set provides graphic, mathematical, scientific, financial, and foreign language characters.

**ASP (Application Service Provider)** An ASP deploys, hosts, and manages access to a packaged application to multiple parties from a centrally managed facility. The applications are delivered over networks on a subscription basis. This delivery model speeds implementation, minimizes the expenses and risks incurred across the application life cycle, and overcomes the chronic shortage of qualified technical personnel available in-house.

**ASSEMBLER** Software that transforms an assembly language source code program into machine language. One assembler instruction code produces one machine language instruction.

**ASSEMBLY LANGUAGE** A lower-level programming language in which one statement is written for each machine language step.

**ASYNCHRONOUS COMMUNICATIONS SERVER** A device on a LAN that provides the capability for network workstations to access ASCII applications via switched communications lines.

**AUDIT TRAIL** A means of locating the origin of specific data that appears on final reports.

**BACKGROUND PROCESS** On a multitasking operating system, an operation that runs in the background while a second operation runs in the foreground.

**BACKUP** A copy of a file, directory, or volume placed on a separate storage device for the purpose of retrieval in case the original is accidentally erased, damaged, or destroyed.

**BAR CODE** A printed pattern of vertical lines used to represent alphanumerical codes in a scannable reading form.

**BATCH PROCESSING** Grouped transactions into a single batch for processing.

**BENCHMARK** A standard measurement used to test the performance of hardware or software.

**BETA TESTING** Using and testing software not yet put on the market by the vendor.

**BIT** A binary digit; must be either a zero (on) or a one (off). The smallest possible unit of information in a digital system.

**BIT ORDER** The order of transmission of a serial system. Typically, the least significant bit (LSB) is sent first.

**BOTTLENECK** A factor restricting the flow of data through a system. When a bottleneck exists, performance is limited.

**BRIDGE** A device used to connect LANs by forwarding packets across connections at the media access control sublayer of the data link layer of the OSI model.

**BROADBAND** A transmission system in which signals are encoded and modulated into different frequencies allowing for transmission of more than one input signal over the same line simultaneously.

**BROADCAST** A LAN data transmission scheme in which data packets are heard by all stations on the network, but are only received by the intended station.

**BROWNOUT** A period with low voltage electric power because of increased demands.

**BUFFER** A memory device holding information temporarily to compensate for differences in speed between computer components.

**BUG** A programming error causing a program or a computer system not to perform as expected.

**BUNDLED SOFTWARE** Software that is included with a hardware system as part of the total price.

**BUS** A common connection. Networks broadcasting to all stations, such as Ethernet broadcasting to ARCnet, are considered bus networks.

**BUS (PC)** The connectors on a PC motherboard into which expansion boards are plugged.

**BYTE** Eight continuous bits representing one character in memory.

**BURSTER** Machine used to separate continuous forms into single-part forms or sets.

**CACHE** To read data into a memory buffer so the information is available whenever needed and does not have to be read from the disk again.

**CACHE BUFFER** An area in RAM used for caching.

**CAD/CAM** Computer-aided design/computer-aided manufacturing.

**CALENDAR TIME** The actual duration of a project, from the date it starts to the date it is completed. This includes both work and non-work days.

**CAMERA-READY COPY** Any material ready to be photographed for reproduction without further change. May be typewritten copy, reproduction proofs, artwork, or previously printed material.

**CD** A compact optical disk with over six hundred and fifty million characters of storage.

**CD READ/WRITE DRIVE** A CD read- and write-only-once device employing compact optical disks.

**CD/ROM DRIVE** A read-only optical storage device employing compact optical disks.

**CLIENT** A computer that accesses the resources of a server. See "client/server."

**CLIENT/SERVER** A network system design in which a processor or computer designated as a server, such as a file server or database server, provides services to clients' workstations or PCs.

**CLIP ART** A collection of graphic images available for use with desktop publishing.

**COAXIAL CABLE** A commonly used cable type that is relatively insensitive to noise interferences, consisting of one or two insulating layers and two conductors. A central conductor wire is surrounded by the first layer of insulation. An outer shielding conductor is laid over the first layer of insulation. Usually the cable is then covered with a second layer of insulation.

**COLLATING** Gathering sheets or computer records in proper preidentified order.

**COLOR CODING** Use of different colored stock, tinting, or printed marks on individual parts of a set to aid in identification and distribution.

**COLUMN HEAD** A heading that identifies a series of entries to be made in columnar sequence below.

**COMMUNICATIONS PROTOCOL** A list of parameters

and standards governing communications between computers employing telecommunications.

**COMPILER** A program that reads high-level program coding statements (source code) and translates the statements into machine executable instructions (object code).

**COMPOSITION** Typographic material that has been set and/or assembled. Also, the process of preparing this material for printing.

**COMPUTER STORE** An IT support unit of information systems providing company employees with the opportunity to view and try out approved hardware and software.

**COMPUTER SYSTEM** A complete computer installation with all the required peripherals needed for elements to work with each other as one system.

**CONCENTRATOR** A 10 BASE-T hub. A multi-port repeater for Ethernet/802.3 used over unshielded twisted-pair cable.

**CONSOLE** A computer display terminal consisting of a monitor and keyboard.

**COPY PROTECTION** The inclusion in a program of hidden instructions intended to prevent unauthorized copying of software.

**CORRUPTED FILE** A file containing scrambled and unrecoverable data.

**COST-BENEFIT ANALYSIS** A projection of the costs incurred in and benefits derived from installing hardware, software, or a proposed system.

**CPM (Critical-Path Method)** A process used in project management for the planning and timing of tasks relying on the identification of a critical path. The time needed for the series of tasks along the critical path determines the total project completion time.

**CRC (Cyclical Redundancy Check)** This ensures the validity of received data.

**CUSTOM FORM** Form manufactured to unique order specifications by a vendor.

**CUT FORMS** Forms delivered as individual sheets, not bound or padded.

**DAT (Digital audio tape)** Popular tape backup format.

**DATA** Units of information stored on some type of magnetic media that can be called into a computer program for use.

**DATA COMMUNICATIONS** The transfer of information from one computer to another.

**DATA DICTIONARY** A list of data elements used in database management programs. Each data element contains information about its use, its size, its characteristics, who can use it, who can alter it, who can remove it, and who can only view it.

**DATA ELEMENT** A field containing an element of information used in records found in database management systems. Examples would be FICA number, name, part number, etc.

**DATA INDEPENDENCE** Data stored in such a way that users can gain access to it in a database system without knowing where the data is actually located.

**DATA MANAGER** A person responsible for the management of all corporate data. The database manager may report directly or indirectly to this person.

**DATA PROCESSING** The preparing, storing, or manipulation of information within a computer system.

**DATA RECORD** A complete addressable unit of related data elements expressed in identified data fields used in files and database systems.

**DATA REDUNDANCY** The same data stored in more than one location.

**DATABASE** An organized collection of information, in random access secondary storage, made up of related data records. There can be more than one database in a computer system.

**DATABASE MANAGEMENT PROGRAM** A data application program providing for the retrieval, modification, de-

letion, or insertion of data elements. Database systems tend to reduce unnecessary "data redundancy" by providing a central location for accessing data.

**DATABASE MANAGEMENT SYSTEM (DBMS)** The operating software system that provides for the access and storage of data.

**DATABASE MANAGER** The person responsible for managing the corporate IT database. This person reports to the manager of corporate information systems, but can report to the corporate data manager, too.

**DATABASE SERVER** The back-end processor that manages the database and fulfills database requests in a client/server system.

**DATAFLOW DIAGRAMS** A method of showing data flows all on one page. It starts at the lowest detail level, which is the system level. Corresponding process parts are all shown in more detail, each on its own page. Dataflow diagrams have their own flowcharting symbols.

**DDOS (Distributed denial of service)** Denial-of-service attacks are attacks whereby a hacker floods a network server with data in an attempt to crash the system. A distributed denial-of-service attack uses multiple computers all attacking at the same time.

**DEBUGGING** The procedure of locating and correcting program errors.

**DECISION TREE** A graphic representation of all possible conditions or processing alternatives and end results. It resembles the branches of a tree growing out from the main trunk.

**DECOLLATOR** Machine used to separate continuous forms into individual piles or to remove interleaved carbon(s).

**DEDICATED FILE SERVER** A file server that cannot be operated as a user's server workstation. See "file server."

**DE FACTO STANDARD** A standard based on broad usage and support.

**DEFAULT** A value or option that is chosen automatically when no other value is specified.

**DEMODULATION** The process of recovering information impressed on a carrier signal by modulation.

**DESKTOP PUBLISHING** The use of a PC to generate camera-ready copy for printing. Requires the use of one of the available desktop publishing software programs.

**DINGBAT** Stock symbol, such as a star, triangle, dot, or arrow, usually used for visual emphasis.

**DIRECTORY** An index to the files stored on a disk that can be displayed on a workstation.

**DISK CHANNEL** All components, including the disk(s), that connect a disk drive or drives to a file server. This includes the host adapter or disk controller and cables.

**DISK CONTROLLER** A hardware device associated with a disk drive that controls how data is written to and retrieved from the disk.

**DISK DRIVE** The unit in a computer that reads and writes information to and from disks.

**DISK DUPLEXING** A method of safeguarding data whereby the data is copied simultaneously to two hard disks on separate channels. If one channel fails, the data on the other channel remains unharmed. When data is duplexed, read requests are sent to whichever disk in the pair can respond faster, decreasing the file server's response time.

**DISK MIRRORING** A method of safeguarding data whereby the same data is copied to two hard disks on the same channel. If one of the disks fails, the data on the other disk is safe. Because the two disks are on the same channel, mirroring provides only limited data protection; a failure anywhere along the channel could shut down both disks and data would be lost. See also "disk duplexing."

**DISTRIBUTED PROCESSING SYSTEM** A computer system designed for multiple users with fully functional computer access.

**DO/WHILE LOOP** A loop control structure that carries out its functions as long as an external condition is satisfied in a program.

**DOCUMENTATION** The instructions and references providing users with the necessary information to use computer programs and systems or alter them at a later date.

**DOCUMENT FLOWCHART** A flowchart constructed all on one page showing the flow of documents used in a given system. It shows the documents traveling from left to right across a page from one user to another. Each user is in its own vertical column.

**DOMAIN NAME SERVICE HIJACKING** A hack in which inquiries seeking one domain are routed to another domain without the user's knowledge. Such attacks on the Internet's control structures could make packets of information undeliverable, quickly snarling traffic on the network.

**DOT-MATRIX PRINTER** An impact printer that causes the ends of pins in the form of characters, numbers, etc., to strike against a ribbon for printing text.

**DOWNLOADING** The reception and storage of data from one computer to another, often via data communications.

**DSL (Digital Subscriber Line)** DSL is a modem technology that transforms ordinary phone lines (also known as "twisted copper pairs") into high-speed digital lines for ultra-fast Internet access.

**DUMP** Transferring the contents of computer main memory to a printer or a secondary storage device.

**DVD (Digital Video Disk)** A high-density compact disk for storing large amounts of data, especially high-resolution audio-visual material.

**ELECTRONIC MAIL (E-MAIL)** A network service enabling users to send and receive messages via computer from anywhere in the world.

**EMULATOR** A computer program that makes a programmable device imitate another computer, producing the same results.

**ENCRYPTION** The scrambling of information for transmission over public communication systems. The receiver requires the same technology key to unscramble the coded information.

**END USER** A person who benefits directly or indirectly from a computer system.

**ERGONOMICS** The science of designing hardware, tools, and the working environment taking into account human factors so as to enable people to interact more comfortably and more productively.

**ERROR MESSAGE** A display on a computer screen or hardcopy stating a computer program is unable to perform as programmed.

**EXPERT SYSTEM** A computer program containing the knowledge used by an expert in a given area that assists non-experts when they attempt to perform duties in that same area.

**FACSIMILE** The exact reproduction of a letter, document, or signature. Usually abbreviated as "fax."

**FAULT TOLERANCE** Resistance to system failure or data loss.

**FAX** The transmission and reception of documents between two locations via telecommunications.

**FAX SERVER** A network device or service providing a LAN workstation access to incoming or outgoing faxes across the LAN.

**FEASIBILITY STUDY** A study to determine the possibility of undertaking a systems project.

**FILE** A name given to a collection of information stored in a secondary storage medium, such as a tape or disk.

**FILE ALLOCATION TABLE** A table on a disk recording the disk location of all the file parts.

**FILE SERVER** A computer providing network stations with controlled access to shareable resources. The network operating system is loaded on the file server and most shareable devices, such as disk subsystems and printers, are attached to it. The file server controls system security. It also monitors station-to-station communications. A dedicated file server can be used online as a file server while it is on the network. A nondedicated file server can be used simultaneously as a file server and a workstation.

**FILE SHARING** The ability for multiple users to share files. Concurrent file sharing is controlled by application software, the workstation operating system, and/or the file server/database server operating system.

**FLOPPY DISK** A removable secondary storage medium using a magnetically sensitive, flexible or firm disk enclosed in a plastic envelope or case.

**FLOWCHART** Analysis tool consisting of a diagrammatic representation of a system process or abstract relationship, normally made up of labeled blocks or keyed symbols connected by lines.

**FORM** A preprinted document available as flat or continuous.

**FORMAT** The size, style, type page, margins, printing requirements, etc., of a printed piece.

**FORMS DESIGN** The art or science of devising a form to efficiently fill a given function or systems need; includes selection of materials, construction, and layout.

**FRONT-END PROCESSOR** A specialized computer that relieves the main CPU, taking over line control, message handling, code conversion, and error control.

**GANTT CHART** A project scheduling tool using graphic representations to show start, elapsed, and completion times of each task within a given project. It can also show the planned scheduled (S) time and the actual completed (C) time. The Gantt chart indicates the status of a given project at any point. A Gantt chart employing dollars can also illustrate money budgeting for given tasks vs. money spent. Gantt chart monitor screen displays are available with most project management software. This allows for online reference of the status of projects that can be networked. Gantt charts can also be drawn on various size sheets of paper. The 8½- by 11-inch size is inserted in binders for project progress recording. Larger size sheets of paper can be used for displaying Gantt charts in the project team work areas.

**GATEWAY** A device providing routing and protocol conversion among physically dissimilar networks and/or computers.

**GIGABYTE (GB, G-BYTE)** A unit of measure of memory or disk storage capacity; two to the thirtieth power (1,073,741,824 bytes).

**HACKER** A technically knowledgeable computer enthusiast who enjoys programming but is not usually employed as a programmer.

**HANDSHAKE** A predetermined exchange between two computer systems in order to establish communication.

**HARDCOPY** Printed output from a computer system or typewriter.

**HARDWARE** Electronic components, computers, and peripherals that make up a computer system.

**HOST ADAPTER** An adapter card that attaches a device to a computer's expansion bus.

**IBM TOKEN RING** IBM's version of the 802.5 token-passing ring network.

**INFORMAL UNIT ORGANIZATION** The unofficial unit organization structure and culture. It also identifies the undercurrent of power within the unit.

**INFORMATION SYSTEMS** The department within a company that is responsible for computer information systems processing and the storage of all centralized data.

**INFORMATION TECHNOLOGY (IT)** The different techniques required to perform the task of information systems processing. The technology units within the information systems organization are required to be orchestrated by the information systems manager.

**IN-HOUSE** Denotes that the task is done within the company.

**INPUT DEVICE** Peripheral hardware that inputs data into a computer system.

**INTELLIGENT WORKSTATION** A terminal containing PC processing capability that runs independently or in conjunction with a host computer.

**INTERFACE** A shared boundary between two systems, such as between data communications (terminating) equipment and data terminal equipment (DTE). Also a boundary between adjacent layers of the ISO model.

**INTERNAL IT AUDITOR** A person representing the company with internal information technology auditing. He/she follows the guidelines provided by the CPA firm's auditors. They are concerned with computer systems audit trails and the security of the hardware, software, and data.

**INTERNET** The largest network in the world. Successor to ARPANET, the Internet includes other large internetworks. The Internet uses the TCP/IP protocol suite and connects universities, government agencies, businesses, and individuals around the world.

**INTERNETWORK** Two or more networks connected by bridges and/or routers; a network of networks.

**ISP (Internet Service Provider)** An ISP is used as your local connection to the Internet. It provide other companies or individuals with access to, or presence on, the Internet.

**JAZ DRIVES** Jaz drives employ secondary storage cartridges that hold one or more gigabytes.

**JUSTIFY** In composition, to space out lines so each is a designated length.

**LAN (Local Area Network)** Typically, denotes a short-distance, high-speed network.

**LASER PRINTER** A high-resolution printer that uses electrostatic reproduction technology, like electrostatic copy machines, to fuse text or graphic images onto plain paper.

**LEASED LINE** A full-time link between two or more locations leased from a local or inter-exchange carrier.

**LIBRARY** A collection of programs and data files for a computer system's off-line storage.

**LOCAL AREA NETWORK (LAN)** The linkage of computers within a limited area so users can exchange information and share peripherals. This linkage can be wired or wireless.

**LSB (Least Significant Bit)** The bit with the least binary weight in a character.

**MAINFRAME** A large computer, generally with high-level and multiprocessing power and the capacity to support many users at once.

**MARGIN** The blank area along any edge of a sheet that must be kept free of printing due to production considerations.

**MEGABYTE (MG, M-BYTE)** A unit of measure for memory or disk storage capacity; two to the twentieth power (1,048,576 bytes).

**MILESTONES** Used with Gantt, CPM, and PERT charting to show when measurable units of task(s) have been completed. With Gantt charts, the actual milestones can be drawn on the charts.

**MINICOMPUTER** A multiple-user computer, generally with more power than a personal computer yet not so large as a mainframe.

**MODELING** An analytical process based on mathematical network behavior formulas

called models used to predict the performance of product designs.

**MODEM** A device converting digital signals to analog and analog signals to digital between computers via telephone transmission.

**MODULAR PROGRAMMING** A style of programming requiring that program functions be broken into modules. It is a form of program segmentation and is the correct way to code procedural programs. This is also a good way to write reusable code. Quick BASIC and Visual BASIC programming require this type of program coding.

**MONITOR** Screen for viewing computer output. It is also called a CRT.

**MULTIPLEXER** An electronic device combining several signals into one to save transmission cost. Time division multiplexing (TDM) and frequency division multiplexing (FDM) are used in various aspects of LAN data communications.

**NETWORK** A series of points connected by communications channels. Public networks can be used by anyone; private networks are closed to outsiders.

**NETWORK ADMINISTRATOR** A local area network manager who is responsible for maintaining a network.

**NETWORK INTERFACE CARD (NIC)** A circuit board installed in each network station allowing communications with other stations.

**NONDEDICATED FILE SERVER** A file server that also functions as a workstation.

**OBJECT CODE** The machine-readable instructions created by a computer or assembler from source code.

**OBJECT-ORIENTED PROGRAMMING** A type of programming in which the data types and the allowed functions for a data type are defined by the programmer.

**OFFSET** An adaptation of stone lithography whereby the design is drawn or photographically reproduced on a

thin, flexible metal plate or other medium from which the design is transferred.

**ONLINE DEVICE** A peripheral device externally attached to a computer or available to other computers on a network.

**PACKET** A basic message unit grouped for transmission through a public network such as ITU-TSS X.25. A packet usually includes routing information, data, and sometimes error-detection information.

**PARALLEL PORT** A printer interface allowing data to be transmitted a byte at a time, with eight bits moving in parallel.

**PASSWORD** A security identification used to authorize users of a computer system or given program.

**PC (Personal Computer)** Smaller computers employing microprocessor chip technology. These can come in various configurations, such as palm devices (PDA), mininotebooks, notebooks, laptops, transportable, desktop, workstations, and microcomputers.

**PC COORDINATOR** An end-user person responsible for the coordination and operation of an end-user PC operation. The person can have full- or part-time responsibility for this duty, and can be hourly or salaried, union or nonunion.

**PC MANAGER** A person responsible for managing and providing support to and training for users of PCs. This person reports to IT management. Since this position is almost always a full-time responsibility, it is advisable it be filled by a salaried worker.

**PDA (Personal Data Assistant)** A small hand-held computer used to write notes, track appointments, and otherwise organize your life. Early PDAs required data to be input using a keypad with keys the size of Chiclets, but more recent models (e.g., the Palm Pilot) use a combination of pen-based input and character-recognition software to accept user input. Many can also be used to send and receive e-mail and browse the Internet.

**PEER-TO-PEER** A network design in which each computer shares and uses devices on an equal basis.

**PERIPHERAL** A physical device (such as a printer or disk subsystem) that is externally attached to a workstation or directly attached to the network.

**PERT (Programmed Evaluation Review Technique)** A planning and control tool for defining and controlling the tasks necessary to complete a given project. The PERT chart and CPM charts are one and the same. The only difference is the manner in which task time is computed. The CPM chart uses only one expected time. With the PERT system, the time required for each task is computed as follows: The longest expected time, the shortest expected time, and four times the expected time are totaled and divided by six. This gives the expected time needed.

**POTS** Plain old telephone service.

**PRINT SERVER** A device and/or program for managing shared printers. Print service is often provided by the file server, but can also be provided from a separate LAN microcomputer or other device.

**PROGRAM RUN BOOK** Operating instructions for the benefit of those who run a given program, including any restart procedures in case of program failure. Most often used by mainframe computer operators, but can also be provided for minicomputer operators and PC users.

**PROJECT SLIPPAGE** Occurs when a project's critical path milestone finish date is not met. The critical path of a PERT or CPM chart determines the project completion time. See "CPM." Projects that are not using PERT or CPM technology can have project slippage, too. It is first recognized when it becomes obvious that the project finish date will be later than planned.

**PROTOCOL** A formal set of rules setting the format and control of data exchange between two devices or processes.

**QUICK BASIC** An improved form of BASIC available from Microsoft. It has been available as part of its DOS/Windows operating system software.

**RECOMMENDED LIST** A list of software that the IT department recommends and for which it provides user support. The list can also contain recommended IT hardware for users.

**RECORD LOCKING** A data-protection scheme preventing different users from performing simultaneous writes to the same record in a shared file, thus preventing overlapping disk writes and ensuring record integrity.

**REDIRECTOR** Device in a workstation that sends data to the network or keeps it in the workstation for local use, as appropriate.

**REPEATER** A device used to extend cabling distances by regenerating signals.

**REUSABLE CODE** Code that is written in a structured modular format allowing it to be used at a later time with no (or minor) changes for other programming efforts.

**RING TOPOLOGY** A close loop in which data passes in one direction from station to station on the LAN. Each workstation on the ring acts as a repeater, passing data on to the next workstation.

**ROM** Read-only memory that is found on CDs and permanent microcomputer main memory.

**ROUTER** Hardware and software routing data between similar or dissimilar networks at the network layer of the OSI model.

**SCANNER** A PC input device that copies documents into computer memory.

**SCHEMA** Schema and subschema are the tools used to define the structure of a database.

**SECONDARY STORAGE** Any place where computer data or program instructions are stored, other than main memory (RAM or ROM).

**SERIAL PORT** A port allowing data to be transmitted one bit at a time.

**SERVER** A network device providing services to client stations. Servers include file servers, disk servers, and print servers. See "client/server."

**SHIELDED TWISTED-PAIR CABLE** Twisted-pair wire surrounded by a foil or mesh shield to reduce susceptibility to outside interference and noise during network transmission.

**SIMULATION** A technique for evaluating the performance of a network before downloading it. Simulation employs timers and sequences as opposed to mathematical models to reproduce network behavior.

**SITE LICENSING** Procedure in which software is licensed to be used only at a particular location.

**SIZE SNOWBALL EFFECT** The larger the project size and/or the longer the required project calendar time, the more likely that additional time and effort will be needed to complete the project. As more time and effort are required, these snowball, which in turn extends the finish date and increases the final cost. The user's needs change over time. The longer a project takes, the more the user can justify changes to the final product, and the number of changes will snowball. In addition, these changes that are required for a useable product also take even more time to install, which can justifiably require more changes.

**SOURCE CODE** Written program code before the program has been compiled into machine instructions.

**SPAGHETTI CODE** The name given to the first method of computer program coding. Program steps were written without any formal structure and meandered through the program. Tracing these program steps was like following a string of spaghetti in a bowl. Contrasted to "structured programming."

**STAR TOPOLOGY** A LAN topology in which each workstation connects to a central device.

**STAR-WIRED TOPOLOGY** A ring network (such as a token-passing ring) cabled through centralized hubs or connection devices to create a physical star topology. Using this, individual stations and whole sections of the network can be removed or added easily.

**STATISTICAL MULTI-PLEXER** A multiplexer that allocates time on the channel to active inputs only. It greatly increases line capacity.

**STRUCTURED PROGRAMMING** A standard requiring programs to be written in modular forms without the use of GO TO statements.

**SURGE PROTECTOR** An electrical device that prevents high-voltage surges from reaching the computer system.

**SYNCHRONOUS TRANSMISSION** Transmission of data during which the components of the network are all controlled by a single timing source.

**TERMINAL** A keyboard and display screen through which users can access a host computer.

**TERMINAL EMULATION** Software enabling a personal computer to communicate with a host computer by transmitting in the form used by the host's terminals.

**THIRD-PARTY VENDOR** A firm marketing hardware for manufacturers.

**TOKEN BUS** A network using a logical token-passing network. A service can only transmit data on the network if it is on the token.

**TOKEN-PASSING RING** A LAN design in which each station is connected to an upstream station and a downstream station. An electronic signal, called the token, is passed from station to station around the ring. A station may not send a transmission to another station unless it has possession of a free token. Since only one token is allowed on the network, only one station may broadcast at a time.

**TURNKEY SYSTEM** A system in which the vendor takes full responsibility for complete system design and provides the required hardware, software, operations manual, and user training.

**TWISTED-PAIR CABLE** Wiring used by local telephone systems.

**UPS (Uninterrupted Power Source)** A device providing electric backup power to a computer system or other devices when the normal electric power fails. This occurs so quickly that the operation of devices that depend on electricity is not interrupted.

**USER-FRIENDLY** A computer system easy for persons with no computer experience to use, causing little or no frustration.

**VISUAL BASIC** A more advanced form of programming than Quick BASIC, available from Microsoft. Program operation is screen-driven, which makes the program user-friendly. As with Quick BASIC, it uses modular programming. Programmed subroutines are available, either for purchase or with the payment of royalties.

**WALK-THROUGH** A technical review of a newly designed program or system. The review is conducted by interested parties such as programmers, systems analysts, users, and/or auditors. Program walk-throughs are conducted by peer programmers to detect program errors. In a walk-through, people play the role of devil's advocate in reviewing another person's/ team's effort.

**WAN (Wide Area Network)** Any network extending more than a few miles. It can use more than one form of message carrying.

**WAP (Wireless Application Protocol)** A standard used by mobile phones and other hand-held devices to access the Internet.

**WIRELESS NETWORK** A LAN system that does not require physical connections—information is transmitted through the air.

**WORK SAMPLING** Consists of a large number of random observations of predetermined tasks that an employee or group of employees perform. Data collected by the work sampling observations identifies the amount of time spent on each task.

**WORKSTATION** A highly intelligent terminal often found on a LAN or client/server system. Some workstations do not require floppy disk drives because data and/or programs are downloaded from a computer server.

**WORM ATTACK** A worm is a program that replicates itself over and over. A worm capable of penetrating networks could quickly overload the Internet.

**ZIP DRIVE** Drives that employ Zip disks that can store 100 to 250 megabytes of data.

# INDEX

*References are to chapters (Ch.), sections, and Exhibits (Exh.). Alphabetization is letter-by-letter (e.g., "Contractors" precedes "Contract personnel").*